AF334610

History, the White House and the Kremlin

Toles copyrighy 1990 Buffalo News. Reprinted with permission of Universal Press Syndicate. All rights reserved

History, the White House and the Kremlin: Statesmen as Historians

Edited by Michael Fry

Pinter Publishers
London and New York

First published in Great Britain in 1991 by
Pinter Publishers, 25 Floral Street, London WC2E 9DS

British Library Cataloguing in Publication Data
A CIP catalogue record for this book is available from the British Library

ISBN 0 86187 129 4

For enquiries in North America please contact PO Box 197, Irvington, NY 10533

Library of Congress Cataloging-in-Publication Data

History, the White House, and the Kremlin : statemen as historians / edited by Michael Fry.
    p. cm.
  Includes bibliographical references and index.
  ISBN 0-86187-129-4
  1. United States--Foreign relations--1945- 2, United States--Foreign relations--1945---Historiography. 3. Statesmen--United States. I. Fry, Michael.
E744.H59 1991
327.73--dc20   90-24904
                                                    CIP

Typeset by The Castlefield Press Ltd., Wellingborough, Northants in Palatino in 10/11 pt.
Printed and bound by Biddles Ltd of Guildford and Kings Lynn

Contents

List of contributors

Jeffry Frieden Department of Political Science, UCLA, author of *Banking on the World. The Politics of American International Finance*, (New York, 1987).

Michael Fry School of International Relations USC, author of *Despatches from Damascus. Gilbert Mackereth and British Policy in the Levant, 1933–1939* (Jerusalem, 1985) with Itamar Rabinovich.

Jonathan Haslam King's College, Cambridge, author of *The Soviet Union and the Struggle for Collective Security in Europe, 1933–1939*, (New York: 1984).

Alan Henrikson The Fletcher School of Law and Diplomacy, Tufts University, editor of *Negotiating World Order: The Artisanship and Architecture of Global Diplomacy* (Wilmington, DE, 1986).

Alex Hybel Department of Political Science, Pitzer College, author of *How Leaders Reason: US Intervention in the Caribbean Basin and Latin America* (Oxford, 1990).

Rashid Khalidi Center for Middle Eastern Studies, University of Chicago, author of *Under Seige: PLO Decision-making During the 1982 War* (New York, 1986).

Diane Kunz Department of History, Yale University, author of *The Battle for Britain's Gold Standard in 1931* (London, 1987).

David Lake Department of Political Science, UCLA, author of *Power, Protection and Free Trade: International Sources of US Commercial Strategy, 1887–1939* (Cornell University Press, 1988).

Dwain Mefford Department of Political Science, Ohio State University, author of *Rationality and Reason in International Relations* (forthcoming).

Condoleezza Rice Department of Political Science, Stanford University, author of *The Soviet Union and The Czechoslovak Army, 1948–1983*, (Princeton University Press, 1984).

Jack Snyder Department of Political Science, Columbia University, author of *The Ideology of the Offensive; Military Decision making and the Disasters of 1914* (Cornell University Press, 1984).

Preface

There are several ways, I suppose, to plan a book of this sort. My choice, born largely of uncertainty, was to ask a mixture of historians and political scientists to think about a series of questions, some of which were fresh enough, others distinctly familiar. All of the participants at one time or another, in their various ways, had asked about the intellectual fit between the sub-discipline of international history and the field of enquiry that is international relations. That question persists, even when it seems enough to conclude that historians use theory implicitly, and may even construct it informally, even involuntarily, while social scientists use history as the laboratory in which to construct theory formally and to test it.

A somewhat different group of us had already explored, in a preliminary way, how history fits into an international relations graduate curriculum. We asked what role historical training should have in the education of young men and women destined for careers in international affairs.[1] From there some of us turned to research questions, particularly to those that seemed relevant to the formulation of policy. They led us to a governing idea — that statesmen and the officials who advise them are all, in their various ways, historians of a kind. If the book has a theme, has a modicum of unity, it lies in the fact that policy communities use history, and may abuse it. History, learned, observed and experienced, plays a role in the formulation of policy. This is the case in both the White House and the Kremlin.

But this central theme did not point to a single approach. Rather it suggested that we examine several questions: how, why and with what consequences a version of the historical record establishes its control over generations of policy-makers; how history shapes beliefs and influences policy; how learning occurs as statesmen and their officials re-examine the historical record of vital events; what forms of broad historical comparison are valuable, and dangerous; and how and with what effect do statesmen and their advisers reason analogically. Perhaps each of these approaches merits a separate volume. Here we may have done no more than introduce them.

Michael Fry
Los Angeles
May 1990

Note

1. Michael G. Fry, *History and International Studies*, (Washington, DC: American Historical Association, 1987).

Acknowledgements

The Exxon Education Foundation provided support for this project with its customary generosity. Arnold Schorr and then Richard Johnson watched over the project. They were invariably helpful and encouraging, always patient and tolerant. I hope that the Foundation and its officers are satisfied, at least to some extent, with the results.

The contributors to the volume helped shape it conceptually, and that was especially true of Dwain Mefford. They wrote in their own good time, but the quality of their work made the task of editing both easy and enjoyable. Robert Keohane and James Piscatori attended the conference that heard preliminary ideas and listened to first drafts. They made significant contributions.

Carl Anthony Watson, a PhD student in the School of International Relations at USC, assisted me, particularly with organizing the conference. I am grateful for his help; I hope he learned something from the experience. Kathy Matthes helped with preliminary editing and typing, in her splendidly efficient way. She knows how much I am in debt to her.

1 Introduction
Michael Fry

Statesmen and their advisers are groups or communities which, in the face of constraints, determine policy. Their debate addresses, essentially, two issues — the nature of problems and the range of alternative solutions to them. Their deliberations are made up of reason and imagination, calculation and comparison, judgment and estimation, and argument about justification for the sake of legitimacy. Their reasoning rests to a great extent on what the community has learned, observed and experienced, and recalls from its semantic and episodic memories, and the insight that such processes give. This is not to argue that time flows in only one direction. Information about a current problem can alter established interpretations and affect memories of past problems. Historical knowledge, in its various forms, is, nevertheless, one of the principal intellectual resources of statesmen, the officials who serve them, and, therefore, of governments. Statesmen are, unavoidably, historians of a kind. They examine formally parts of the past as they formulate policy. They use history habitually if unevenly as an aid, and it is intellectually respectable to do so.

To examine the purposes to which statesmen put historical knowledge is to judge whether they use it wisely. That remains a controversial subject. Perhaps statesmen are generally unsophisticated and naïve in terms of their sensitivity to history, but not necessarily so. Many may deserve George Kennan's slashing attack on that score, but not without exception.[1] Certainly statesmen vary widely in the extent of their historical training, consciousness, understanding and accomplishments. Few perhaps either reason counterfactually or mix history with imagination to good effect. It is not at all clear which forms of historical knowledge are most influential with and useful to statesmen — history learned (when, where, from whom, formally or casually, about what period or region, and of what type), history observed (when and from what vantage point), and history experienced personally, in office (in what capacity, and as a positive or traumatic episode).[2] It is not at all clear either how these three forms of history relate to each other in the mind of a statesman; they might reinforce or conflict with one another. Indeed, some might carp at the idea of observation of the experience of contemporaries or personal experience being seen as 'history'. But to understand statesmen as historians is to open a window on the political mind at work, on the intent, motive and purpose behind actions, on the conceptual worlds and mental experiments of these who determine policy, very much as historians since Thucydides have tried to do.

Statesmen have a reserve of stored knowledge that is historical information about a very wide range of relevant subjects — the national experience and the national interest, foreign governments and societies, prominent individuals and enduring structures, important events and significant trends. They put it to several uses and call on it for many purposes. It provides a basis for their casual opinions, general attitudes, predispositions, perceptions, images, beliefs, convictions and axioms, and for their values, preferences and expectations. History is, therefore, central to their ideas, oratory and actions, to how they think and interpret, to that they declare and to what they do. When they think of individuals, factors, events and situations and ask why did it turn out that way, why did we get the results we got, they construct narratives that become authoritative and compelling, and are the foundation of confident extrapolation. When history provides governing concepts, propositions and seemingly powerful theories of how the world works, it helps statesmen construct their 'mental maps'[3]. As statesmen see parallels and discern patterns in the historical record they find grounds for comparison, and for reasoning comparatively. Metaphors and precedents provide analogies and thus a basis for reasoning analogically. The supposed lessons of history mark out paths to policy, and furnish comforting reassurance if they provide moral guidance and evidence of progress. Historical knowledge, in fact, helps statesmen construct reality. In the world of policy, deadlines and stress, of uncontrollable agendas, of challenges and opportunities, statesmen must cope. These assertions are quite different of course from the quaint, antiquarian notion that apprentice bureaucrats and statesmen consciously ground themselves in historical studies in order to prepare themselves for the challenge of serving the state. But as statesmen, for example, compare, reason analogically and extrapolate, do they do so judiciously and appropriately? As historical knowledge is itself less than complete and even fragmentary, and always selective, and is set alongside current information that is also partial and ambiguous, do statesmen elevate it to the level of evidence about the problem at hand carefully and perceptively? If history is used habitually but abused repeatedly, as some argue, why is that the case? And all this in a complex, uncertain and urgent world which is both pathological and civilized, and for which, to varying degrees, statesmen shoulder enormous burdens and immense responsibilities rather than seek emancipation from them.

As they decide on policy, statesmen are aware that history is a judge, sooner or later, in a rough and ready way, with or without precision, adequate evidence or consensus, and a formidable one in the hands of political enemies. Errors, like sins, grow on the tongue and under the pen. There is no haven either in determinism or in Greek rather than Roman tragedies, when there was no choice. There is only flimsy shelter in being one's own historian, as Otto von Bismarck, David Lloyd George and Winston Churchill were; any version of the historical record is always in contest with other sources of information and forms of judgement. Statesmen, especially if they are determined to free themselves from history, to break out and break loose, to change history's course, are portrayed and portray themselves as responsible and influential agents. They can be judged severely, not only as inept or foolish but also as lacking in honor and being evil. Nations as well as individuals can feel and be made to feel shame and guilt — history will never forgive us if we . . . because we have . . . because we have failed to . . ., and so on. Reputations matter, so do verdicts. History remains a formidable constraint even now for those who, if they involve the world in nuclear war, cannot quite see how they will be able to be judged. And it matters hardly at all that some of them sit in Washington and others in Moscow.[4]

It should be remembered that while every member of a policy community is, individually, a historian of a kind, each mind at work politically is the preface to collective debate, argument, calculation and judgment. And group discussion affects individual reasoning as the sequences unfold. Policy communities are heterogeneous in their composition. Their members, each in their way, have particular views and perceptions, images and beliefs, in part because they are informed by different histories and experiences. They may have different inventories of crucial examples, precedents and analogies. Their memories are variously extensive, sharp, selective and versatile. It is likely, therefore, that they will find different patterns and apparent lessons in the past as they grapple with a current problem. The fact that members of a group have different roles, varying political skills and intellectual powers, competitive cognitive styles and uneven abilities to cope compounds the lack of uniformity. Yet policy communities are formed and find incentives to hold together, beyond merely the desire to retain office and wield power. Coalitions that come together within a group, particularly if they are transitory, reflect the existence of certain commonalties in, for example, values and goals, and preferences for certain means and courses of action. A shared view of history provides both a degree of homogeneity and a basis for consensus that is far more authentic than that fashioned by the psychological pressures of group debate.

The historical record is part of the 'central intelligence' of every policy problem.[5] How far the mind must range back in time is debatable, but it is incumbent on statesmen and officials, in a very straightforward way, to understand the specific history of a problem that is to 'get it right'. Those who do not are at a distinct disadvantage either in debate or negotiation; they are not in command of the subject because they have not mastered an essential part of the brief. To 'get it right' is to identify the principal participants and their perceptions, to isolate the critical factors involved, the parameters of a problem, to establish the contingent relations between them and to construct an impeccable analytical narrative. If that is done, statesmen know the history of a problem and can begin to comprehend its current status and the significance of the present state of affairs. They will be able to answer such questions as where are we, how did we get here, and even how is it that we are not somewhere else? That is because the history of a problem lies particularly in its complexity and uncertainty, in its contingencies, in how and why alternative courses of action were ignored or neglected, and identified to be discarded, in how risks and probabilities were accessed, in outcomes that seemed probable but did not occur. This suggests that there are critical junctures and, on occasions, substantial changes of direction in a policy process. Results that do occur are often unpredictable and unanticipated. What might yet unfold is not clear and extrapolation may not provide ready answers. That is why, perhaps, statesmen and their advisers still reach back into history for insight and lessons, to find comparable situations, parallels, precedents and analogies, even when they have command apparently of the specific history of the problem at hand. Yet these two forms of historical knowledge may well compete with rather than complement one another.

Mastering the brief is a relatively simple, seemingly obvious prescription. But statesmen do not always 'get it right'. That they do not can, apart from the predictable debilitating consequences (e.g. the damage to US–Soviet relations and prospects for the SALT treaty brought about by the failure of the Carter administration to master the brief in the summer of 1979), result in the triumph of an *idée fixe* over the evidence. It can bring about devotion to a version of history, to a particular script, which crowds out and even excludes an alternative history, which may be more valid. And thus one can speak of the invention of history, of repeated coloring of events and interpreting of situations in ways that are meant to and do distort. Rashid Khalidi argues that this is the case when United States officials approach the question of Palestine. Policy-makers remain devoted to a flawed but powerful narrative for a host of unsound and even unworthy reasons.[6] They may be judged irrational.

The application of psychology to politics has been attempted essentially to test the limits of and constraints on the idealization that is rationality by examining the relationship between perceptions, images and beliefs and behavior, and particularly between politically relevant beliefs and policy choice. All statesmen work with psychological constraints. Beliefs exist and influence the direction of policy. Such explorations have tended to ignore not the structure and content of belief systems (the relationship between central and peripheral, and primitive and sophisticated beliefs, the open or closed nature, the rational content and the logical consistency of belief systems, and the differences between empirical and normative beliefs), but their origins and formulation.[7] It is generally agreed, for example, that statesmen seize on established images and rely on beliefs and preconceived views as they initially and intuitively respond to a problem, attempt to grasp the current situation and form perceptions about it. It should be noted that in this context 'misperception' is not the antithesis of 'perception'. Perceptions, intuitive responses, are the mind using ideas, insights, beliefs and convictions, not processing information. They are, by definition, faulty guides by themselves as to how to proceed. They cannot be part of a purely rational process. *Ex post facto*, with hindsight and information, historians may conclude that a particular perception of a statesman or official was unsound and judge it to be a misperception. But at the time, when it was important, it was merely and actually a perception. Beliefs help statesmen handle information, whether they seek the reassurance of consistency or causal relationships that suggest solutions to a problem. Images and beliefs, therefore, connect the present and the past in a very formal way because they are part of memory, of a person's mental repertoire, of his or her state of mind at any particular point in time.[8] Experience helps shape disposition. Yet while no one questions the fact that history, learned, observed and experienced, helps form images and beliefs, few have explored exactly how the education of a statesman takes place.[9]

If one knows how beliefs change then one can infer how they are formed. But belief systems are usually regarded as highly stable and resistant to change, largely because of the need psychologically to maintain consistency between beliefs and information. Conviction born of historical knowledge is a particularly potent source of such stability. Yet the assumption of enduring beliefs about foreign policy has been challenged convincingly.[10] Changes in personnel, statesmen relinquishing power and officials losing influence, are not the only ways the beliefs that help determine government policy mutate and are replaced. The beliefs of those who retain office and authority can be discredited and displaced; new beliefs can be adopted.

If the issue is also individual statesmen and officials operating as a group, as a policy community, which it is, then the relationship between the beliefs of an individual which are discrete and those beliefs which are shared in common by the group becomes important. And logically one must then explore the relationship between the beliefs of those in office and power and the beliefs of their contemporaries at home and in other states and societies. From those vantage points the degree of conformity and the extent of deviance can be explored, as biographers always have in their interest in men and women and their times. More mundanely, and to reconstruct Sam Rayburn's aphorism, statesmen are politicians who have been elected and seek re-election, or have been elevated by other than democratic processes. All of them require legitimacy and seek support. Those who occupy the White House and the Kremlin have much in common.

Jonathan Haslam argues that history observed and experienced, and reinforced through learning, can be traumatic and establish enduring beliefs which affect behavior profoundly and irrationally over a sustained period of time. This would appear to be the case at several levels, embracing, for example, individuals, ethnic groups and societies. Dwain Mefford, in the first of his two essays, examines how Soviet and United States scholars and practitioners are cooperating in an attempt to understand the Cuban Missile Crisis of 1962 and agree on an analytical narrative about it. He argues that that crisis, that traumatic event, more than any other single event, shaped the strategic relationship between the Soviet Union and the United States by creating in its aftermath a regime of assumptions, rules, conventions and bargaining strategies. Soviet and American statesmen, as they recoiled from the specter of nuclear war, learned and began to behave differently. A theory of learning, Mefford argues, is essential, therefore, if we are to understand how history shapes policy. It can be argued, and it has been, that these are psychological rather than historical processes but the dichotomy may be a false one. Condoleezza Rice sees the Soviet General Staff as an institution with a seventy-year history of dominance over the individual services and of carving out a sphere of control and action, but being vulnerable to and dependent on political influences and the preferences of individual leaders.

Twenty-five years ago Donald Watt began his examination of the governing beliefs of trans-Atlantic elites, their effect on policy in Britain and the United States and on the prospects for Anglo-American cooperation. Implicit in his original and subsequent work was the idea that beliefs have power, and that the influence of the beliefs of either elite at particular times reflects to some extent the relative distribution of power between Britain and the United States. In that way the leadership of any Pax Anglo-Americana would be determined. Political scientists are now exploring why different governments adopt the same new policies, simultaneously or sequentially, and agree on joint strategies, at crucial times in history. They may merely be responding to changing structural circumstances common to both or to the special circumstances of their own state. Or they may be adopting the fresh theories and new doctrines spreading out from a dominant state. That process could reflect some combination of intellectual coercion, adoption out of self-interest or mutually reciprocal, transnational learning. The resulting changes of policy and their general adoption could come with or without drama and crisis, but somehow old beliefs are discarded, a consensus forms around new beliefs, and a new strategy is pursued. Those who follow Donald Watt's lead, unknowingly it would seem, have yet to examine the influence on these processes of adaptation and learning by different states of historical knowledge learned, observed and experienced, and of divergent inventories of precedents and analogies of respective elites. They affect how policy within a state is changed and, if viewed transnationally, how policy coordination occurs between states.

Statesmen, aware of historical examples, seeing regularities and recurring phenomena, discovering parallels and patterns, make broad comparisons as they attempt to cope with complex agendas. Structural change, for example, occurs in the international political-strategic and economic systems, and in domestic arrangements. New states, Germany for example in 1870, enter the system; others are partitioned, redefined or actually eliminated. The relative distribution of power between states alters, forcing states into new positions in the rank order. Britain faced that predicament at the turn of the century.[11] Both the United States and the Soviet Union, each in their way, at different rates and for varied reasons, are experiencing such change today. Their prominence after the Second World War was based on sharply different combinations of economic, strategic and ideological imperatives. The challenges now facing the Soviet Union are more dramatically dangerous, but the foundations of American power were rocked first and the readjustments facing the United States may be more difficult to bring about. This estimation may seem to be in defiance certainly of media coverage and even of realities, but paradox is rarely absent from international affairs. And the United States must take on the consequences of the problems of the Soviet Union; the Soviet Union can evade those of the United States.

Whatever the truth of that, structural factors, such as changing distributions of power in the international system, do not by themselves explain a great deal nor in any way specific developments. Policy choice intervenes decisively between structures and results. It is never irrelevant to the rise or decline of states. It may contribute initially to or exacerbate a trend, enhancing relative rise or decline. Thus the relative position of states is littered with sound decisions and policy error. And so are less stark and dramatic changes than relative decline and rise. Indeed, the idea that a package of indicators, economic, political, strategic and ideological, will unite in pointing in the same direction at the same time, toward rise or decline, is convenient but not necessarily persuasive. That elites will invariably see it that way is even less probable. And there are many areas that require major policy adjustments without necessarily being made part of a formal calculus of rise or decline. But it is axiomatic that as statesmen grapple with the need to make such adjustments, they turn to the historical record, to comparison. They are to some degree, in the White House and the Kremlin, caught up in their versions of history. They look back into the experience of their own states and try to learn from the experience of others, the United States from Britain, for example. David Lake and Diane Kunz suggest that the United States, grappling with relative decline and the novel status of being a debtor, faces predicaments that resemble those confronting Britain generally after 1870 and, specifically with respect to financial strain, in 1931 and 1956. Current problems take on features of the past, and elements of previous cases appear in the present. How British statesmen adapted and coped deserves careful scrutiny by the White House and the bureaucracy, they argue, with as much attention being paid to crucial differences as to similarities.

Pressures and constraints come also from domestic sources and they may conflict with or reinforce those from the international environment. Presidents of the United States and leaders of the Soviet Union must, Janus-like, look outward to the world and inward into society. In the United States, the current contradiction between international market and security incentives for cooperation and domestic preferences for protectionism and unilateralism has intensified. In the Soviet Union, domestic pressures demand various economic, political and military innovations, and even make them virtually impossible to effect gradually. Greater degrees of integration into the world economy, forms of competition from outside, and comparisons made with developments in the non-communist and communist worlds mandate the adaptation of policy and even more dramatic and comprehensive change. Things are sufficiently serious for pundits to speak wistfully of controlled evolution or darkly of disintegration. These predicaments are not new in their essence, only in their intensity and urgency. There have been similar situations historically, several examples of corresponding circumstances either at home or abroad. Jeffry Frieden and Jack Snyder examine the significance of domestic factors. Frieden compares United States behavior, driven, he argues, by domestic economic interest groups, after each World War, in terms of fulfilling its responsibilities in the international financial system. He uses the comparison to assess what the world should now expect of Japan, and how Japan might respond, and why. The comparison might help Japan learn from the United States experience, but more particularly it should help the United States learn how to influence Japanese policy as Japan faces or evades its 'international responsibilities'. Snyder argues that an explanation for Soviet expansion and restraint lies in domestic political influences on policy rather than in systemic factors or cognitive processes. He suggests, implicitly, that Mikhail Gorbachev has learned from history observed and experienced, and that the United States can learn to adapt its policies toward the Soviet Union so as to help induce cooperative and restrained international behavior.

Analogies are a particular form of comparison. Statesmen and their advisers reason analogically and find reassurance in schema and stereotypes. They do so habitually as they formulate policy. Historical analogies, in the absence of homologies, take shape as similarities are found in earlier situations that were in fact different. Discrepancies may also be detected or confirmed as patterns are matched.[12] Historical analogies need not be narrow and confined. They can be elaborate. They may, in burst of enthusiasm mixed with relief, extend from narratives of events and actions to estimations of cause, from assessment of intent, purpose and motive of foreign governments to prediction of the behavior of other states, and to the prescribing of responses and strategies that will result in desirable solutions. Analogies can be, therefore, about relationships and take on explanatory power. A set of events in the past led to a particular result; a similar, current set of events will have the same outcome. The causes of a historical event were clearly the following; the problem now being faced, which mirrors the historical case, has equally discernible causes. The current protagonist resembles a previous competitor; its motives and purposes are, therefore, similar. A particular course of action proved to be an appropriate response before; it will work again.

Historical analogies, then, are not called upon merely to substantiate established beliefs and preferences. They affect the choice of policy as they interact with other factors. What it is to reason analogically, therefore, must be understood, for individuals and groups. To begin to understand it is to appreciate its value as much as to deplore its negative consequences. Statesmen use analogies to interpret situations and to formulate and frame problems. They define and re-define current problems in terms of corresponding and seemingly relevant problems of the past. They look for contexts for problems and what is apposite and fitting in previous examples. The exercise is, and is meant to be, comforting, for the familiar is a welcome sight. And an analogy may well provide initially a sound enough, general response to a problem by identifying reoccurring phenomena, and not necessarily to the exclusion of the specifics of the current situation. Problems are made more manageable initially if they can be simplified by being made members of known, established categories.

Statesmen and their officials require and acquire at the outset, therefore, information essentially about the nature of a problem. Historical knowledge about past analogous problems, called up from memory, is set alongside information gathered about the problem at hand, its recent history and current status. Both are forms of data that must be elevated to the status of evidence. Gathering information requires the expenditure of scarce resources. Recall from memory, on the other hand, is a particularly efficient though not necessarily sound way to acquire knowledge. As they weigh new, freshly presented information of various types and forms (statistical, literary, vivid, unimpressive) about a current problem, statesmen must judge both its source and content so as to determine its validity, and its relevance and completeness so as to test its value. What is recalled from memory is relatively free of such scrutiny and tests. And the historical record has the advantage of known outcomes. There are dangers here.

How problems are structured affects how alternative causes of action and strategies to implement them are ultimately viewed. Historical analogies are used to identify credible courses of action. Conceivably, alternatives range from the obvious to the obscure, from the plausible to the fantastic. Historical comparison helps restrict the universe of choice and narrows down the range of alternatives that deserve consideration. It helps statesmen differentiate between what is intellectually imaginable and what is politically feasible. It simplifies the challenge. Statesmen use historical analogies as one way to develop arguments about the respective merits of alternative courses of action so as to evaluate and rank them, if only in some rough and ready way, to see whether they are particularly promising. It is a matter of efficient and, it is hoped, effective evaluation, where analogical reasoning reinforces up to a certain point what rational calculations statesmen, limited by intellect, ability and resources can make. Rational processes involve the weighing of costs and benefits, means and ends, risks and probabilities, causal relations and consequences, and the significance of the actions of other parties involved in the problem. An argument that rests on the evidence that a strategy has worked in the past, can be implemented effectively once again, with results that are likely to be comfortingly incremental rather than disturbingly radical, may be powerfully persuasive. The case will be no less strong if it is made in negative terms, in order to banish a proposed course of action. Such an argument may contribute to logical debate and rational processes, but not necessarily so. If analogical reasoning alone identifies which alternative should be chosen, and, in effect, dictates policy, then a precedent-based choice has been made. The issue, during and as an integral part of decision sessions and not as a mere postscript, is also whether and how a policy can be legitimated effectively.[13] That is, is there ample precedent to justify the policy, and will the policy be seen to have legitimacy and earn support? Those considerations will be served also be analogical reasoning but rational choice may well be the casualty. Dwain Mefford and Alex Hybel reconstruct the way analogical reasoning occurs, using examples from Soviet and American decision-making. They chart a path not toward a new middle-level, policy relevant theory, but toward a refinement of established cognitive theories.

This attempt to tie the use of analogical reasoning to the generally recognized stages of the decision-making process is somewhat mechanical. There are also other problems. Although analogical reasoning is regarded as habitual, it is not enough simply to assert that statesmen use analogies pervasively, out of necessity, unavoidably, as standard fare. In fact, the records preserved, the archival evidence of policy debate, tend not to capture it. Archival records also fail to distinguish clearly the use of analogies from extrapolation. This may well be a problem of how procès-verbaux are generally recorded, but it nonetheless leaves behind a formidable research challenge. Moreover, because precedent is a most powerful tool of justification, memoirs and oral histories tend to distort the record. If analogical reasoning is difficult to detect, than its relationship to rational behavior in decision sessions is not immediately obvious. This does not matter at all to those who refuse, resolutely, to use archives. It matters less to those who place the use of historical analogies unreservedly in the cognitive and cybernetic rather than the rational realm. If statesmen reason analogically in order to develop simplified rules to handle information, and to deal with complexity, uncertainty, ambiguity and resulting stress, the issue can be left there. But if decision-making processes are hybrids and not strictly sequential, and they are,[14] and if the use of historical evidence can be seen as a part of rational behavior, and it can, then the balance is unclear and judgment of it becomes highly subjective. Indeed, for every abuse of history there is, apparently, a sensible use. In order to reduce the degree of subjectivity historians may ask what types of statesmen and officials, in what circumstances and over what types of issues, are more likely to use, in sensitive and discriminating fashion, historical analogies. And thus they can compare cognitive styles (contemplative, intuitive, collegial), roles and circumstances in which statesmen find themselves (individual and lonely authority, in groups), personalities (assured, confident, decisive, diffident), in crisis and routine situations, facing political and strategic as opposed to economic and social policy problems, and control for cultural and linguistic differences. But even then problems remain. Are there master analogies — 1914, Munich, Vietnam — high in representativeness and compelling, that take hold of the minds of a generation and on occasions overwhelm more specific analogies? Do analogies vary with generations? Do stereotypes identify individuals — Nasser as Mussolini or even Hitler — serve as analogies, and determine to a significant extent the formulation of policies to deal with them?

Those who have examined the use and abuse of history by statesmen and their officials have generally come to pessimistic conclusions.[15] Beyond the tendency of the naïve to look to history for moral guidance or to find evidence of progress, the abuses are, apparently, legion. The most common picture painted is of statesmen who are either simply unsophisticated, or who drop down to lower analytical standards in government service and under the pressures of office. As the higher standards are set, supposedly, in various non-governmental settings, including universities, academics report fluently on the lapses into sloth.

More specifically, criticism of the use of history in the policy process takes three forms that are not, however, always sharply distinguished. First, it is suggested that statesmen find in history, unjustifiably, a particular form of evidence that they regard as authoritative. That is because historical knowledge, a principal source of their sense of both constraint and opportunity, is part of their intellectual capital. It can be impressively vivid and seem compellingly salient. When statesmen call on the past they do so with singular confidence, whether they speak of individuals, governments, nations or societies. That is why historical information being used for advocacy and illustration rather than analysis still manages to impress. The *gravitas* of history may also undermine the search for new and relevant information. Statesmen have reason to resist fresh evidence as they find validity and truth in history. A small body of historical information may be allowed to outweigh a larger and more relevant body of evidence that contains, as it should, inconsistencies and as many dissimilarities as similarities. To the extent that history crowds out and outflanks other information, it undermines creativity and critical analysis. Historical evidence, initially having promoted a sense of understanding, then provides a ready source of *apologia, ex post facto* self-justification and rationalization. What has happened before is unfolding again; my views surely will be vindicated, and so on. In a word, statesmen, supposedly, prefer narrative to theory, sequence to science, a sense of the predictable, even the inevitable, to complication.[16]

One might ask, by way of illustration, how much, for example, of Henry Kissinger's acknowledged profundity comes from this apparent grasp of history, to which he turns without a trace of pedantry.[17] Yet even as he claims that history is the only meaningful source of experience, he can seem out of touch with much historical research and even unread as he compares the past and the present. But that criticism is a far cry from asserting, as some do, that the less history a statesman knows the more likely he is to make comparisons and pronounce with certainty on the relevance of the historical record to a current problem. It is not the same as suggesting that statesmen who do not master the recent history of a current problem and do not guard against serious lapses of individual, group and institutional memory, use historical analogies all the more freely. It is different from insisting that ignorance breeds analogies, that statesmen who do not know what has recently happened, what has been agreed upon in careful negotiation, resort to analogical reasoning. Such is the authority of history, however, that a group's 'historian', a status achieved or ascribed, may well dominate debate. This notwithstanding the fact that historical knowledge may lead to lengthy, even profound explanation of the past at the cost, not of failing to identify desired courses of action and solutions, but of inhibiting the ability to prescribe the choice that should be made. George Curzon's role as Foreign Secretary in the Lloyd George cabinet demonstrates the point. Members of policy groups find it difficult to argue against a version of the historical record when it is pronounced with authority by a dominant figure. Its author, impressive and seemingly disinterested, compares well with shifty lawyers, urgent scientists and eager strategists, even though he is grinding axes as he uses history. And when a respected or feared leader invents history, propagates myth, builds falsely an aura of invincibility and lapses into fatalism it seems to matter less than it should.

Yet, depending somewhat on the cognitive style of statesmen, historical knowledge, as was suggested above, can help them organize their thinking effectively as they confront a current problem. Memory can sharpen understanding. There is no reason a priori why the historically informed should discourage the search for information. Time might do that but not history. 'Getting it right' is, in part, by definition, searching for recent, specific historical information. It may also stimulate recall of comparative information from analogous, historical cases, but not necessarily with detrimental results. Validity of source and value of content remain the issue. There is no reason a priori why comparative historical information should be elevated over information about the problem at hand, including its recent, specific history, in the structuring of argument about alternative courses of action and strategies. Both types of information can be used appropriately, critically, discerningly, in discriminating fashion. Historical knowledge does not have to be a source of diagnosis rather than prescription, of elaborate pedantry rather than decisive advice. To know the recent history of a current problem is to have a decided and legitimate advantage in group argument and in negotiation. No one has yet tackled, however, the unfolding of negotiations when, for example, both parties are either well or badly informed historically, or one party is demonstrably better or worse informed than the other. Can A who is well informed really believe that B is so uninformed about the historical record? Will A then look for hidden agendas and concealed motive, and assume B is being provocative and confrontational rather than naïve and, therefore, disingenuous and irresponsible? The dynamics are compounded in multilateral negotiations. And what of the wisdom or danger of assuming that an opponent must be making the same comparisons, must have drawn the same analogies and must have seen the same lessons in the past as one has oneself? This might result in a particularly significant error of attribution.

Second, statesmen are said to find in history a certainty where uncertainty reigns. Certainty has many faces — causes that explain undeniably effects and point to predictable, even inevitable results; processes of change that are simple, continuous and at even rates, without subtlety, discontinuities and variations of tempo; extrapolations that make the possible inevitable and conjecture irrelevant; inexorable developments that make counterfactuals and imagination unnecessary; patterns and parallels that *exist*; indubitable trends that unfold without interruption; and regularities that will not be disturbed. Statesmen, supposedly, see, in fact, what historians do not. But at least they join in solemn, tacit alliance to give history greater significance than theory. They do this whether or not they recognize that history is a principal source of theory, that questions about problems are informed by theory, and that theory underpins, if only implicitly, decisions. Historians, surprised that their work is taken so seriously, bewildered by the fact that what is to them a matter of interpretation and contingency and may already be discredited, is accepted as truth, have been more vocal in their criticism of theorists than of historically naïve statesmen. Some see their task actually as studying the rise and fall of theories.[18] The rapidity and ease with which theories in international relations bite the dust, some of it from archives, gives their professional lives a rare dose of excitement. There may be euphoria among historians when war is seen to be obsolescent without there every having been a plausible theory of war.

Yet anarchy, the axiom of the international system, is not chaos; it has rules. Certain problems, relationships, dilemmas, the security dilemma for example, as well as structures, the coral reefs of the system, endure and reoccur. It is not imbecilic to look for patterns and regularities. History is the record of uncertainty as individuals make choices given the presence of prevailing structures, but that points to the value of counterfactual reasoning, to the promise of fusing history and imagination, not to abandoning the business of government to the argument that everything is marked by its uniqueness. Are statesmen unable, necessarily, to distinguish between what is novel and what is enduring, what is unique from what is replicable, what should be compelling and what is deviant? Are they unable to differentiate between a flimsy pattern and a sound generalization? Can they not develop a healthy scepticism about confident predictions and facile or premature assurances about results? Do they have to be insensitive to change over time, to differentiated rates of change and discontinuities, and to the way the meaning of words or the significance of concepts changes over time and culture? And is it not sensible to extrapolate, to attempt to get a more acute sense of risks, probabilities and consequences, of where a course of action might lead?

Third, statesmen are reputed to extract from history comparisons that they see as powerfully instructive and lessons that are clear and unambiguous. The comparisons made may well be simplistic, misleading and even irrelevant and the lessons feeble, superficial and unsound. Whether history experienced is more compelling in this regard than history observed or learned is not clear. In the Reagan administration, apparently, the President remembered California; Caspar Weinberger, the Secretary of Defense, would not forget the Second World War; while Fred Ikle of the NSC and John Lehman, when Secretary of the Navy, posed as resident historians, pedantic and frequently wrong.[19]

Analogical reasoning is a particular type of comparative reasoning. Analogies that simplify the past so that the present resembles it, or simplify the present so that it mirrors the past, are said to entrance rather than warn, divert rather than focus attention. They conjure up similarities that do not exist, or give quite trivial similarities undue significance. It matters little to statesmen, apparently, that the similarities may have been deduced from a limited set of examples, or even from one past event, and that the risks of bias and distortion are correspondingly high. Analogies ignore important dissimilarities which may be the critical specifics of the current situation. It is said to be particularly dangerous to assume that when problems seem familiar, when cases seem similar, then causal relationships are comparable. That at the very least may blur the distinction between necessary and sufficient cause. That fact is that while historical outcomes are known, the reasons for them often remain obscure. Certainty of consequence is not matched by certainty of cause. Equally contentious is the assumption that because a certain current action resembles a past action then motive, intent and purpose have remained constant. The policies of others are made to appear to be what they are not, especially when statesmen and officials are set on advocacy, on reinforcing favorite ideas and securing the acceptance of entrenched views. Individuals in foreign governments are assigned motives and given intent, or consistency of motive and firmness of intent, which they may well lack.

To reason analogically, therefore, is to be imprecise, to be superficial and facile, to be impressed with broad and general interpretations, to fail to monitor new circumstances, to find false validity or infer incorrectly, even when the analogy is valid. The presence of seeming consistency leads to a level of confidence that is unwarranted and thus to policy error. A thorough search for viable alternative ways of handling a current problem seems less necessary. Statesmen will be loath to eliminate a strategy that has worked in the past. It is convenient, inherently plausible and readily at hand. An alternative course of action that worked in the past may in fact be inappropriate now; one that failed before may now be entirely appropriate. Earlier success can impress unduly; failure can be attributed to the wrong reason. Benefits can be exaggerated, costs trivialized. In effect, the use of analogies is debilitating because it undermines rationality. It represents a short-cut to interpretation and judgment which leads invariably to decisions that are unsound and unwise, and sometimes disastrous.

Yet can this condemnation of historically based reasoning be turned into a call for statesmen to be ahistorical? Historically based reasoning can be seen as undermining rational decision-making and resulting in unsound decisions. The participants in a game theoretic situation behave, as they are meant to do, without ethics, history or psychology; options are set out in advance. But it can be argued that exploring similar historical problems, using the record of the past and comparing present with previous situations, with all their dissimilarities and uncertainties, to arrive at policy alternatives can be consistent, up to a point, with rational processes of choice. If one breaks, as one should, with the strict canons of classical rationality and recognizes that statesmen have limited intellectual skills and computational abilities, and finite resources, then one should ask of them only that they attempt, to the best of their ability and in the circumstances, to reach sound decisions. In other words, accept the fact that a statesman is not *homo economicus*, begin at a reasonable point of departure, with the realistic assumptions of bounded rationality as defined by Herbert Simon, and work with the degrees of incrementalism and satisficing that will result. No statesman sets out to be irrational, no official sets out to be ignored.

Learning through controlled comparison presents significant, possibly unsurmountable, challenges even to the most careful and talented of policy communities.[20] But analogical reasoning can assist the decision-making process and help statesmen, up to a point, make decisions of high quality. Analogies, as President Eisenhower demonstrated in his handling of the Suez crisis in 1956, do not have to dominate debate. Flimsy analogies can be and were dismissed out of hand. Egypt in 1956 was not Iran in 1953; Nasser was not Musaddiq.[21] Analogies may well limit the range of alternative courses of action statesmen consider, mask important options, and give the less apt an unfounded degree of prominence. But they need neither eliminate the apposite not restrict careful examination of seemingly credible alternative strategies and their consequences. Analogies can illuminate choice without dictating it. It would be irrational to use historical analogies to the exclusion of other factors to decide on a course of action. It may well be that statesmen find excessively attractive courses of action that can be repeated without serious modification, as they exaggerate the beneficial results from an act of satisficing. But to examine solutions that have worked in the past in order to handle a current problem, especially if values and goals are relatively stable, does not mean that the statesmen will choose a course of action in a dangerously mechanical way. Indeed, as statesmen contemplate how their predecessors, using their best judgment, handled comparable problems, they might develop a wise, cautious and sensible sense of restraint.

This is not to argue that experience is necessarily profitable or that learning from comparison and analogy invariably promotes understanding. Learning in that fashion may confirm established views that are unsound and alter views that are sound. Knowing the past never inoculated anyone from error. Thus judgment on this score, on whether historically based reasoning undermines or contributes to rational processes, remains highly subjective and inadequately explored. In its place we have advice, from a very few historians and political scientists, on how statesmen might use history more effectively, both to master the recent history of a current problem and to compare and use analogies. These prescriptions are usually eminently sensible and appropriately modest.[22] They are consistent both with the proposition that historically based reasoning is efficient and can be effective, and that, strictly speaking, it is unwise to expect history to provide lessons. Perhaps useful advice is always somewhat banal.[23]

Notes

1. For a splendid restatement of this theme see Frank Ninkovich, 'Interests and Discourse in Diplomatic History', *Diplomatic History*, **13**, 2, Spring 1989, pp. 135–61. Kennan, diplomat turned historian, believed that statesmen, if they were to understand power, its evolving configurations and role in international relations, and the national interest, must grasp in a profound way historical trends, processes and logic. If they had not, from Woodrow Wilson on, disaster had followed.
2. Robert Jervis argued that history observed directly, early in adult life, that affected an individual or his country, and experienced, especially when it was vivid, dramatic and even traumatic, is more potent than history learned, for several reasons — it is more readily available from memory, it is recognized earlier as relevant information and evidence, it has helped form perceptions and analogies, and it is less dismissible because it is seemingly more concrete and relevant, especially when a statesman retains power over an extended period of time and faces a series of similar problems. Jervis does not disengage history observed, the experience of others, sufficiently from history personally experienced. The exceptions may well be significant. Personal experience is sometimes suppressed for psychological reasons. And occasionally statesmen face challenges for which observation and personal experience provide no guide. When governments in the First World War grappled with the fact of the Bolshevik Revolution, they turned to the French Revolution. When they compared the war with earlier conflicts they evoked the American Civil War and the Napoleonic Wars, not the Boer War or the Russo-Japanese War. A second question is which kind of history is likely to provide the surer guide. To attempt to answer this involves one in assessing the value of detachment and perspective as opposed to involvement and exposure.

3. Alan K. Henrikson, 'The Geographical "Mental Maps" of American Foreign Policy Makers', *International Political Science Review*, **1**, 4, 1980, pp. 498–500.

4. Ada Bozeman, *Politics and Culture in International History* (Princeton: Princeton University Press, 1960); Klaus Knorr, ed., *Historical Dimensions of National Security Problems* (Lawrence: University Press of Kansas, 1976); Michael Fry, *History and International Relations* (Washington, DC: American Historical Association, 1987); and Christopher Thorne, *Border Crossings: Studies in International History* (Oxford: Basil Blackwell, 1988), pp. 3–55. My impression is that statesmen and politicians read, and write, biographies, memoirs and diaries. They prefer individuals to structures, politics to economics, narrative to theory. Cultural rather than ideological differences may well, however, point to other preferences.

5. The phrase is Alan Henrikson's.

6. Bernard Lewis, *History — Remembered, Received, Invented* (Princeton: Princeton University Press, 1975), and Charles S. Maier, *Wargames: 1914–1919*, in Robert I. Rotberg and Theodore K. Rabb, eds, *The Origins and Prevention of Major Wars* (Cambridge: Cambridge University Press, 1989), pp. 249–79.

7. Richard Little, 'Belief Systems in the Social Sciences', and John Maclean, 'Belief Systems and Ideology in International Relations: A Critical Approach', in Richard Little and Steve Smith, *Belief Systems and International Relations* (Oxford: Basil Blackwell, 1988), pp. 37–56 and 57–82. See also Ernest R. May, 'The Nature of Foreign Policy: the Calculated Versus the Axiomatic', *Daedalus*, **91**, 1962, pp. 653–67.

8. Richard Wollheim, *The Thread of Life* (Cambridge: Cambridge University Press, 1985), and Eric Hobsbawm, *The Age of Empire, 1875–1914* (London: Weidenfeld and Nicolson, 1987), pp. 1–12.

9. Michael Fry, *Lloyd George and Foreign Policy, Volume I: The Education of a Statesman, 1890–1916* (Montreal: McGill-Queen's University Press, 1977).

10. Deborah Welch Larson, *Origins of Containment* (Princeton: Princeton University Press, 1985).

11. Robert Gilpin, *War and Change in World Politics* (Cambridge: Cambridge University Press, 1981); P. Kennedy, *The Rise and Fall of the Great Powers* (New York: Random House, 1987); and Aaron Friedberg, *Weary Titan* (Princeton: Princeton University Press, 1988).

12. Philip A. Schrodt, 'Adaptive Precedent-Based Logic and Rational Choice: A Comparison of Two Approaches to the Modelling of International Behavior', in Urs Luterbacher and Michael D. Ward, eds, *Dynamic Models of International Conflict* (Boulder: Lynne Reinner, 1985), pp. 373–400. He demonstrates how analogies and precedents are used in decision-making by 'pattern matching', which relates a current situation to an analogous past situation by certain rules. Thus precedents and analogies have similar functions to standard operating procedures. Statesmen have an inventory of experiences stored in the memory and when they face a current problem they turn to that inventory to find the closest match. This enables them to see what has been and should be done, to act and to evaluate the results to see whether the inventory should be changed. Recall in fact continues to assist reasoning in a formal, rule-based way, even when the inventory changes.

13. Michael Fry, *Facing Both Ways: Foreign Policy and the Legitimation Imperative: Eisenhower and the Suez Crisis* (forthcoming), and Paul A. Anderson, 'Justification and Precedents as Constraints on Foreign Policy Decision-Making', *American Journal of Political Science*, **25**, 4, November 1981, pp. 732–61.

14. Janice Gross Stein and Raymond Tanter, *Rational Decision Making* (Columbus, Ohio State University Press, 1980).
15. Herbert Butterfield, *History and Human Relations* (London: Collins, 1951); Peter Geyl, *The Use and Abuse of History* (New Haven: Yale University Press, 1955); Glenn D. Paige, *The Korean Decision* (New York: Free Press, 1968); Ernest R. May, *'Lessons' of the Past: The Use and Misuse of History in American Foreign Policy* (New York: Oxford University Press, 1973); Robert Jervis, *Perception and Misperception in International Politics* (Princeton: Princeton University Press, 1976), pp. 217–87 and his 'Hypotheses on Misperception', in Klaus Knorr, ed., *Power, Strategy and Security* (Princeton: Princeton University Press, 1985), pp. 152–77; Glenn H. Snyder and Paul Deising, *Conflict Among Nations* (Princeton: Princeton University Press, 1977), pp. 369–74; Miles Kahler, 'Rumors of War: the 1914 Analogy', *Foreign Affairs*, **58**, Winter 1980, pp. 374–96; John P. Lovell, 'Lessons from US Military Involvement: Preliminary Conceptualizations', and James P. Bennett, 'Data Stories: Learning About Learning From the US Experience in Vietnam', in Donald A. Sylvan and Steve Chan, eds, *Foreign Policy Decision Making* (New York: Praeger 1984), pp. 129–57 and 227–79; Richard Neustadt and Ernest R. May, *Thinking in Time: The Uses of History for Decision Makers* (New York: Free Press, 1986); and Yaacov Y. I. Vertzberger, 'Foreign Policy Decisionmakers as Practical-Intuitive Historians: Applied History and its shortcomings', in *International Studies Quarterly*, **30**, 1986, pp. 223–47. Of course, many scholars recently interested in decision processes, such as Charles Lindblom, Graham Allison, Alexander George and Morton Halperin, have touched on the subject, while others have noted the similarity between the use of analogical reasoning and standard operating procedures in cybernetic and organizational models (J. Keegan, 'The Human Face of Deterrence', *International Security*, **6**, 1981, pp. 136–51).
16. For an argument that policy-makers think either in sequential or systemic terms, as historians, or as political scientists, but never as both, see John Lewis Gaddis, 'Expanding the Data Base: Historians, Political Scientists and the Enrichment of Security Studies', *International Security*, **12**, 1, Summer 1987, pp. 3–21.
17. Henry Kissinger, 'The Lessons of the Past: A Conversation with Walter Laqueur, *The Washington Review*, **1**, 1, January 1978, pp. 1–9.
18. Thorne, *Border Crossings*, p. 6.
19. Interview with Lawrence Korb, Washington, DC, July 1986.
20. David H. Fischer, *Historians' Fallacies: Toward a Logic of Historical Thought* (New York: Harper and Row 1970); Paul Gordon Lauren, 'Crisis Management; History and Theory in International Conflict', *The International History Review*, **1**, 4, October 1979, pp. 342–556; Alexander George, 'Case Studies and Theory Development: The Method of Structured, Focused Comparison', in Paul Gordon Lauren, ed., *Diplomacy* (New York: Free Press, 1979), pp. 43–68, and W.W. Rostow, 'Beware of Historians Bearing False Analogies', *Foreign Affairs*, **66**, Spring 1988, pp. 863–8.
21. Roger Hilsman suggested that Lyndon Johnson resorted fairly freely to analogies whereas John Kennedy did not, but Kennedy was not immune to the appeal of analogies presented by the military and the CIA when dealing with Cuba. The Bay of Pigs example came up frequently (interview with Roger Hilsman, New York, 1988).
22. May and Neustadt make six points. First, look before you leap; do not over-

react; do not lock into hastily constructed assumptions; seek perspective; guard against excessive zeal; frame the problem carefully before looking for solutions; do not rush to act. Second, avoid dependence on fuzzy analogies; look for differences as vigorously as for similarities; get to the really salient questions; what comes to mind is not necessarily what is relevant; do not let analogies cloud vision. Third, know the history of the problem; know how it arose; sort out the facts; distinguish between the known, the unclear and the presumed. Fourth, analyze alternatives carefully; think about the basic presumptions behind alternatives; analyze rather than advocate solutions which one has already decided on prior to the debate; ask about alternative solutions the following questions — will it work, will it stick, and, if not, turn to what other solution; know the history of one's own society as well as that of others and thus have a sense of what society, in light of its traditions, values and precedents, will accept. Fifth, do not use stereotypes to 'place' persons or organizations; get a clearer picture of them so as to be able to understand their conduct. Sixth, see choice as part of a historical sequence; connect events over time and see if the connection makes sense; understand the nature of change over time; see time as a stream where what is now has flowed from the past but is now, in certain critical ways, different from the past; get a clear sense of the extent to which the present is and is not different from the past. Vertzberger, warning against the use of 'instant analogies', urges use of a 'control group' (additional similar events and deductive logic) and seeking ways to avoid unwarranted group consensus (check with professional historians and turn the relationships contained in an analogy into a puzzle).

23. If statesmen and their advisers are to 'get it right', if the presidential and institutional memories are to be sharp and clear, if knowledge is to be comprehensive, if continuity is to be maintained between administrations, then records have to be made, preserved, retrieved and used fully, efficiently and effectively. Official, authoritative records in the most appropriate form of past transactions, negotiations, debate, decision and implementation must be kept. They must not be a matter initially of oral reports and then of casual, episodic recall. Every administration must work on the assumption that all other governments manage their records effectively and may enjoy, therefore, a decided advantage in negotiation. This must be done despite the legitimate concern for secrecy, the fear of leaks, the risk of unauthorized or premature disclosure and other forms of abuse. Officials leaving office must turn over their records and papers. Fear of condemnation, greed and the determination to be one's own historian must not be allowed to stand in the way. The problems of transition in Washington are, on this score, by all accounts, horrendous. Each wave of decision-makers, therefore, must learn anew, and surely with debilitating consequences for the conduct of the nation's business.

2 United States policy and the Palestine problem: historical dimensions and the creation of an 'alternative narrative'
Rashid I. Khalidi

In moments of crisis, political leaders fall back on unspoken assumptions, and their intentions can often only be judged in the light of what we can discover about these assumptions.' (James Joll, '1914: The Unspoken Assumptions', in H.W. Koch, ed., *The Origins of the First World War*, London: Macmillan, 1972, p. 309)

Three propositions illuminate the way in which the United States has related to the historical dimensions of the Palestine problem over more than four decades. They are particularly relevant to the more recent past, but have some validity even for the earliest stages of meaningful American involvement, in the mid 1940s. They are:

1. History has in most cases not served as a guide for the formulation of United States policy. Rather, other considerations have tended to prevail.
2. In the past, and even more in the present, much energy has been devoted to obscuring lessons and precedents derived from history, generally with the objective of implementing policies which are politically expedient, and frequently to great effect.
3. Success in dealing with the Palestine issue in the future will depend increasingly on a correct appreciation of its historical dimensions, as aspects of it which were purposely obscured for much of the past four decades re-emerge and demand solution.

In practice, these three propositions boil down to an argument that the American policy-making process on this issue has become almost ahistorical with the progression of time. This process has suffered also from the familiar, chronic American foreign policy malaise of starting *ab initio* as virtually every new president and his foreign policy advisors learn on the job about the issues facing them, and about the precedents by which they are supposed to be bound. This happens with regard to many foreign policy areas. Quite frequently precedent is deliberately ignored when a new president believes that he has a mandate to change policy.

Beyond that, however, policy-making with regard to the Palestine problem has suffered particularly severely from its historical and other specificities being ignored. In time, what amounts to an 'alternate narrative' of the history of this issue, one quite distinct from that accepted by many experts, and even from that enshrined in the institutional memory of the foreign-policy bureaucracy, and one based largely on the official Israeli position, has established itself in Washington and become 'reality' in political terms. This took place first in the political arena and on Capitol Hill, and then in parts of the executive branch starting in the 1960s, and came to impinge in ever more significant ways on policy-making.

The first two propositions apply with increasing validity to virtually every period of American policy-making towards the Palestine problem which, for most of the past four decades, has been subsumed under the rubric of the Arab–Israeli conflict. The very wording here is a perfect illustration of what has occurred, for the power to name often means control over process. What was originally called the Palestine problem became the Arab–Israeli conflict for a variety of reasons, some objective and some less so. Objectively, after their crushing military defeat in the months leading up to May 1948, and the expulsion of over half of the Arab population of the country from their homes, the Palestinians ceased to be the main Arab protagonists in the conflict, being replaced by the Arab states.

However, crucial aspects of the conflict continue to this day and concern the final disposition of the former territory of mandated Palestine, and its people. This reality is reflected in United Nations terminology and resolutions which for over forty years have consistently referred to a 'Palestine question,' even in the 1950s when the United States almost completely dominated that organization. The United States regularly voted for many such resolutions, notably those which from 1948 onwards annually called for the 'repatriation or compensation' of the 750,000 Palestinians who were made refugees in 1948.[1] Nevertheless, within the United States foreign policy establishment and in American discourse, the term Palestine rapidly disappeared.

Not coincidentally, this meshed with the thrust of Israeli policy, which consistently tried to define the conflict as being between Israel and its Arab neighbors, rather than the Palestinians. The very existence of the latter was an embarrassment, as it recalled the ambivalent circumstances in which Israel was born, and the fact that the conflict had roots deeper than the ongoing disputes between the Arab states and Israel. Out of such motivations came Israel's long-standing attempts to delegitimize the Palestinians, symbolized by Golda Meir's infamous remark that there were no Palestinians, an assertion which found a concrete echo in the increasing blindness of American policy to their existence.

Furthermore, beyond this development, there was a deterioration in the American policy-making process regarding the Palestine issue over time, and distinct variations in different periods. These periods have tended to coincide with changing presidential administrations.

Most of the first crucial decisions relating to Palestine taken by the Truman administration from 1946–1949 fit this pattern. These were the decisions to call for the immediate entry of 100,000 European Jewish death-camp survivors to Palestine in 1946; to advocate the partition of the country in 1947 and recognize Israel the year after; to acquiesce in the tacit understandings between Israel and Transjordan, and between Transjordan and Great Britain, to prevent the establishment of a Palestinian state alongside Israel as called for in the 1947 partition plan[2]; and to address the conflict after the 1948–9 Arab-Israeli war as one between the Arab states and Israel to which the Palestinians were no longer a party, but simply refugees.

These decisions defined crucial parameters for American policy towards the conflict, some of which are still in place. In these decisions, history was generally not taken into account, notably the history of the complications for Britain of her relations with the Arab states because of the Palestine issue. In his one major intervention over the Palestine question, President Roosevelt in 1945 had promised Saudi King 'Abd al-'Aziz Ibn Sa'ud that the United States would take no action on Palestine 'hostile to the Arab people'.[3] At the same time, Roosevelt repeated his endorsement of the Zionist program for Palestine, which at that stage was to create there a 'Jewish commonwealth'.[4] The impossibility of reconciling these contradictory imperatives was never resolved by Roosevelt, who died only weeks after giving both pledges, but it was to dog his successors, as it had dogged British policy-makers for three decades.

Equally important in the taking of American decisions, the imperatives of the local situation in the region tended to be downplayed in favor of influences from elsewhere. This was true whether these influences came from the extension to the Middle East of the growing US-Soviet rivalry, from relations with European allies, the plight of Jewish refugees in Europe, or domestic political considerations relating to the support of the American Jewish community for the Yishuv, and later for Israel.

Thus, the call for the entry into Palestine of 100,000 Jews, made in the heat of the 1946 election campaign, and at a time when US immigration laws kept out most Jews desirous of coming to the United States, ignored the crucial fact that the issue of immigration had been bitterly contested between Palestinians and Zionists for over half a century. Just before the Second World War, it had sparked off the Arab revolt of 1936–9 in which 5000 Arabs had died, 15,000 were wounded and over 5000 detained.[5] The Arab revolt had impelled the British to issue the May 1939 White Paper which instituted immigration controls. This issue therefore had a local resonance in Palestine and the region, quite distinct from that derived from humanitarian considerations related to Nazi crimes against the Jews of Europe which tended to prevail in the United States.

Similarly, the partition of Palestine was anathema to the Arabs for many reasons, not least because the UN plan to do so gave 55 per cent of the country to a Jewish minority which constituted about one-third of the population, and owned under 6 per cent of the land. American support for partition was a function mainly of domestic considerations and the strong pressure of the Zionist movement, reinforced by the nascent competition with the Soviet Union in the Middle East, rather than of a reading of local considerations or of the history of the issue, notably the British experience with partition plans. Most Foreign Service professionals acquainted with the Arab world foresaw the problems that would arise for US policy. The State Department thus argued for caution, but was ultimately overruled.

Finally, the decision to acquiesce in Jordan's attempt to assert hegemony over the Palestinians, which fitted into a broader trend of downplaying the Palestinian aspects of the conflict, was largely a response to the approval for such an outcome of both the new Israeli state and America's ally, Britain. It ignored a historically based reading of the fundamentals of the case, notably the strength of Palestinian nationalism, even after the calamitous adversity which befell the Palestinians in 1948, and the limitations on the legitimacy and capabilities of the Jordanian state. Both of these factors were soon to pose serious problems, first for British and later for American policy-makers, after the United States, in the late 1950s, took over the task of providing the subsidies on which Jordan for so long depended.

This pattern of both ignoring the local specificities of the problem and its history (both the genesis of the problem itself and the experience of Great Britain), and of according influences from elsewhere greater importance, continued. Indeed, it intensified with succeeding administrations as they confronted new aspects of the Arab–Israeli conflict, and as Israel grew stronger and its influence in American public life expanded. Even if one or another of these factors was inoperative in a given period others would prevail, as became clear during the Eisenhower years. The nature of the electoral base of the Republican Party in this period insulated the Eisenhower administration to a large degree from domestic political pressures in relation to the Palestine issue which had strongly affected the Democrats. The Eisenhower administration nevertheless tended to be preoccupied with the Soviet Union and with relations with Britain and France. Thus, even when it took harsh measures against Israel in the wake of the 1956 war, it did so more out of global strategic considerations than for ones derived from a regional calculus. This global, Cold War preoccupation of United States policy with things non-Middle Eastern had already poisoned relations with Egypt and thus neutralised any possible positive impact of the United States stand over Suez. It did so again after the 1956 Suez war, when it resulted in the issuance of the entirely Cold War-derived Eisenhower Doctrine, which was highly unpopular in the Arab world.[6]

At the same time, the Eisenhower administration went further than the preceding one in dealing with the Palestinian refugees. John Foster Dulles saw them as no more than a nuisance, and expressed the belief that within a generation they would cease to be a coherent group and would integrate into the surrounding Arab societies, following international efforts at resettlement.[7] Under Dean Acheson, Truman's secretary of state, a modicum of effort had been devoted to attempting to persuade Israel to accept the repatriation of more than token numbers of refugees. This reflected the UN General Assembly resolutions voted for annually by the United States from December 1948 which called for repatriation of or compensation for Palestinians made refugees in 1948. Although such votes continued under Dulles's stewardship of the Department of State (and indeed through the 1980s), under his impetus the permanent resettlement of these refugees outside their homeland became United States policy, thinly disguised under the rubric of the Johnston irrigation plan.[8] Although it absorbed the energies of American Middle East policy-makers for years, this was a futile effort. That was because of the resistance of the refugees themselves to anything but repatriation or compensation, the strong sympathy which the populations of the Arab countries felt for the Palestinians, and the resulting reluctance of the prospective host governments which, virtually without exception, had been initially favorable to the idea. This episode provided a near perfect example of the creation of a myth which became a central part of the 'alternate narrative' of the Palestine problem: the idea that the Arab governments concerned opposed Palestinian refugee resettlement. In fact, the governments of Lebanon, Jordan and Syria initially gave the idea a favorable reception.[9] They reversed their position only as a result of popular pressure in the wake of strong protests by the Palestinians themselves.

Harmful though Dulles's futile efforts to evade and ignore the Palestinians had been, more damage was probably done by him and his successors through their looking at the problem of Palestine and seeing the Soviet Union rather than regional specificities. During the Democratic administrations which followed that of Eisenhower, there was a confluence between this ideological factor and the domestic considerations to which Democrats were traditionally more responsive. During the Vietnam war in particular, this led to a situation in Middle East policy-making where the interests of Israel came to be identified with those of the United States, and opposed to those of the Soviet Union and the key Arab states involved in conflict with Israel. These Arab states were perceived as clients of the Soviet Union. It was against this background that important elements of the 'alternate narrative' so favorable to Israel first established a beach-head in sectors of the executive branch such as the National Security Council and the Department of Defense. This occurred under presidents who had come out of the Congress, where the 'alternative narrative' was already well established. Thus, during the Kennedy and Johnson administrations important decisions such as supplying Israel with weapons, which the United States had never overtly done before, responding in particular ways to the 1967 Arab–Israeli war, and putting forward a basis for dealing with the new situation which arose from that war were largely determined by superpower rivalries exacerbated by Vietnam, and by a new view of Israel emanating from this 'alternative narrative'. The impact of the newly galvanized American Jewish community, especially after Israel's victory in 1967, was also important in these decisions.[10] The community influenced foreign-policy-making circles during the Kennedy and Johnson administrations by way of a number of fervent supporters of Israel who served or counseled the presidents, including Clark Clifford, Abe Fortas, Arthur Goldberg, and Walt and Eugene Rostow.

During these Democratic administrations there was a reprise of the influence of domestic factors on policy towards the Palestine issue, as had been the case under Truman, in contrast to the situation under Eisenhower. But under Kennedy and Johnson, as under Eisenhower, strategic considerations, notably an obsessive preoccupation with the Soviet Union, tended to drive policy, rather than domestic factors. This was strongly accentuated by Johnson's growing preoccupation with the Vietnam war as the 1960s wore on. It was evidenced by the increased level of direct and indirect American involvement in the Yemeni civil war, which matched growing Soviet involvement.

When the 1967 Arab-Israeli war broke out, it was treated primarily against the background of the crisis in South East Asia, and the need to 'take a stand' in the Middle East against the Soviet Union and those Arab states seen as its regional pawns, a perception we now know to have been utterly baseless.[11] Though some of Johnson's advisors were affected by their deep sympathy for Israel's position, and influenced by the popular apocalyptic view of Israel's vulnerability on the eve of the 1967 war (a view now known to be demonstrably false),[12] their influence on policy was enhanced because it was couched in the polarized terms of East–West conflict prevalent in the Vietnam era.

The questions of Israel's vulnerability on the eve of the 1967 war, and of its responsibility for starting that conflict are further instances of the encroachment of the 'alternative narrative' on policy-making. For while American intelligence had determined in late May that the Arab states were not about to attack, and 'both the CIA and Pentagon were convinced that Israel would easily win if hostilities were to begin, no matter who struck first',[13] quite different propositions established themselves in the political arena. These were derived essentially from the Israeli propaganda barrage launched in support of its military offensive, and from the folly of the Arab states which provided Israel with a provocation, a *casus belli*, and goaded Israel with huge amounts of warlike rhetoric, while being utterly unprepared themselves for war.

Regrettably, whatever lessons might have been learned from the history of the problem to that point, and its treatment by earlier administrations, were ignored in the wake of the 1967 war. Both the line taken by the United States during the negotiations for peace which followed the 1948 war (of pressing Israel to give up some areas which it had captured, and to accept limited refugee repatriation in return for peace), and the firm stand opposing Israel's occupation of Egyptian territory in 1956–7, were abandoned. Instead, under the icy impact of Cold War stereotypes applied to the Middle East, combined with the sympathy of key officials for the Israeli position, and the growing salience of the 'alternative narrative' in the political arena, the Johnson administration adopted a policy of allowing Israel to retain the occupied territories and their populations until the Arab states accepted Israel's position on crucial issues still in dispute. This policy has been upheld by succeeding administrations, with negative consequences for US regional policy. They grew worse over time as Israel became totally dependent on US arms and aid, a situation which meant concretely that the United States was underwriting whatever Israel did in these territories, whether it approved publicly or not.

This flawed policy was consecrated in Security Council resolution 242 of 22 November 1967, which , while drafted by the British Ambassador to the UN Lord Caradon, closely reflected the view of the Johnson administration. Its flaws were most glaring with regard to the Palestine refugee question, a subject not mentioned by name in a resolution purporting to lay down a framework for peace in the Middle East. Instead, resolution 242 refers only to 'a just solution to the refugee problem'. This is a formulation so ambivalent as to permit some to claim that it applied as well to Jewish refugees forced to leave the Arab world after the creation of Israel — and it may indeed have been intended to mean that by its drafters. While the resolution does not mention the Palestinian refugees' right to repatriation or compensation, which several Arab governments had urged be done during the many months in which this resolution was being hammered out, that is from June until November 1967,[14] it does not fail to address a single Israeli preoccupation. Although resolution 242 has often been invoked since its adoption with the reverence normally accorded scripture, and although it has served as an element in some successful and unsuccessful efforts since then to defuse aspects of the Arab–Israeli conflict, the extent to which it has been ignored in practice over more than two decades is remarkable. After all this time, it has still not been implemented with regard to the most heavily populated and controversial of the territories occupied in 1967, that is the West Bank, including Jerusalem, the Gaza Strip, and the Golan Heights. Indeed, various Israeli governments have disputed its applicability to them.

Moreover, neither Secretary of State Henry Kissinger's three disengagement accords of 1973–5 between Israel and Egypt and Syria, nor the Camp David accords and the Egyptian–Israeli separate peace which resulted from them, pay much more than lip-service to the core principles of the resolution. This may not seem true of the Egyptian–Israeli peace treaty, inasmuch as a trade of 'land for peace', which is in many ways at the heart of resolution 242, would seem to be its main result. Nevertheless, other key precepts of resolution 242, such as the inadmissibility of the acquisition of territory by war, and the requirement for withdrawal of Israeli forces from areas occupied during the 1967 conflict could only be implemented in the Egyptian case via a decoupling of Egypt from the solution of the problems at issue between Israel and its other neighbors, and via one-sided limitations on Egypt's sovereignty and freedom of action in the areas it recovered.[15] Furthermore, the deliberate failure of resolution 242 to address what one party to the conflict had since 1948 felt to be the central question at issue — a resolution of the Palestinian–Israeli problem — continues to bedevil the situation to this day. The violence this resolution did to history, and its recasting of the problem as solely one of frontiers between Israel and its neighbors, was the primary American contribution, and one which introduced further complications into an already complex situation.

Henry Kissinger's vicarship over foreign policy under Presidents Nixon and Ford, which lasted for the next eight years, built on these precedents, adding to them new elements. These, in turn, have been elaborated on by succeeding administrations. Kissinger raised the practice of ignoring the Palestinians and the Palestinian core of the dispute, initiated under Truman, intensified by Dulles, and enshrined in resolution 242 under Johnson, to the level of a binding commitment to Israel. This was delivered secretly in 1975 as part of the bargaining over the Egypt–Israel disengagement accord of that year, and later raised to the level of a solemn public undertaking. As a result, the Palestinians, in contrast to all other parties to the conflict, could only participate in negotiations, if at all, (and their absence has always seemed to be the preferred situation from the American point of view) after meeting certain stringent preconditions. The Palestinians were obliged, moreover, to accept the fact that negotiations would have to be on the basis of resolution 242, which categorically excluded the solving of their national problem from the agenda for a settlement, while never mentioning them as a party, as a people, or otherwise by name. Israel, by contrast, was rarely pressed to commit itself to resolution 242 by Kissinger and his successors. Ironically, the commitment to Israel of 1975 was made by Kissinger soon after the PLO, at the 12th Palestine National Council in 1974, had begun moving towards acceptance of the principle of a negotiated settlement and a two-state solution. Just as they were moving towards participation in possible peace negotiations, the Palestinians were in effect excluded from such negotiations by US policy.[16]

Yet another element of Kissinger's approach, an almost exclusive focus on Egypt (except when he was forced to pay attention to Syria by a three-month 'war of attrition' launched by President Asad in 1974), established what was to become a constant in American policy. At the same time, Kissinger ignored the rich historical record, compiled in 1948, 1956 and 1967, of the futility of attempting to achieve a Middle East settlement on any basis other than a comprehensive one, involving all questions and all concerned regional and external actors. For while the argument can be made that bringing all the parties together encourages irresponsibility and extremism on the Arab side, and perhaps also on the part of the

Israelis, the same factors apply as well in a bilateral context. Moreover, multilateral diplomacy does not necessarily involve bringing all the parties together, but rather taking all of them seriously and dealing with all of them. And in bilateral negotiations other problems arise. Any Arab state which has tried to deal with Israel on its own, as did Jordan under King 'Abdallah from 1948 until his death, or Egypt under Anwar Sadat, or Lebanon during Amin Gemayel's presidency, has found itself subject to intense pressures from domestic public opinion, the Palestinians, and other Arab states.

This pattern, like many others, goes back before 1948 to the involvement of the Arab states in the Palestine conflict in the late 1930s. It was clearly understood by British statesmen at the time, as was shown by their skilful manipulation of the Arab governments against the interests of the Palestinians during the Arab revolt in Palestine. But American policy-makers in the post-war era, suffused with a holier-than-thou attitude toward the colonialist British, acted as if the lessons of the British experience in Palestine before 1948 were inapplicable to the involvement of the United States in the problem. British policy-makers, trapped between the various contradictory lines of policy embodied in the Husayn–McMahon correspondence and the Sykes–Picot accords of 1915–16, the Balfour declaration of November 1917, and their innumerable sequels, had very quickly realized their dilemma. Indeed, they had frequently succeeded in benefiting from the contradictions resulting from their own decisions.

As early as August 1919, Arthur Balfour wrote of these conflicting lines of policy:

> The contradiction between the letter of the [League of Nations] Covenant and the policy of the Allies is . . . flagrant in the case of the 'independent nation' of Palestine . . . For in Palestine we do not propose even to go through the form of consulting the wishes of the present inhabitants of the country . . . The four Great Powers are committed to Zionism. And Zionism, be it right or wrong, good or bad, is rooted in age-long traditions, in present needs, in future hopes, of far greater import than the desires and prejudices of the 700,000 Arabs who now inhabit that ancient land. In my opinion that is right. What I have never been able to understand is how it can be harmonised with the declaration [to Arab leaders], the Covenant, or the instructions to the [American King-Crane] Commission of Enquiry. In short, so far as Palestine is concerned, the Powers have made no statement of fact which is not admittedly wrong, and no declaration of policy which, at least in the letter, they had not always intended to violate.[17]

Although American policy-makers undoubtedly were ignorant of this memorandum, published only in 1952, most of them would probably have refused to recognize that it applied to their situation, even though it perfectly described the contradictions inherent in US policy from the time of Roosevelt. Kissinger tried to maintain the appearance of even-handedness between the Arab states and Israel, but his policy contained not even a pretence of even-handedness between the Palestinians and

Israel. And like Britain, although most probably unconscious of the parallel, the United States frequently benefited from the contradictions inherent in its approach, perhaps never more than during the Nixon–Ford administrations. Thus, while maintaining and indeed raising to a much higher level the unique special relationship with its ally Israel, the United States was able to establish good relations with key Arab countries such as Egypt, Saudi Arabia, Jordan and even Syria. All the while, it supported the Israeli position on a number of contentious issues. And the post-1973 increases in aid to Israel meant that the latter's actions were to a large extent financially underwritten by the United States.

Yet another element of the 'alternate narrative' emerged during the Kissinger years — the idea that Israel can only be induced to offer concessions, or even to begin negotiations, by massive bribes, while the employment of pressure against Israel is invariably counter-productive. This nugget of wisdom was derived from Kissinger's experience with the 1975 Sinai II disengagement accord. It was to be applied in a fashion exceedingly costly to US taxpayers at Camp David and in the Egypt–Israel peace treaty. Yet it ignored the experience of most American policy-makers from the days of Acheson and Truman. They had frequently succeeded in exerting pressure on Israel to accept American proposals. But even as Israel was becoming more dependent on the United States in concrete terms, it was gaining even greater freedom of action. This unhealthy, paradoxical situation resulted in part from the increasing pervasiveness of an 'alternative narrative' favorable to it which buried some of the lessons of the history of the conflict.

During their first year in office, President Carter and his key advisors appeared to be willing to challenge crucial elements of this 'alternative narrative' by raising issues which had long been obscured in American Middle East policy. The most notable were the adoption of a comprehensive settlement approach involving all the parties, including the Soviet Union, and bringing the Palestinian issue back into the realm of serious policy discussion after decades of neglect. This was signalled in the US–Soviet joint communiqué of 1 October 1977. It stressed the necessity of a comprehensive settlement involving all parties, including representatives of the Palestinian people, and the need to ensure 'the legitimate rights of the Palestinian people'.[18] The United States had not supported such language about the Palestinians since the 1947 partition resolution.

In spite of this unconventional but promising beginning the Carter administration ultimately produced results little different from those of its predecessors as far as the Palestine question was concerned. Its attempts to bypass the 'alternate narrative' aroused the ire of Israel's supporters, and of the Israeli government. They, in a matter of days, forced the Carter administration into a humiliating retreat from the terms of the joint communique. Soon afterwards, Sadat and Begin picked up the idea of an Egyptian–Israeli separate settlement where Kissinger had left it in 1975. The Carter administration quickly followed along.

Appearing at the outset to have learned from the experience of their predecessors in office, and thus to have appreciated some of the historical dimensions of this problem, the Carter team, by the end of 1977, was back in the rut of focusing on Egypt and Israel. It was soon involved with them in bilateral negotiations which not only left out the other Arab parties and infuriated them, but also again ignored the Palestinians. Thus a radically different initial approach on the part of the Carter administration resulted merely in the completion of a bilateral, separate Egypt–Israel peace which the Rogers plan had pointed toward, and which Kissinger had done so much to further. The Carter administration, however, showed some independence from elements of the 'alternate narrative' by its forceful reaction to Israel's invasion of South Lebanon in 1978, by exerting pressure to obtain Israel's withdrawal from most of the territory it had occupied, and by rejecting the invocation of 'terrorism' as justifying Israel's action.[19]

Nevertheless, the cornerstone of Carter's Middle East policy was the Camp David agreements. For all its benefits to the United States, Israel and Egypt, this outcome of efforts that went back to Rogers and Kissinger did not solve the Arab–Israeli conflict in its entirety. In some ways it made it harder to solve by obscuring the Palestinian–Israeli dimension that is at its core. Moreover, its benefits had to be seen against a background of growing Palestinian nationalism, the pronounced unwillingness of Arab states other than Egypt under Sadat to accept exclusive American brokerage of negotiations with Israel, and a regional situation which got worse after 1977. This deteriorating situation centered around the escalating conflict in Lebanon between Israel, Syria, the PLO and various Lebanese factions, which seemed to expand in direct proportion to the quiescence on the Egyptian–Israeli front.

The most severe post-Camp David fallout, however, took place during the Reagan administration, whose monumentally inept handling of the Middle East exacerbated an already grave set of regional problems. Reagan's advisors combined a commitment to a Cold War view of the Middle East starker than that of Dulles, an unprecedented level of ignorance of the region, its languages and cultures, and the history of the problem, and a preoccupation with the domestic resonance of foreign policy. Not surprisingly, they were captivated by the 'alternative narrative', and did less to restrain Israel than had any other American administration. During Reagan's two terms, Israel was awarded the status of a strategic ally. It was emboldened to the point that it carried out a devastating series of attacks on Lebanon in 1981, and then invaded Lebanon in 1982 and besieged Beirut. Those acts brought on the disastrous American involvement there, the withdrawal of the United States from Lebanon, and Israel's retreat from most of the country. Israel also annexed the Golan Height, and launched air raids on Tunis and Baghdad, while its oppressive, continued occupation of the West Bank and the Gaza Strip, marked by settlements and land seizures, finally provoked the Palestinian uprising which began in 1987.

By blindly accepting and even endorsing many key Israeli objectives regarding the PLO, Lebanon and Syria, the Reagan administration contributed significantly to the carnage — in 1982, 19,000 people were killed in the seventy-day Israeli offensive in Lebanon,[20] the longest Arab–Israeli war since 1948 — and to the damage to American interests that resulted. The Reagan administration had the signal distinction of completely substituting for the first time the 'alternative narrative' for the accepted American position on a number of issues. Some of them were major, like the invasion of Lebanon, or the Israeli–Iranian connection pioneered by Oliver North. Others were less notorious, but nevertheless significant. The latter included a down-playing of the illegality of Israeli settlements in the occupied territories and in occupied Arab West Jerusalem, a position which had been adhered to since 1967 but which was eroded significantly under Reagan. These developments left the Bush administration with the problem of having to reassert the traditional US posture on Jerusalem in early 1990.[21]

The Middle East policy of the Reagan administration marked perhaps the most extreme point in the American move away from the conclusions reached by a General Assembly majority in 1947, which, after seriously assessing the experience of the preceding decades, voted to partition Palestine and set up a Jewish and an Arab state there. For all the injustice to the Palestinians embodied in this plan, it at least recognized the historically incontrovertible fact that there were two peoples involved in the conflict, the morally inescapable conclusion that neither should be allowed to dominate the other, and that partition was therefore perhaps the least deplorable of many deplorable alternative courses of action.

Since 1947, American policy-makers have gradually drifted away from the historically derived propositions summed up in that UN resolution, and in other resolutions on the subject which the United States has supported and in may cases fashioned itself. From the mid-1960s onwards, the United States did so under the growing influence of an 'alternative narrative' with variegated roots in the midst of a strategic obsession with the Soviet Union, in ignorance of the specificities of the conflict, and in a commitment to the narrowest possible definition of the interests of Israel, which were seen as being indistinguishable from those of the United States. After Truman and Acheson allowed the Palestinian state called for by the partition resolution to disappear in the face of an unholy confluence of interests between Israel, Jordan and Britain, this direction in US policy continued under Eisenhower and Dulles. Through sponsorship of the Johnston plan for refugee resettlement, they compromised on the principle of Palestinian refugees having the right to repatriation or compensation embodied in General Assembly resolution 194 of 1948, even though that principle was restated in UN resolutions which the United States voted for annually. Under President Johnson, the principle of the inadmissibility of the acquisition of territory by war, which was at the heart of Security Council resolution 242, was diluted by support of Israel's use of such territory as a bargaining chip, even while providing it with advanced weaponry. This was all in stark contrast to Eisenhower's use of threats to force Israel to withdraw from Sinai in 1957.

Kissinger was responsible for circumventing the principle that Middle East peace negotiations should involve all the concerned regional parties, with multilateral international mediation, a principle put forward in Security Council resolution 242 and later restated in Security Council resolution 338. This last resolution ended the 1973 war and called for immediate negotiations under 'appropriate' — meaning international — auspices.[22] Although this was the origin of the Geneva conference, Kissinger soon brought Middle East peace-making under exclusively American auspices. It has remained there ever since under each administration, to some advantage to the United States at the expense of the Soviet Union, but without ending a conflict which seems no nearer to resolution at this time.

Similarly, the Reagan administration watered down the long-standing American rejection of the legality of Israel's absorption of Arab East Jerusalem and its settlements in the occupied territories, both of which the United States had joined in condemning in the Security Council.[23] It did this by ceasing to describe Israeli settlements as 'illegal' (they were now merely 'obstacles to peace'), and by stating (in the 1982 Reagan plan), that 'Jerusalem must remain undivided'. This constituted the first official American acquiescence in Israel's seizure of Arab East Jerusalem, disguised in the positive-sounding term 'unification'.[24]

The 1982 Israeli invasion of Lebanon marked how far things had come. Far from utilizing the framework of the UN to stop the conflict, the Reagan administration, for the first time in any Arab–Israeli war, actually prevented the UN from taking action.[25] Worse, the United States not only gave Israel a green light for the invasion, but tried to help it reap advantage from it. This contrasted starkly with the stern measures taken both through the UN and bilaterally by the Truman and Eisenhower administrations to force Israel to stop its victorious advances in 1948–49 and 1956. It went much further than President Johnson and Arthur Goldberg in 1967, or Nixon and Kissinger in 1973. They had allowed the Israelis a few hours and days of 'rolling cease-fire' advances respectively, before allowing the UN to put an effective halt to hostilities.[26] And it was a far cry from Carter's rapid moves to halt Israel's invasion of Lebanon in 1978 and force its withdrawal through Security Council resolution 425.

The prevalence in Washington of the idea that American interests in the Middle East were best served by the United States allowing Israel in effect to dictate events, as in the invasion of Lebanon, or the opening to Iran in an attempt to recreate the American–Israel–Iranian *entente* shattered by the fall of the Shah, was symptomatic of the situation under Reagan. For all their failures to study and learn from the history of this conflict, successive policy-makers up to and including the Carter administration would have shrunk from such behavior. But by the 1980s, the bureaucracy's institutional memory of the history of the conflict, which might have been invoked to prevent such a catastrophic policy, had been replaced, at the highest levels at least, with a simpleton's narrative. That narrative accepted virtually every Israeli assertion on key issues, saw the Middle East in Cold War terms, and described Israeli and American interests as completely identical. The substitution of hysterical invective on terrorism for any substantive policy towards the Palestinian people was the natural outcome of such an approach.

Cemented by a formidable congressional majority on every issue related to Palestine (but not always on strategic questions like arms sales to Arab states) on which AIPAC chose to call out its troops, this new 'consensus' was the quintessence of the ahistorical trend which had developed in American policy over the past four decades. Even as American public opinion, including a significant proportion of American Jewish opinion, began to shift in the wake of the 1982 war and the Palestinian uprising,[27] and even as contemporary Israeli revisionist historians, together with historical writings by other scholars, were dissolving some of the myths which lay at the core of this consensus,[28] Congress and Reagan administration policy-makers were mouthing the same tired old slogans. They thereby gave notice that reality, and the lessons of history, had yet to penetrate the American political process.

In the second year of the Bush administration, the question remains — what will change this pattern and bring to the fore the third of the propositions set out at the beginning of this chapter? In the waning years of the Reagan era the Palestinian issue imposed itself on the debate. Reagan and his advisors bequeathed to their successors an equivocal legacy. Secretary of State George Shultz, who for years had focused obsessively on terrorism to the virtual exclusion of the Palestine problem *per se*, authorized in December 1988 contacts with the PLO. This took place only weeks after Shultz had denied PLO Chairman Yasser Arafat entry into the United States to address the United Nations on the ground of his terrorist past. True to the prevailing standards of the administration, Shultz's perusal of history was clearly selective. The rich terrorist past of Begin, Yitzhak Shamir and some of their colleagues had apparently escaped his attention, or been ignored.

The Bush team nevertheless was spared the embarrassing necessity of adhering to the ban on contacts with the PLO initiated by Kissinger. It imposed upon itself, however, a self-denying ordinance by continuing to restrict these contacts to meetings in Tunis, and by maintaining restrictions on visits by PLO officials to the United States. In substantive terms, George Bush and Secretary of State James Baker committed the United States to an Israeli proposal for elections to choose Palestinian representatives to participate in negotiations with Israel. That proposal was meant by Shamir to delay substantive negotiations as long as possible, to bypass the PLO, and to restrict the whole process to Palestinians under occupation, to the exclusion of those in the diaspora. The proposal thus undercut much of the impact of the opening of contacts with the PLO. Although the proposal, as understood by Washington, at least accepted that the Palestinians must be involved directly in the negotiations, it failed to address the comprehensive aspects which are necessary to make a settlement a success. It also raised at the very outset highly contentious issues such as the status of Jerusalem.

Whatever the merits and possible fate of the Shamir plan, the fact that it brought rapidly to the fore crucial, long-buried substantive problems such as Jerusalem, the status of Palestinians expelled in 1948, Jewish immigration and the population balance in Palestine/Israel as a whole, and Israeli settlements in the occupied territories, meant that the situation was being clarified substantially. The hard substantive issues, fudged for so long, most outrageously under Reagan, were once again exposed. An obsessive preoccupation with procedure, which had almost obliterated some questions of substance, was now again linked to substantive matters. As a result the historical precedents, and the genesis of this conflict over more than four decades, were now being returned inexorably to the policy debate.

It is worth repeating, in conclusion, the proposition that success in dealing with the Palestine question will depend, for the Bush administration as for its predecessors, on a willingness to examine these precedents and this genesis as a guide to policy. The major changes in public opinion already alluded to, and subtle but important shifts in perceptions of the history of the conflict, may have made this more possible, and allowed for an opening up of subjects which under Reagan had remained buried. Certainly, the decline of the Cold War ideology which was central to Reagan's approach to the Middle East, and indeed to the American–Israeli relationship since the late 1960s, has lifted a miasmic cloud hanging over this issue.[29] It has undermined the political coalition which championed the 'alternate narrative'.

But the alternate narrative is not dead. It still stalks Capitol Hill and parts of the bureaucracy, and still has powerful bases in important American institutions and organs of opinion. Should it regain the position of hegemony which it enjoyed until recently, there will be a return to the immobility of the past. That would mean that there would be no movement towards resolution of the conflict. But even if it continues the retreat which has begun, one indispensable precondition will exist for a just and lasting settlement — that it be based on the lessons of history. The challenge of fashioning such a settlement will still remain, and history tells us that that will not be an easy process.

Notes

1. This is the wording of UN General Assembly resolution 194 of 1948, wording repeated annually in resolutions voted for by the United States.
2. These understandings can best be followed in Avi Shlaim, *Collusion Across the Jordan: King Abdullah, the Zionist Movement, and the Partition of Palestine* (New York: Columbia University Press, 1988). See also Mary Wilson, *King Abdullah, Britain and the Making of Jordan* (Cambridge: Cambridge University Press, 1987), and the earliest primary source to reveal details of them, 'Abdallah al-Tal,

Karithat Filastin: Mudhakkirat 'Abdallah al-Tal, qa'id ma'rakat al-Quds (The Palestine Disaster: Memoirs of 'Abdullah al-Tal, Commander in the Battle for Jerusalem), Vol. 1 (Cairo: Dar al-Qalam, 1959), by the Arab Legion commander in Jerusalem in 1948.

3. The text of Roosevelt's letter to Ibn Sa'ud, setting down the commitment made during their meeting aboard an American warship in the Suez Canal in February 1945, is dated 5 April 1945, and is cited in John Snetsinger, *Truman, the Jewish Vote and the Creation of Israel* (Stanford: Hoover Institution Press, 1974), p. 19.

4. Snetsinger, ibid., p. 20, cites a letter to this effect dated 16 March 1945 from Roosevelt to Stephen Wise, co-chairman of the American Zionist Emergency Council.

5. These figures are complied by Walid Khalidi in Appendix IV of his *From Haven to Conquest: Readings in Zionism and the Palestine Problem until 1948*, 2nd printing (Washington: Institute for Palestine Studies, 1987), pp. 846–9, mainly from official British statistics.

6. For more on the impact of the Suez crisis, see Rashid Khalidi, 'Consequences of the Suez Crisis in the Arab World', in Wm Roger Louis and Roger Owen, eds, *Suez 1956: The Crisis and its Consequences* (Oxford: Clarendon Press, 1989), pp. 377–92. On the effect of the Cold War on the Middle East, see R. Khalidi, 'An Arab View of Containment', in John Gaddis and Terry Deibel, eds, *Containment: Concepts and Policies* (Washington: National Defense University, 1986), pp. 415–23; Miles Copeland, *The Game of Nations* (London: Weidenfeld and Nicolson, 1969); and Wilbur Crane Eveland, *Ropes of Sand* (New York: W.W. Norton, 1980). The latter two books are invaluable sources regarding this period by intelligence personnel who often knew more than the diplomats about US policy. They must nevertheless be used carefully.

7. Dulles expressed this opinion in a speech to the Council on Foreign Relations on 26 August 1955, published in the *New York Times*, 27 August 1955.

8. Eveland, *Ropes of Sand*, p. 68, gives a good description.

9. According to Eveland, who worked for both the Defense Department and the CIA in the Middle East at different times during this period, Syria, Jordan and Lebanon, as well as Israel, all informed Ambassador Eric Johnston of their acceptance of his plan during his trip to the region in October 1954 (Eveland, *Ropes of Sand*, p. 90.)

10. Nathan Glazer, *American Judaism*, rev. 2nd edn (Chicago: University of Chicago Press, 1989), pp. 169–86, discusses the impact of the 1967 war on the American Jewish community. The centrality of the myth of Israel being on the brink of extermination to this impact is striking.

11. One of the best studies exposing this idea is Alvin Z. Rubinstein, *Red Star on the Nile: The Soviet–Egyptian Influence Relationship since the June War* (Princeton: Princeton University Press, 1977). It shows that far from dominating Egypt, the Soviet 'patron' more often did what its 'client' wanted.

12. The Israeli military (and US intelligence — see note 13 below) knew this view was groundless. In 1968, the then Chief-of-Staff Gen. Yitzhak Rabin stated: 'I do not believe that Nasser wanted war. The two divisions he sent into Sinai on May 14 would not have been enough to unleash an offensive against Israel. He knew it and we knew it', (*Le Monde*, 29 February 1969). Gen. Matti Peled, a senior military commander in 1967 later asserted: 'To claim that the Egyptian forces concentrated on our borders were capable of threatening Israel's existence not only insults the intelligence of anyone capable of analysing this sort of situation, but is an insult to the IDF', *Maariv*, 24 March 1972, cited in

David Hirst, *The Gun and the Olive Branch*, 2nd ed (London: Faber, 1984), p. 211.

13. William B. Quandt, *Decade of Decisions: American Policy Toward the Arab–Israeli Conflict, 1967–1976* (Berkeley: University of California Press, 1977), pp. 49–50. This is a thoroughly reliable account of the period.

14. Arthur Lall, *The UN and the Middle East Crisis, 1967*, rev. edn (New York: Columbia University Press, 1970), although dated, is still the most comprehensive account. It has the virtue of being written by a participant in the events.

15. Begin would not even allow the wording derived from resolution 242 regarding 'the inadmissibility of the acquisition of territory by war' to be included in the Camp David Accords (Steven Spiegel, *The Other Arab–Israeli Conflict: Making America's Middle East Policy, from Truman to Reagan*, Chicago: University of Chicago Press, 1985, pp. 355, 358).

16. See Rashid Khalidi, 'The Resolutions of the 19th Palestine National Council', *Journal of Palestine Studies*, **19**, 2, Winter 1990, pp. 29–42, for details.

17. Balfour memorandum, 11 August 1919, Great Britain, Foreign Office, *Documents on British Foreign Policy, 1919–1939*, 1st Series, Vol. IV, 1919, E.L. Woodward and R. Butler, eds (London: Her Majesty's Stationery Office, 1952,) p. 345.

18. Department of State, *Bulletin*, 7 November 1977, pp. 639–40.

19. Carter's policy in 1978 is analysed in Fredric C. Hof, *Galilee Divided: The Israel–Lebanon Frontier, 1916–1984* (Boulder: Westview, 1985), pp. 87–95.

20. These figures, from an official Lebanese police report, were cited in the *Washington Post*, 2 December 1982. By 1985, Israel had suffered 655 soldiers killed in Lebanon and about 4000 wounded. For details on this conflict, see R. Khalidi, *Under Siege: PLO Decision-making During the 1982 War* (New York: Columbia University Press, 1986), and Ze'ev Schiff and Ehud Ya'ari, *Israel's Lebanon War* (New York: Simon and Schuster, 1985).

21. At a news conference on 3 March 1990, Bush stated US opposition to Israeli settlements in the occupied territories, including East Jerusalem (*New York Times*, 4 March 1990). He stood firm ten days later, saying that he was merely 'reiterating United States policy' (*New York Times*, 14 March 1990).

22. The wording is that of resolution 338, which was adopted on 22 October 1973, and which was the basis for Security Council resolution 344 of 15 December 1973. As a result the United Nations took a role in the Geneva peace conference, which held a single meeting that same month.

23. The United States voted for Security Council resolutions 267 of 1969 and 298 of 1971, which censured Israeli measures to change the status of Jerusalem, and for resolution 465 of 1980 which called on Israel to dismantle all settlements in occupied territories, including Jerusalem. Carter later claimed that the United States intended to abstain (Spiegel, *The Other Arab–Israeli Conflict*, pp. 377–8). The United States had abstained on the milder resolution 446 of 1979.

24. The Reagan plan is in *Weekly Compilation of Presidential Documents*, 6 September 1982, pp. 1081–5.

25. US policy at the United Nations is described in R. Khalidi, *Under Siege*, pp. 105–10 and 135–47.

26. The wording was used by an enraged Presidential envoy Ambassador Philip Habib to Begin protesting similar Israeli tactics in 1982; (cited in an interview with Patrick Seale, *Asad, The Struggle for the Middle East*, Berkeley: University of California Press, 1985, p. 385.)

27. The *New York Times*, 10 February 1990, reports a survey by the Tel Aviv-based Israel-Diaspora Institute of leaders of local and national Jewish groups, of whom 780 responded. The results were remarkably dovish in some respects: 74 per cent approved of Israel–PLO negotiations. See also Washington Jewish Week, 15 February 1990, 'Survey Finds US Jewish Leaders are more Dovish than they Admit'. This is only the latest of a consistent series of polls over a period of at least three years showing a growing open-mindedness among the American Jewish community on the Palestine issue. It remains to be seen when and if this shift will affect Congress, although recent polls of their constituents by Congressmen like Sidney Yates (9th–IL) and Ted Weiss (17th–NY) show strong evidence of similar trends.

28. The best of this Israeli revisionist scholarship is represented by works such as Shlaim, *Collusion Across the Jordan* (note 2); Benny Morris, *The Birth of the Palestinian Refugee Problem, 1947–49* (Cambridge: Cambridge University Press, 1988); Tom Segev, *1949: The First Israelis* (New York: The Free Press, 1985); Simha Flapan, *The Birth of Israel: Myths and Realities* (New York: Pantheon, 1987); Gershon Shafir, *Land, Labor and the Origins of the Israeli–Palestinian Conflict 1882–1914* (Cambridge, Cambridge University Press, 1989); and Shimon Shamir, 'The Collapse of Project Alpha', in Louis and Owen, eds, *Suez 1956*, pp. 73–100. For assessments of some of this scholarship see R. Khalidi, 'Revisionist Views of the Modern History of Palestine: 1948', *Arab Studies Quarterly*, **10**, 4, Fall 1988, pp. 425–32; Zachary Lockman, 'Original Sin', *Middle East Report*, **152**, May–June 1988, pp. 57–64; and 'Redefining the Past', in Fouad Moughrabi, *Under Israeli Eyes* (Syracuse: Syracuse University Press, forthcoming).

29. In 'Retrospect and Prospects: Forty Years of US Middle East Policy', *Middle East Journal*, **41**, 1, Winter 1987, pp. 7–25, Bruce R. Kuniholm comes to similar conclusions to those reached in this essay regarding the impact of a preoccupation with the Soviet Union and of American political imperatives on the making of Middle East policy, although his wording is more circumspect: '. . . most postwar presidential administrations, because of their concern for geopolitical factors (and their responsiveness to domestic political pressure) have been unable either to understand or to respond constructively to the needs of the region's emerging national and transnational forces . . .'

3 *The boundaries of rational calculation in Soviet policy towards Japan*
Jonathan Haslam

The aim of this chapter is to explore the limits of rational calculation in Soviet policy towards Japan.[1] This is not an arbitrary choice. It arises from evidence that 'irrationality' has had a significant impact on the conduct of Soviet relations with Japan. The first section questions the prevailing assumption that the behaviour of states can be reduced to a 'rational actor' model. The second section focuses on the impact of history on Soviet attitudes towards Japan. The conclusion draws the two together and argues the case for a less mechanistic approach to international relations.

Is it feasible to separate out the limits of rational calculation from other determinants of Soviet policy towards Japan? In dealing with the ethereal and abstract, one should not expect precise answers. One cannot, of course, quantify such findings and this is perhaps no bad thing. It is all too tempting to focus on factors that can be quantified, or attempt to quantify the unquantifiable. In an attack on the 'Utilitarian Theory of Government' in 1829, Macaulay argued that terms such as 'power' could not be talked about 'as if the meaning of the word power were as determinate as the meaning of the word circle'. Far less was there any justification in reasoning mathematically 'about things which had not been, or perhaps could not be, defined with mathematical accuracy'.[2]

By focusing on qualities rather than quantities, one methodological trap is avoided. But other snares still lie in wait. It is all too easy to slip into assumptions — blandly taken to be self-evident — as to the true extent of the supposed 'rationality' of the political process: theories 'based on the assumption that the participants coolly and "rationally" calculate their advantages according to a consistent value system', in Thomas Schelling's definition. Schelling goes on to argue not that this approach produces the answers, but 'that the assumption of rational behavior is a productive one in the generation of systematic theory'.[3] In other words, the assumption of rationality makes it easier to theorise about reality, nothing more. The reason for assuming rationality thus appears to be tautological: rationality is the best working assumption because it makes theory-building easier. This leaves aside the awkward question as to whether, by making the theories easier to construct, we might in fact be creating false and ultimately misleading images of reality.

The philosopher Searle has attacked the fallacy of assuming too much in the social sciences. Motivation or — as he terms it — 'intentionality' is generally taken as given: the 'science' consists of working out the consequences of the 'intentionality'. Searle's critique of economics is equally applicable to all the social sciences: 'Economics as a science presupposes certain historical facts about people and societies that are not themselves part of economics. And when those facts change, economics has to change.'[4] In this sense the structure of the social sciences is precariously balanced on historical variables rather than securely anchored in ahistorical constants. We should therefore be wary of accepting reasoning based on first principles. One such axiom is that of presumed rationality.

Scholars are notoriously given to see the world as a rational place. Recently those scientists working on 'fractals' even claim to have found order in 'chaos'[5]. They may well be right. But we are a long way from the crude certainties of most natural science and, indeed, of science fiction. In Asimov's *Foundation*, for example, we encounter Hari Seldon who has developed the science of psychohistory on the basis of thousands of years of events recorded in the history of the galaxy, which allow him to make predictions of human actions through the employment of mathematical probability.[6] Unfortunately some political scientists, without the aid of the 'Encyclopaedia Galactica', assume they are as omniscient as Seldon. Intent on revealing the regularities underlying mass behaviour in the more complex and impenetrable world of human affairs, they ignore or iron out the awkwardly unpredictable irregularities — relegated as 'x' factors — that threaten the well-ordered but artificial mechanics of 'models' and 'paradigms'.

Such criticism should not be mistaken as an appeal for blind empiricism. There is clearly an advantage in simplifying reality; this has to be done to make sense of anything. The question is whether the degree of simplification is so great that the model loses its essential explanatory capacity and in fact misleads rather than enlightens. For academic observers, secluded from the rough and tumble of the outside world, it is all too easy to construct models in which 'rational' actors behave according to some preconceived pattern dictated purely by 'interests'. If ever they stopped, however, to consider how they and, indeed, their colleagues make decisions, they might reconsider hasty acceptance of such a mechanistic philosophy.

A good example of the traumatic impact of the real world on the ordered academic mind can be found in the case of former US budget director David Stockman. In his autobiographical epitaph suitably entitled *The Triumph of Politics* Stockman describes how he came into office with a 'Grand Doctrine'. Soon he made an important discovery: 'Governance was not a realm of pure reason, analysis, and the clash of ideologies. It really did involve the brute force of personality, the effrontery of bloated egos, the raw will-to-power.'[7]

The argument here is not that Soviet policy towards Japan has been entirely irrational, but that the policy cannot be accurately explained purely within the limits of a rational-actor model of behaviour. At least in theory some noted political scientists accept that there are strict limits to the rational-actor model. Most recently international relations theorist James Rosenau has rightly acknowledged that 'the rational actor who only calculates interest . . . is an ideal type'.[8] In other words, one must expect to find instances in reality where policy results from factors other than a rational calculation of interests. And political scientist Aaron Wildavsky has decisively rejected 'a social science that begins at the end by assuming interests'. He has forcefully argued that we make *what people want* — their desires, preferences, values, ideals . . . the central subject of our inquiry'.[9]

This brings us into uncharted territory. But here we are not entirely alone and without landmarks. And it is striking that it is a much respected historian of international relations who saw the problem. He found wanting what we would now call the rational-actor model as a complete explanation for the foreign policy of the Great Powers. In the *American Historical Review* over thirty years ago William Langer directed historians to

> the problem whether major changes in the psychology of a society or culture can be traced, even in part, to some severe trauma suffered in common, that is, with the question whether whole communities, like individuals, can be profoundly affected by some shattering experience. If it is indeed true that every society or culture has a 'unique psychological fabric', deriving at least in part from past common experiences and attitudes, it seems reasonable to suppose that any great crisis, such as famine, pestilence, natural disaster, or war, should leave its mark on the group, the intensity and duration of the impact depending, of course, on the nature and magnitude of the crisis.[10]

Langer suggests we 'shall have to learn to reckon with the concept of "collective mentality," even on the unconscious level . . . .'.[11]

It is one aspect of the 'collective mentality' that leads us to Soviet policy towards Japan. The evidence for 'irrational' factors is not hard to find. Even the Soviet government newspaper *Izvestiya* has now openly acknowledged that relations with Japan have been damaged by 'prejudice'.[12] And *Izvestiya* made no attempt to attribute this fault exclusively to the Japanese. If 'prejudice' is at work on an unconscious level, its origins appear to date from the 'trauma' of the 1904–5 war. One does not have to go far to find evidence for this. Asked for his opinion on a Marshall Plan for Eastern Europe, a Soviet academician recently and somewhat cryptically responded: 'We don't want another Port Arthur.'

This is more than an obscure reference to the distant past made by an intellectual out of touch with policy or public sentiment. In memoirs published in 1988 by former Foreign Minister Andrei Gromyko we read: 'History has reinforced a sense of caution in the consciousness of our people towards the good intentions expressed by the politicians of that country. They know about the treacherous attack by Japan in 1904 on Port Arthur, that led to the start of the Russo–Japanese war.'[13] More than forty years after the end of the Second World War, the Soviet Union and Japan have yet to sign a peace treaty. Precisely how important a role has 'prejudice' played? What have been the boundaries of rational calculation in Soviet policy towards Japan?

By the turn of the century Tsarist Russia and Meiji Japan were the two main rivals for the domination of North East Asia. After months of futile negotiation between Tokyo and Petersburg, and in a bold if not reckless attempt to settle the Russian problem once and for all, Japanese admiral Togo launched a pre-emptive strike against the Russian squadron at Port Arthur at 4.00 p.m. on 8 February 1904. The Russian government issued a communiqué expressed in terms that were to be reiterated repeatedly half a century later:

> Eight days have now elapsed since all Russia was shaken with profound indignation against an enemy who suddenly broke off negotiations, and, by a treacherous attack, endeavoured to obtain an easy success in a war long desired. The Russian nation, with natural impatience, desires prompt vengeance, and feverishly awaits news from the Far East.[14]

But worse news was to follow and, in November 1904, after observing a long series of reverses on land and at sea, senior officials at the Quai d'Orsay — responsible for the foreign policy of Russia's anxious ally, France — noted: 'Public opinion in Russia feels the humiliation very deeply. In all ranks of society, including the rural masses, and in every part of the Empire irritation is becoming more and more pronounced.'[15] The sense of humiliation did not assist the war effort, however; on the contrary, it fed widespread discontent with the entire system of authority which ultimately precipitated an abortive revolution. The disastrous defeat of Russian naval forces at Tsushima on 27–8 May 1905 added insult to injury. And, although Japan was also weary of war, the resulting peace settlement at Portsmouth, New Hampshire, on 5 September, underlined Russia's humiliation by the cession of South Sakhalin to Japan.

The weakness of Russia after the Bolshevik revolution then proved too great a temptation for the Japanese to resist. What followed merely reinforced the bitterness experiences in 1904–5. From 1918 to 1922 Japanese forces occupied the Russian maritime province and withdrew from North Sakhalin only with the establishment of diplomatic recognition of the new Soviet regime under the Peking convention of 1925. Inevitably the Japanese war of intervention left a further stain on Russian attitudes towards Japan. The Soviet government ostentatiously refused to recognise any responsibility for the Portsmouth Treaty signed by its Tsarist predecessor; though as yet it had no power to avenge 1904–5 nor secure the return of South Sakhalin.[16] In September 1931 Japanese forces overran Manchuria and once more threatened the Soviet maritime province. The Russians built up their military power in the area to offset

Japanese offensive capabilities; but, while holding firm on the Soviet frontier, Stalin studiously tried to avoid any action that might lead to open conflict.[17] Border disputes broke out nonetheless. Indeed they developed into major battles in 1938 and 1939; but they were undertaken on the Soviet side only in the sure knowledge that Japan, too, could not risk a full-scale war.[18]

Soviet caution *vis-à-vis* Japan arose in large part because the Russians faced a major adversary in the West: Nazi Germany. The Nazi–Soviet pacts of August and September 1939 thus enabled the Russians to confront Japan from a position of strength. Stalin and his foreign minister, Vyacheslav Molotov, tried to use this shift in the balance of power to secure the revision of the Portsmouth treaty in 1940 in return for a non-aggression pact earnestly sought by the Japanese in the face of a growing confrontation with the United States. Japan never secured a non-aggression pact; all it could get — without abrogation of the Portsmouth treaty — was a neutrality pact.[19] The German invasion of Russia in June 1941 then threatened to tilt the scales in the Far East to Soviet disadvantage. But friction between Japan and the United States was accelerating at such a speed that the choice was made to attack Pearl Harbor rather than the Soviet Far East. And with the outbreak of war between Japan and the United States in December 1941 the Americans acquired a direct investment in securing Soviet participation in an alliance against Japan. The terms demanded by the Russians caused little surprise; it was the manner in which those terms were couched and what this indicated of Soviet thinking that raised Western eyebrows.

The issue of Soviet participation in the Pacific war was raised by President Roosevelt at Tehran in November 1943. It was raised again, this time by US ambassador Averell Harriman, in Moscow a year later. On 14 December Stalin told Harriman: 'The Soviet Union would like to receive South Sakhalin, i.e. restitution of what was handed over to Japan in the Portsmouth Treaty, and also receive the Kurile islands.'[20] Both of these conditions made strategic sense. The Russian navy had been pressing for the reacquisition of South Sakhalin since the 1930s to obtain a secure egress for the Pacific fleet stationed at Vladivostok from the Sea of Japan. The reacquisition of the Kurile islands (ceded in 1875) would then secure egress from the Sea of Okhotsk into the Pacific beyond.[21] Stalin also raised the matter of access to warm water in the Pacific: rental of Port Arthur and Dalny from the Chinese, plus reacquisition of the Chinese Eastern and South Manchurian Railways that linked these ports to the Soviet hinterland. Once again, all this made sense in purely strategic terms.[22]

Harriman promised to pass all this on to Roosevelt. At the Yalta conference on 8 February 1945 Stalin was again asked about Soviet entry into the Pacific war. The record of his reply reads: 'all this is fine, but he (Stalin) wanted to know how matters stand with the political conditions upon which the Soviet Union will enter the war against Japan. This concerns those political questions which he, Stalin, discussed with Harriman in Moscow.' Roosevelt agreed. But Stalin was insistent upon having something on paper. He said 'that if Soviet conditions were accepted, then the Soviet people would understand why the USSR will enter the war against Japan. Therefore it is important to have a document, signed by the President, Churchill and Stalin himself, in which the aims of the Soviet Union's war against Japan would be expressed.'[23] All of this can be explained as perfectly rational, though Stalin's suspiciousness was very much a reflection of his personality rather than a rational response to the situation. What followed is less predictable in terms of rational-actor theory.

The terms agreed were communicated by letter delivered by special messenger from Roosevelt to Stalin. Andrei Gromyko, then polpred (ambassador equivalent) to the United States, was present at the Yusupov palace when the messenger arrived. In his memoirs Gromyko describes what he calls 'a notable episode'. 'I want you to translate this letter for me orally. Before the meeting I want to know its contents to the letter [khotya by na slukh].' Gromyko began translating. He recalls: 'While I was speaking, Stalin asked me to repeat the content of this or that phrase.' Stalin was extremely pleased. 'He paced up and down the study and repeated out loud: — Good. Very good!.' Gromyko then played on Stalin's obsession with the Russo–Japanese war to the advantage of improved relations with the United States. He recalls: 'I pointed out: — The position now taken by the USA in a way rehabilitates them in our eyes, in that they sympathised with Japan in 1905 . . . At that time the USA in essence helped Japan to snatch territory from Russia.' Gromyko adds: 'Everything pointed to the fact that Stalin completely concurred in the view that the USA were rehabilitating themselves.' 'Several times he passed through the room serving as the study with it (the letter) in his hands, as though he did not want to let go of what he had received. And he was still holding the letter in his hand at the moment I left him.'[24]

Why was this concession so special to Stalin? Why did Gromyko think it so worthy of recording? Neither before nor after this date is there clear evidence that the Far East was ever at the top of Stalin's order of priorities. Had this been Germany, it might have been another matter. But Japan? The key lies in the phrase Stalin had inserted in the Yalta agreement with reference to Russia's entry into the Pacific war: 'The restoration of the rights belonging to Russia that were broken by Japan's treacherous attack [verolomnym napadeniem] in 1904'[25] — a curious insertion by the leader of a party that had condemned Russia's part in that war and had made use of the war to attempt a revolution. It is striking that the reference to Japanese treachery recalls the Tsarist government communiqué of 18 February 1904.

Once again, none of this dismisses the strategic significance of the gains Stalin sought and obtained at Yalta. The secure possession of warm-water ports in the Far East and the reacquisition of South Sakhalin and the Kurile islands gave the Soviet Union the edge in North East Asia lost by the Tsars during the twilight of empire. Indeed, in negotiation with the Chinese government Stalin told foreign minister T.V. Soong: 'We are closed up. We have no outlet. One should keep Japan vulnerable from all sides, north, west, south, east, then she will keep quiet . . . Japan will be crushed but she will restore her might in 20, 30 years.'[26] And after Russia's entry into the war, on 16 August, Stalin tried to enhance Soviet gains still further by requesting a landing of Soviet troops on Hokkaido. This would, together with possession of the Kuriles, provide additional security for egress from the Sea of Okhotsk to the Pacific. The Americans simply let the matter drop and Stalin did not persist.[27]

The expansion of Soviet power in the region fitted a geostrategic pattern evident elsewhere — in the Baltic (re-annexation of the Baltic states and the acquisition of bases in and territory from Finland), and the Eastern Mediterranean (attempts to limit entry into the Black Sea through the Dardanelles). But, as Stalin's odd behaviour in front of Gromyko and the Yalta statement attest, this was also something special. More evidence follows. Stalin's declaration of victory over Japan on 2 September 1945 also echoed the Tsarist communiqué:

" . . . we have a special account to settle with Japan.

Japan began its aggression against our country as early as 1904 at the time of the Russo–Japanese war. As you know, in February 1904, when talks between Japan and Russia were still under way, Japan, taking advantage of the weakness of the Tsarist Government, unexpectedly and treacherously, without a declaration of war, set upon our country and attacked the Russian squadron in the Port Arthur region . . . As you know, in the war with Japan Russia than suffered defeat. Japan took advantage of the defeat of Tsarist Russia to seize South Sakhalin from Russia, to consolidate itself on the Kurile islands and, by these means, put under lock and key for our country in the East all egress to the open sea — consequently also all egress to the ports of Soviet Kamchatka and Soviet Chukotka. It was clear the Japan set itself the task of tearing away from Russia its entire Far East.

But this does not exhaust Japan's predatory actions against our country. In 1918, after the establishment of a Soviet regime in our country, Japan . . . once again set upon our country, occupied the Far East and for four years tormented our people, plundered the Soviet Far East.

But that is not all. In 1938 Japan once more set upon our country at Lake Khasan . . . and in the following year repeated its attack this time somewhere else, in the region of the Mongolian People's Republic, around Khalkhin-Gol . . .

True, Japan's attacks in the region of Khasan and Khalkhin-Gol were liquidated by Soviet forces to the great shame of the Japanese. Equally the Japanese military intervention of 1918–1922 was successfully liquidated, and the Japanese occupiers were thrown out of our Far Eastern regions. But the defeat of Russian forces in 1904 in the period of the Russo–Japanese war left painful memories in the consciousness of the people. It left a black stain on our country. Our people believed and waited for the day when Japan would be beaten and the stain would be liquidated. We waited forty years, the people of the old generation, for this day. And here we are, this day has come.[28]

These attitudes continued to shape Soviet policy towards Japan despite the attainment of victory in 1945. At the onset of the Cold War in Europe it is striking how rapidly the Russians raised the banner of German nationalism as a means of undermining the continued American presence in Central Europe. What is equally striking in contrast, is how the Russians failed to do the same with respect to Japan, despite the fact that it soon became evident that the Americans were going to turn Japan into a base for operations against the Soviet Union in the Pacific. Not until early 1950 did Stalin insist that the Japanese Communist Party take action against the US forces of occupation, and even then the Russians remained wary of fuelling Japanese nationalism.[29] In effect they surrendered the initiative to the United States which easily brought about the San Francisco peace treaty with Japan in September 1951 in the face of Soviet opposition.[30] The Americans thus outflanked the Russians, representing themselves as the defender of Japanese rights in world affairs.

Not until Stalin died in March 1953 did it become possible for the Soviet government, now led by Georgii Malenkov (until February 1955), to explore closed terrain in foreign as well as domestic policy. Concerned at the continued armed presence of the United States on Japanese soil that had been guaranteed concurrently with the San Francisco treaty, the Russians belatedly moved to secure a separate peace treaty with Japan. In August 1953 US diplomats in Tokyo learned that the Russians were about to initiate talks with Japan on a peace treaty. They had an obvious interest in doing so: as a result of the US–Japanese Security Treaty of September 1951 'The United States had a base in Okinawa but the Soviet Union had none in the Caribbean', as Deputy Foreign Minister Jakob Malik complained.[31] And with the overthrow of the pro-American Yoshida government in Japan in December 1954 the road was open. Under the leadership of Premier Hatoyama the new coalition of Liberals and Democrats was determined to normalise relations with both the Soviet Union and the People's Republic of China. In retrospect it is all too easy to forget the potent force of neutralism and nationalism uniting left and right in Hatoyama's Japan. Japanese deference to US hegemony postdates this period; it dates essentially from the US–Japanese security treaty of 1960. One only has to look at the diplomatic correspondence of the period to see how tenuous the Americans believed to be their hold on Hatoyama's Japan.[32]

Talks with the Russians finally opened in London on 1 June 1955. The Japanese wanted a quid pro quo in return for a peace treaty: retrocession of the Kurile islands and South Sakhalin seized by Stalin by agreement with Roosevelt and Churchill in 1945. At the talks the Russians initially tabled a draft that indicated no concessions would be forthcoming. On the sidelines the British expressed amazement — and relief — at such ineptitude. 'To me the most interesting feature of this whole business is that the Russians should have been stupid enough to stand pat on the position they took up in S(an) F(rancisco) four years ago. By so doing they missed what could have been a real opportunity,' commented Sir Esler (Bill) Dening, Britain's ambassador to Japan.[33] All Russians had difficulty swallowing the notion that the defeated power — Japan — was the one laying down conditions for the peace treaty. But foreign minister Molotov was the most obdurate of all. Two years later he was openly attacked for having been 'against the normalisation of relations with Japan'.[34]

First secretary of the Soviet Communist Party Nikita Khrushchev forced Molotov to back down sufficiently to secure greater flexibility. Finally, in August, the Russians offered to restore to Japan the Habomais and Shikotan islands on condition they and the surrounding seas were demilitarised. Accepting that they were unlikely to secure all the Kurile islands and South Sakhalin, the Japanese insisted only on the addition of Etorofu and Kunashiri.[35] But the Russians had quickly reached the limits of their flexibility and the expression of their irritation soon indicated a visceral resentment that had been only partially suppressed in the immediate interests of *realpolitik*.

'One must understand the psychology of our people,' Khrushchev insisted. 'The Soviet Union was a victor in the war. Now the defeated side doesn't want to accept our proposal.'[36] Even the dismissal of Molotov from the Foreign Ministry in June 1956 made no difference to the Soviet attitude on territory. Chairman of the Soviet Council of Ministers Nikolai Bulganin made clear that memories of Japan's unprovoked attack on Russia in 1904 still rankled.[37] In August foreign minister Dimitry Shepilov emphasised that Japanese rights to the Kuriles under the treaties signed in the nineteenth century was nullified by Japan's attack on Russia in 1904.[38] In the end a lesser agreement was reached on 19 October providing for full establishment of diplomatic relations but leaving the peace treaty open to further negotiation.[39]

But those negotiations never really got under way. The Russians were never prepared to concede more than two sets of islands. Given the importance of winning the Japanese away from the Americans, to neutralism rather than to the Soviet sphere of influence, it is striking how inflexible Soviet diplomacy remained and has remained up to 1990. Clearly the issue of territory was more than a matter of geopolitics. It was not a simple question of precedent, either; otherwise the Russian would have never offered anything at all. The puzzle was, why offer two but not four groups of islands?

Khrushchev was never inhibited in expressing his thoughts. And on the matter of a peace treaty with Japan he reiterated in 1957 the Soviet position more than once in terms that Stalin and, indeed, Tsar Nicholas II would have found remarkably familiar. Here the impact of history is only too apparent.

> It is impossible to view the fact that the Soviet Union took action against Japan in the last war apart from the pre-existing history of relations between our countries. You say that the USSR acted in breach of the neutrality pact. But remember how Japan attacked Port-Arthur in 1904, attacked without a declaration of war and with no warning.
>
> In 1918 Japan attacked the maritime province.
>
> I don't know how to term this in the language of diplomats but I personally would use the word impudence [naglost´], when speaking of the

behaviour of the Japanese consul in Vladivostok. This consul told the chairman of the maritime province executive committee Butsenko: — What are you doing here on your backsides; this land is vast; you make poor use of it. Get out! Otherwise we will chuck you out.'

'We put up with this at the time. But all this left its traces,' Khrushchev added. Only at the very end of this interview with the *Asahi Shimbun* did he mention the fact that the islands had an 'important strategic significance' (for the Soviet Pacific fleet).[40] The strategic imperative was, and is still, real enough. And Khrushchev may well have exaggerated for effect. But what strikes the reader is the framing of the Soviet case very much in terms of the past rather than present contingencies. And why would he do this if there was no resonance in Soviet (Party) opinion? Again, this time in a letter to Premier Ikeda on 8 December 1961, Khrushchev vented this age-old grievance once more: Japanese aggression in 1904 'inflicted a great deal of grief on the Russian people'.[41]

The repeated appeal to emotion by those at the highest level of the Soviet regime is surely evidence enough that the phenomenon of 'trauma' suggested by Langer has some relevance to the evolution of Soviet policy towards Japan, at the very least into the early 1960s and almost certainly into the 1980s. When Sino–Soviet relations broke down in 1969 and the Chinese moved to mend fences with the Japanese, Moscow was prompted into discussing once more the issue of territory, despite the agreements only very recently obtained with West Germany on the inviolability of the post-war frontiers in Europe. The joint communique issued at the close of the visit of Premier Tanaka to Moscow on 10 October implied Soviet willingness to make territorial concessions: 'both sides have recognized that the conclusion of a peace treaty by settling the various pending problems since World War II will contribute toward the establishment of truly good-neighbourly relations between the two countries.'[42]

But once again Moscow went to the brink of agreement only to step back at the last moment: no sooner was this concession extracted by the Japanese than the Russians reneged on it. By then the fear of creating a precedent had compounded the impact of the sentiments originally aroused in 1904–5. And these sentiments appear until very recently to have had a life of their own, even if one would naturally expect their influence to have waned over time. Gromyko retired from the Foreign Ministry in 1985 and remained in the Gorbachev leadership for a further three years. His recollections of 1904–5 ware derived from the tales of his peasant father, who had fought the Japanese in that disastrous conflict.[43] They buttressed attitudes forged in the 1930s when the Soviet Union was once more in open conflict with Japan, shutting out realistic assessments and foreclosing more enlightened options. And although he found Stalin's behaviour at Yalta over the avenging of 1904–5 somewhat strange, his memoirs indicate that he too ultimately shared many of the same sentiments that fired 'the boss'.

This is the case for arguing that those who work in the field of international relations, whether as historians, political scientists, or policy-makers should not ignore or brush aside awkward inconsistencies that raise questions about the rational-actor model of foreign policy-making. The danger is that an apparently common-sense assumption that may fit the generality of circumstances is all too easily and all too often raised to the status of dogma and applied a priori to all international actors in every conceivable situation. In this particular case unthinking acceptance of such a dogma would ride roughshod over the evidence adduced in support of the case laid out in the preceding pages.

If, indeed, Langer is right and that at certain points in history societies can be 'profoundly affected by some shattering experience' — in this case Russian society and the 1904–5 war — then the discovery and description of the impact of such traumas and their consequences might have a sobering effect on those who all too often presume the 'rationality' of foreign policy decision-making. At the very least the tidy assumption that states act consistently with their interests to the exclusion of the prejudices of their leaders has been called into question.

The message for scholars is that instead of continuing to reduce the study of international relations to the scale of simple models, which might work for physics but are inadequate for the complexities of human and political behaviour, those in the field should surely accept the challenge and take a fresh look at what motivates political man and explore primary sources familiar to the diplomatic historian in an effort to recast the study of international relations as a more complex yet more accurate reflection of that outer world.

The conclusions for those actively engaged in the formulation and execution of foreign policy are as follows: first, avoid the assumption that the world looks the same through the eyes of others — a case nicely made by Robert Jervis in his path-breaking work on misperception;[44] second, for any given action some powers will be seen in less rational terms than others; third, past relations with such powers may have had undue emotional influence on current policy; and, lastly, the onlooker or, indeed, the decision-maker may well benefit from the services of the historian to clarify the likely impact of history on the decisions of the 'non-rational actor', particularly where — at first sight — those decisions appear to make no sense at all.

Notes

1. This chapter is based on research for two future monographs on Soviet relations with Japan, the first dealing with the 1930s, the second focusing on the post-war period.
2. *Macaulay's Complete Works, Essays, Biographies*, VII (London, 1898), p. 422. For a recent example in the most readable form: B. Bueno de Mesquita, *The War Trap* (New Haven, 1981). It is as if Macaulay wrote the attack after reading Bueno de Mesquita.

3. T. Schelling, *The Strategy of Conflict* (New York, 1960), p. 16. See also Bueno de Mesquita, 'The Rationality Assumption', in *The War Trap*, p. 29.

4. J. Searle, *Minds, Brains and Science* (Cambridge, Mass., 1984), pp. 82–3.

5. J. Gleick, *Chaos: Making a New Science* (London, 1988).

6. I. Asimov, *Foundation* (New York, 1951); *Foundation and Empire* (New York, 1952); and *Second Foundation* (New York, 1953). Asimov is still adding to the series.

7. D. Stockman, *The Triumph of Politics: The Inside Story of the Reagan Revolution* (New York, 1986), p. 263.

8. J. Rosenau, 'Before Co-operation: Hegemons, Regimes, and Habit-driven Actors in World Politics', *International Organisation*, **40**, 4, (Autumn 1986), p. 862.

9. A. Wildavsky, 'Choosing Preferences By Constructing Institutions: A Cultural Theory of Preference Formation', *American Political Science Review*, **81**, 1, March 1987, p. 5.

10. W. Langer, 'The Next Assignment', *American Historical Review*, **LXIII**, 2, January 1958, p. 291.

11. ibid., p. 290.

12. *Izvestiya*, 3 Jan 1989.

13. A. Gromyko, *Pamyatnoe*, Vol. 2 (Moscow, 1988), p. 145.

14. Quoted in *The War in the Far East 1904–1905 By the Military Correspondent of 'The Times'* (London, 1905), p. 68.

15. Diary entry, 14 Nov 1904: M. Paleologue, *The Turning Point: Three Critical Years, 1904–1906* (London, 1935), p. 145.

16. Declaration by Deputy Commissar for Foreign Affairs Lev Karakhan attached to the Soviet–Japanese convention establishing diplomatic relations, 20 Jan 1925: *Dokumenty Vneshnei Politiki SSSR*, Vol. VIII (Moscow, 1963), doc. 30.

17. J. Haslam, *Soviet Foreign Policy 1930–33: The Impact of the Depression* (London/New York, 1983) pp. 83–4.

18. F. Volkov, 'Legendy i deistvitel'nost' o Rikharde Zorge', *Voenno-Istoricheskii Zhurnal*, No.12, 1966, p. 100; F. Volkov, *Podvig Rikharda Zorge* (Moscow, 1976), p. 38.

19. L. Kutakov, *Istoriya sovetsko-yaponskikh diplomaticheskikh otnoshenii* (Moscow, 1962), p. 276.

20. Record of a conversation between the Chairman of the Council of People's Commissars and the ambassador of the United States in the USSR, 14 Dec 1944: *Sovetsko-amerikanskie otnosheniya vo vremya velikoi otechestvennoi voiny 1941–1945: dokumenty i materialy v dvukh tomakh*, Vol. 2 (Moscow, 1984), doc. 164.

21. K Simonov, 'Glazami cheloveka moego pokoleniya: iz materialov ko vtoroi chasti — "Stalin i Voina": Besedy s admiralom flota Sovetskogo Soyuza I.S. Isakovym, 21 May 1962', *Znamya*, 5 April 1988, pp. 71–2.

22. As in note 21. This is confirmed by Harriman's account summarised in W. Averell Harriman and E. Abel, *Special Envoy to Churchill and Stalin 1941–1946* (London, 1976), p. 380.

23. Record of a conversation between the Chairman of the Council of Ministers of the USSR and the President of the United States, 8 February 1945, 3.30 p.m., Livadia palace: *Sovetskii Soyuz na mezhdunarodnykh konferentsiyakh perioda velikoi otechestvennoi voiny 1941–1945 gg*, Vol. IV: *Krymskaya konferentsiya rukovoditelei trekh soyuznykh derzhav — SSSR, SshA i Velikobritanii (4–11 fevralya 1945g.): sbornik dokumentov* (Moscow, 1984), doc. 12.

24. Gromyko, *Pamyatnoe*, Vol. 1, p. 189.

25. *Krymskaya konferentsiya*, doc. 27.
26. 7 July 1945 — 'Notes taken at Sino–Soviet conferences, Moscow 1945': Victor Hoo Papers, Box 2, Hoover Institution Archives, Stanford University.
27. W. Sebald, *With MacArthur in Japan: A Personal History of the Occupation* (London, 1965), pp. 45–6.
28. 'Obrashchenie k narodu', *Pravda*, 3 Sept 1945.
29. The opening salvo was an article that appeared in the Cominform journal written by 'Observer' and entitled 'Concerning the Situation in Japan': *For a Lasting Peace, For a People's Democracy*, 6 January 1950. It was published 'on Stalin's personal initiative': letter from the Soviet Politburo to the Central Committee of the Japanese Communist Party, 18 April 1964: *Partiinaya zhizn'*, No.14, 16 July 1964, p. 16.
30. *Text: J. Grenville, ed., The Major International Treaties 1914–1973* (New York 1974), pp. 283–6.
31. Memorandum of a conversation between John Foster Dulles and Jakob Malik, 26–27 Oct 1950: *Foreign Relations of the United States 1950*, Vol. 6 (Washington, DC, 1976) p. 1335.
32. J. Allison, *Ambassador from the Prairie* (Boston, 1973), pp. 272–3.
33. Dening (Tokyo) to Allen (London), 22 June 1955: Public Record Office, London, Foreign Office (hereafter FO) 371/115233. The British were very thoroughly briefed by the Japanese on every aspect of the negotiations with Moscow.
34. 'Postanovlenie plenuma TsK KPSS: Ob antipartiinoi gruppe Malenkova G.M., Kaganovicha L.M., Molotova V.M.', 29 June 1957: *Pravda*, 4 July 1957.
35. Minute by Higgins, 15 Sept 1955: FO 371/115234; also, by Crowe, 12 Aug: ibid.
36. *Pravda*, 24 Sept 1955.
37. Dening (Tokyo) to London, 11 June 1956: FO 371/121039.
38. 'The Territorial Issue in Moscow', *Japan Quarterly*, October–December 1956, pp. 401–5. The information came from official sources in Tokyo.
39. *Pravda*, 20 Oct 1956.
40. Interview with the *Asahi Shimbun*, 18 June 1957: N.S. Khrushchev, *Za prochnyi mir i mirnoe sosushchestvovanie* (Moscow, 1958), pp. 97–105.
41. *Vneshnyaya politika Sovetskogo Soyuza i mezhdunarodnye otnosheniya: sbornik dokumentov 1961 god* (Moscow, 1962), doc. 99.
42. *Diplomatic Bluebook for 1973* (Tokyo, 1974), pp. 23–4.
43. Gromyko, *Pamyatnoe*, p. 16.
44. R. Jervis, *Perception and Misperception in International Politics* (Princeton, 1976).

4 The Cuban Missile Crisis twenty-five years later: the learning continues
Dwain Mefford

The impact of historical episodes on Soviet–American relations

The front page of the 29 January 1989 *New York Times* carried a picture of Robert McNamara, President Kennedy's secretary of defense, arm in arm with Sergei Mikoyan, the son of the late Soviet president and former first deputy premier. The place was Moscow; the occasion was a conference on the Cuban Missile Crisis officially sponsored by the Soviet government. This was the third in a series of meetings that began with an exclusively American conclave of former Kennedy advisors,[1] followed by a second conference at Harvard University in which three highly placed Soviet analysts took part.[2] The third and largest conference became a three-way affair with the participation of key Cuban officials.[3] These conferences, particularly the Moscow meeting, revealed dramatic new facts about the events of October 1962. But as important as these revelations are, the most significant fact is undoubtedly the conferences themselves. The exercise of reconstructing the events has a political significance that goes well beyond its contribution to modern history.[4] As Raymond Garthoff observes, 'the conference was most significant as the start of a dialogue and a process of collaborative historical analysis', motivated, in Garthoff's view, by 'growing Soviet awareness of the value of careful historical and political analysis in dealing with current and future problems'.[5] The same might be said of awareness in the United States. The careful analysis of the past, especially collaborative analysis, can correct and complete the record as to who said what to whom. But, more fundamentally, the dialogue exposes beliefs and assumptions that have remained immune to scrutiny for a quarter of a century. This corrected understanding may make a difference in how policy is conducted in the future. The careful reconstruction of past episodes is not an idle exercise for scholars; historical analysis and political education are inseparable as Clausewitz told us. In a moment of crisis an improved ability to anticipate and interpret the thinking of the other side may prove of inestimable value.

The Berlin and Cuban crises of the early 1960s mark a watershed in the history of US–Soviet relations. Looking back twenty-five years later, the confrontations over the status of Berlin, in August 1961, and over the emplacement of missiles in Cuba a year later, are not only remote in time, but belong, in an important sense, to another era. There are good reasons that make it unlikely that confrontations of this order will be repeated in the 1990s. Among them is the fact that by virtue of the earlier experiences the United States and the Soviet Union can jointly invoke the examples of those strategic encounters. To chart the history of the strategic relationship between the Soviet Union and the United States over the past four decades is to invite a number of questions regarding the impetus, direction, and rate of change that is evident in that relationship. That some form of political learning has taken place seems beyond question. Explaining change of this order, and accounting for how the present relationship has emerged from repeated encounters over the decades, is a major conceptual challenge for theorists and policy-makers alike.

Realism, neorealism and learning

Despite the importance of the question and the considerable effort that has gone into the analysis of Soviet–American relations, at present we lack even the rudiments of a theory of learning that might realistically apply to the Soviet–American case. For that matter, it is doubtful whether a theory currently exists which satisfactorily explains qualitative change of this type in any area within international affairs. Learning in animals, in human beings, and in machines, is the subject matter of a number of scientific disciplines. Yet, to date, little in the way of theory from this vast body of work has been convincingly applied to international relations, let alone applied to the specific learning process that may be at work in shaping the relationship between the United States the Soviet Union.

For the purpose of devising a theory of political learning, existing theories of international relations are less than helpful. Because of its level of abstraction and its static character, the pre-eminent approach in the American literature, structural realism or neorealism, cannot describe, let alone explain, the complex, qualitative change occurring in US–Soviet relations. Structures, in Kenneth Waltz's sense, because of their magnitude and temporal scale, are insensitive to the abrupt, qualitative change in the rules and norms that is evident in international relations. Critics have argued that structuralists not only fail to account for regularity and change in the conduct of foreign relations, but that structuralist theory is inherently incapable of accounting for change at this or any other level, including change at the systemic level, where one might expect a structuralist theory to excel.

In a backhanded fashion it is possible to force realist theory to address cognitive questions, including the issue of learning. A structuralist would explain a shift in strategic doctrine or behavior as a reflection of an underlying change in the distribution of power. It might be argued, for example, that the tactic of brandishing nuclear weapons in contexts like Berlin, Cuba, or North East Asia, is no longer likely to achieve results. This realization, coupled with the principle of rationality, dictates that the United States and the Soviet Union should abandon nuclear confrontation as an option. The risk outweighs the conceivable gain. Such an explanation works *post hoc*, but it is hardly satisfactory. As has been pointed out at least since Thomas Macaulay's pitiless critique of John Stuart Mill, to maintain that individuals, or states, act in accordance with their interests is to say very little unless, and until, an account is given as to what these interests are recognized to be. In other words, the structuralist explanation of shifts in Soviet–American relations is compelling only if structural realists can show how leaders and publics come to rethink the choices before them. But structuralists eschew such a level of analysis, as was apparent in Waltz's critique of Stanley Hoffman and Raymond Aron. Because, as Waltz maintains, structures cannot themselves act, if there is to be activity in the system, including change in strategic relationships of the order examined here, it is necessary to go outside the scope of neorealist theory. Committed to the image of a system which functions like a market above or behind the calculations of individuals or firms, neorealist theory is seriously deficient. It must be supplemented by a theory of action or agency. But to raise questions about action or agency, and about the strategic calculations these entail, requires penetrating the structuralist's world of macro forces and comparative statics.

For the purpose of developing a theory of political learning, a second framework holds out greater promise. Robert Keohane's neoliberal institutionalism[6] focuses on the function that institutions serve in shaping and facilitating the interplay of international relations. Neoliberals like Keohane retain realism's and neorealism's core agenda, but add to it significantly. Like realists they are concerned with the management of power and the issues of war and peace, but they expand the notion of power considerably to embrace a wide range of interactions including those which appear, on the surface, to be purely economic in character. Pursuing this expanded agenda, neoliberals investigate the function of institutions in mitigating transaction costs, including the cost of acquiring information and controlling uncertainty. To cope with these issues, they draw heavily from bargaining theory and from the formal models of coordination and cooperation that have been developed by game theorists. Because of their concern with the function of institutions as mechanisms for reducing the uncertainty and costs of transactions, those who adhere to the theoretical program initiated by Keohane and others — Oran Young and Friedrich Kratochwil, for example — investigate systematically the principles, norms and rules which make possible, and which sustain, complex international relationships.

Within this context, which involves, broadly, the question of regime formation and function, Keohane points to the issue of how rules emerge in and through repeated interactions. He cites James March and Johan

Olsen, and John Rawls to the effect that rules embody the history of a practice or relationship: 'history is encoded in rules' and 'rules are pictured as summaries of past decisions'. Institutions, which are compilations of rules, in effect carry the past in their very structure. History is encoded in the operational principles that govern the activity of institutions.[7] Though Keohane does not use the term 'learning' to refer to this process of acquiring and shaping principles of action as a function of past experience, the acquisition of rules is unmistakably a learning process.[8] A process similar to the one Keohane sees in the formation of international economic regimes is likely to be at work in the strategic relationship between the Soviet Union and the United States. The task for the theorist is to find a systematic way to formulate the idea of rule acquisition and regime formation/transformation.

A first attempt at a theory of political learning: a rule-based approach.

International politics, like any set of social relations, depends fundamentally on thought and perception. Cognition is not a residual variable that is usefully examined only once 'structure' has been extracted. The two are inseparable because structure must be recognized if it is to have an effect on action. What is to count as structure is problematic; and itself requires explanation.

As has been documented at length by students of US and Soviet foreign policy, mutually recognized rules and norms of restraint give structure to the relationship. These norms have emerged in and through repeated encounters, including, especially, episodes that verged on disaster. Confrontational tactics that threaten war are no longer viewed as either necessary or acceptable by a sizeable proportion of the US population. From all indications a similar sentiment pervades the Soviet Union. Over the decades, tacit principles have developed that serve to impose bounds upon what is considered prudent or permissible. These principles include what Joseph Nye, following Alexander George, calls 'de facto rules of prudence'. An example of such a rule is the attempt on the part of both the United States and the Soviet Union strictly to avoid Third World interventions that are likely to result in direct encounters between their armed forces. This norm has held in several regions of conflict: the Middle East, the Horn of Africa, and North East and South East Asia. While such rules are largely tacit and imprecise, they nevertheless exert a real influence and can be discerned in the patterns of US and Soviet behavior. Like rules and principles in other areas of human affairs, they lack the certainty of laws of nature. That is, unlike physical laws, they can be violated. But despite this they nevertheless profoundly affect behavior by structuring expectations. As Emile Durkheim insisted in his defense of the 'objective' character of social structures in general, such rules exist independent of the subjective control of individuals; while they must be believed to be effective, the fact that they are widely held means that they cannot be disregarded or wished away voluntarily.[9] Because these structures of expectation and meaning have entered into the fabric of international affairs, they are part of the world in which states act. The product of past actions, they actively shape and constrain what is recognized as possible, prudent and perhaps desirable.

Accounting for their operation, and, more particularly, accounting for how they are acquired and modified in the face of experience is an important practical and theoretical task. Although there have been significant efforts to describe and chart the behavioral evidence for these rules and principles, both in single-case and multi-case studies, by Alexander George and Richard Smoke, and Neil Matheson, for example, there has been little progress in the development of a theory of how such rules are acquired or applied.

The limitations of the rule-based conception of learning

The existence of patterns in the strategic relationship between the United States and the Soviet Union suggests that there may be some underlying rule-like structure, at least in such areas as armed interventions. If this is true, than a theory of political learning in this domain might be constructed around the acquisition and modification of rules. But a rule-based approach of the type frequently used in the expert systems of the 1970s cannot reproduce important dimensions of the qualitative learning that seems endemic to international politics. There are also serious empirical questions since rules are rarely explicitly stated in either documents or policy debates. If they are present at all, their existence and their form must be inferred by the analyst. This might be called the 'rule identification problem'. A further difficulty is the question of the flexible use and creative application of rules. MYCIN-like rules take a fixed form and function essentially independent of specific contexts. As as result, unanticipated situations present severe problems for conventional rule-based systems, which have been generally designed for well-structured and essentially closed domains.

In addition to the issues of rule identification and rule flexibility, there is the problem of consistency and coherence. Contradiction and ambiguity seem inherent in political reasoning, as evidenced in US and Soviet actions in complex situations like the Middle East or Latin America. Because political reasoning may be prone to contradictions, the rules employed, if they are in fact 'rules' as used in expert systems, are also likely to be inconsistent. Consequently, a rule-based system would require mechanisms for adjudicating and limiting the scope or precedence of individual rules, and this added element of judgment may be context-sensitive. Because it is comparatively easy to program rule-based systems which mimic sophisticated political behavior in limited contexts, the rule-based approach has considerable appeal. But, though a modicum of performance can be programmed at low cost, it is questionable whether rule-based systems can be scaled up to become full-bodied models of political decision-making. And it is unclear what the theoretical contribution would be even if large-scale, rule-based systems could be built.[10] For these reasons, and because of the inherent difficulty of capturing important cognitive mechanisms in rule-like form, it is reasonable to conclude that the rule-based approach is an insufficient basis for building a theory of political reasoning.

A second attempt: a script-based approach — its appeal and limitations

The alternative to formulating the problem of learning in terms of the acquisition and modification of rules is to utilize larger cognitive structures. Within Artificial Intelligence, the most developed examples of such structures are 'scripts', 'schema' and 'frames', formulated in the 1970s. But, as a basis for a theory of political reasoning and learning, these too prove insufficient. The existence of 'scripts' in memory is not only problematic, as the developers of the concept such as Roger Schank acknowledge, but the script-based approach is radically incomplete unless mechanisms are specified for acquiring, composing and restructuring scripts. This latter set of issues drives much of the recent effort within script-oriented research, both in AI systems and in psychological studies.[11] The script-inspired research that is perhaps most relevant to the issue of political learning, that of Gerald DeJong, concerns the acquisition of scripts in the context of story understanding. That line of enquiry has broadened into an entire subfield within machine learning, that of Explanation-Based Generalization or Explanation-Based Learning. While the work on scripts in the 1970s assumed pre-given, fixed structures in memory, the work that derives from these earlier efforts is focused on the dynamics inherent in the acquisition and modification of structures in memory. These efforts are represented in the areas of Case-Based Reasoning, Case-Based Learning, and Explanation-Based Learning.[12] This concern with the organization and change of structures in memory begins to address precisely those questions which are most relevant to political learning.

A Soviet model of the 'Caribbean Crisis': Sergeev and Parshin's theory of reasoning and metaphor

In an attempt to apply the concept of script to official statements of Soviet foreign policy, Vicktor Sergeev and his colleagues encounter several of the limitations of that concept.[13] In their work on the 'Caribbean Crisis' they reconstruct the political reasoning implicit in official Soviet statements of that period.[14] In criticizing a script-based representation, they point out that, contrary to what script-based models appear to require, political leaders rarely speak of sequences of actions which culminate in the satisfaction of particular goals. Policies are not described or justified with explicit reference to the type of concrete events, plans or goal structures characteristic of the scripts of Roger Schank and Robert Abelson. Rather, as reflected in the language of the Central Committee Reports published in *Pravda*, political reasoning typically operates at a conceptual level which is much less literal. In the Soviet case, Sergeev asserts, political leaders rely heavily on the notions of 'process', 'trend', 'tendency', and the like. These abstractions are occasionally exemplified by particular events, but such references only serve to illustrate an argument that is cast at an entirely different level.

In his public statements before and after the 'Caribbean Crisis', Nikita Khrushchev, for example, does not explicitly mention causal factors or goals at all. In the place of specific events and strategies, he refers to overarching concepts that describe political developments and tendencies. His Report to the Supreme Soviet of 12 December 1962 is not only laced with metaphors, but is sustained throughout by a linked set of images: peace-loving Socialists manage to curb the reckless policies of imperialists who, but for the restraint and clear-headedness of the Soviet leadership, would endanger world peace by stoking the spreading fire of war. Only at rare intervals in the text does Khrushchev actually name specific actors or refer explicitly to actual historical events.[15]

In criticizing the script-based approach, Sergeev argues as though there must be an immediate correspondence between cognitive structures and the expressions used in speeches or texts. Ultimately, there must be some connection, but it need not be isomorphic. Because Khrushchev does not choose to, or does not happen to, mention specific actions or events in his published statements does not, in itself, demonstrate that Khrushchev reasoned in some mode in which actions and consequences do not figure. This may in fact be the case, but the text itself is not sufficient proof. Thus, it is important to distinguish between the task of modeling the text and the task of reconstructing the reasoning of which the text is a product. As Sergeev and Parshin show, scripts are clearly inadequate for the former task in this case. Whether they are also inadequate to model the reasoning behind the text, as they claim, is an open question.

In contrast to the fine-grained, action- and event-oriented representation which they associate with both scripts and cognitive maps, Sergeev and Parshin propose a representation designed to capture the high-level, process-like statements that Khrushchev uses.[16] In place of the causal linkages and explicit goals, Sergeev emphasizes the inferential function of metaphor. He proposes a split-level scheme consisting of a 'processual map' within a 'metaphorical space' and an 'exemplificative space'. A 'metaphorical engine' govern inferences in the first space while, apparently, metaphors from that space are mapped into concrete examples in the 'exemplification space' via a set of procedures collectively called the 'exemplificator'.[17] The structures that occupy these spaces and the procedures which invoke and manipulate them, are not fully specified in the technical papers by Sergeev and Parshin, but the underlying intuition nevertheless is clear.

Their representation, which Sergeev labels 'processual-evaluative' to emphasize its departure from the cause- and action-oriented structures indicative of scripts, is specifically designed to portray the process-oriented and metaphorical character of Soviet political rhetoric. Sergeev speculates that, in this regard, Soviet political rhetoric is qualitatively different from the American, for which he suggests scripts are a better representation. In fact the discrepancy Sergeev finds between what scripts are capable of expressing and the structures that political texts, and political reasoning in general, utilize is not unique to the Soviet Case. Metaphor and abstraction are universal attributes of political and other discourse. The stock of metaphors and images may differ, but similar inferential patterns are very much in evidence in American policy statements. If scripts fail in this regard as a medium for representing Soviet reasoning, then they must also fail, for the same reasons, to capture the imagery and structure of argument in the American case.

But recognizing that scripts, as generally conceived, are rigid and overly literal does not warrant abandoning the insights that motivated the original work on scripts, schema and the like. Rather, what is required is an extended representation which integrates what is cognitively valid about scripts with the incomplete and open-ended character of metaphorical and analogical reasoning. A representation minimally sufficient for modeling political texts or modeling the evolution of political reasoning, such as that which marks the evolution of the strategic relationship between the Soviet Union and the United States, must address forms of inference at several levels, ranging from the literal or factual to the abstract and poetic. Scripts, as they have been designed, speak to the former but virtually exclude the latter. A representation which is focused on metaphor alone would be equally one-sided. What is needed is a representation that integrates the several dimensions of political cognition.

Scripts are essentially defined in terms of their cognitive function.[18] They are structures in memory that facilitate judgment and inference. As such, they constitute a form of semantic or 'episodic' category. Because they are category-like, they have properties like those which Eleanor Rosch and her colleagues have demonstrated in the case of common semantic categories such as color and species. In this conception, rather than being rigid and fixed, scripts are flexible and admit to variations. The relevance of a particular script to a situation would be a matter of degree in the same sense that semantic categories can be judged to apply to an object to some degree, i.e. some instances would be judged as representative of the category while others would be seen as marginal examples. This suggests that criticisms leveled at the script-based approach which attack its fixed character and literal-mindedness may apply to a particular implementation of the notion, but not to the basic theoretical point. The cognitive theory that motivates the work with scripts goes well beyond the data structures and examples which were employed in the AI programs produced at Yale in the 1970s by, for example, Richard Cullingford and Jaime Carbonnell. In particular, the underlying conception need not be tied to the implementation in Schank's Conceptual Dependency, which, as Sergeev and others have pointed out, is cast at a level well below that which political leaders seem to employ. Schank and Carbonnell realized this when, in their attempt to encode Lincoln's Gettysburg Address, they were forced to add new primitives to the original set in Conceptual Dependency.[19]

Learning within the framework of heuristic search: the acquisition of new scripts from historical episodes

The connection between the literal character of historical events and the abstract properties of the metaphors that Sergeev points to might be captured using the notion of *procedural abstraction*. Through procedural abstraction as it has been developed in several areas of machine learning, a system acquires a concept or stratagem by generalizing a particular example or experience. This form of abstraction may resolve the apparent conflict between scripts and metaphors; it may also serve as the core principle for a theory of historically based political learning. Procedural abstraction is closely related, if not identical in essentials, to several major ideas that have emerged in Artificial Intelligence. 'Chunking', particularly the 'chunking' of procedural knowledge as demonstrated in the SOAR project by John Laird, Paul Rosenbloom and Allan Newell, is a form of procedural abstraction and is rooted in basic features of the class of programming languages to which LISP belongs.

Applied to international relations, this form of learning abstracts a structure from a particular episode, which, subsequently, can be reapplied to construct plans and arguments. What was formerly a sequence of concrete actions in a specific context becomes a concept or category that can be applied more generally. Specific cases in Soviet–American relations have been elevated to a such a status. The Cuban Missile Crisis, which Sergeev and Parshin analyze, is an example. The experience of that crisis results in a qualitative change in the assumptions and norms that inform political and strategic judgment. That is, events of this magnitude have an impact on political cognition such that perception and reasoning after the event is qualitatively different from what prevailed before. To handle this order of change theoretically one needs to spell out what it is that is acquired cognitively through such experiences, and how, once such structures have been compiled into memory, they inform intuitions and expectations at later points in time.

In the framework of heuristic search, learning consists essentially of retaining copies of prior search. These are then available to be reused or avoided as the case may be. In Allan Newell's work, the operation of copying or abstracting this problem solving effort is called 'chunking' and relates, as the word implies, to George Miller's concept of a 'chunk' of information. Learning via 'chunking' is by no means restricted to the tasks or mechanisms that Newell has investigated in the SOAR project and elsewhere. The core idea is ubiquitous and has surfaced under different vocabularies. For example, it is explicit in the work on macro-operator acquisition via a technique of plan abstraction embodied in ABSTRIPS, the successor to the original work on robotic planning at SRI. Much the same idea developed not within the planning and problem-solving context, but *vis-à-vis* the theory of computer languages. Harold Abelson and Gerald Sussman, for example, speak of procedural abstraction as a basic feature of functional languages like LISP. The essential mechanism, whether described in terms of procedural abstraction, 'chunking', macro-operator induction, or memorizing, implies that a problem-solving system can acquire whole new strategies or operators by observing its own problem-solving steps, or by observing sequences of steps in the problem-solving activity of another intelligent agent.[20] What this amounts to is that experience can be 'compiled' or abstracted, and subsequently applied in a rule-like way. It should be emphasized that, unlike behavioural learning theory or learning as it is generally conceived in pattern recognition, this form of learning can be single-shot and qualitative; it does not involve incrementing parameters or adjusting weights in the fashion characteristic of behavioral learning theory.

Political episodes, like the Cuban Missile Crisis, represent the codification of traumatic political experience. Such episodes become an intimate part of the reasoning mechanism that informs political intuition and judgment. Events of this order function much like lemmas in mathematics. That is, although they are discovered or encountered at a discrete point in time, they subsequently become a working part of the body of principles, rules and examples that intelligent agents use in solving problems. Viewed psychologically, events of this magnitude are elevated to a type of semantic category. As such, they enter into the cognitive construction of the political world we recognize and inhabit. Evidence of this is that episodes such as the Cuban Missile Crisis, or 'Vietnam' and 'Afghanistan', becomes an integral part of the language of politics. These terms function like conventional semantic categories.[21] While they initially resemble the type of cognitive structure that Lawrence Barsalou calls 'ad-hoc categories', with usage they take on a generic status and serve as standards or exemplars for the classification of other events. Thus , critical historical episodes impact on political reasoning by altering the very language in which politics is conceived. The consequence is, for better or worse, that they fundamentally alter strategic relationships. To live through a nuclear crisis is, for the members of an entire generation, vividly to acquire a new concept, which, potentially, may partially determine the parameters of future encounters.

To explain what is involved in acquiring such a 'political category', and how this form of learning affects subsequent judgments and perceptions, requires a new theoretical approach. A framework sufficient for capturing this form of political or institutional learning can be devised by integrating the insights associated with the work on scripts with the learning mechanisms, 'chunking' and its variants, that have been developed within the framework of heuristic search. The object is to conceptualize how change occurs in the fundamental representation that informs political judgment and strategic calculation. As Herbert Simon pointed out, the space that is searched may itself consist of search spaces. By extension, the activity of modifying the search space falls within the heuristic search paradigm. This permits a fundamental form of learning. If the space to be searched consists of script-like structures, then the insertion of an event like the Cuban Missile Crisis may have the effect of fundamentally altering the space in which the problem-solving characteristic of foreign policy takes place. If this happens, as it has in the history of Soviet–American relations, then the joint experience of a particular episode can conceivably have immense impact on the formulation and interpretation of subsequent policies, because it impacts on the space of possibilities that inform political reasoning.

Delineating the concept of learning: innovation in the game of chess

Before tackling the complexities of the issue of learning in the concrete case of the Missile Crisis, the concepts introduced to this point need to be sharpened. This requires first applying them in a simplified context. The game of chess is a good candidate, because, in addition to the process of learning it illustrates, it also involves reasoning at several levels of representation. These levels range from that of the actual moves, through that of gambits and variations, to metaphorical readings of the competition and conflict that the game embodies. Moreover, chess, if viewed not simply as a board game but as an artful practice with its own history, shares a number of essential features with political institutions. As such, if it proves possible to outline a theory of learning sufficient to capture what may be called 'institutional learning' in the game of chess, then there is reason to believe that much the same conception might suffice to explicate the evolution of a strategic relationship, which can be considered as a particular form of regime or institution.[22]

Multiple, simultaneous representations in the game of chess

Consider chess openings such as that of Ruy Lopez. Using standard notation, this opening is recorded as a sequence of moves involving White's and Black's king's pawns, followed by their respective knights, followed by White's attack with the bishop on Black's knight, etc.

1. P-K4, P-K4
2. Kt-KB3, Kt-QB3
3. B-Kt5, . . .[23]

This representation, familiar from chess columns in newspapers, is fine-grained or literal in much the same sense as Axelrod's Cognitive Maps or Schank's scripts — the point that Sergeev and Parshin make in their critique. Each action, in this case the move resulting in a new board position, is completely specified. As chess has evolved, a body of commentary has collected that is organized around segments of games, e.g. openings, gambits and end games. These basic patterns or stratagems, for example, the Ruy Lopez opening named after the twelfth-century Spanish bishop, consist of the core moves in the actual or legendary games in which they were first used. Such compiled strategies figure in the stock of openings and gambits that all serious chess players know. What is important here is the process by which new game strategies are added to this collective knowledge. Related to this is the question of how openings and variations are represented, and subsequently used strategically in the play of the game. The discovery and subsequent use of new gambits in chess has in fact much in common with the learning that may potentially result from the experience of major crises in international relations.

In identifying strategic patterns, like that of the five-move sequence called Ruy Lopez, chess players overlay a more abstract representation onto the underlying one that conveys board positions and moves. This effectively extends the overall representation of the game by imposing a space of variations onto the space of moves. This can be construed as a simple form of 'chunking' or abstraction. The chunks corresponding to the opening and defense are represented in Figure 4.1 as boxed-in

	White	Black	
1.	P-K4	P-K4	
2.	Kt-KB3	Kt-QB3	Ruy Lopez
3.	B-Kt5	P-QR3	
4.	B-R4	Kt-B3	
5.	0-0	B-K2	
6.	R-K1	P-Qkt4	Marshall's Counterattack
7.	B-Kt3	0-0	
8.	P-B3	P-Q4	
9.	P x P	Kt x P	
10.	Kt x P	Kt x Kt	
11.	R x Kt	Kt-B3	
12.	R-K1	B-Q3	

Capablanca vs. Marshall
New York, 1918.

Figure 4.1 The initial sequence of moves in the Capablanca–Marshall game with the White's opening and Black's defense identified.

segments of the sequence of moves. The effect of the added representation is to shift the problem-solving activity from the level of the moves to that of choosing among gambits and variations. For example, if White elects to play Ruy Lopez, which translates into a particular sequence of moves, then Black must decide whether to reply with a standard defense like Petroff, or with something more daring. In general, variations are not fixed recipes of moves, but are more general and more flexible patterns which admit significant variability. There are, for example, hundreds of variations of the Petroff defense. What makes these actual move sequences instances of a single opening or gambit is that they share a common strategic pattern. This point regarding flexible structure relates back to the issues raised by Sergeev and Parshin in their criticism of the rigidity of scripts.

The historical dimension of chess: the acquisition of new gambits

Chess has a historical dimension. When viewed as a collective activity with a history, the game has the basic features of an institution that evolves over time. That is, chess, with its community of practitioners and its body of theory, can be viewed as a living institution of the kind described by James March and Johan Olsen. Certain important games live on in the annals of chess and, as such, become part of the strategic problem-solving of subsequent generations. The game of chess, as played today, is intimately related to the history of all prior games of chess in the sense that momentous games of the past ushered in innovations — variations and stratagems — which have been incorporated into the theory and lore of the game. These particular games have an impact on how chess is played by all those who are expert enough to belong to the community of chess players that extends back through the history of the game. The sense in which an individual game can alter the way all subsequent games are played is the fundamental principle of abstraction and learning emphasized here.

A particular game of chess, the famous Capablanca–Marshall encounter, for example, in New York in 1918, is sensitive not only to the history of past encounters between those two players, but is also profoundly sensitive to the history of all historically important games that have been recorded and analyzed.

The significance of the Capablanca–Marshall match is that Marshall had discovered a new variation for Black in response to White's use of the Ruy Lopez opening. By his own account, Marshall hit upon the counterattack ten years earlier while analyzing prior games he had lost to Capablanca. Knowing that once the new variation was used in tournament play it would enter into the stock of knowledge available to all serious chess players, Marshall carefully sequestered his discovery until he could spring it on Capablanca. The tournament in 1918 was to be the occasion. When, as Capablanca records in his autobiography, Marshall did not choose one of the standard defenses, Capablanca immediately suspected that Marshall had discovered an unprecedented line of play. At that point, Capablanca's decision problem involved not only board position and variations, as depicted in Figure 4.2, but also entailed a strategic estimate of what was and was not known by the chess community regarding possible defenses against this particular opening. On top of this multilayered interpretation of the strategic situation, Capablanca adds yet another dimension, that of his personal competition with Marshall. In his description of the game, he speaks of

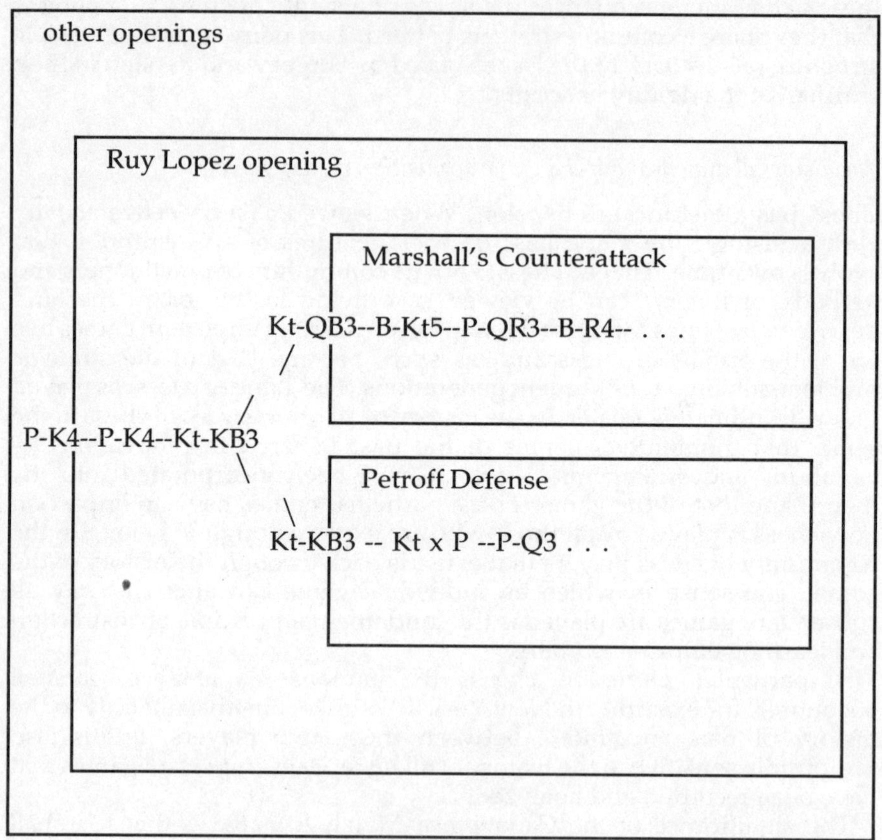

Figure 4.2 'Marshall's Counterattack'

'risk', 'honor' and the drama of 'mortal combat' between adversaries well known to each other. All of this is imposed on the mundane problem-solving activity of moving wooden objects on a flat surface. In effect, there are at least three representations compounded into the multilevel cognitive activity that chess embodies. In Capablanca's autobiography essentially only the most metaphorical dimension registers. For example, when describing what went through his mind during the match with Marshall, he records that:

> The lust for battle . . . had been aroused within me. I felt that my judgment and skill were being challenged by a player who had very reason to fear both . . . but who wanted to take advantage of the element of surprise and of the fact of my being unfamiliar with a thing to which he had devoted many a night of toil and hard work. I considered the position and then decided that I was honor bound, so to speak, to take the Pawn . . .[24]

Because the counterattack that Marshall used in response to Capablanca's Ruy Lopez opening marked a major innovation, this individual game altered the history of chess. It illustrates the manner in which a concrete episode can impact on the working principles that define an institution. In this case, a category was literally added to the body of chess knowledge — the category of the 'Marshall Counterattack'. As a result, in principle, all subsequent games that follow from White's choice of the Ruy Lopez opening involve a new strategic element, namely the possibility that Black might respond with the stratagem that Marshall inaugurated in the 1918 tournament. The parallel to be drawn is between an epic event like this one in the domain of chess and epic events in the domain of strategic politics.

In addition to the sense in which the past becomes a living part of the present, the game of chess also illustrates the ways in which multiple levels of cognitive activity can proceed simultaneously. The reasoning is, in effect, multilayered and complex to an extent scarcely revealed in a textual account, e.g. Capablanca's single-dimensional description. This point bears on the issues raised by Sergeev and Parshin regarding the choice of representation for modeling political texts. Over and above behavior which can be observed, the actors involved can superimpose levels of representation, such as doctrine or personalized conflict, like that which unfolded between Nikita Khrushchev and John Kennedy. This causes problems for empirical analysis, whether of events or of texts. As in Khrushchev's choice of language, reference to actual board positions and the movement of pieces disappears under an all-encompassing metaphor of personal anguish and struggle.

In sum, this example illustrates the several layers of representation that are simultaneously active in the game of chess. They range from the most literal, consisting of moves and board configurations, to metaphors involving honor and risk. There is, in addition, a qualitative dynamic through which the game of chess, as a living institution, may be profoundly changed as the result of a particular instance or episode of the game. A new gambit or variation, once exhibited in tournament play, is added to the stock of variations that condition how expert players subsequently play the game. Moreover, because the new line of play interacts with previously known stratagems, the change that a new gambit exerts is not simply additive. The institutional change or learning is qualitative. It resembles the type of change that has occurred as the result of certain episodes in Soviet–American relations, of which the Cuban Missile Crisis is perhaps the most vivid. Examining Figure 4.2 suggests how this form of learning might be conceptualized. Before the match in 1918 the universe of possible game trees which emanated from the Ruy Lopez opening did not include Marshall's variation. After the match that stratagem, now named the 'Marshall Counterattack', exists not only as a segment of the actual game played between Marshall and Capablanca, but as a strategic pattern which belongs to the community of chess players as a whole. In effect, a sub-universe has been grafted onto the space of chess strategies, as pictured in the figure. As suggested earlier, a particular episode of the game has gained the status of a category, and, as such, affects all subsequent play.

International politics shares with the chess example a complex process by which episodes from the past serve as examples or prototypes which become inextricably part of strategic reasoning in the present. The process is bootstrap-like. The core mechanism can be formalized using procedural abstraction. But the cognitive change that results from the application of this learning mechanism depends fundamentally on the characteristics of the concrete episodes. Moreover, the process is path-dependent. The order in which concrete episodes are encountered makes a profound difference in the evolution of a strategic relationship. That the Cuban Missile Crisis happened as it did, when it did, matters. A historical episode reverberates in the assumptions and principles that inform the strategic relationship.

Extracting lessons from the Cuban Missile Crisis

The chess metaphor is applied so often to politics that it threatens to degenerate into a cliché. Nevertheless, there are important and valid parallels between the artificial world of chess and the real one of politics and war that it emulates. McGeorge Bundy, for one, employed the image of chess in his detailed account of the missile crisis to underscore the sequential and interactive character of that episode. What the chess image suggests, in a revealing if simplified way, is that the course of play is the result of an interaction that is never fully under the control of either of the players. As Bundy observes, each step by each of the players is taken within the immediate context that is the product of the history of play to that point. The chess metaphor also serves to underscore the cognitive and problem-solving dimensions. As in game theory, the problem-solving task is an interdependent one: whether the structure of the situation is competitive or cooperative, the essential cognitive task forces each player to solve the other player's problem as he solves his own. Each player's interpretation of the game is based on the interpretation attributed to the other. How these interpretations interact determines what transpires.

Bundy is quick to point out the limitations of the chess metaphor when applied to events as complex and plastic as those of the Cuban Missile Crisis:

> The analogy to chess oversimplifies, because the process had more than two dimensions, and the possible moves were far more varied than in chess. The element of chance was high, and so was the possibility of intervention by third parties like Castro. The two sides were engaged in a set of actions and communications vastly more complex than any game conducted by two players making alternating single moves.[25]

Among others, Graham Allison has also used the chess metaphor to focus attention on the dynamics of the situation. But Allison extends the metaphor considerably. In fact, at one point he renders each of his three models in the chess metaphor, thereby pointing out how they overlap and complement each other. He suggests that we

> Imagine a chess game in which the observer could see only a screen upon which moves in the game were projected, with no information about how the pieces came to be moved. Initially, most observers would assume — as [the rational actor model] does — that an individual chess player was moving the pieces with reference to plans and tactics toward the goal of winning the game. But a pattern of moves can be imagined that would lead some observers, after watching several games, to consider [an organizational process] assumption: the chess player might not be a single individual but rather a loose alliance of semi-independent organizations, each of which moved its set of pieces according to standard operating procedures. For example, movement of separate sets of pieces might proceed in turn, each according to a routine, the king's rook, bishop, and their pawns repeatedly attack the opponent according to a fixed plan. It is conceivable, furthermore, that the pattern of play might suggest to an observer a [bureaucratic politics] assumption: a number of distinct players, with distinct objectives but shared power over the pieces, could be determining the moves as the resultant of collegial bargaining. For example, the black rook's move might contribute to the loss of a black knight with no comparable gains for the black team, but with the black rook becoming the principal guardian of the palace on that side of the board.[26]

But the game embodied in the Cuban Missile Crisis is an odd one if chess is to be the standard. At several points new players suddenly intervene, changing the state of the board in major or minor ways. It is as though the United States and the Soviet Union are not playing chess, but a game like chess in which pieces are moved, and even added, by events outside the control of, and perhaps even unknown to the players. Aleksandr Fomin's critically important meeting with John Scali on 26 October is an example, as is the shooting down of the U-2 over Cuba on 27 October. The chess board, and the pieces on it, have a life of their own. This new game must be played under the rule that regardless of how the board changes or who interferes, the players must proceed from the new board position as best they can. But there is not only the added uncertainty due to interference, there is also the fact that the players' knowledge and control of the pieces is only partial. The strategic game is effectively played not by two individuals, but by loose committees, each 'embedded in enormous complex organizations whose outline they barely discern and whose detailed operations they scarcely control'.[27]

In addition to the complexity imposed by this motion, confusion and multiplicity, the real-life game is complex in yet another way, and reveals one dimension of possible learning. As was the case with Capablanca and Marshall, in the course of play opponents reveal to each other — in fact may instruct each other — as to what kind of players they are. That newly acquired knowledge feeds back and significantly alters the character of the interaction. Not only do the players learn in the course of the game, but their actions and innovations, like the famous Capablanca–Marshall encounter, become a living part of the history and mythology of international relations. Later generations play a game that bears the deep imprint of critical episodes like that of the Cuban Missile Crisis. Thus the issue is the lessons that have been drawn, or, more precisely, the process of *lesson-making* itself, both in the immediate aftermath of the crisis and in the efforts twenty-five years later to interpret the historical significance of the crisis. But the lessons drawn depend intimately on the analysis of decisions and events. The questions most often addressed can be grouped into three clusters, only the third of which is pursued here.

1. Why did Khrushchev decide to put missiles in Cuba; what motivated that action; why did Khrushchev not anticipate the US reaction?
2. How did Kennedy and his advisers fix on the policy of a blockade rather than airstrike, invasion or diplomacy?
3. Where did the formula of missiles-for-pledge originate. How did it relate to the missiles-for-missiles trade? Why did Khrushchev accept the former terms after proposing the missile quid pro quo? And why did he do so with such apparent haste?

Efforts in 1962 and in 1987–9 to explain Khrushchev's 'switch'

This third issue contains two essential puzzles: the question of how the missiles-for-pledge formula emerged, on which, according to the official record, the crisis was resolved, and the question of the origin of the second formula, that of missiles-for-missiles, which vastly complicated the negotiations at the very height of the crisis. The question of how these formulas were first introduced and subsequently handled has been central to the analysis of the crisis since the accounts of Arthur Schlesinger and Theodore Sorensen, published in 1965. But time has not solved these riddles, nor diminished their interest. In fact, twenty-five years later at the conferences in Florida, Cambridge and Moscow, the veterans of the crisis — American, Soviet and Cuban — intently questioned each other on these crucial matters.

At the height of the Cuban Missile Crisis four days after President Kennedy's televised address, Aleksandr Fomin, counselor at the Soviet embassy, but known to be the senior KGB official in Washington, met ABC's State Department correspondent John Scali. Authoritative accounts of the Fomin–Scali meeting were given by Schlesinger and Sorensen, and by Roger Hilsman who, as Director of the Bureau of Intelligence and Research at the State Department, conveyed Scali's report to Dean Rusk and the ExComm.[28] There is little question as to what Fomin said to Scali; Schlesinger reports it almost verbatim. But there is, in retrospect, considerable question as to the interpretation that Kennedy and the ExComm put on both the content and the fact of Fomin's initiative.

In the literature up to and including McGeorge Bundy's book, it was assumed that Fomin was an unofficial but authorized channel between the two governments, one of the five channels used during the crisis. In 1987 Fomin reported that, in approaching Scali, 'his probe was strictly his own'.[29] Fomin repeated this assertion at the Moscow conference in 1989. If this is to be believed, then the crucial signal that Fomin sent via Scali to the American leadership may in fact have been neither authorized nor known by Khrushchev.[30] At the time, of course, Kennedy and the Excomm were unaware of this. Splicing together Fomin's very specific offer with the 'germ of a reasonable settlement' contained in Khrushchev's 'first' letter that began to arrive just hours after the Scali–Fomin meeting, President Kennedy, Robert McNamara, McGeorge Bundy *et al.* arrived at the firm conviction that Khrushchev had proposed a basis for resolving the crisis on terms acceptable to the United States.[31] The Americans reached this conclusion by coupling the two communications, and by literally conjoining elements of the one, i.e the promise of UN verification from the Fomin conversation, with elements of the other. In short, Kennedy and his advisers used Fomin's concrete offer to guide their interpretation of Khrushchev's conciliatory, but unspecific proposal for resolving the crisis. Because Fomin's proposal resonated with other informal gestures at the United Nations, and because it seemed to dovetail with Khrushchev's serious concerns passionately expounded in the letter received in Washington on the evening of 26 October, the Americans concluded that the two messages were part of a package.[32] In combination the two communications constituted a specific Soviet offer, namely to remove the missiles in exchange for a public US pledge not to invade Cuba.

Khrushchev's letter of 26 October is one of the most remarkable documents in the annals of international relations. But it is extraordinary for the appeal it makes, not for the proposal it contains. In fact, in the letter Khrushchev makes no concrete offer. He attempts only to persuade Kennedy of his own motivation and reasoning, arguing that if the United States would stop threatening Cuba, then 'the necessity for the presence of our military specialists in Cuba will be obviated'. But no plan for the removal of Soviet forces is spelled out. In substance, the letter simply repeats the proposal that Secretary General U Thant had put forward at the United Nations on 24 October as a stop-gap measure to de-escalate the crisis. U Thant had urged a cooling-off period during which arms shipments to Cuba would cease in return for a suspension of the quarantine. What Khrushchev's letter powerfully conveys is the frank expression that both he and Kennedy would lose control and that war would result. This is driven home by an arresting metaphor:

> Mr. President, you and I should not pull on the ends of the rope in which you have tied a knot of war, because the harder you and I pull, the tighter this knot will become. And a time may come when this knot is tied so tight that the person who tied it is no longer capable of untying it, and then the knot will have to be cut. What that would mean I need not explain to you, because you yourself understand perfectly what dread forces our two countries possess.
>
> Therefore, if there is no intention of tightening this knot, thereby dooming the world to the catastrophe of thermonuclear war, let us not only relax the forces straining on the ends of the rope, let us take measures for untying this knot.[33]

Kennedy and the ExComm believed that Khrushchev had signaled a way out of the crisis. The *fact* of that belief was to result in confusion and dangerous recrimination when the ExComm was faced with the offer in the 'second letter', broadcast the morning of 27 October (5 p.m. Moscow time) on Radio Moscow, demanding a quid pro quo: missiles in Turkey for missiles in Cuba.

Perhaps the most dramatic moment of the crisis in Washington, captured verbatim on tape, occurred the morning of 27 October as McNamara, Bundy and the members of the ExComm puzzled through the meaning of these three communications: Fomin's offer to Scali, Khrushchev's letter of 26 October, and the Soviet position broadcast on Radio Moscow on Saturday morning (Washington time), 27 October. The question of how the messages related and what they portended, including what they indicated about confusion and conflict within the Soviet leadership, was a profound problem for Kennedy's advisers. It remained so twenty-five years later at the conferences. To respond to Khrushchev the members of the ExComm had to explain to themselves what lay behind Khrushchev's 'switch'.

The American understanding of the situation, at least the working understanding of the members of the ExComm, was seriously in error because it was based on assumptions that were either false or incomplete, i.e. the belief that Fomin's message was an integral part of Khrushchev's offer, and the assumption that there had been no high-level communication between Washington and Moscow on the night of 26 October that would explain the abrupt *démarche* signaled in Khrushchev's second letter. The error was due in part to lack of clarity from the Soviet side. Sorensen, Kennedy's principal speech writer and a close adviser, described Khrushchev's first letter as 'long, meandering, full of polemics'. But the misunderstanding was due in larger part to what, in retrospect, looks like a double-game that the Kennedys, John and Robert, were inadvertently playing *vis-à-vis* their chief advisers. Indications of this are apparent in the transcribed tape of the 27 October ExComm meeting. As Bundy and Blight note in their commentary on the transcript, on the morning of 27 October Kennedy appears to be pursuing an entirely different track from that of his advisers.[34] He focuses on the missiles-for-missiles trade, asking questions about the negotiations with the Turks, and arguing that '. . . to any man at the United Nations or any other rational man it will look like a very fair trade'. Bundy, McNamara, Sorensen and Llewelyn Thompson, former American ambassador to the Soviet Union, question the direction in which Kennedy appears to be moving. They raise a host of objections and attempt to find an alternative to the missiles-for-missiles trade. Bundy questions whether this second offer is in fact a serious one. McNamara is deeply concerned about what this tactic of abruptly changing the terms of the offer reveals about Khrushchev's intentions, and, ultimately, about the prospect of negotiating any type of settlement with the Soviets. He asks Rusk:

> How do you interpret the addition of still another condition over and above the letter that came in last night? We had one deal in the letter, and now we've got a different deal . . . How can we negotiate with somebody who changes his deal before we even get a chance to reply and announces publicly the deal before we receive it?[35]

On scrutinizing Khrushchev's first letter, McNamara realizes fully that it does not contain a genuine offer:

> When I read that message of last night this morning, I thought, *My God* I'd never sell — I'd never base a transaction on *that contract*. Hell, that's no offer. There's not a damned thing in it that's an offer. You read that message carefully. He didn't propose to take the missiles out. Not once — there isn't a single word in it that proposes to take the missiles out. It's twelve pages of — of fluff.[36]

After considerable effort to fathom what lay behind the surprising change from the first letter to the second, the ExComm, following a suggestion of Robert Kennedy and Sorensen, hit on the 'Trollope Ploy': to reply to the first letter, interpreted in light of the Fomin initiative, while effectively ignoring the proposal in the second. That Rusk, Bundy and McNamara truly believed that Khrushchev had in effect doubled-crossed the United States by proposing one thing privately and quite another publicly is confirmed by the fact that Rusk sent Scali back to Fomin for an explanation. Schlesinger reports in great detail what Scali subsequently conveyed to Fomin, both with body language and blunt words. 'Scali, fearful that he had been used to deceive his own country upbraided Fomin, accusing him of a double cross. The Russian said miserably that there must have been a cable delay, that the Embassy was waiting word from Khrushchev at any moment.'[37]

Twenty-five years later, prior to the revelations at the conferences in Cambridge and Moscow, the contradiction between Khrushchev's two letters remained as enigmatic as it had been for the ExComm on the morning of 27 October 1962. In the literature there are at least three hypotheses. The first in effect denies that the 'first letter' was in fact first. Because of a mix-up in communication, the letter received on 26 October was the final Soviet position. It superseded the public statement made on 27 October. Schlesinger, relying on Henry Pachter's close textual analysis of the second letter and its connections to Khrushchev's Thursday message to U Thant, offers this explanation in his *A Thousand Days*. But, in a footnote in his book, Sorensen discounts the idea that the second letter had actually been written first on the grounds that 'the far greater length of time required to send a private, coded message made this possibility highly doubtful'.[38]

The second hypothesis suggests that there was a struggle in the Kremlin between Khrushchev and the hard-liners. Noting that the Soviet defense minister, Marshall Rodion Malinovksy, had linked Cuba and Turkey earlier in the week — a connection repeated on Friday in the army newspaper, *Krasnaya Zvezda* — Schlesinger speculates that 'the military had taken over in Moscow'. This was Bundy's immediate reaction as the transcripts of the 27 October ExComm meeting shows.[39] One of the most astute and psychologically penetrating analyses of this line of reasoning was constructed by the former *Le Monde* correspondent in Moscow, Michel Tatu. Using indirect evidence from the Soviet Press, Tatu, in his book on Khrushchev, constructs an elaborate battle within the Kremlin. He explains why Khrushchev reconstructed events as he did in his official account delivered before the Supreme Soviet on 12 December 1962.[40] Tatu emphasizes that the missile-for-missiles trade not only contradicted Khrushchev's letter to Kennedy, but starkly contradicted the official position taken by the Soviet government, as presented in V. Mareyev's column in *Izvestia* the same day as the broadcast of Khrushchev's second letter. Tatu observes that

> The confusion reached its height late on Saturday afternoon, when *Izvestia* came out. On page one was Khrushchev's message proposing the Cuba–Turkey deal, and on page two the following comment by V. Mareyev: 'Measuring things by their own cynical bargaining standard, some persons in the United States are plotting schemes whereby, in exchange for the abandonment by Cuba of the means to counter an American aggression, some American base near Soviet territory might be abandoned . . . Such "proposals", if they deserve the name, only reveal the impure conscience of their authors' (*Izvestia*, October 27 1962; October 28 in the foreign edition). The contradiction between this commentary and the note on Turkey is due to the fact that the latter was handed to the newspaper at the last minute and the editors had no time, or forgot, to jettison their columnist's article.[41]

Tatu is struck by the remarkable fact that in the Supreme Soviet speech Khrushchev completely suppressed any mention of the missiles-for-missiles trade though it had been broadcast in Russian and English on Radio Moscow. Tatu explains this and Khrushchev's claim that he had initiated the terms of the final settlement as not simply a self-serving defense, but as 'a belated recital of the facts — not as they actually were, but as they should have been if his advice had been heeded'. Tatu reasons that Khrushchev had been outvoted on 27 October by a hard-line majority. As a result

> he did not approve of anything that was done that day, not even the Turkish proposal, and chose subsequently to regard the events of the day as an interlude of no significance . . . His aim was to record for history the thesis that he had unsuccessfully defended before his colleagues that day and to vindicate his own line, not theirs . . . he was bringing a semblance of consistency into a series of chaotic happenings.[42]

The third hypothesis focuses on the possibility that Khrushchev may have interpreted a statement by a third party as an indirect signal that the United States was willing to trade missiles in Turkey for missiles in Cuba. Llewelyn Thompson, the one Soviet expert in the ExComm, thought this might be likely. Responding to Lyndon Johnson's question about the switch in Khrushchev's bargaining position during the ExComm meeting on 27 October, Thompson ventured that 'it's one of two things. Either Khrushchev was overruled or Khrushchev and/or his colleagues were deceived by the Lippmann pieces and the fact that Kreisky put this out which made them think that *we* were putting this, that we were willing to — to make a trade'.[43] From what we know now, the hypothesis regarding a signal in fact explains Khrushchev's switch. But the signal did not arise from a third party, but from Robert Kennedy in a secret meeting with Ambassador Dobrynin late on the night of 26 October.

THE STRANGE CAREER OF THE MISSILES-FOR-MISSILES FORMULA: DOBRYNIN'S REVELATION

At the Cambridge conference in 1987 McGeorge Bundy said that in his view the crucial moment in the crisis came on 26 October 'when we received that long but encouraging telegram — which we all assumed at the time had been written by Khrushchev himself — essentially proposing the terms on which we finally settled. Of all the communications in the crisis, this one seems to me to have been the most important'.[44] But, twenty-five years later he was still puzzled by the change in tone and content from this first letter to the one received the next day. Bundy, backed by Allison and Garthoff, pumped the three Soviet participants, Mikoyan, Burlatsky and Shaknazarov, for an answer. Allison asked: 'let me put it to Sergei [Mikoyan] and Fyodor [Burlatsky]. If you read the two letters, what would you think? Tommy Thompson thought for sure that the first letter was written by Khrushchev himself, and that the second had been written by a committee. Is that correct? Do we know who was involved in the two letters?' Garthoff further amplified the question by asking: 'do you have any thoughts on whether Khrushchev *himself* thought of raising the ante in the second letter, or were others *urging* him? We tend to think the latter, that a harder-line group was pushing him to demand the Turkish missile trade.'[45]

Burlatsky's answer was to suggest that there may have been a signal from the Americans, either through Scali or Robert Kennedy, which 'hinted that there might be some possibilities for trading missiles in Turkey'. But to this speculation Bundy stated matter-of-factly that 'We have no information to that effect. We certainly hadn't authorized anybody to do it'. John Scali was a possible source, but Bundy suggested that 'Scali was acting as an independent, but even then, he was pretty hard-line, so it's difficult to imagine him doing anything like that'. Overall, Bundy pointed out that 'The President himself decided not to make a public trade, but undertook to get them out, which was hard work. It involved a lot of secret, delicate negotiations. We needed to be very careful about our own public opinion'.[46]

At this point Shaknazarov related what Dobrynin had told him in Moscow shortly before the Cambridge conference: 'He . . . told me that the Turkish idea was born here in the Soviet embassy, in a conversation, maybe with Robert Kennedy. It was suggested to Moscow, and then it came back . . .'[47] Dobrynin was himself present at the third conference in Moscow and provided further details regarding his meetings with Robert Kennedy. Dobrynin maintained that he and Robert Kennedy met secretly on the night of Friday, 26 October 'as part of a series of private, late-night back-channel discussions between the two'. On that night, according to Dobrynin, he had

> remarked to the attorney general that the administration's extreme reaction to the deployment of Soviet missiles in Cuba was puzzling in view of the fact that the United States had deployed similar missiles in Turkey, next door to the Soviet Union. In raising the issue, Dobrynin said, he was acting entirely on his own initiative, not expecting it to be interpreted as part of a negotiating position. He was merely attempting to make the point that the Soviet side had an equal right to provide for its own security.

From memory Dobrynin quoted Robert Kennedy:

> Robert Kennedy said, 'You are interested in the missiles in Turkey?' He thought pensively and said, 'One minute, I will go and talk to the President.' He went out of the room . . . [He] came back and said, 'The President said that we are ready to consider the question of Turkey, to examine favorably the question of Turkey.'[48]

Dobrynin immediately reported this development to Moscow. At the conference in 1989, Dobrynin said that he believed that this was the source of the missiles-for-missiles formula, though he also suggested that the idea may have occurred to Khrushchev independent of Dobrynin's cable of 26 October. Andrei Gromyko was present at the conference and did not contradict Dobrynin as he made his statement.

The fact that there were several secret, late-night meetings between Robert Kennedy and Dobrynin will be corroborated no doubt when the Soviet archives are opened to scholarly research. On the assumption that the conversation on that critical night of 26 October was as Dobrynin remembers it, then the version of the crisis, given, for example, by Schlesinger and Robert Kennedy, and now generally accepted, is seriously incomplete. The narrative they offered is so seriously skewed that the lessons projected may well be fundamentally erroneous. Contrary to established opinion, it may simply not be the case that the Soviet Union backed down in the face of tough American diplomacy backed by the threat of force. The truth may be that the crisis was resolved on the basis of a secret deal that, for complex reasons, neither party chose to reveal. This deal was kept secret not only from the American public, but from some of President Kennedy's most highly placed advisers — several of whom subsequently became the chief historians and *lesson-makers* of this most dramatic episode.

The secret meeting between Robert Kennedy and Dobrynin on the night of 26 October explains John Kennedy's preoccupation with the Turkish missiles in the ExComm meetings the next day. By 27 October, 'the ExComm had become largely irrelevant to the president's decision-making . . . Crucial decision were being made by the president and a few close advisers, well away from — and unknown to — the ExComm as a whole'.[49] Unknown to McNamara, Bundy *et al.*, President Kennedy had not only seriously considered the missiles-for-missiles trade, but had communicated this position to the Soviet leadership via the Soviet ambassador. This action by Kennedy was consistent with a second initiative that he directed — also unknown to the members of ExComm with the exception of Dean Rusk. In a letter which was read at the first conference in Florida in 1987, Dean Rusk stated that he was instructed by President Kennedy to approach the Secretary General of the United Nations via Andrew Cordier with a proposal to trade missiles in Turkey for missiles in Cuba.

> [The President] instructed me to telephone the late Andrew Cordier, than at Columbia University, and dictate to him a statement which would be made by U Thant, the Secretary General of the United Nations, proposing the removal of both the Jupiters and the missiles in Cuba. Mr. Cordier was to put that statement in the hands of U Thant only after a further signal from us. That step was never taken and the statement I furnished to Mr. Cordier has never seen the light of day. So far as I know, President Kennedy, Andrew Cordier and I were the only ones who knew of this particular step.[50]

ULTIMATUM OR DEAL?

The popular version of the Missile Crisis is based largely on the account dramatically reconstructed in Robert Kennedy's posthumously published *Thirteen Days*. This account, assembled from Robert Kennedy's diary by Theodore Sorensen, contains a vivid description of the meeting with Dobrynin on 27 October. The thrust of this conversation is the basis for what is perceived to be perhaps the pre-eminent example of the successful use of a compellent threat. The narrative depicts Robert Kennedy delivering an ultimatum to the Soviet Ambassador:

> The Soviet Union had secretly established missile bases in Cuba while at the same time proclaiming privately and publicly that this would never be

done. We had to have a commitment by tomorrow that those bases would be removed. I was not giving them an ultimatum but a statement of fact. He should understand that if they did not remove those bases, we would remove them. President Kennedy had great respect for the Ambassador's country and the courage of its people. Perhaps his country might feel it necessary to take retaliatory action; but before that was over, there would be not only dead Americans but dead Russians as well.[51]

In this account, the issue of a missiles-for-missiles trade arose in the conversation only tangentially, and only in the context of a private assurance and not as a quid pro quo. According to Robert Kennedy,

> [Dobrynin] raised the question of our removing the missiles from Turkey. I said that there could be no quid pro quo or any arrangement made under this kind of threat or pressure, and that in the last analysis this was a decision that would have to be made by NATO. However, I said, President Kennedy had been anxious to remove those missiles from Turkey and Italy for a long period of time. He had ordered their removal some time ago, and it was our judgment that, within a short time after this crisis was over, those missiles would be gone.[52]

Throughout the conversation Robert Kennedy emphasized that 'Time was running out. We had only a few more hours — we needed an answer immediately from the Soviet Union, I said we must have it the next day'.

One of the most important, and most contentious, questions raised at the conferences twenty-five years later concerned what Robert Kennedy said to Dobrynin on the evening of 27 October. Did he, in effect, trade the missiles in Turkey for the ones in Cuba? Or did he issue an ultimatum with a definite deadline? Or did he convey something that was neither a trade nor an ultimatum, but yet had elements of both? Up until the Moscow conference in 1989 the official Soviet version of the Kennedy–Dobrynin meeting, though different in emphasis, had been sufficiently circumspect that it did not challenge the American version.[53] But in Moscow Dobrynin directly contradicted the accepted version of history. Dobrynin insisted that 'it was Robert Kennedy who pursued the idea of an explicit "deal" on the Turkish missiles; that he wished to portray it as a significant concession by the United States; and that he never said that the president had already ordered their removal'.[54] The discrepancy between Dobrynin's version and that published in *Thirteen Days* was partially cleared up by Sorensen: 'Sorensen confessed that the missile trade had been portrayed as an explicit deal in the diaries on which the book was based, and that he had seen fit to revise that account in view of the fact that the trade was still a secret at the time, known to only six members of the ExComm.'[55]

The deliberations over the possible trade of the missiles had been kept secret until the publication of Robert Kennedy's book in 1969. Bundy, in his account of the Cuban Missile Crisis published in 1988, wrote that the inner circle of the ExComm had met briefly in the Oval Office to consider the instructions to Robert Kennedy for his meeting with Dobrynin on the evening of 27 October. The discussion was not taped.

The afternoon meeting of ExComm adjourned . . . and a smaller group moved from the Cabinet Room to the Oval Office to talk over the second means of communication — an oral message to be conveyed to Ambassador Dobrynin . . . One part of the oral message we discussed was simple, stern, and quickly decided — that the time had come to agree on the basis set out in the president's new letter: no Soviet missiles in Cuba, and no US invasion. Otherwise further American action was unavoidable . . . The other part of the oral message was proposed by Dean Rusk: that we should tell Khrushchev that while there could be no deal over the Turkish missiles, the president was determined to get them out and would do so once the Cuban crisis was resolved. The proposal was quickly supported by the rest of us and approved by the president. It was also agreed that knowledge of this assurance would be held among those present and no one else. Concerned as we all were by the cost of a public bargain struck under pressure at the apparent expense of the Turks . . . Robert Kennedy was instructed to make it plain to Dobrynin that the same secrecy must be observed on the other side, and that any Soviet reference to our assurance would simply make it null and void.[56]

At the Cambridge conference McNamara described that same meeting and the instructions given to Robert Kennedy:

Four or five of us were there in the room and we all agreed that Bobby should inform Dobrynin that the Jupiters would be withdrawn, though he shouldn't conclude a public deal to that effect. And by the way, right away I went back to the Pentagon and ordered them withdrawn, cut up, and photographed, so that I could personally see that those missiles had been destroyed . . . it was clear that Bobby was told to communicate that we had unilaterally agreed to withdraw the Turkish missiles, though not as part of a public deal . . .[57]

It is clear from the tape of the ExComm meeting on 27 October that McNamara, Sorensen and Bundy *intended* that the Soviet leadership not interpret any mention of the Turkish missiles as part of a trade. Yet it appears that this is precisely what the Soviets understood at the time from Robert Kennedy's conversations with Dobrynin on 27 October in light of what had been said in the meeting of 26 October. At the Moscow conference Andrei Gromyko underscored the fact that the question of the Turkish missiles was 'not trivial'. Gromyko maintained that

the Soviet Union had a solid foundation to consider that their removal was part of the terms on which the crisis was resolved. Indeed, Khrushchev sent the president a letter after the conclusion of the crisis, in which he described the withdrawal of the Jupiter missiles from Turkey as an integral part of the agreement on which the crisis was resolved.

The reasons why this letter does not appear in the 'complete' set of letters published in 1973 in the *Department of State Bulletin* was explained by Sorensen at the Moscow conference:

Sorensen conceded that this letter had been received, but explained its absence from the collected Kennedy–Khrushchev correspondence by noting that the administration decided against acknowledging the withdrawal of the Jupiters as a quid pro quo, and returned the letter as if it had never been opened.[58]

In sum,

> It appears . . . that the withdrawal of the Jupiter missiles from Turkey in the spring of 1963 was indeed part of a private deal that led to the withdrawal of Soviet missiles from Cuba in November, 1962. However, both the United States and the Soviet Union have subsequently found it expedient not to insist on this point, the United States because of the complications and ill-will it would cause among its NATO allies (and because of the domestic political consequences to the president had he publicly acknowledged the trade of the missiles), and the Soviet Union because of Castro's objection to being treated like a 'bargaining chip' on a par with a 'minor' NATO ally such as Turkey.[59]

The fine art of drawing historical lessons

With the possible exceptions of the outbreak of the First World War in August 1914 and Chamberlain's mission to Munich in September 1938, there is perhaps no other case that has spawned more 'lessons' than that of the Cuban Missile Crisis. For the conduct of Soviet–American relations, among the most important consequences is the popular understanding that the public took away from this televised confrontation. Within minutes of the announcement that the crisis had been resolved, network anchormen were interpreting the event for millions of Americans. For example, a CBS documentary aired on 28 October concluded with the statement:

> The danger of war over Cuba seems to have ended with Premier Khrushchev's remarkable letter to President Kennedy. Moreover, it has ended, if it has ended, on our terms — which can only be a victory for United States policy. It can only be read as a humiliating defeat for Soviet policy.[60]

In the scholarly literature, as in public understanding, it is clear that the lessons drawn depend fundamentally on what was perceived to have been the issue, and what was understood to have transpired. There are a number of tactical lessons as to what worked and what did not, including questions of near-misses.[61] But these questions aside, the basic lesson drawn depends fundamentally on an understanding of the narrative. The consensus that has prevailed for a quarter of a century holds that the Soviet Union challenged the United States but was forced to retreat in the face of firm and well-calibrated American pressure. This reading of the case as the premier example of a successful compellent threat is built upon two premises: that Khrushchev's action was a challenge — and was intended as such — and that the US response was to employ its military superiority to compel the Soviets to retreat. In light of what has been revealed twenty-five years after the event, these premises are open to serious question. And therefore the lessons that have been drawn are suspect.

For many analysts the 'problem', as seen from the American perspective, was an obvious one: to remove the missiles. The decision problem for the Kennedy administration consisted essentially of the search for a means to achieve this objective. In an interview with Richard Neustadt, General Maxwell Taylor listed three basic options: '"talk the missiles out," "squeeze the missiles out," or "shoot the missiles out."'[62] Garthoff characterizes these alternatives as

> (1) destroy the missiles by attacking; (2) *compel* the Soviet leaders to remove the missiles by pressure; and (3) *induce* the Soviets to remove the missiles by negotiation, probably a trade involving American concessions. The latter two are not entirely exclusive; there could be pressure *and* negotiation, but there was a clear difference.[63]

In this analysis the basic lesson of the crisis is one regarding the conditions under which a compellent threat can be effective in the nuclear age. For example, in Hilsman's view, the Soviets 'backed down in the face of a threat that combined both conventional and nuclear power' because

> Cuba is close to the sources of American strength and distant from the sources of Soviet strength. With vastly shorter lines of communication, the United States could apply overwhelmingly preponderant conventional power at the point of contact — Cuba — and do so under an umbrella of nuclear power that foreclosed any possibility of the Soviets trying to use nuclear weapons to redress the imbalance at the contact point. It was this combination of overwhelming conventional power on the spot and adequate nuclear power overall that proved irresistible.[64]

More generally to Hilsman, 'the first and most obvious lesson of the Cuban missile crisis is that of power. The United States had both the power and the will, and the Soviet Union suffered a defeat'[65].

If this is the general lesson, then the particular tactical lessons of the case are irrelevant for today's world since we now live in a situation of nuclear parity — a situation wholly unlike that of 1962. For this reason, some of the American participants in the first conference in 1987 felt that

> the crisis holds no significant lessons for today. In their view, the reason why the Soviets capitulated, agreeing to withdraw the missiles from Cuba, and the main reason the Soviets would not have retaliated militarily even if the missiles had been removed by an air strike and if necessary by an invasion of the island, was the overwhelming American superiority at the strategic nuclear level.

Because this is no longer the case 'the missile crisis is thought to be no more (or less) relevant to present concerns than, say, the Peloponnesian Wars'[66].

In relation to the earlier discussion of learning as exemplified in the game of chess, the lessons extracted by Hilsman and others speak only to the 'game' in its most literal sense. These lessons concern only the configuration of pieces, the relative distribution of power and strategic maneuver. But, as in the actual game of chess, there are additional dimensions, and, just as with the strategic dimension, these additional levels can conceivably be areas in which learning takes place. In addition to the strategic level that has received the greatest attention by analysts, there are at least four of these other dimensions. In essence, the crisis can serve to foster political learning

1. At the level of the use of power to achieve outcomes.
2. At the level of principles governing play.
3. At the level of knowledge of oneself and of the other player(s).
4. At the historical level, i.e. at a level that embraces the evolution of the game itself.

In his *A Thousand Days* and again at the first conference in 1987, Schlesinger reported President Kennedy's thoughts on the lesson to be taken away from the Cuban Missile Crisis. This lesson concerned the principles and beliefs that would govern the conduct of Soviet–American relations in light of the crisis. Kennedy saw well, as Khrushchev did in his 12 December speech to the Supreme Soviet, that the American public, and the world at large, could easily conclude that the correct policy is to be 'tough with Soviets'. To avoid reinforcing this facile conviction, Kennedy 'issued immediate instructions that there should be no claiming of victory, no cheering over the Soviet retreat'. That night he limited himself on nationwide television to a few unadorned words about 'Chairman Khrushchev's statesmanlike decision' and the 'compelling necessity for ending the arms race and reducing world tensions'. The day following the resolution of the crisis, Kennedy confided to Schlesinger that he feared 'that people would conclude from this experience that all we had to do in dealing with the Russians was to be tough and they would collapse'. But Kennedy reasoned that this would be a deep misunderstanding. The Cuban Missile Crisis was a special case not only because of the conventional and strategic factors that favored the American position, but also because of the moral and political dimensions that reinforced the American case. In placing missiles in Cuba, 'the Russians lacked a case which they could plausibly sustain before the world. Things would be different . . . if the situation were one where they had the local superiority, where their national security was directly engaged and where they could convince themselves and others they were in the right'. Kennedy was cognizant of the norms involved: 'I think there is a law of equity in these disputes . . . When one part is clearly wrong, it will eventually give way . . . They had no business in putting those missiles in and lying to me about it. They were in the wrong and knew it.'[67]

In the course of the interaction, and in the immediate aftermath of the crisis, Khrushchev and Kennedy, and their inner circles, learned a great deal not only about each other's interests, but also about their respective levels of political sophistication. The new understanding acquired in this regard belongs to the level described as knowledge of oneself and of the other player. At the Cambridge conference McNamara emphasized that in such situations it is imperative that leaders 'recognize that human beings are fallible . . . prone to misjudgement, misinformation, miscalculation, and emotion'.[68] Recognizing that information and control are made problematic by all of these factors, Blight, Nye and Welch concluded that the blockade 'was successful largely because it provided the flexibility that enabled the Administration to "learn" about its adversary as the crisis progressed'. In this regard they report that McGeorge Bundy recalled that as the missile crisis wore on, President Kennedy expressed increasing curiosity about Khrushchev, and about the ways the man's personality might interact with the Soviet system and with the deep crisis they both were in to produce various Soviet actions. Llewelyn Thompson provided the indispensable judgment and intuition regarding Soviet thinking. Thompson was the one member of the ExComm who was intimately familiar with the language, history and culture of the Soviet Union. Thompson's influence on the decision-making was indirect. But, nonetheless, as Abraham Chayes emphasized, Thompson was the 'unsung hero' of the ExComm deliberations. Blight, Nye and Welch concluded that 'perhaps in no other two-week period has any American administration learned so much about the Soviet Union and its leaders as Kennedy's did during the Cuban missile crisis'.[69]

Acknowledging limitations in the ability either adequately to interpret Khrushchev's motivations or to anticipate Soviet responses to American overtures and actions is itself a vital lesson. It concerns the recognition of the complexity and open-ended character of interactions of this order. This makes Soviet–American relations inherently complex and uncertain. Unlike the idealized world of strategic planning, real cases have the open-ended character that the philosopher Hans–Georg Gadamer attributes to human conversation in general. Gadamer makes the point by insisting that conversations are not controlled.

> We say that we 'conduct' a conversation, but the more fundamental a conversation is, the less its conduct lies within the will of either partner. Thus a fundamental conversation is never one that we want to conduct. Rather, it is generally more correct to say that we fall into conversation, or even that we become involved in it. The way in which one word follows another, with the conversation taking its own turnings and reaching its own conclusion, may well be conducted in some way, but the people conversing are far less the leaders of it than the led.[70]

This realization has much in common with the one that the participants in the crisis took away after the fact.

The open, uncontrollable character of the drama of the Cuban Missile Crisis is apparent in the facts that were revealed at the conferences. Initiatives were undertaken independent of, and sometimes unknown to, President Kennedy, Khrushchev and their closest advisers. Fomin's conversation with Scali is perhaps the most critical example. But there were a host of other actions that helped determine the ultimate settlement. Dobrynin's inadvertent signal to Robert Kennedy during their late-night conversation of 26 October regarding the missiles in Turkey was a vital link in the chain of events. Other inadvertent and unauthorized signals included the strong message — verging on an ultimatum — that Scali conveyed to Fomin at their second meeting. Allyn, Blight and Welch are correct in stressing that much more attention must be directed to the consequences of 'free-lance diplomacy' and 'inadvertent *diplomatic* acts'.[71] It is important to realize that the members of the ExComm were convinced that Fomin's message and Khrushchev's first letter were parts of a package offer. They conjoined two communications to draw an inference that, as we now see, did not reflect Soviet intentions or understanding. In retrospect, an extremely important lesson that emerges is the recognition that, by the sheer accident of timing, messages can be combined to yield interpretations that were never intended with the result that consequences follow that surprise both parties. Something like a 'garbage can' principle of political communication seems to be at work.[72]

At the fourth level, that is the historical perspective that examines the impact of the event on the subsequent course of history, both Americans and Russians expressed the view at the conferences that the Cuban Missile Crisis, as dangerous as it was, was a profoundly beneficial experience. So much so that had it not happened, it should have been concocted. In Cambridge, Mikoyan summed up his view with the statement: 'I would draw your attention to the fact that the missile crisis was a result of our adventurism. We may now confess it. But happily, it did not result in war. Paradoxically, it has helped us lower the risks of war. If there had been no Cuban missile crisis, we should perhaps have organized it.'[73] At the first conference in Florida, Thomas Schelling made a very similar observation:

> I want to state something I firmly believe . . . that the Cuban missile crisis was the best thing to happen to us since the Second World War. It helped us avoid further confrontation with the Soviets . . . it established new basic understandings about US–Soviet interaction . . . I don't think the Cuban missile crisis should be repeated, but I do think it was a good crisis.[74]

Among the long-term benefits of the crisis resides the very fact that statements like this can be made by Soviet and American participants and experts. Communication of this order is a testimony to the unprecedented state that US–Soviet relations have reached in the last decade of the twentieth century. The Cuban Missile Crisis, and the effort to understand it, must be counted as one of the historical causes of this development.

Notes

1. For a report on this conference see James G. Blight, Joseph S. Nye, and David A. Welch, 'The Cuban Missile Crisis Revisited', *Foreign Affairs*, **66**, 1, 1987, pp. 170–88. The transcript is available in David A. Welch, ed., 'Proceedings of the Hawk's Cay Conference on the Cuban Missile Crisis', Center for Science and International Affairs, Working Paper 89–1 (Cambridge, MA: John F. Kennedy School of Government, 1989).

2. For the transcript of the Cambridge meeting see David A. Welch, ed., 'Proceedings of the Cambridge Conference on the Cuban Missile Crisis', Center for Science and International Affairs, Working Paper 89–2 (Cambridge, MA: John F. Kennedy School of Government, 1989). See also James G. Blight and David A. Welch, *On the Brink: Americans and Soviets Re-examine the Cuban Missile Crisis* (New York: Hill and Wang, 1989).

3. Reported in Bruce J. Allyn, James G. Blight, and David A. Welch, 'Essence of Revision. Or: Moscow, Havana, and the Cuban Missile Crisis', *International Security*, **14**, 3, 1989, pp. 136–72.

4. A separate series of conferences, involving US and Soviet historians rather than policy-makers, commenced last year. The result is to be a series of volumes entitled *Soviet–American Dialogues on United States History*. The first is devoted to Soviet accounts of the New Deal and will match chapters by Soviet historians with commentary by American historians. Other volumes in the series will address the American Revolution and Constitution, United States–Soviet relations before 1917, the two-party system in the United States, and additional topics yet to be decided.

5. Raymond L. Garthoff, 'Cuban Missile Crisis: The Soviet Story', *Foreign Policy*, **72**, 1988, pp. 61–80.

6. Keohane is sometimes identified as a neorealist, for example by Richard Ashley, but this ignores fundamental differences between Keohane's research program and that of Waltz. For an account of the genealogy of neoliberal institutionalism, see Robert Keohane, 'Neoliberal Institutionalism: A Perspective on World Politics', in *International Institutions and State Power: Essays in International Relations Theory* (Boulder, CO: Westview Press, 1989), pp. 1–20. Also see his description of his own intellectual career for the light it throws on the substantive agenda of this school of theory and its position *vis-à-vis* the narrower agenda characteristic of contemporary forms of realism (Keohane, 'A Personal Intellectual History', ibid., pp. 21–32).

7. James G. March and Johan P. Olsen, 'The New Institutionalism: Organizational Factors in Political Life', *American Political Science Review*, **78**, 1984, pp. 734–49; John Rawls, 'Two Concepts of Rules', *Philosophical Review*, **64**, 1955, pp. 3–32; and Robert Keohane, 'International Institutions: Two Approaches', *International Studies Quarterly*, **32**, 4, 1988, pp. 379–96.

8. Ernst Haas's conceptual and empirical work on the impact of knowledge, innovation and learning on international politics has exerted considerable influence on neorealists and neoliberals alike. Haas, who was one of the original neofunctionalists, is difficult to fit into the present landscape of international relations theory. He is neither a realist nor a neorealist. But, with his interest in systemic thinking, it is not altogether clear that he is a neoliberal institutionalist in Keohane's sense, though this is a likely label, if labels are needed. Haas's work on adaptation and learning points to the essential agenda addressed here. In his work on intergovernmental and societal learning,

especially with regard to changes in the conception of system interdependence, Haas investigates the varieties of 'system' concepts. (Ernst B. Haas, 'On Systems and International Regimes', *World Politics*, **27**, 2, 1975, pp. 147–74; 'Is There a Hole in the Whole? Knowledge, Technology, Interdependence, and the Construction of International Regimes', *International Organization*, **29**, 1975, pp. 827–76; 'Words Can Hurt You; Or, Who Said What to Whom About Regimes', *International Organization*, **36**, 2, 1982, pp. 207–43; and *When Knowledge is Power* (Berkeley: University of California Press, 1990). For an account of Haas on political learning see Dwain Mefford and Brian Ripley, 'The Cognitive Foundations of Regimes: The Advantages of Applying Artificial Intelligence to International Political Economy' (paper presented at the annual meeting of the American Political Science Association, Chicago, 1987); and Mefford, 'Knowledge, Power, and Argument: A Formal Interpretation of Ernst Haas' (forthcoming).

9. Durkheim conceived of social facts as distinguished by several criteria, including externality, constraint, generality, and independence (Emile Durkheim, *The Rules of Sociological Method* (1895), Steven Lukes, ed., W.D. Halls, trans, New York: The Free Press, 1980, p. 59).

10. This has also been the experience apparently of other political scientists who have designed and built rule-based systems, though the builders of these systems will have to speak for themselves.

11. For efforts to demonstrate empirically the existence of such cognitive procedures, see James A. Galambos, Robert P. Abelson and John B. Black, eds, *Knowledge Structures* (Hillsdale, NJ: Lawrence Erlbaum, 1986). For a survey of conceptual efforts to induce dynamics into script-based reasoning, including Schank's MOPs, Dyer's TAUs and the Thematic Organization Packets (TOPs) used in the experiments reported in the article, see Collen M. Siefert, Gail McKoon, Robert P. Abelson and Roger Ratcliff, 'Memory Connections Between Thematically Similar Episodes', *Journal of Experimental Psychology: Learning, Memory and Cognition*, **12**, 2, 1986, pp. 220–31.

12. Schank introduces a number of procedure-like devices for reorganizing script. See Roger C. Schank, *Dynamic Memory: A Theory of Reminding and Learning in Computers and People* (New York: Cambridge University Press, 1982); Janet Kolodner, 'Maintaining Organization in a Dynamic Long-Term Memory', *Cognitive Science*, **7**, 1983, pp. 243–80; Kolodner, 'Reconstructive Memory: A Computer Model', ibid., pp. 281–328; Kolodner, *Retrieval and Organizational Strategies in Conceptual Memory: A Computer Model* (Hillsdale, NJ: Lawrence Erlbaum, 1984); and Janet Kolodner and R.L. Simpson, Jr., 'Problem Solving and Dynamic Memory', in Janet Kolodner and C.K. Reisbeck, eds, *Experience, Memory and Reasoning* (Hillsdale, NJ: Lawrence Erlbaum, 1986). For the study of political reasoning, Kolodner's Ph.D. thesis is of particular interest. She develops a variation of Schank's MOP (Memory Organization Packet) scheme for the organization of memory, which she calls E-MOPs for Episodic Memory Organization Packets. As events are entered, they are indexed as a function of the match between the event and the current stock of MOP structures. As a function of this match, new E-MOPS may be generated and old ones updated, i.e. the frame of norms, or defaults, may be revised. The object of the system is to support retrieval for a question–answer system whose performance does not degrade as the number of items in memory increases. CYRUS, named after the former US Secretary of State, is a system built to exercise this approach to dynamic memory. It is linked, in one of its versions, to DeJong's FRUMP, a story processing and summarizing

program that reads the UPI wire. The substantive domain is current events, specifically the comings and goings of former US Secretaries of State, Cyrus Vance and Edmund Muskie. See also Janet Kolodner, ed., *Proceedings of the DARPA Workshop on Case-Based Reasoning* (Palo Alto, CA: Morgan–Kaufmann, 1988); Gerald DeJong and Raymond Mooney, 'Explanation-Based Learning: An Alternative View', *Machine Learning*, **1**, 2, 1986, pp. 145–76; and Dwain Mefford, 'Steps Toward Artificial Intelligence: Rule-Based, Case-Based, and Explanation-Based Models of Politics', in Valerie M. Hudson, ed., *Artificial Intelligence and International Politics* (Boulder, CO: Westview Press, 1990).

13. Vicktor M. Sergeev, V.P. Akimov, V.B. Lukov and P.B. Parshin, 'Interdependency in a Crisis Situation: Simulating the Caribbean Crisis', paper presented at the First US–USSR Workshop on Models and Concepts of Interdependence Among Nations, Washington, DC, January 1988; Vicktor M. Sergeev and P.B. Parshin, 'Acquiring "The Sense of Interdependence" Through Crisis: An Essay in Cognitive Analysis of the Soviet Position in the Caribbean Crisis of 1962', paper presented at the Second Joint US National Academy of Sciences–Academy of Sciences of the USSR Workshop on Models and Concepts of Interdependence Between Nations, Tallin, Estonian SSR, USSR, January 1989; and Sergeev and Parshin, 'Processes, Metamorphoses, and Procedures: The New Thinking as Reflected in Linguistic Structures', paper prepared for the Third Joint Workshop, Berkeley, CA, January 1990. They also refer to Robert Axelrod's cognitive maps as 'scripts', but while there are a number of links between Axelrod's work in the early 1970s and that of Robert Abelson and C.M. Reich, such as the use of graph structures and the application of principles taken from Fritz Heider's psychological theory, Abelson's subsequent work, which culminates in the collaboration with Schank, introduces fundamentally different structures that have no analog in Axelrod. For this reason the two should be kept distinct.

14. They model the central themes in two official statements: the Report of the Central Committee to the XXII Congress of the CPSU of 17 October 1961 and Khrushchev's Report to the Supreme Soviet on 12 December 1962 (*Pravda*, 13 December 1962; for an abridged translation of the second speech, see Ronald Pope, ed., *Soviet Views of the Cuban Missile Crisis: Myth and Reality in Foreign Policy*, Lanham, MD: University Press of America, 1982, pp. 71–107).

15. Sergeev and Parshin, 'Acquiring "The Sense of Interdependence" Through Crisis'. Though in the pair of documents that Sergeev *et al.* chose to model Khrushchev's language is exceptionally abstract and metaphorical, it should be noted that the public context in which the statement was delivered may largely account for the Soviet leader's choice of phrasing. On other occasions Khrushchev was not adverse to describing events, strategies and personalities. For example, see his account of the 'Caribbean Crisis' in the two volumes of his memoirs. Nikita Khrushchev, *Khrushchev Remembers*, Strobe Talbot, ed. and trans. (Boston: Little Brown, 1970), pp. 554–8, and Nikita Khrushchev, *Khrushchev Remembers: The Last Testament*, Strobe Talbot, ed. and trans. (Boston: Little Brown, 1974), pp. 581–7.

16. Robert Abelson's initial conception of 'script' had much in common with the metaphorical structures that Sergeev attributes to Khrushchev. For example, Abelson's master Cold War script pits 'weak liberal dupes' against insidious 'Communist powers'. As Abelson sets up this script, 'there is a great struggle taking place between the Free World and the forces of Communism . . . which the Communists fully expect to pursue until they totally control the

world . . . Liberal and left-wing-dupes who dominate many Free World governments . . . are playing into the hands of Communist designs. It is the task of good Americans to oppose and expose these fuzzy-thinking liberals . . . With determination, we can rid the Free World of their influence . . . and a strong American can then establish a cooperative relationship with other free peoples . . . in order to block Communist schemes and bring about a Free World Victory' (Robert P. Abelson, 'The Structure of Belief Systems', in Roger C. Schank and K.M. Colby, eds, *Computer Models of Thought and Language,* San Francisco: W.H. Freeman, 1973, pp. 287–339). Abelson reconceptualizes the idea of script in his later work. In his collaboration with Schank, scripts figure as one category within a hierarchy of interrelated structures. Scripts are concrete realizations of high-level 'themes'. As such, they are exemplifications of more general ideas in much the same sense as Sergeev and Pashin's system constructs exemplifications of metaphors. While scripts *per se* in this formalization fail to correspond to the structures Sergeev wants to model, other structures within Abelson's broad conception do seem to capture what he has in mind. In sum, while scripts, in the narrow sense, are insufficient for modeling political text, a script-based representation complete with additional levels of abstraction may suffice. But even this extended representation runs into difficulties, and so may ultimately fall short of what is required. (Roger C. Schank and Robert P. Abelson, 'Scripts, Plans, and Knowledge', in *Proceedings of the Fourth International Joint Conference on Artificial Intelligence,* Los Altos, CA: Morgan Kaufman, 1975, I, pp. 151–7, and Schank and Abelson, *Scripts, Plans, Goals, and Understanding: An Inquiry into Human Knowledge Structures,* Hillsdale, NJ: Lawrence Erlbaum, 1977).

17. 'Three zones of political position [are distinguished], namely [the] Processual Map (PM), Metaphorical Space (MS), and Exemplificative Space (ES). The interplay between PM and MS, and PM and ES is mediated by the Metaphorical Engine and the Exemplificator, respectively. The Metaphorical Engine works in several modes, at least two of them relevant to the case: the first one is metaphor introduction, and the second is metaphor derivation resulting in derived metaphors. The Processual Map includes four abstract processes each of them named more or less metaphorically' (Sergeev and Parshin, 'Acquiring "The Sense of Interdependence" Through Crisis', p. 9).

18. 'We said there that a script was a kind of data structure that was useful in the processing of text to the extent that it directed the inference process and tied together pieces of input. Input sentences were connected together by referring to the overall structure of the script to which they made references. Thus, scripts were, in our view, a kind of high level knowledge structure that could be called upon to supply background information during the understanding process. Scripts, as embodied in the computer programs that we wrote, were essentially sets or predictions of event sequences. A script was constituted as a list of events that comprise a stereotypical episode. Input events that matched one or more of the events in the list would cause the program to infer that the other events in the list had also taken place' (Schank, *Dynamic Memory*, p. 3).

19. Roger C. Schank and Jaime G. Carbonnell, 'The Gettysburg Address, Representing Social and Political Acts', in N.V. Findler, ed., *Associative Networks* (New York: Academic Press, 1979). Schank's original Conceptual Dependency is not sufficiently expressive to render much of what is

important in political discourse. Other efforts to apply Conceptual Dependency to political and social relations have also run up against the limitations of that formalism. See, for example, Seth R. Goldman, Michael G. Dyer and Margot Flowers, 'Learning to Understand Contractual Situations', in *Proceedings of the Ninth International Joint Conference on Artificial Intelligence* (Los Altos, CA: Morgan Kaufmann, 1985), I, pp. 291–3, and 'Precedent-based Legal Reasoning and Knowledge Acquisition in Contract Law: A Process Model', in *Proceedings of the First International Conference on Artificial Intelligence and Law* (Boston, 1987).

20. The notion is much the same in Explanation-Based Learning where the essential idea is that concept attainment involves the construction and retention of the proof structure which establishes that an object is an instance of a class or category. (Gerald DeJong and Raymond Mooney, 'Explanation-Based Learning: An Alternative View', *Machine Learning*, **1**, 2, 1986, pp. 165–76, and DeJong, 'An Introduction to Explanation-Based Learning', in Howard E. Shrobe, ed., *Exploring Artificial Intelligence: Survey Talks from the National Conference on Artificial Intelligence* (Palo Alto, CA: Morgan Kaufmann, 1988).

21. The work in category theory, as exemplified in the studies of categories of color across cultures, tends to concentrate on distinctions acquired quite early in childhood. These concepts are embedded in language and have almost grammatical status. (Eleanor Rosch and C.B. Mervis, 'Family Resemblances: Studies in the Internal Structure of Categories', *Cognitive Psychology*, **7**, 1975, pp. 573–605; Rosch 'Principles of Categorization', in Rosch and B.B. Lloyd, eds, *Cognition and Categorization*, Hillsdale, NJ: Lawrence Erlbaum, 1978, pp. 27–48; Rosch, 'Prototype Classification and Logical Classification: The Two Systems', in E. Scholnick, ed., *New Trends in Cognitive Representation: Challenges to Piaget's Theory*, Hillsdale, NJ: Lawrence Erlbaum, 1983, pp. 73–86; and Edward E. Smith and D.L. Medin, *Categories and Concepts*, Cambridge, MA: Harvard University Press, 1981.) Of the little work that has been done on artificial categories, like those that adults create and modify, Barsalou's investigations into made-up classes of objects, such as that of 'things to see in a yard sale', are perhaps of greatest relevance to the study of political reasoning and political learning. The case of the Cuban Missile Crisis can be viewed as such a category, one into which later situations are mapped. See Lawrence W. Barsalou, 'Ad-hoc Categories', *Memory and Cognition*, **11**, 1983, pp. 211–27.

22. The game of chess has had a distinguished career as a medium for developing concepts in mathematics. It has also served as a laboratory for some of the most important work in Artificial Intelligence, from Turning and Shannon to Newell and Simon. The justification for using chess to help spell out the learning mechanisms in fundamental shifts in politics is that the chess metaphor opens doors onto a number of fields. If learning of the scale explored here can be rendered via the example of chess, then mathematics and other formalisms that have been similarly developed through analogy with the game of chess become immediately accessible. The common medium of chess may prove an efficient way not only to illustrate the learning mechanism, but to integrate it with certain basic principles in several fields, including Artificial Intelligence.

23. Where P, Kt, and B, designate pawn, knight and bishop, respectively, and where K4, KB3, QB3 and Kt5 denote squares on the chess board indexed from White's and Black's sides of the board. 'B–Kt5' means that White moves

a Bishop to the fifth square in the knight file counting from White's end of the board. Each file is designated by the piece that occupies the first square as the board is initially set up; rows are labeled 1 to 8. By convention, in each numbered line, as in Figure 4.1, the first entry is White's move, followed by Black's. The 'O–O' in move 5 in Figure 4.1 denotes that White castled kingside.

24. Jose R. Capablanca, *My Chess Career* (London, 1920), quoted in Harold C. Schonberg, *Grandmasters of Chess* (Philadelphia: J.B. Lippincott Company, 1973), p. 174. See also Edward Lasker, *Modern Chess Strategy* (Philadelphia: David McKay Company, 1945), p. 132. Anatol Rapoport uses this same example to convey the drama of interdependent choice which is the subject matter of game theory (Anatol Rapoport, *Fights, Games, and Debates* (Ann Arbor: University of Michigan Press, 1960), pp. 2–5).
25. McGeorge Bundy, *Danger and Survival: Choices About the Bomb in the First Fifty Years* (New York: Random House, 1988), p. 427.
26. Graham T. Allison, *Essence of Decision: Explaining the Cuban Missile Crisis* (Boston: Little Brown, 1971), p. 7.
27. Blight, Nye and Welch, 'Cuban Missile Crisis Revisited', p. 186.
28. Arthur M. Schlesinger, *A Thousand Days* (New York: Houghton Mifflin Company, 1965), pp. 825–6; Theodore C. Sorenson, *Kennedy* (New York: Harper and Row, 1965), p. 712; and Roger Hilsman, *To Move a Nation: The Politics of Foreign Policy in the Administration of John F. Kennedy* (New York: Doubleday, 1967), pp. 217–9. See also John Scali, 'I was the Secret Go-Between in the Cuban Crisis', *Family Weekly*, 25 October 1964, pp. 4–5 and 12–14, and Robert F. Kennedy, *Thirteen Days* (New York: Norton, 1971), pp. 163–71.
29. Raymond L. Garthoff, *Reflecting on the Cuban Missile Crisis* (Washington, DC: The Brookings Institution, 2nd edn, 1989), p. 80.
30. Allyn, Blight and Welch, 'Essence of Revision', p. 156.
31. Sorenson, *Kennedy*, p. 712.
32. Schlesinger, *Thousand Days*, ch. 31, and Marc Trachtenberg's note in Welch, ed., 'Proceedings of the Cambridge Conference on the Cuban Missile Crisis', pp. 75–7.
33. Pope, ed., *Soviet Views of the Cuban Missile Crisis*, p. 49.
34. McGeorge Bundy and James G. Blight, eds, 'October 27, 1962: Transcripts of the Meeting of the Ex Comm', *International Security*, **12**, 3, 1987, pp. 35–8.
35. ibid., p. 79.
36. ibid.
37. Schlesinger, *Thousand Days*, p. 828.
38. ibid., p. 828; Henry M. Pachter, *Collision Course: The Cuban Missile Crisis* (New York: Praeger, 1963); and Sorensen, *Kennedy*, p. 712.
39. Bundy and Blight, 'October 27, 1962', p. 42.
40. Speech to the Supreme Soviet, 12 December 1962, reported in *Pravda* and *Izvestia*, 13 December 1962, translated in *The Current Digest of the Soviet Press*, 16 and 23 January 1963, and reprinted (abridged) in Pope, *Soviet Views of the Cuban Missile Crisis*, pp. 71–107.
41. Michel Tatu, *Power in the Kremlin: From Krushchev to Kosygin* (New York: Viking, 1969), pp. 268–9.
42. ibid., pp. 270–1.
43. Bundy and Blight, 'October 27, 1962', p. 81.
44. Welch, ed., 'Proceedings of the Cambridge Conference on the Cuban Missile Crisis', p. 42.

45. ibid.
46. ibid., p. 43.
47. ibid., p. 44.
48. Allyn, Blight and Welch, *Essence of Revision*, p. 158.
49. ibid., p. 158.
50. Welch, ed., 'Proceedings of the Hawk's Cay Conference on the Cuban Missile Crisis', p. 75.
51. Kennedy, *Thirteen Days*, p. 108.
52. ibid., pp. 108–9.
53. Anatoly A. Gromyko, 'The Caribbean Crisis', *Voprosy isotorii*, Nos. 7 and 8, 1971, trans. by William Mandel and reprinted in Pope, *Soviet Views of the Cuban Missile Crisis*, pp. 161–226, and Gromyko, *1036 dnei prezienta Kennedi* (Moscow: Politzdat, 1971), reprinted in *The United States as Through Russian Eyes: Kennedy's 1,036 Days*, trans. by Philip Gavon (Washington, DC: International Library, 1973).
54. Allyn, Blight and Welch, 'Essence of Revision', p. 164.
55. ibid.
56. Bundy, *Danger and Survival*, pp. 432–3.
57. Welch, ed., 'Proceedings of the Cambridge Conference on the Cuban Missile Crisis', pp. 49–50.
58. Allyn, Blight and Welch, 'Essence of Revision', p. 164.
59. ibid., pp. 164–5.
60. Welch, ed., 'Proceedings of the Hawk's Cay Conference on the Cuban Missile Crisis', p. 9.
61. The seven points that Robert Kennedy underscored at the end of *Thirteen Days* are recognized to be as valid today as they were then. They include:

    (a) Take time to plan; do not go with your first impulse.
    (b) The president should be exposed to a variety of opinion.
    (c) Depend heavily on those with solid knowledge of the Soviet Union.
    (d) Retain civilian control and beware of the limited outlook of the military.
    (e) Pay close attention to world opinion.
    (f) Do not humiliate your opponent; leave him a way out.
    (g) Beware of inadvertence-the Guns of August scenario.

    See Kennedy, *Thirteen Days*, pp. 111–28; Sorenson, *Kennedy*, pp. 716–17; and Blight, Nye and Welch, 'Cuban Missile Crisis Revisited', p. 172.
62. Welch, ed., 'Proceedings of the Hawk's Cay Conference on the Cuban Missile Crisis', p. 70.
63. Garthoff, *Reflecting on the Cuban Missile Crisis*, pp. 44–5.
64. Hilsman, *To Move a Nation*, p. 227.
65. ibid.
66. Blight, Nye and Welch, 'Cuban Missile Crisis Revisited', p. 175.
67. Schlesinger, *A Thousand Days*, p. 831.
68. Welch, ed., 'Proceedings of the Hawk's Cay Conference on the Cuban Missile Crisis', p. 71.
69. Blight, Nye and Welch, 'Cuban Missile Crisis Revisted', p. 183. See also Welch, ed., 'Proceedings of the Hawk's Cay Conference on the Cuban Missile Crisis', p. 42, and Abraham Chayes, *The Cuban Missile Crisis: International Crisis and the Role of Law* (New York: Oxford University Press, 1974).
70. Hans-Georg Gadamer, *Truth and Method* (New York: Seabury Press, 1975), p. 345.

71. Allyn, Blight and Welch, 'Essence of Revision', p. 166.
72. Michael D. Cohen, James G. March and Johan P. Olsen, 'A Garbage Can Model of Organizational Choice', *Administrative Sciences Quarterly*, **17**, 1972, pp. 1–25, and James G. March and Johan P. Olsen, *Ambiguity and Choice in Organization* (Bergen: Universitetsforlaget, 1976).
73. Welch, ed., 'Proceedings of the Cambridge Conference on the Cuban Missile Crisis', p. 73.
74. Welch, ed., 'Proceedings of the Hawk's Cay Conference on the Cuban Missile Crisis', p. 100.

5 *The Soviet General Staff: an institution's response to change*
Condoleezza Rice

How critical is it to know an institution's history in order to understand the factors that might constrain its future development? If, in fact, institutions respond readily to new environmental stimuli, reshaping themselves in accordance with new demands and challenges, the history of an institution provides an interesting backdrop but little more. But if, as James March and Johan Olsen pointed out in a seminal article in the *American Political Science Review* in 1984, institutional development is better thought of as a historical process of adaptation or, in many cases, maladaptation, then it is the cumulative experience of an institution that holds the key to understanding its true nature and its future.[1]

Military institutions would seem to be ideal examples of the value of understanding historical patterns. They are among the most self-conscious of all institutions about transmitting traditions and values. Cohesion is the *sine qua non* of an effective military and, more often than not, connection with past glories and long-established patterns of behaviour are the chief means to that end. Yet, studies of militaries and how they adapt still tend to underestimate the weight of historical patterns in institutional responses to new challenges.

The often stormy history of the Soviet General Staff's struggle to adapt simultaneously to the changing requirements of warfare and to the political circumstances of its domestic environment is examined here. It is primarily the story of how the Soviet General Staff acquired jurisdiction over most of the functions of military planning in a country that is inherently distrustful of the political potential of a strong military. The clear lesson is that, relative to other institutions that might control military planning, the General Staff has been powerful and dominant. But in relation to political authority, the General Staff's position has been and continues to be fragile. Though resilient enough in the face of repeated assaults on its authority, the General Staff's role has nevertheless always been in large part dependent on the political leadership's attitude toward it.

This history is especially interesting today in the midst of the Gorbachev revolution. So many established patterns of behavior are being broken that it is fair to ask whether the Soviet General Staff is not, in fact, a prime candidate for analyzing the question — when does history cease to be a reliable guide? What is the power of history and what limits its influence?

The nature of the dependent variable

The method of tracing historical processes to understand institutional development is useful only if it leads to a clearer understanding of how an institution responds to specific new challenges. This requires a more finely tuned definition of the dependent variable — the somewhat ambiguous term 'institution'. Precisely what is being affected as each new challenge is met?

An institution is defined here in terms of four characteristics: jurisdiction, competence, norms and traditions. *Jurisdiction* is a claim to some set of functions and establishes a legitimate realm for the institution. As such, this characteristic defines the position of a general staff in relation to other institutions in the system. In the case of general staffs, this may be in relation to higher political authority, other military sub-institutions or other governmental actors (foreign ministries or intelligence institutions, for example).

Competence is the claim that the institution possesses information and expertise relevant to its jurisdiction. Institutions defend their jurisdiction through claims of competence. Those that monopolize expertise are well positioned to ward off potential competitors.

Norms are accepted modes of behavior: the guiding principles of conduct and views of the right way to do things. Institutional norms may or may not be consonant with those of the larger society. Arguably, however, an institution whose norms run counter to those of the larger polity will have more difficulty operating effectively within it.

Traditions are the means by which all other characteristics of an institution are preserved and communicated to new members. Traditions are a means of providing institutional memory and ensuring that the institution will survive with the passage of time and people.

The institutional characteristics of the Soviet General Staff

Among modern European military staffs, the Soviet General Staff comes closest to the 'Prussian ideal', centralizing and integrating all planning functions within it. It has self-consciously labored to become the 'brain of the army', capable of performing the full range of tasks associated with military planning. To date, even in the midst of the Gorbachev revolution, there is no comparable institutional base in the civilian sector. Nor have the individual services been able to assert a claim to jurisdiction over key military planning functions. At the level of planning the details of military power — force structure and military strategy (what the

Soviets call the military–technical level) — the General Staff has traditionally had no competitors.

The operative norms of the General Staff are centralization of responsibility and authority, 'scientific' or rational planning and compartmentalization of knowledge and information. As a result of that centralized authority, the General Staff has been capable of distributing and redistributing assets among the services to produce realignment when new military technologies have required it.

But the General Staff's relationship to the services and to other military planning institutions belies its role in the polity as a whole. The Prussian General Staff and its successor in Wilhelmian Germany were 'brains of the army' powerful enough to ensure that the army could, without political interference, walk and talk by itself. The central political institutions during the period of the German General Staff's ascendance before 1914 were, more often than not, weak and ineffective.

An analysis of the organizational structure of the Soviet General Staff would almost certainly give rise to similar assumptions about its power *vis à vis* political authority in the Soviet Union. But that would be misleading. Careful attention to the history of the Soviet General Staff shows that the similarities between the Prussian model and Soviet reality are superficial. Soviet political authorities, because of ideological prejudices against the centralization of military power, kept a watchful eye on the development of the General Staff. There was, in fact, as part of this surveillance, conscious reference to the problems associated with the German model.[2] There has thus been a fragile and oft broken compact by which the General Staff was allowed to acquire control of the functions required to do its important but narrowly defined job, but the parameters of that autonomy were always determined in an intensely political process. It is not an exaggeration to say that the General Staff has been powerful and autonomous when and only when political authorities have allowed it to be so.

The evolution of the Soviet General Staff

The General Staff acquired its dominance of military policy through a slow, evolutionary and above all political process in which it developed the competence to handle the critical functions of military management. In doing so, it arrived at a key historical juncture — the fall of Nikita Khrushchev in 1964 — with a solid claim to competence and expertise in the military–technical sphere. The General Staff was able to eliminate institutional competitors largely because parallelism and overlapping authority could not be tolerated. The Soviet Union had to acquire military power fast and in a race with technologically and economically superior states; the result is a streamlined system for military planning. Other powerful norms in the larger polity, secrecy and compartmentalization of knowledge, reinforced the strict hierarchy and centralization. Competitive institutions and diffusion of authority would have demanded access to information for another set of actors entirely. Serial rather than parallel institutions maximized information control. In a country that tried to plan an entire economy from the top down, preference for centralization is not surprising.

Interestingly, these were not the dominant norms at the time of the creation of the Red Army. The argument for centralization had flourished under the Tsars. The dominance initially of the Staff by officers of the old regime helped to preserve those tendencies. But the legacy of the tsarist General Staff was, at least in principle, rejected by those who played the biggest role in structuring the Soviet staff system. The early Bolsheviks intended to disband the army altogether once the danger to the regime — first from Germany, and then from the White forces, supported by the Entente powers, in the civil war — had disappeared. But history took a different turn and the Red Army slowly developed into a fighting force in accordance with the prevailing trends for European armies of the day.

This evolution took place in spite of extreme suspicion firmly grounded in both ideological and historical realities. Ideologically, the professional military was viewed both as an anachronism which would pass away with the victory of socialism and as an institution that was potentially dangerous. The unflattering term (still in the Soviet lexicon) 'Bonapartism' expressed the fear that standing armies were a threat because they were likely to engage in counter-revolutionary activities. Experiments with forms other than a professional army, though, came to a screeching halt in 1918 when the Soviets realized that without effective armed forces they would be unable to defend the revolution. The Red Army was created as a temporary institution.

From the very beginning, the Soviet leadership employed political commissars and secret police moles within the army to make certain that officers were politically loyal. But the commissars never developed into a 'competitive' institution either in matters of strategy, organization and force posture or in command. With the breakup of 'dual command' in warfare (where a commander could not make a decision or issue an order without the concurrence of the political officer) the commissar lost his equal rank with the commander. The reason for the breakup of dual command is clear: it was simply inefficient. Overly zealous commissars with little or no military knowledge could not be tolerated in the regime's fight for survival.

As the regular army developed, so did the broadening jurisdiction and competence of the central staff. The creation of the Red Army Main Staff in 1918 centralized key functions in that body. While the reforms of 1924–5 actually redistributed some of the functions, the Staff for instance lost its role in the direction of mobilization and training, the reforms of Mikhail Frunze did solidify its jurisdiction in matters of strategy, organization and force posture.[3]

However, in its attempts to expand its role in the economics of defense, the professional military staff did not fare well. Early treatises on staff organization by Mikhail Tukhachevsky, as Chief of Staff, and Boris Shaposhnikov (who later became Chief of the General Staff) envisioned a unified military–political organ that would have wide-ranging powers. In Tukhachevsky's model, the General Staff would have played an extensive role in determining economic policy through the integration of industrial and war plans. Reversing priorities, Tukhachevsky developed a thesis on how the General Staff should enjoy great authority during the massive industrialization and militarization drive of the early 1930s. But the military's role in this area was never very secure.[4]

Defense-related industrial concerns were kept under the watchful eye of a trusted political lieutenant — who in Tukhachevsky's time was K.Y. Voroshilov. That arrangement exists in some form even today. While there are no parallel institutions for the development of strategy and force posture, there is a Central Committee Department and a member of the Politburo who holds the portfolio for managing the industrial concerns associated with defense policy.

It is perhaps surprising that the Party, especially under Joseph Stalin in the 1930s, did not create a Central Committee apparatus to parallel even those limited functions of the General Staff. Such departments were created for other governmental functions, for example, education and foreign affairs.[5] Therefore, with no institutional competitors, matters of military strategy became the Staff's exclusive preserve. The reforms of 1935, renaming the Red Army Staff the General Staff and expanding its functions, further strengthened its role. The Soviets now had a General Staff seemingly in the great German and Russian imperial traditions to which they often looked. But the development was not automatic or inevitable. And in fact, concerns about the 'German' model dominated the debate. Thus, the General Staff, while secure in the realm of military strategy, was continually challenged for control of mobilization, intelligence and training.

In 1937, the fragility of the General Staff's position became clear. The lesson of the period was that when political authority decided to intrude on the prerogatives of the General Staff there was no protection. Stalin politicized Soviet military strategy, dominating its development and forcing the understandably cowed General Staff to bend their military analyses in accordance with his views. That timidity was reinforced by a reign of terror that resulted in the liquidation of three of five marshals of the Soviet Union and approximately 70 per cent of generals at the division level or above.[6]

Because Stalin distrusted the military so intensely, he divided the functions that the General Staff had slowly accumulated among several institutions. Responsibility for mobilization and for training was given to a new organization, Glavupraform (Main Administration for Forming and Bringing Up to Strength the Forces of the Red Army). But in June 1942, the competition between the General Staff and Glavupraform was so fierce that Stalin personally issued a directive delineating their functions. The measure created greater confusion, however, and with the exigencies of the war dominant, mobilization and organizational matters were returned to the General Staff.[7]

Similar challenges occurred in the area of intelligence. The purges left the General Staff's Main Intelligence Directorate (GRU) depleted and nervous. The NKVD began to take on many of the GRU's functions and sowed distrust of it with Stalin. Only after several months of warfare was the position of the GRU re-established in matters of military intelligence.

But even at this darkest moment for the General Staff, Stalin chose not to create an institution fully parallel to it and capable of managing the range of military–technical functions. Rather, Stalin exercised his personal power through the demoralized General Staff. Calling its members to report to him, berating them and personally altering their plans, Stalin asserted his authority over the military. Later, facing the possible loss of the war, he relied increasingly on the expertise of his staff officers; it was the General Staff to which Stalin delegated, for example, the task of generating options. But there was never any doubt — Stalin was the Supreme Commander and all decisions rested ultimately with him.

Yet, the General Staff emerged from the Second World War as the focal point for the direction of the Soviet military forces in peace and war. That position was short-lived, however, for the General Staff soon faced the continuous but haphazard interference of Nikita Khrushchev.

The primary problems arose in connection with the assessment of the impact of nuclear weapons on warfare. Though there were certainly those in the General Staff who held the radical views that became the basis of Khrushchev's missile diplomacy, the General Secretary drew conclusions that were not popular with military professionals. Most importantly, he believed that nuclear weapons obviated the need for balanced military forces. He planned to cut manpower by 2 million men, abolished the Ground Forces Command, ravaged Soviet surface naval programs in favor of submarine forces, fired the Chief of the General Staff, and ordered cuts in it and other staffs of 25 per cent.[8]

The General Staff was powerless to do anything about this assault, however, until Khrushchev's own errors led to his demise. It did not take the recently retired Chief of the General Staff, Marshal Zakharov, long to point out that Khrushchev's disregard for military advice lay at the base of the failure in the Cuban Missile crisis and the dangerous confrontation in Berlin. Khrushchev had, in fact, taken the Soviet Union to the brink of war without adequate conventional military forces and, in Cuba, had finally had to back down. Zakharov's forceful argument for non-interference in the military's legitimate realm found a sympathetic listener in Khrushchev's successor, Leonid Brezhnev, who believed that there was no substitute for effective military power in shaping a successful foreign policy.

Brezhnev's understanding of the link between diplomacy and military power was perhaps best expressed in the Soviet view of *détente*. *Détente* was not a policy choice on the part of the West but an objective condition created by the strength of the Soviet Union. Soviet diplomats became fond of saying, as Alexei Kosygin did in 1971, that there was no major decision that could be taken without the participation of the Soviet Union.[9]

The Soviet leadership under Brezhnev was willing to expend whatever resources were necessary to give the Soviet Union effective military power. Assessments of Soviet military spending vary and are, at best, guestimates. But the most conservative estimates would seem to suggest that the Soviets were spending at least 15 per cent of their GNP on defense from 1967 to 1974 and perhaps beyond. Some in the Soviet Union now estimate that military spending during those years was over 25 per cent of GNP.[10] Currently, with the domestic environment in the Soviet Union so hostile to the military burden of the Brezhnev years, those figures are suspect. Thanks to subsidization of the military sector and the lack of real prices, the Soviets may not really know how much they spent. One can be agnostic about that question, however, and point out simply that the burden of defense, gladly borne by a leadership group under Brezhnev in search of superpower status, was indeed very great.

The expenditure of resources to make the Soviet military second to none ran parallel to political tolerance of military autonomy in structuring those forces. The professionalization of military planning in the Soviet Union took on a normative character in the General Staff's almost slavish worship of scientific planning. This normative defense of 'military science' in turn helped to insulate the General Staff both from political interference and from any claim to competence by those who were not members of the guild.[11]

Rejecting the notion of war as a series of random and mysterious events, the General Staff argued that there were laws that could be discovered through research and debate. In support of this position, they invoked the Marxist assertion that all of history developed scientifically. Scientific socialism, they argued, demanded that all phenomena, including warfare, be studied systematically. The military, led by the General Staff, embraced 'scientific' approaches to planning and operations research, systems analysis and decision theory. Other scientific methods were instituted in all planning and operations agencies.

The worship of scientific methods actually produced a backlash in the military itself as the role of the 'commander–engineer' came under scrutiny. Less technically educated officers argued that attributes like bravery and courage and even historical analysis were being undervalued.[12] But their voices were few as the General Staff pressed ahead with 'scientific planning'. The message was also there for those who might attempt to intrude for political reasons — only military scientists knew enough about warfare to create a rational and efficient military force.

Under Brezhnev, the General Staff profited from a prolonged period of being relatively free from political interference. It was able to use that opportunity to solidify its jurisdiction over military affairs, particularly *vis à vis* the individual services. Efforts to integrate planning and to create a single strategic view were pursued aggressively. The primacy of combined-arms doctrine provided the rationale for the General Staff's dominance of strategy. The relationship of various levels of strategy was, and remains, strictly hierarchical in the Soviet Union. An all-service strategy governs and while the main staffs of the individual services are responsible for developing the operational art and tactics that are service-specific, the General Staff reviews any changes to make certain that it is consistent with the overall thrust of national military strategy.

In order to prevent diversions from national strategy, the General Staff has steadily improved its input into the individual service staff's planning processes and has created a unified training program for senior officers. As early as 1960, an already strong all-service perspective was strengthened with the abolition of separate service faculties at the Voroshilov Academy (the Academy of the General Staff).[13] Instead, all senior officers were put through a unified arms course. There have also been extensive efforts to standardize methods of planning. Planning indices have long required the General Staff's approval. In 1965, this requirement was extended to the development of textbooks on planning methods for use in all agencies, staffs, academic institutions, and military–scientific societies. This effort to integrate planning is reflected in the designated role of the General Staff.[14]

The most significant challenge to the authority of the General Staff came from the Soviet Navy which twice had its own ministry. Like most army-dominated staffs, the General Staff has tended to view naval power as an appendage of ground power, best used in a support role. This position became increasingly unacceptable for an increasingly sophisticated navy. Several altercations took place and the General Staff responded in 1963 by designating a Special Assistant to the Chief of the General Staff for Naval Affairs. Since 1972, an admiral has always been a deputy chief of the General Staff.[15]

In the early 1970s it appeared that the Soviet Navy was about to break free of its maritime support role and match the American Navy as a blue water naval force. The Soviets began construction of a full-sized carrier. Admiral S.G. Gorshkov, Deputy Defence Minister and Commander of the Navy, believed to possess great political acumen in winning support for the Navy, began to press for a 'naval strategy' that recognized the unique character of naval forces. Gorshkov made essentially a political argument for a blue water navy: superpowers, like the United States, have blue water navies and the Soviet Union is a superpower. This argument resonated with the Soviet political leadership, locked as it was in a battle to secure 'equal status' with the United States largely on the basis of growing military power.

Gorshkov argued that navies could influence events without ever firing a shot by showing the flag in far corners of the world, and lamented that these characteristics had been largely ignored in Soviet military planning (by unnamed culprits). For a while, those elements of the Soviet Navy not associated with traditional missions, carriers and amphibious landing forces, received resources. But since this was at a time when the military's share of the budget was extraordinarily high there were arguably enough resources available for the General Staff to tolerate this divergence. With the more stringent budgets of the latter half of the 1970s, however, naval programs began to be stretched out and possibly some were cancelled. Gorshkov, himself, was forced to admit that only military strategy existed and that the navy, like the other services, could claim only a unique operational art (one level below strategy).

This period in Soviet history should probably be considered the military's 'golden age'. But the significant degree of autonomy that military professionals enjoyed gave rise to arguments that Brezhnev had become captive of a powerful military whose historical legacy was that of the Prussian and German General Staffs. Clearly, until 1985, the General Staff was secure and dominant within its domain — military strategy and force posture. The historical record seemed to support the idea that political interference usually led to disaster and that centralization and hierarchical structures maximized efficiency in military planning. The General Staff did what it could to support that claim, excoriating both Stalin and Khrushchev for unwarranted and harmful interference in military affairs, and trumpeting the importance of 'scientific planning'.[16]

Then, the rules of the game began to change.[17] The final chapter of the Gorbachev revolution and its impact on the Soviet military in general and the General Staff in particular is yet to be written. But it is already a gross understatement to say that it has had a profound impact on the jurisdiction and norms of that institution.

The essence of the 'institutionalist' approach is that institutional characteristics, acquired over an extended period and hardening over time, are remarkably resilient and persistent even in the face of large-scale environmental changes. It is even more remarkable, then, that recent developments in the Soviet Union have had the rapid and powerful impact on the institutional characteristics of the General Staff that they have. What has happened to the Soviet General Staff in the current period is more akin to what one would expect after the loss of a great war. But there has been no war. Thus, what does Gorbachev's Soviet Union say about the power of an institution's history, or, perhaps more correctly, the lack thereof?

The General Staff's weakened position can be explained by two factors. The first has historical parallels but the second does not. The current political leadership, like others before it save that of Brezhnev, has established a connection between its own control of the defense agenda and the professional military's role in decision-making. This has led both to greater direction from the top and to a tendency to start with a political answer to a military problem, a fact which constrains tightly the potential military responses. That lesson did not simply occur to the Gorbachev leadership. It was forced upon it by a deepening economic and political crisis at home and a series of foreign policy disasters abroad. More than at any time before, the lessons of history favored those who argued that a military left to its own devices would do more harm than good. This realization essentially undermined the General Staff's claim to unchallenged jurisdiction in matters of military strategy and force posture.

Second, and in the long term more important, the norms of the General Staff are for the first time in Soviet history badly out of phase with the direction of the norms of the polity as a whole. In the past, centralization of authority, tight secrecy and hierarchical structures throughout the political system helped to prevent the rise of institutional competitors to the General Staff, even when wanton political interference was present. But as the Soviet polity changes, natural jurisdictional competitors to the General Staff are emerging as the discussion of military matters is opened up.

The two factors are related. The mistakes of the Brezhnev period, particularly in foreign policy, are in large part responsible for the vocal critique of the decision-making structures of his government. That, in part, has fuelled sentiment for opening up defense decision-making as a part of the broader democratization of politics.

The critique of decision-making in the Brezhnev period portrays the leadership as captive of a structure that generated limited options, narrowly military in perspective. The argument is not that the military acted outside of its authority or challenged the political leadership. Rather, the argument goes right to the heart of the General Staff's hard-won bargain with the political leadership — the neat division between political and military issues. The boundary between the military–technical and political aspects of policy, preserved in an institutional separation that left the former to the General Staff, is said to have created a dangerous tendency myopically to prepare for war without understanding the foreign policy implications.[18]

Soviet commentators now point readily to the deployment of the SS-20 missile as a prime example of a militarily sound decision — modernization of the aging SS-4 and SS-5 forces — that led to a perception of an enhanced threat to Western Europe. That, in turn, created support for the NATO deployment of ground-launched cruise missiles and the Pershing II, which both qualitatively increased the threat to the Soviet Union and helped to solidify NATO's political cohesion. Likewise, the enormous Soviet military presence in Eastern Europe was always a thorn in the side of the Soviet Union's political relationship with those countries. And try as they might to convince the West that there was no threat, the deployment of a military force ready and able to invade Western Europe at a moment's notice made such protestations extremely weak.

These problems in foreign policy were coupled with the pervasive and growing sense throughout the latter half of the 1980s that the Soviet military's view of the prevailing threat to the Soviet Union was fuelling a defense budget that was bankrupting the economy. Both Stalin and Khrushchev, consciously or not, kept threat assessment within their personal grasp. As noted above, Khrushchev did this to the extreme, perhaps prematurely dismissing the importance of conventional force balances in favor of nuclear sabar rattling. Nonetheless, in his drive to control Soviet defense spending, he was able to impose his view of the prevailing threat on Soviet defense planning.

Likewise Stalin, with an almost disastrous outcome, personally assessed both the political direction of the threat and its imminence. This led to the miscalculations of the summer of 1941, when Stalin, despite repeated and incontrovertible evidence, ignored the military's warnings of a German attack. What is more, Stalin so thoroughly cowed the General Staff that no one was willing to tell him that he was wrong. Stalin's insistence that military realities would not undo his diplomatic initiatives with Nazi Germany almost resulted in the destruction of the Soviet Union.

The evidence is increasing that under Brezhnev the pendulum swung the other way, leaving the military to determine requirements based largely on its own threat assessment. The documentary evidence for this claim is not complete but both by inference from events and from comments of Soviet leaders, a picture emerges of Soviet foreign policy driven by the mistaken assumption that a stronger Soviet Union would produce an effective foreign policy without creating a significant backlash. Moreover, the political leadership, like the military, fell more and more into a paranoiac fear that coalitions forming against the Soviet Union had to be countered by Soviet military might.

Perhaps the best example of the latter development can be seen in Soviet policy toward Asia at the end of the 1970s. The Soviets were convinced that Japan, the United States and China were forming an iron triangle against the Soviet Union. This led the Soviet military to engage in a buildup of forces in the Far East, including on the disputed islands with Japan. The effect was predictable. The Soviets succeeded in forcing the Japanese and the United States into closer military cooperation, leading in 1980 to a Japanese decision to interpret its self-defense limitations more broadly. Similarly, the Chinese, in accordance with their long-held preference for allying with the weaker against the stronger, developed closer military ties with the United States.

The Soviets, in turn, adopted a military strategy to 'prepare the Soviet Union to defend against all possible enemies, either in coalition or individually, that the motherland might face'.[19] Since that potential coalition included the United States, Western Europe, Japan and China, the strain on Soviet defense budgets was enormous. Consequently, as Steven Meyer put it, the Soviet leadership knew that in order to reduce defense spending it had to get a handle on the defense agenda.[20] Threat assessment had lost its political dimension. If there were diplomatic ways to encourage rather than to coerce other states to improve relations with the Soviet Union, that strategy was not likely to be developed within the General Staff. Militaries know only one way to meet a threat, and that was head on. The fact that the decision-making structure was found wanting led the political leadership, particularly Foreign Minister Eduard Shevardnadze, to seek other sources of ideas and options.[21]

But the creation of effective counter-institutions is a long-term process. The four characteristics mentioned above, once in place — jurisdiction, expertise, norms and traditions — are not easily undermined. The problem is especially acute for the Soviet Union where there has been, to date, extremely limited expertise outside of the military to deal with these issues. Access to information has always been a barrier to the creation of new military planning institutions.[22]

The growth of pluralism in the larger polity is likely to have a lasting effect on the way that the General Staff operates. The Soviet political system is in tremendous flux and it is sufficient to note that the development of new institutions, the Presidential Council, the Congress of Peoples' Deputies and a rejuvenated Supreme Soviet, all with responsibilities in defense affairs, has served to stimulate debate about issues in what has been the General Staff's sole domain. Similarly, the loosening of ties between the Union and the republics has created an entirely new layer of institutions and interested parties relevant to matters of defense. Decentralization in the Soviet polity ensures that there are many eyes, ears and voices concerned with questions of military force posture and strategy.

As important as these developments are, these institutions tend to be more reactive to what the General Staff does than to be capable of structuring viable alternatives. That could change over time. The rapidly shifting norms of political behavior in the Soviet Union, with a premium on openness and debate, may, in the long-term, imperil the General Staff's hold on its domain perhaps more than any other development. It may not be necessary to create institutions exactly parallel to the General Staff. Rather, simply opening up the debate on issues of military strategy and force posture can have the effect of producing alternative views and challenging established patterns of how alternative course of action are developed.

Currently, in the absence of institutions fully capable of tackling the details of military strategy and force posture, the political leadership has had to play a much more active role in dictating to the General Staff what outcomes are acceptable. While this pattern does have historical antecedents, the effect this time has been much more dramatic. It is no exaggeration to say that the General Staff's world has been turned upside down by decisions taken by the political leadership. Could the General Staff, in its wildest scenarios, have figured on the absorption of the GDR into a unified Germany within the NATO Alliance?

Reliance on political direction does have its drawbacks, however, and there is some evidence that this approach is not wholly satisfactory. First, the political leadership is thinly stretched across the range of policy issues within its domain and cannot pay attention in a sustained fashion to the details of military policy. When the political leadership is distracted, the absence of expertise outside the military tends to allow bureaucratic inertia to set in rapidly, with a consequent return to General Staff dominance of the process. This is most notable in arms control negotiations, where, several times, the General Staff's preferences have reasserted themselves at critical junctures, requiring the highest-level intervention to dislodge them.[23]

Conservative spokesmen see little reason to question the General Staff's role in arms control negotiations. Military experts must be intimately involved, alongside the political leaders in discussions leading to the dismantling of the armed forces. That view notwithstanding, the lack of institutions other than the General Staff which can handle the details of arms control planning can backfire and, ultimately, undermine implementation of defense policy. It is widely believed that such an episode occurred in February 1990 when during a US–Soviet ministerial meeting the Foreign Ministry, in the absence of General Staff clearance, accepted a US START position on ALCMs. The Soviet Union retreated from that position at the next ministerial meeting in April, and, after some confusion, agreement was reached, with the General Staff heavily represented at the table. None of this alters one basic fact, however. The General Staff's institutional role is changing as a new Soviet Union emerges.

What is the lesson of this period for those who are interested in understanding the impact of history on an institution's future? There have always been those cases where massive changes in the environment — the loss of a war or the onset of revolution — create conditions in which an institution must define itself *de novo*. Though the situation is not quite that severe for the General Staff, the combined circumstances of the end of the Cold War, reversing seventy years of confrontation with powerful enemies, coupled with the rapidly changing norms of the internal polity, confront the General Staff as an institution with an imperative to redefine itself.

The evidence so far is that it is already doing that and beginning a new phase in its development with new norms and, though uncomfortably, shared jurisdiction for matters that it once controlled completely.[24] The General Staff is still served well by the fact that it has no coherent institutional competitors for the things that it does best. That is perhaps the most lasting element of the historical legacy. But, barring a reversal of prevailing major international and domestic trends, it will have to transform itself into a very different institution than it has traditionally been. It remains to be seen whether the General Staff's characteristics, now so badly out of phase with current trends, are an impediment to a timely and effective response to the new environment in which it finds itself. That these challenges exist is beyond question. As they are met they will provide both an indicator of the state of civil–military relations in the Soviet Union and of how Soviet defense policy is being made, and a guideline for the United States in dealing with the Soviet Union of Mikhail Gorbachev.

Notes

1. James G. March and Johan P. Olsen, 'The New Institutionalism: Organizational Factors in Political Life', *American Political Science Review*, **78**, 3, September 1984, pp. 734–49.
2. See especially the commentary of Boris Shaposhnikov in *Mogz Armil* (Brain of the Army) (Moscow: Izdatelst'vo, 1928) and a scathing critique of the General Staff System in 'Nam Nado Generalnyi Stab?' (Do we need a General Staff?), *Krasnaia Armii*, 1 December 1918.
3. The protracted debate about how 'regular' the Red Army should be raged for almost ten years between Mikhail Frunze and the brilliant but utopian Leo Trotsky. Frunze's vision eventually won out with the reforms of 1924–5 which laid the foundation for the modern staff system. The reforms are chronicled in M. A. Gareyev, *Frunze: Voennyi teoretik* (Moscow: Voenizdat, 1985).
4. The problems that Tukhachevsky encountered in restructuring the Red Army and bringing it up to the standards of modern-day armies are explored in an increasing number of works by Soviet scholars. Pre-glasnost sources include: S. A. Tyushkevich *et al.*, *Sovetskiye Vooruzhennykh sil'* (Moscow: Voennoe izdatet'stvo, 1978); and I. A. Korotkov, *Istoriya Sovetskoi Voennoi Mysli: Korotkii ocherk* (Moscow: Nauka, 1980). Recently, the treatment of Tukhachevsky and other military heroes of the 1930s has become a *cause célèbre* both in popular and scholarly journals. See, e.g., interviews with military historian D. A. Volkogonov, e.g., 11 July 1990, p. 3, in *Izvestiya*.
5. In 1944, The Soviets considered creating a Secretariat for the Council of Labor and Defense as a civilian counterpart to the General Staff. The plan was rejected, however, because it would have infringed upon the General Staff's responsibilities and caused 'disconnections' (otrivi) in the strategic plan. (M. A. Garayev, op. cit., pp. 180–1.)
6. Volkogonov, op. cit., John Erickson, *The Soviet High Command* (New York: St. Martin's Press, 1967) is still the best Western source for this period.
7. S. M. Shtemenko, *General'ny i stab v god y voini*, 2 vols. (Moscow: Voenizdat, 1973).
8. While Khrushchev's 'reforms' are viewed somewhat more favorably in the Gorbachev era as an attempt to cut a bloated — military he is despised by military historians as one who haphazardly dictated a military policy based on illusory military power. The argument is not without merit. See David Holloway and Condoleezza Rice. 'The Evolution of Soviet Forces, Strategy, and Command', in Kurt Gottfried and Bruce G. Blair, eds, *Crisis Stability and Nuclear War* (New York: Oxford University Press, 1988), pp. 126–58.
9. For the clearest explication of this link, see Coit D. Blacker, 'The Kremlin and Detente: Soviet Conceptions, Hopes, and Expectations', in Alexander George, ed., *Managing US–Soviet Rivalry: Problems of Crisis Prevention* (Boulder, CO: Westview Press, 1983), pp. 119–37.
10. See the condemnation of Prime Minister N. I. Ryzhkov's argument that Soviet defense spending was 77 billion rubles in 1989.

11. There is a voluminous literature on this issue. See, e.g., K. Ivanov, 'Nauchniye printsipy rukovodstra zashchiniye socialist-icheskogo otechestra', *Kommunist vooruzhenykh sil'*, No. 16, 1969: and V. V. Druzhinin and I. A. Korotkov, *Ideiya, algorithm i resheniya* (Moscow: Voenizdat, 1972). David Holloway noted this trend in *Technology and Military Management in the Soviet Union*, Adelphi Paper No. 76 (London: International Institute of Strategic Studies, 1977).

12. V. Bondarenko and S. Tyushkevich, 'Soveremennyi etap revolutsii v voennom dele itrebovaniya k voennym Kadram', *Kommunist vooruzhenykh sil'*, No. 6, 1968.

13. V. I. Kilikov, *Akademiya general'nogo staba* (Moscow: Voenizdat, 1976).

14. ibid., p. 208.

15. See James McConnell, 'The Gorshkov Articles, the New Gorshkov Book and Their Relation to Policy', in Michael MccGwire and James McConnell, eds, *Soviet Naval Influence* (New York: Praeger, 1977), pp. 565–617.

16. The most direct attack was that of M. V. Zakharov, who was fired by Khrushchev as Chief of the General Staff and rehired by Brezhnev (*Krasnaia Zvezda*, 4 February 1965.)

17. For explanations of the changes in decision structures, see Stephen M. Meyer, 'The Sources and Prospects of Gorbachev's New Political Thinking on Security', *International Security*, **13**, 2, Fall 1988, pp. 124–63; and Condoleezza Rice, 'Is Gorbachev Changing the Rules of the Defense Decision-making Game?', *Journal of International Affairs*, **42**, 2, Spring 1989, pp. 377–97.

18. The critique has exploded onto the front pages of popular and scholarly journals. See *Moscow News*, January 1990. One of the most interesting exchanges of views took place on television in a *Literaturnaia gazeta*-sponsored roundtable, 29 June 1988.

19. D. F. Ustinov in speech to military *aktiv*, January 1979.

20. Meyer, op. cit.

21. E. A. Shevardnadze's speech reported in *Vestnik Ministertva Inostrannykh del SSR*, 26 August 1987. Also personal conversations with researchers at the Institute for USA and Canada Studies and at the Central Committee's International Department, July 1988.

22. In the *Literaturnaia gazeta* roundtable, Sergei F. Akhromeyev, former Chief of the General Staff and now advisor to Gorbachev, defended control of information. Members of the Supreme Soviet still complain about problems of access to information and many Soviet civilians still find themselves dependent on Western sources.

23. Members of the Bush administration, as well as European diplomats, have commented on this phenomenon.

24. The most important development is a widening role for members of the General Staff as soldier-diplomats in arms control, military to military contacts and events like the Military Doctrine Seminar of the CSCE last March in Vienna.

6 British and American hegemony compared: lessons for the current era of decline
David Lake

America's decline has gained new prominence in the current political debate. There is little doubt that the country's economic competitiveness has, in fact, waned since its hegemonic zenith in the 1950s. The immediate post-Second World War era was anomalous; with Europe and Japan devastated by the war, the United States enjoyed a period of unchallenged economic supremacy. As other countries rebuilt their economies, this lead had to diminish. Yet, even in the 1970s and 1980s, long after the period of 'catch up' had ended, America's economy continued to weaken relative to its principal trading partners.[1]

Popular attention has focused on the appropriate policy response to this self-evident decline. One critical issue, which cuts across the traditional liberal–conservative spectrum, is America's relations with its allies. Should the United States maintain a policy of free trade premised on broad reciprocity as in the General Agreement on Tariffs and Trade (GATT), or must it 'get tough' with its trading partners, demand equal access industry-by-industry to foreign markets, balance trade between specific countries, and retaliate if others fail to abide by America's understanding of the international trade regime? This is a question which all present and future American governments will have to address — and the answer is by no means ideologically predetermined or, for that matter, clear.

The issue of American decline is not new, despite the recent attention devoted to it. It has been a topic of lively academic debate for almost twenty years — a debate which, while not directly focused on such issues, can shed considerable light on the question of America's relations with its trading partners. The so-called theory of hegemonic stability was developed in the early 1970s to explain the rise and fall of the *Pax Britannica* and *Pax Americana*, periods of relative international economic openness in the mid-nineteenth and mid-twentieth centuries respectively. In its early form, the theory posited that hegemony, or the existence of a single dominant economic power, was both a necessary and sufficient condition for the construction and maintenance of a liberal international economy. It followed that once the hegemon began to decline, the international economy would move toward greater conflict and closure.[2] The theory has since been refined and extended, with nearly all revisions concluding that a greater potential exists for non-hegemonic international economic cooperation than was allowed for in the original formulation.[3] All variants of the theory of hegemonic stability suggest, nonetheless, that Britain's relative decline after 1870 is the closest historical analogy to the present era and a fruitful source of lessons for American policy. Many have drawn pessimistic predictions about the future of the liberal international economy on the basis of this comparison, with the implication that a more nationalist foreign economic policy is necessary to halt the breakdown of the open international economy into a series of regional trading blocs.[4] To understand and judge this, one must recognize and begin with the parallels between the *Pax Americana* and the *Pax Britannica* and their subsequent periods of decline. Yet, one must also recognize that the differences between these two cycles of hegemony are just as important as the similarities. The two periods of declining hegemony are similar, but not identical — and the differences have tremendous import for the future of the liberal international economic order and the nature of American policy.

The historical analogy

From the sixteenth to the eighteenth centuries, the international economy was dominated by mercantilism — a pervasive set of state regulations governing the import and export of goods, services, capital, and people. Britain was no exception to this general trend and, in fact, was one of its leading proponents. While restrictions on trade may have been adopted largely as a result of rent-seeking by domestic groups, they also stimulated home production and innovation and allowed Britain to build an industrial base from which to challenge Dutch hegemony.[5]

With the industrial revolution, and the resulting economic take-off, Britain slowly began dismantling its mercantilist system. Various restraints were removed, and by the 1830s few industrial tariffs and trade restrictions remained. Agricultural protection persisted, however, until industry finally triumphed over landed interests in the repeal of the Corn Laws in 1846.[6] Britain's shift to free trade ushered in a period of international economic liberalization. For reasons discussed below, the repeal of the Corn Laws facilitated the rise of free trade coalitions in both the emerging Germany and the United States. Moreover, Britain finally induced France to join in the emerging free trade order in 1860, trading its acquiescence in France's military excursions into Northern Italy for lower tariffs in a bargain which underlay the important Cobden–Chevalier Treaty.[7] Interlocking trade treaties premised on the unconditional most-favored-nation principle then served to spread these reductions throughout Europe.[8]

British hegemony peaked in approximately 1870, after which its national product, trade and labor productivity — while continuing to grow in absolute terms — began to shrink relative to its principal economic rivals. With Britain's decline, the free trade order began to unravel. The United States returned to a policy of high protection after the Civil War. Germany adopted high tariffs in its coalition of Iron and Rye in 1879. France followed suit in the Meline Tariff of 1892.[9]

Just as Britain had used mercantilism as a weapon against Dutch hegemony, the United States and Germany used protection to build up their infant industries, which were then able to challenge and defeat British industry in global competition. Despite a large measure of protectionist rent-seeking by various uncompetitive groups in both countries, this strategy of industrial stimulation was successful. By the late 1890s, the United States surpassed Britain in relative labor productivity and other key indicators of industrial production. Germany also emerged as a major threat to British economic supremacy, particularly in the race for colonies in the developing world.[10]

Despite these threats, Britain continued to dominate and manage the international economy until the outbreak of the First World War. With its industrial base slipping, Britain moved into services — relying on shipping, insurance and international finance to offset its increasing trade deficits. The British pound remained the international currency and the City of London the core of the international financial system.[11]

British weakness, however, was revealed and exacerbated by the First World War. Britain sold off many of its overseas assets to pay for the necessary wartime supplies. As a result, repatriated profits were no longer sufficient to offset its trade deficit. Moreover, the war generated several deep and insidious sources of international economic instability — war debts, German reparations, America's new status as a net creditor nation, and, at least partly through Britain's own mistakes, an overvalued pound.

Eventually, the international economy collapsed under the weight of its own contradictions, despite futile efforts at joint Anglo–American international economic leadership in the 1920s.[12] American capital, previously channeled to Germany, which in turn used its international borrowings to pay reparations to Britain and France, was diverted to the stock market after 1927, feeding the speculative fever and precipitating a wave of bank closures in Austria and Germany. As the banking panic spread across Europe and eventually across the Atlantic, the stock market became its own victim.[13] While the crash of 1929 did not cause the Great Depression, it certainly exacerbated the underlying instabilities in international commodity markets. As the depression worsened, each country turned inward upon itself, adopting beggar-thy-neighbor policies in a vain attempt to export the pain to other states.

The roots of American hegemony lie in the period following the Civil War.[14] With the defeat of the South, government policy shifted in favor of the North and industrialization. By the First World War, the United States had emerged as Britain's equal. The two competed for international economic leadership (and occasionally for the abdication of leadership) throughout the inter-war period.

The United States began the process of liberalization in 1913 with the passage of the Underwood Tariff Act. While pressure for freer trade had been building for over a decade, this was the first concrete manifestation of reform. This nascent liberalism, however, was aborted by the war and the international economic instability it engendered; tariffs were raised in 1922 and again in 1930. The United States returned to international liberalism in the Reciprocal Trade Agreements Act of 1934. While free trade remained politically tenuous throughout the 1930s and early 1940s, it was locked securely in place as the centerpiece of American foreign economic policy by the end of the Second World War.

Like Britain, the United States was the principal impetus behind international economic liberalization.[15] It led the international economy to greater economic openness through the GATT, the International Monetary Fund (IMF), the World Bank, and a host of United Nations-related organizations. The United States also made disproportionately large reductions in its tariffs and encouraged discrimination against its exports as a means of facilitating economic reconstruction. Real trade liberalization was delayed until the 1960s, when the Kennedy Round of the GATT substantially reduced tariffs in all industrialized countries. This success was soon followed by the equally important Tokyo Round, which further reduced tariffs and rendered them essentially unimportant impediments to trade.

Despite these successes, and in part because of them, challenges to international liberalism began to emerge in the late 1960s. As America's economic supremacy receded, the exercise of international power became more overt and coercive. This was especially true in the international monetary arena, where the series of stop-gap measures adopted during the 1960s to cope with the dollar overhang were abandoned in favor of a more unilateral approach in the appropriately named 'Nixon Shocks' of August 1971. More importantly, as tariffs were reduced and previously sheltered industries were exposed to international competition, new pressures were placed on governments for trade restrictions. These pressures have been satisfied, at least in part, by the proliferation of non-tariff barriers to trade, the most important of which take the form of 'voluntary' export restraints by foreign producers. While the net effect of reduced tariffs and increased non-tariff barriers to trade is difficult to discern, it is clear that domestic political support for free trade in the United States and other advanced industrialized countries has eroded.[16]

In summary, during their hegemonic ascendancies, both Britain and the United States played leading roles in opening the international economy. And in both cases, brief successes were soon followed by increasing challenges to global liberalism. The parallels are clear. The historical analogy suggests a period of increasing economic conflict, a slide down the 'slippery slope of protection', and a return to the beggar-thy-neighbor policies of the inter-war period.

The historical reality

Despite the plausibility and attractiveness of this historical analogy, it is deeply flawed. The similarities between the *Pax Britannica* and *Pax Americana* have over-shadowed the differences, but those differences may in the end prove to be more important. The points of contrast between the two periods of hegemony can be grouped into four categories.

I. International political structures

In the nineteenth century, and throughout the period of British hegemony, the United Kingdom, France, and then Germany all pursued empire as a partial substitute for trade within an open international economy. No country relied entirely on intra-empire trade, but as the international economy became more competitive in the late nineteenth century all three countries turned toward their colonies. This stimulated a general breakdown of the international economy into regional trading blocs and substituted government legislation and regulations for international market forces.

At the height of its hegemony, for instance, Britain pursued an open door policy within its colonies. Parliament repealed the mercantilist Navigation Laws in 1828 and soon thereafter opened the trade of the colonies to all countries on equal terms. Despite the absence of formal trade restrictions in the colonies, however, Britain continued to dominate their trade through informal means, counting on the ties between colonial administrators and the home state to channel trade in the appropriate directions.

Beginning in the late 1890s, however, Britain began to accept and, later, actively to promote preferential trade measures within the empire.[17] While the earliest preferences took the form of unilateral reductions in colonial tariffs on British exports, by the First World War, Britain, under pressure from the colonies, began to reciprocate. The McKenna Duties, passed in 1915, and the Safeguarding of Industry Duties, enacted after the war, all discriminated against non-empire trade. In 1932, Britain returned to protection and adopted a complete system of Imperial Preference. In short, as its economic strength deteriorated in the late nineteenth century, even Britain, the paragon of international liberalism, turned inward to its empire.

Since 1945, on the other hand, formal imperialism has all but disappeared. Instead of a system of geographically dispersed empires, there now exists a system of sovereign states. As the American-dominated 'Dollar bloc' of the 1930s attests, a formal empire is not necessary for the creation of a regional trade bloc. Yet the present international system is less likely to break down into regional economic blocs for two reasons.

As Hobson, Lenin and other theorists of late nineteenth-century imperialism correctly pointed out, imperialism is a finite process, the end point of which is determined by the quantity of available land.[18] Once the hinterland is exhausted, countries can expand only through the redistribution of existing colonies. Thus, the quest for imperial trading blocs transforms exchange, at least in part, from a positive into a zero-sum game and increases the level of economic conflict endemic in the international system. Despite the decline of American hegemony, the gains from trade today are both more visible and less exclusive, helping to make the liberal international economy more durable than in the past.

In addition, colonies are not fully sovereign and have, at best, abridged decision-making powers. As a result, intra-imperial trade and trade agreements are not subject to the same possibilities for opportunism as are trade arrangements between independent states. Today, even if two countries undertake a bilateral trade treaty, as in the case of the United States and Canada, each remains fully sovereign and capable of cheating and exploiting the other. Indeed, as regional specialization expands, the quasi-rents potentially appropriable by either party will also increase, thereby raising the gains from opportunism.[19] The higher the gains and, therefore, the risk of opportunism, the less likely it is that two countries will enter into binding bilateral relationships. As a result, trade blocs between sovereign states will always be more fragile, less beneficial and, it follows, less prevalent than those based upon imperial preference.

II. International economic structures

A. THE BASES OF BRITISH AND AMERICAN HEGEMONY

While both Britain and the United States enjoyed a position of international economic dominance, the bases of their economic hegemony differed in important ways. Britain's share of world *trade* was substantially larger than that obtained by the United States, while America's share of world *product* was far larger than Britain's.

In 1870, Britain controlled approximately 24 per cent of world trade, declining to less than 15 per cent by the outbreak of the First World War. The United States, however, accounted for only 18.4 per cent of world trade in 1950, and its share fell to less than 15 per cent by the mid 1960s. Collective goods theory suggests that Britain had a stronger interest in acting as a benevolent hegemon and, specifically, in regulating and maintaining an open international economy.[20] This interest in providing the international economic infrastructure, furthermore, was reinforced by Britain's higher dependence on trade, which reached 49 per cent of national product in 1877–85 and 52 per cent in 1909–13. For the United States, trade accounted for only 17 per cent of national product in the 1960s, although this ratio has risen in recent years.[21] These figures indicate that Britain also faced a considerably higher opportunity costs of international economic closure.

While British hegemony was based upon control of international trade, the United States — still the largest trader of its era — relied on the relatively greater size of its domestic economy. Throughout its hegemonic rise and decline, the British economy (measured in terms of national product) was relatively small compared to its trading rivals, and to that of the United States at a similar stage in its hegemonic cycle. In 1860, Britain's economy was only three-quarters the size of America's. Conversely, in 1950, the domestic economy of the United States was over three times larger than the Soviet Union's, its next largest rival.[22] This difference between British and American hegemony, while highlighting variations in the opportunity costs of closure, also have important implications for the international political processes discussed below.

B. THE TRAJECTORIES OF DECLINE

Not only were the economic bases of British and American hegemony different, but their respective declines have also followed alternative trajectories. In the late nineteenth century, Britain was confronted by two dynamic, vibrant and rapidly growing rivals: the United States and Germany. Perhaps because of its latecomer status or its geographical position in Europe, Germany was singled out as Britain's principal challenger for hegemony. With the eventual assistance of the United States, Germany was defeated in war and eliminated as an important economic actor.[23]

The waning of British hegemony thus found the United States and the United Kingdom in roughly equal international economic positions. In the years immediately before the First World War, an economic *modus vivendi*, grounded in substantial tariff reductions in the United States, appeared possible between these two powers. Yet, Anglo–American cooperation and the potential for joint leadership of the international economy were cut short by the war and its aftermath. The breakdown of the international economy during the war created difficult problems of reconstruction and generated high international economic instability, which shortened time horizons in both the United States and Britain and rendered post-war cooperation substantially more difficult.[24] In the absence of such cooperation, the conflicts over reconstruction were insoluble, and the international economy eventually collapsed in the Great Depression.

The decline of American hegemony has occurred primarily through a general levelling of international economic capabilities among the Western powers. Today, the international economy is dominated by the United States, the Federal Republic of Germany, France, and Japan, all substantial traders with a strong interest in free trade, even if they desire some protection for their own industries. The greatest structural threat to continued cooperation is not the absence of partners capable of joint management, but too many partners and the corresponding potential for free riding that this creates.

Despite the instability generated by the oil shocks of the 1970s, moreover, these four economic powers have successfully managed the international economy — or at least muddled through. They have coped with a major change in the international monetary regime, the rise of the Euromarkets, and the Third World debt crisis. The most immediate threats to continued cooperation are the large and, apparently, endless budget and trade deficits of the United States. Barring any further increase in international economic instability, however, even these problems may be manageable.

III. *International political processes*

A. THE THREE FACES OF HEGEMONY

Elsewhere, Scott James and I have distinguished three 'faces' or strategies of hegemonic leadership.[25] The first face of hegemony, as we define it, is characterized by the use of positive and negative sanctions aimed directly at foreign governments in an attempt to influence their choice of policies. Through inducements or threats, the hegemon seeks to alter the international costs and benefits of particular state actions. Economic sanctions, foreign aid and military support (or lack thereof) exemplify the strategic use of direct and overt international power central to this first face.

In the second face, the hegemon uses its international market power, or the ability to influence the price of specific goods, to alter the incentives and political influence of societal actors in foreign countries. These individuals, firms, sectors, or regions then exert pressure upon their governments for alternative policies, which — if the hegemon has used its market power correctly — will be more consistent with the interests of the dominant international power. This is a 'Trojan Horse' strategy in which the hegemon changes the constellation of interests and political power within other countries in ways more favorable to its own interests.

The third face focuses on the hegemon's use of ideas and ideology to structure public opinion and the political agenda in other countries so as to determine what are legitimate and illegitimate policies and forms of political behavior. In other words, the hegemon uses propaganda, in the broadest sense of the word, to influence the climate of opinion in foreign countries.

In the mid-nineteenth century, Britain used its dominance of world trade to pursue an essentially second face strategy of hegemonic leadership. By repealing its Corn Laws, and allowing unfettered access to its markets, Britain effectively restructured the economic incentives facing producers of raw materials and foodstuffs. Over the long term, by altering factor and sector profit rates, and hence investment patterns, Britain augmented and mobilized the political influence of the interests within non-hegemonic countries most amenable to an international division of labor. All this was premised on complementary production and the free exchange of primary goods for British manufactures. Thus, in the United States, repeal of the Corn Laws facilitated the rise of a free trade coalition between Southern cotton growers, the traditional force for international economic openness in the American politics, and Western grain producers who had previously allied themselves with the more protectionist North-Eastern industrialists. This South–West coalition was reflected in almost two decades of freer trade in the United States, begun with the passage of the Walker Tariff in 1846. A similar process can be identified in Prussia, where the repeal of the Corn Laws reinforced the political power and free trade tendencies of the Junkers. This is not to argue, of course, that Britain relied exclusively on the second face of hegemony, only that it was an important theme in British trade policy and international leadership.

The United States, as noted above, has never dominated international trade to the same extent as Britain, but instead bases its leadership and influence upon its large domestic market. American strategy follows from this difference. Where Britain used its trade dominance to pursue a second face strategy, the United States relies to a larger extent on a first face strategy, trading access to its own market for reciprocal tariff reductions abroad. Accordingly, the United States did not unilaterally reduce tariffs, except for the period immediately after the Second World War, but instead linked reductions in, at first, bilateral treaties under the Reciprocal Trade Agreements Act and, later, in the GATT.

The explicitly reciprocal nature of American trade policy facilitates greater multilateral openness. British liberalization was spread throughout Europe by the unconditional most-favored-nation principle, but free trade remained fragile. As soon as alternative political coalitions obtained power, as in the United States in the aftermath of the Civil War and in Germany in the coalition of Iron and Rye, liberal trade policies were quickly jettisoned in favor of protection. Committed to free trade, Britain made clear its reluctance to retaliate against new protectionism by its trading partners. As a result, it allowed countries like the United States and Germany to free ride on its leadership — specifically, to protect their domestic industries while continuing to take advantage of British openness.[26] The reciprocal trade policy adopted by the United States has brought more countries into the fold, so to speak, by linking access to American markets to participation in the GATT system. This system of generalized reciprocity, as well as the increasing willingness of the United States to retaliate against unfair foreign trade practices, acts to restrain protectionism in foreign countries. Paradoxically, a trade strategy based upon the first face of hegemony, despite its more overt use of international power, may prove more resilient.

B. INTERNATIONAL REGIMES

A second and related difference in the international political processes of British and American hegemony is the latter's greater reliance upon international institutions and international economic regimes. Britain led the international economy in the nineteenth century without recourse to any formal international institutions and with few international rules governing exchange relations between counties. The nineteenth century, in other words, was a period of weak or, at best, implicit international economic regimes.

In the present period, on the other hand, international economic regimes are highly prevalent, even pervasive. The GATT, the IMF, the World Bank, and many United Nations organizations all give concrete — and lasting — substance to America's global economic leadership. As a result, international liberalism has been institutionalized in international relations.

As Robert Keohane has persuasively argued, international regimes are instruments of statecraft and are created to facilitate cooperation, specifically, by (a) providing a legal liability framework, (b) reducing transactions costs, and (c) reducing uncertainty by providing information and constraining moral hazard and irresponsibility. States comply with their dictates, Keohane continues, because of reputational considerations, because regimes provide a service which is of value, and because they are easier to maintain than to create.[27] For these same reasons, Keohane suggests, international regimes are likely to persist even though the interests which brought them into being change. International regimes are thus important because they create more consistent, routinized and enduring international behavior.[28]

To the extent that this argument is correct, the greater reliance of American hegemony on international regimes can be expected to preserve the liberal international economic order for some unspecifiable period, not only in the United States but throughout the international economy as well. America's hegemonic 'afterglow' may well be longer than Britain's.

C. ISSUE LINKAGE

The 'low' politics of trade have always been linked with the 'high' politics of national security — the views of certain liberal economists notwithstanding.[29] Military issues have been linked with trade treaties, as in the Cobden–Chevalier treaty between Britain and France in 1860. Trade policy also impinges upon economic growth and the basis for long-term military strength.

The free trade order constructed under British leadership bridged the political divide by including both allies and antagonists, friends and foes. In this system, not only was British influence over its military competitors limited, but the free trade order benefited all participants, often stimulating growth in antagonists and undermining the long-term strength of the United Kingdom. As Robert Gilpin noted, perhaps the most important contradiction of a free trade order, and international capitalism more generally, is that it develops rather than exploits potential competitors for international leadership.[30]

The liberal international economic regimes of American hegemony, on the other hand, have been built exclusively on one side of a bipolar political divide.[31] All of America's important trading partners are also its allies. This provides great potential leverage for the United States in trade issues. America's contributions to the public good of common defense can be diplomatically and tactically linked to liberal trade policies.[32] In addition, the greater benefits derived from specialization and the international division of labor are confined to allies of the United States. All economic benefits, in other words, reinforce America's security needs. As a result, challengers to American hegemony are less likely to emerge. And the United States, in turn, may be willing to make greater economic sacrifices to maintain the long-term strength and stability of the Western alliance.

IV. International economic processes

A. THE PATTERN OF SPECIALIZATION

The nineteenth-century international economy was built upon a pattern of complementary trade. Britain, and later a handfull of other industrialized countries, exported manufactured goods and imported raw materials and foodstuffs. To the extent that complementary products were not available within any particular economy, or available only at a substantially higher cost, this system of North–South trade created conditions of mutual dependence between core and peripheral states and, in turn, high opportunity costs of closure. As the Great Depression of the early 1930s clearly demonstrated, the economic costs of international closure were considerable.

The largest and most rapidly growing area of international trade after 1945, on the other hand, has been intra-industry trade — or the exchange of similar commodities between similarly endowed countries.[33] Accordingly, the United States is both a major importer and exporter of chemicals, machine tools and numerous other products. Similar patterns can be found in Europe and, to a lesser extent, for Japan.

This pattern of intra-industry trade creates two important but offsetting pressures, the net impact of which is unclear. First, intra-industry trade has a lower opportunity cost of closure than does complementary trade. The welfare loss of trade restraints on automobiles in the United States, for instance, is considerably less than it would be in the absence of a significant domestic car industry. In short, countries can more easily do without intra-industry trade. Second, the primary stimulus for intra-industry trade is economies of scale in production.[34] To the extent that these economies are larger than the domestic market, and can be satisfied only by exporting to foreign countries, they create important domestic political interest in favor of free trade and international openness. This restraint on protection, of course, will vary across countries, weighing more heavily in, say, Switzerland, than in the United States.

B. INTERNATIONAL CAPITAL FLOWS

In both the mid-nineteenth and mid-twentieth centuries, Britain and the United States, respectively, were the centers of the international financial system and the primary source of foreign investment. Both hegemons invested considerable sums abroad, perhaps at the expense of their own domestic economies.[35] Nonetheless, an important difference exists between the two cases. Britain engaged almost exclusively in portfolio investment; the United States relied to a greater extent upon foreign direct investment.

During the period of British decline, a deep conflict emerged between the City of London, the primary source of international capital, and British manufacturers. As the latter found themselves less competitive within the international economy, they began to demand and lobby for a return to protection. The protectionists, or so-called tariff reformers, had grown strong enough to split the Conservative Party by 1903, costing it the parliamentary election of January 1906. By 1912, the tariff reformers dominated the party and, before the trade issue was displaced on the political agenda by Irish home rule, appeared likely to win the next legislative battle. The City, on the other hand, remained solidly liberal. Increasingly, financial profits depended upon new capital outflows and prompt repayment of loans made to developing countries. With an international horizon stretched before it, the City would bear the costs of protection in the form of higher domestic prices and, more importantly, in the reduced ability of exporting countries to repay their loans, but would receive few if any benefits. Where the manufacturers desired to return to an industrially based economy and a trade surplus, the City was content with the reliance on services and recognized the need for Britain to run a trade deficit for the foreseeable future. This conflict lasted throughout the inter-war period, with the City emerging triumphant with the return of pre-war parity in 1925, only to be defeated on the question of protection in 1932.

Until the 1970s, on the other hand, the United States engaged primarily in foreign direct investment. The export of both capital and ownership alters the nature of America's political cleavages, creating intra-industry and capital–labor conflicts rather than an industry–finance division. The overseas manufacturing assets, globally integrated production facilities, and enhanced trade dependence of multinational corporations reduce the demands for protection by firms engaged in foreign investment, but not by labor employed in those sectors.[36] In this sense, the trade interests of multinational corporations are more similar to those of the international financial community than they are to domestic or non-internationalized firms. While nationally oriented firms and labor may still seek rents through domestic protection, the presence of a large multinational sector creates offsetting trade policy pressures within manufacturing and, indeed, often within the same sector, thereby strengthening the free trade lobby in the United States.[37]

Whither the *Pax Americana*?

The differences between British and American hegemony are considerable, and serve to call into question the appropriateness of the historical analogy. The decline of the *Pax Americana* will not follow the same path blazed by the decline of the *Pax Britannica*. Simplistic historical analogies fully deserve the scepticism with which they are greeted. What then is the likely future of the international economic order? Will openness endure, or is closure imminent?

The international constraints discussed above point in different directions. The absence of formal imperialism, the emerging structure of the post-hegemonic international economy, the moderate (so far) level of international economic instability, greater American reliance on a first face strategy of explicit reciprocity, the institutionalization of liberal international economic regimes, the overlap between the security and economic issue areas, and the importance of foreign direct investment, all suggest that international liberalism is robust and likely to endure. The potential for free riding among the great economic powers, the pattern of economic specialization, and the growing importance of intra-industry trade, are the most important challenges to the liberal international economy — and are a source of caution about the future.

While certainly more fragile than in, say, the 1960s, the open international economy has several underlying sources of resiliency. Even though America's economic competitiveness has declined, relatively free and unrestricted commerce is likely to remain the international norm. The international economy is not being held open simply through inertia; there are real interests supporting international liberalism.

This relatively optimistic view of the future of the international trading order supports continued commitment by the United States to free trade and generalized reciprocity as found in the GATT. Japan or Korea-bashing is unnecessary; other countries share America's interest in maintaining free trade within the international economy. The United States does not carry the burden of maintaining international openness alone.

Narrow policies of reciprocity, which seek equal access industry-by-industry or balanced trade between specific countries, may prove counterproductive, encouraging a decline into bilateralism that will redound to everyone's disadvantage and create the result which pessimists fear. As recent work on iterated prisoners' dilemma shows, cooperation can be sustained best by reciprocating cooperation.[38] To the extent that the United States is perceived as defecting from the open international economy, it encourages similar behavior in others. Economic instability enhanced this problem in the 1920s, but it is inherent in the current system as well.

On the other hand, the United States cannot benefit by being the 'sucker' in international trade. It must make clear that the continued openness of the American market is contingent upon similar degrees of openness in other countries. A broad or generalized policy of reciprocity is sufficient for this task, and promises to calm rather than exacerbate international economic tensions.

Conclusion

Statesmen and stateswomen undoubtedly base their decisions on theories of international politics, even if such theories are so implicit and amorphous as to resemble nothing more than 'world views'. No policy is made in a theoretical vacuum. Rather, beginning from selected assumptions or principles of human action, all policy-makers rely upon means–ends relationships and estimates of costs and benefits either derived from or validated by historical experience. These theories can be quite wrong or poorly understood, in which case the policy is likely to fail. Good theories, well employed, lead to more positive outcomes — or at least one hopes they do.

Scholars are an important source of the theories upon which decision-makers base their policies. This is especially true of the theory of hegemonic stability. Developed just as the first signs of American decline were becoming apparent and long before the pattern and its implications were recognized in diplomatic circles, the theory of hegemonic stability has slowly crept out of the ivory tower and into the public consciousness. It has helped spark a debate on the limits of American power in the late twentieth century. It has also led to demands for more aggressive trade policies under the generally accepted but nonetheless dangerous standard of 'specific reciprocity'.

No theory is widely accepted unless it has some empirical support and intuitive plausibility. The danger is, however, that even theories that meet these criteria may be underdeveloped and inadequately specified by their scholarly progenitors or over-simplified by those who translate academic jargon and subtlety into the language of public debate. The theory of hegemonic stability has been poorly served on both counts, leading to overly pessimistic predications on the future of the international economy and to far too aggressive trade policies which threaten to bring about the results they are supposedly designed to prevent.

Notes

1. The issue of American decline is raised most clearly in the controversy surrounding Paul Kennedy's *The Rise and Fall of the Great Powers* (New York: Random House, 1987). This academic tome has received surprisingly wide circulation. For an alternative view on the extent of American decline, see Bruce Russett, 'The Mysterious Case of Vanishing Hegemony: or, Is Mark Twain really Dead?', *International Organization*, **39**, 2, Spring 1985, pp. 207–31.

2. See Charles P. Kindleberger, *The World in Depression, 1929–1939* (Berkeley: University of California Press, 1973); Robert Gilpin, *US Power and the Multinational Corporation: The Political Economy of Foreign Direct Investment* (New York: Basic Books, 1975); and Stephen D. Krasner, 'State Power and the Structure of International Trade', *World Politics*, **28**, 3, April 1976, pp. 317–47.

3. See Robert O. Keohane, *After Hegemony: Cooperation and Discord in the World Political Economy* (Princeton: Princeton University Press, 1984); David A. Lake, *Power, Protection and Free Trade: International Sources of US Commercial Strategy, 1887–1939* (Ithaca: Cornell University Press, 1988); and Duncan Snidal, 'The Limits of Hegemonic Stability Theory', *International Organization*, **39**, 4, Autumn 1985, pp. 579–614.

4. See, for example, Gilpin, *US Power*; and Stephen D. Krasner, *Asymmetries in Japanese–American Trade: The Case for Specific Reciprocity* (Berkeley: Institute of International Studies, 1987).

5. On mercantilism and rent-seeking, see Robert B. Ekelund and Robert D. Tollison, *Mercantilism as a Rent-Seeking Society: Economic Regulation in Historical Perspective* (College Station: Texas A & M University Press, 1981). For mercantilism as a weapon against Dutch hegemony, see Charles Wilson, *Profit and Power: A Study of England and the Dutch Wars* (New York: Longmans, Green, 1957).

6. The complex politics of the repeal of the Corn Laws are examined through endogenous tariff theory in Cheryl Schonhardt, 'Politics, Politicians, and Policymaking: Domestic Determinants of the Repeal of the Corn Laws', Ph.D. dissertation, UCLA, forthcoming.

7. A.A. Iliasu, 'The Cobden–Chevalier Commercial Treaty of 1860', *Historical Journal*, **14**, March 1971, pp. 67–98.

8. Charles P. Kindleberger, 'The Rise of Free Trade in Western Europe', *The Journal of Economic History*, **35**, 1, March 1975, pp. 20–55. For a view which questions the importance of British hegemony in creating the free trade regime of the nineteenth century, see Timothy J. McKeown, 'Hegemonic Stability Theory and Nineteenth Century Tariff Levels in Europe', *International Organization*, **37**, 1, Winter 1983, pp. 73–91.

9. See Peter A. Gourevitch, 'International Trade, Domestic Coalitions, and Liberty: Comparative Responses to the Crisis of 1876–1896', *Journal of Interdisciplinary History*, **8**, Autumn 1977, pp. 281–313; and Percy Ashley, *Modern Tariff History: Germany–United States–France* (New York: Dutton, 1920).

10. On the United States, see Lake, *Power, Protection and Free Trade*, pp. 91–118. On the Anglo–German competition, see Ross J. S. Hoffman, *Great Britain and the German Trade Rivalry, 1875–1914* (Philadelphia: University of Pennsylvania Press, 1933).

11. On late nineteenth-century Britain, see Eric J. Hobsbawm, *Industry and Empire: The Making of English Society*, Vol. 2, *1750 to the Present* (New York: Pantheon, 1968).

12. These are reviewed in Lake, *Power, Protection and Free Trade*, pp. 178–82.

13. See Kindleberger, *The World in Depression*.

14. This discussion follows from Lake, *Power, Protection and Free Trade*.

15. For a brief treatment of American hegemony and international openness, see Keohane, *After Hegemony, inter alia*, pp. 135–216.

16. See Edward John Ray, 'Changing Patterns of Protectionism: The Fall in Tariffs and the Rise in Non-Tariff Barriers', *Northwestern Journal of International Law and Business*, **8**, 2, Fall 1987, pp. 285–327.

17. See Lake, *Power, Protection and Free Trade*, pp. 149–52 and 163–6.

18. John A. Hobson, *Imperialism: A Study* (1902; third ed rev., London: G. Allen and Unwin, 1938); V.I. Lenin, *Imperialism: The Highest Stage of Capitalism* (New York: International Publishers, 1939).

19. On asset specificity and opportunism, see Oliver Williamson, *The Economic Institutions of Capitalism* (New York: Free Press, 1985). For an application of this argument to international relations, see my 'Predatory States and the Pursuit of International Security', UCLA, mimeo, 6 April 1988.

20. See Duncan Snidal, 'Limits of Hegemonic Stability Theory', Mancur Olson and Richard Zeckhauser, 'An Economic Theory of Alliances', *Review of Economics and Statistics*, **48**, 3, August 1966, pp. 266–79. I am aware of the criticism that free trade is not a collective good. See John A.C. Conybeare, 'Public Goods, Prisoners' Dilemmas, and the International Political Economy', *International Studies Quarterly*, **28**, 1, March 1984, especially pp. 8–9; and Arthur A. Stein, 'The Hegemon's Dilemma: Great Britain, the United States and the International Economic Order', *International Organization*, **38**, 2, Spring 1984, pp. 355–86. Yet, this criticism mis-reads the theory of hegemonic stability. Kindleberger, in *The World in Depression*, for instance, did not write that free trade was a collective good, but that certain infrastructural needs were — such as a reserve asset, international finance and a market for distress goods. These needs, in turn, have attributes of a collective good — or at least substantial positive externalities — which lead to their under-supply in the absence of a hegemonic leader willing to provide the necessary service. This argument is developed further in my *Power, Protection, and Free Trade*, pp. 33–8.

21. These figures are from Kenneth N. Waltz, *Theory of International Politics* (Reading, MA: Addison-Wesley, 1979), p. 212.

22. Figures are from Krasner, 'State Power and the Structure of International Trade'.

23. On challengers to hegemony, see Mark Brawley, 'Challenging Hegemony: How Cycles of Hegemony, Hegemonic Decline, Major War and Hegemonic Transitions are linked', Ph.D. dissertation, UCLA, 1989.

24. See Lake, *Power, Protection , and Free Trade*, pp. 148–83.

25. See Scott C. James and David A. Lake, 'The Second Face of Hegemony: Britain's Repeal of the Corn Laws and the American Walker Tariff of 1846', *International Organization*, **43**, 1, 1989, pp. 1–29.

26. See Lake, *Power, Protection , and Free Trade*, pp. 91–147.

27. See Keohane, *After Hegemony*.

28. See also Stephen D. Krasner, ed., *International Regimes* (Ithaca: Cornell University Press, 1983).

29. See, for instance, Richard N. Cooper, 'Trade Policy is Foreign Policy', *Foreign Policy*, No. 9, Winter 1972–73, pp. 18–36.

30. Gilpin, *US Power*.

31. See Joanne Gowa, 'Rational Hegemons, Excludable Goods, and Small Groups: An Epitaph for Hegemonic Stability Theory?', *World Politics*, **41**, 3, April 1989, pp. 307–42; and 'Bipolarity, Multipolarity and Free Trade', *American Political Science Review*, **83**, 4, December 1989, 1245–56.

32. See Robert Pahre, 'The Process of Hegemonic Leadership in Economic and Security Affairs', Ph.D. dissertation, UCLA, forthcoming.

33. For a recent review of the political issues created by intra-industry trade, see Charles Lipson, 'The Transformation of Trade: The Sources and Effects of

Regime Change', in Krasner, ed., *International Regimes*, pp. 233–71.
34. See Elhanan Helpman and Paul R. Krugman, *Market Structure and Foreign Trade: Increasing Returns, Imperfect Competition and the International Economy* (Cambridge: MIT Press, 1985).
35. Gilpin, *US Power*.
36. See Helen Milner, 'Trading Places: Industries for Free Trade', *World Politics*, **40**, 3, April 1988, pp. 50–76; and G.K. Helleiner, 'Transnational Enterprises and the New Political Economy of US Trade Policy', *Oxford Economic Papers*, **29**, 1, 1977.
37. See I.M. Destler and John S. Odell, *Anti-Protection: Changing Forces in United States Trade Politics* (Washington: Institute on International Economics, 1987).
38. Robert Axelrod, *The Evolution of Cooperation* (New York: Basic Books, 1984). On the effects of uncertainty, imperfect information and misperception, see George W. Downs, David M. Rocke and Randolph M. Siverson, 'Arms Races and Cooperation', in Kenneth A. Oye, ed., *Cooperation Under Anarchy* (Princeton: Princeton University Press, 1986), pp. 118–46.

7 *Being a borrower: the re-emergence of the United States as a debtor nation*
Diane B. Kunz

It cannot be a law that all nations shall fall after a certain number of years. God does not work in that sort of way; they must have broken some law of nature which has caused them to fall. But are all nations to sink in that way? As if national soil, like the soil of the earth must lie fallow after a certain number of crops.

(Florence Nightingale, Letters From Egypt)1

In 1985 a milestone was reached: from being the world's largest creditor nation the United States transformed itself into a debtor on international account, a position it had jettisoned during the First World War. Thereafter, the American financial position has continued to deteriorate. Its balance of payments deficits have grown worse while simultaneously, individually and as a nation, Americans have embarked on a massive borrowing binge. The statistics tell a frightening story. During the two decades before 1982 total debt had held steady at 160 per cent of Gross National Product. But in the years 1982–6 the ratio of total debt to GNP leapt to 200 per cent.[2] In 1981 the federal deficit stood at what then seemed the frightening figure of $79 billion. During the Reagan years, however, it ranged from a low of $128 billion in 1982 to a high of $221 billion in 1986; the average for the years 1982–7 was $184 billion.[3] At the same time American corporate debt has grown apace. More worryingly, borrowers spent much of the money not on productive investment but on costly takeover battles. Increasingly the United States has relied on foreigners to fund these massive amounts.

Although eschewed in the 1988 presidential election, this problem has been the subject of numerous articles and books; for example, Felix Rohatyn in the *New York Review of Books*, Peter Peterson's series in *The Atlantic*, and *Day of Reckoning* by Benjamin Friedman. The eroding American financial position has also contributed to the popularity of such books as *The Rise and Fall of the Great Powers* by Paul Kennedy which discusses the change in the position of the United States within a historical framework. These accounts had in common a negative assessment of current American policies. In contrast, during the last eighteen months a more optimistic view has emerged. The most elaborate exposition of this approach is found in *The Debt and the Deficit* by Robert Heilbroner and Peter Bernstein.[4] The authors indicate their viewpoint by their subtitle, 'False Alarms/Real Possibilities'.

As Heilbroner and Bernstein point out, the twin deficits and the issues of public and private debt have often been confused and confounded. They can be clarified. It is possible, using historical analogies, to show what might result when the financial grasp of the world's leading power exceeds its reach. As decision-makers in Washington consider how to cope with the implications of the mounting tide of debt for American global policies, the example of Great Britain, specifically two dissimilar ways in which it coped with financial crisis during the twentieth century, provides useful instruction. Both in 1931 and 1956 the British economic plight took center stage. Different reasons had brought matters to that point; as a result British governments made different decisions. Each example has its lessons for American policy-makers today. However, the objective is not to find an exact road map for the future. History is not biology — patterns do not exactly replicate themselves. Rather, by examining two examples of how another nation attempted to cope with the same problem, officials can examine the effects of being a borrower on a leading world power in two distinct situations.

Prior to 1914 London had been the unquestioned center of the world financial community. One of the many changes wrought by the Great War was the erosion of Britain's financial position. A total war expenditure of £8,215 million above the £1,000 million estimated as the total peacetime budget for the period 1914–18 ensured that Britain's post-war financial house would not be in order. Exacerbating London's difficulties, only about 10 per cent of the cost had been paid by taxation.[5] Borrowing, both from other governments and on world markets, had paid for the rest.[6] Potentially this financial state of affairs could have led to post-war retrenchment. However, Britain's responsibilities during the immediate post-war period expanded; with the granting of various League of Nations mandates, ever more areas of the globe were colored red. Among other things, this expansion had the effect of hiding Britain's true financial position from itself. Psychological factors also inhibited British officials from admitting that their nation was no longer the financial titan that it had been. Moreover, the large overhang of outstanding debt combined with the obvious indications of the serious erosion of Britain's industrial supremacy created a general consensus that rebuilding the position of the City of London was imperative.

Therefore, the most important task for British government and financial leaders appeared to be the return of sterling to the gold standard, from which it had slipped during the war.[7] Even before the war's end the Committee on Foreign Exchanges After the War (known as the Cunliffe Committee) declared: 'In our opinion it is imperative that after the war the conditions necessary to the maintenance of an effective gold standard should be restored without delay.'[8] That this statement represented a generally held consensus of opinion became increasingly clear during the seven years from the war's end that it took for Britain to return to the gold standard. During the first decade following the Versailles Treaty of 1919 it also became apparent that politicians remained content to accept the bifurcation stated by Montagu Norman, Governor of the Bank of England: they would deal with the political issues while the Bank dealt with fiscal matters. Such a division of responsibility pleased Conservative, Liberal and Labour politicians alike who, by delegation, could rid themselves of much of the burdensome problems associated with budgetary decisions. It would take the 1931 crisis for them to realize that they had also renounced a considerable amount of power.

Norman cultivated their passivity. He had a *Weltanschauung* that prescribed cooperation between central banks built around a reconstituted gold standard and its variant, the gold exchange standard, which would extend the influence of the Bank of England and the City of London. On 28 April 1925, with the help of Norman's allies, Governor Benjamin Strong of the New York Federal Reserve Bank (FRBNY) which served as the American central bank for international transactions, and the bankers who were members of the House of Morgan, the pound was returned to the gold standard at the pre-war parity of £1 = \$4.86.[9]

One of the most interesting aspects of Britain's return to the gold standard is that there was no discussion about returning to a gold standard at a lower parity, as the French government would later do. Because British policy-makers intended that the pound regain its formerly unchallenged financial supremacy, they refused to take an action which would have seemed like admitting defeat before the exercise had begun. For the first eighteen months after the return to gold, the Bank of England encountered smooth waters. But after January 1927 Norman faced continual turmoil as he strove to keep the pound on the gold standard. Many different factors were responsible; these included the effects of the war on both Britain and the European economy, the war debts and reparations imbroglio, the rise of the American economy, and the problems of Third World economies.

Among other things, Norman enlisted American help to keep the pound on the gold standard. The July 1927 summit of central bankers remains perhaps the most notable example of such cooperation. As this Long Island meeting, Strong agreed to lower the FRBNY's discount rate in order to encourage funds to flow to London.[10] Unfortunately, the succeeding year proved even worse for the Bank of England and the British economy as the Wall Street boom sucked ever larger amounts of funds into the call money market. It was for this reason that Keynes, in response to the Wall Street crash, could say: 'We in Great Britain cannot help heaving a big sigh of relief at what seems like the removal of an incubus which has been lying heavily on the business life of the whole world outside America.'[11]

But the world financial situation continued to deteriorate and the

British economy continued to nosedive through 1930. The 1931 financial failures which began with the collapse of Austria's Creditanstalt Bank in May 1931 proved a significant blow especially as a panic at the German Reichsbank followed immediately. That led to the 13 July failure of the Danat Bank and the closing of all German financial institutions.

That day, 13 July 1931, was a crucial one for Britain as well: it marked the publication of the report of the Committee on Finance and Industry, popularly known as the Macmillan Committee. This report revealed, among other things, that the exposure of British banks to borrowers was £267 million or almost twice Britain's gold reserves which fluctuated between £130 and £150 million.[12] As much of this lending had been to German borrowers, the winds of financial panic now blew across to London where the Bank of England began losing gold at an alarming rate. Norman arranged to borrow £25 million from both the FRBNY and the Bank of France. However, these unprecedentedly large credits did not suffice. Several factors kept gold reserves flowing out of London. Chief among them was the publication on 31 July 1931 of the May Report, which indicated that the British government had a deficit of £120 million.

The Labour government headed by Ramsay MacDonald found itself ill equipped to face this crisis. The Conservative Party simply accepted the dogma that sound money and the gold standard were financial and moral imperatives. MacDonald and his colleagues questioned the effect of this philosophy but had no alternative system of beliefs to justify jettisoning the gold standard. The immediate problem faced by the government in August 1931 was that, according to the Bank of England, Britain required immediate new loans from private American bankers. However, Bank officials also informed the Prime Minister that such credits would neither be efficacious nor even obtainable unless the Cabinet authorized significant budget cuts. Given the nature of the British budget these reductions could only come from unemployment benefits. The Labour cabinet split eleven to nine over this issue. The next day MacDonald, at the request of King George V, formed a national government. Composed of representatives of all three parties, saving the gold standard provided its *raison d'être*.

One month later, on 21 September, despite massive private American and French credits of £80 million ($400 million), the British government announced that it was going off the gold standard. What had happened? The story told for fifty years was that Britain was pushed off the gold standard by the flood of speculation which had engulfed sterling. In reality it would appear that Norman and his associates, believing that the battle to stay on the gold standard could only further erode British strength, decided that once the borrowed monies had been used up, a strategic retreat was the best offense.[13]

Thus ended Britain's thirteen-year struggle to regain its financial primacy. Instead of being the leader of an integrated world system, Britain now was yet another nation following the path of autarky. Yet, instead of depressing Britain both economically and psychologically, this change proved to be a totally liberating event for Britain's economy and society. The 1930s were a far more prosperous decade for Britain than the previous decade had been. In large part the cheap money policy which kept the Bank rate at 2 per cent from July 1932 until September 1939 deserved credit for the recovery. Not only did the low cost of funds allow a massive construction boom which transformed the face of Britain, but it also fueled a consumer boom which greatly increased ownership of automobiles, radios and domestic appliances.

What factors made it possible for Britain to adapt so well to these changed conditions? The first is that the fight to maintain the gold standard had been the incubus around Britain's neck. Walking away from the battle had proved immensely liberating for the nation, both economically and psychologically. Policy-makers knew that, given the current political and economic realities, Britain would continue to wield a strong influence in monetary circles. Indeed, over twenty countries followed Britain off the gold standard. Comprised of the Empire, Commonwealth and Scandinavian countries, they joined together in the so-called 'sterling bloc', linking their currencies to the pound instead of the dollar. Britain thereby retained much of the influence which it had enjoyed while on the gold standard without many of the problems. The sterling bloc also helped Britain in another way — it formed the nucleus of the countries which together with Britain joined in the Ottawa agreements of October 1932 which created an imperial preference system. Erecting tariff walls protected the trade of Britain, its Empire and Commonwealth.

That the early 1930s was a period of *sauve qui peut*, when each country pursued its own strategy as best it could, helped make Britain's chosen path tenable. British leaders faced neither domestic nor foreign criticism for being the country which had wrecked international monetary cooperation. Moreover, London could not lose out in the race to be the center of world finance — in the 1930s no one center could exist.

Finally, the British government and financial circles easily accepted the departure from the gold standard because the strength of sterling did not yet represent an indispensable element of prestige. Inter-war British society did not doubt its pre-eminence in the way it would be forced to do after the Second World War. To the extent that the British leadership or public needed reassurance as to Britain's importance, indications were readily available, particularly the Empire whose viability as a whole was not yet doubted. Twenty-five years later the situation would be very different.

The financial effects of the Second World War on Britain were in some ways the most devastating of the conflict. From a net creditor, Britain ended the war as the world's largest debtor. Among other things, London had in large measure paid for the war through enforced loans, known as 'sterling balances', from the Empire and the Commonwealth. Virtually bankrupt, the British government was forced to go to the United States, hat in hand, for a loan in the autumn of 1945.[14] This credit of $3.75 billion did not suffice to protect the British government from a major financial crisis in 1947 — only the American Marshall Plan enabled Britain to avoid financial disaster. Nonetheless the British government was forced to devalue the pound in September 1949 from £1 = $4.03 to £1 = $2.80.

The 1950s brought a renewed British determination to retain the sterling area and to maintain the system whereby sterling remained the most frequently used international trading currency. In part economic self-interest provided the explanation for this policy. During the early post-war period Britain's trade with the Empire and the Commonwealth greatly expanded.[15] But psychological factors played an equally important role. In British minds the sterling area and the strength of the pound had begun to serve as a major factor which could offset the difference in power between the United States and the Soviet Union on the one hand, and Britain on the other.

The British government, during the 1950s, continued to emphasize the important role of sterling and the sterling area. The Bank of England, therefore, now under government control, returned the pound to de facto convertibility in February 1955. Sterling almost immediately confronted serious difficulties. British reserves of dollars and gold were not very large, hovering around $2,000–$2,400 million, and they were declining as a percentage of British trade in goods.[16] The British economy also faced strong inflationary pressures which led many holders of sterling to doubt whether the current exchange rate could be maintained. With the dollar shortage ending, non-resident holders of sterling could choose alternative currencies; that many foreigners had been severely burnt by the 1949 devaluation stimulated a tendency to move out of sterling sooner rather than later. To stem the pressure on the pound the British government raised the Bank rate during 1955, thereby resorting to the use of this tool for the first time since 1931. However, the strain on sterling remained fearsome until February 1956 and then only partially subsided.

The end of the Second World War had brought also the beginning of severe pressure on Britain to begin a retrenchment from empire; this process began in 1947 when India and Pakistan were granted independence. In 1954 the Conservative government signed the Anglo–Egyptian Base Accord which stipulated that Britain would evacuate its Suez Canal base by June 1956. Foreign Secretary, Sir Anthony Eden was one of the main movers behind this agreement. He had realized that Britain had neither the military nor financial capability to remain in Egypt indefinitely. However, when Gamel Abdul Nasser nationalized the Suez Canal on 26 July 1956, a combination of motives led Eden, now Prime Minister, to decide that military force should be used to regain control over the Canal.[17]

The United States successfully managed to restrain Britain until 29 October 1956 when the unlikely trio of Britain, Israel and France executed a plot to invade Egypt.[18] President Eisenhower and his colleagues were furious both at being misled and at the stupidity of the British plan.[19]

After all, if they were unable to hold onto the base, how could they control all of Egypt? The American administration also thought that this move could undermine all Western influence in the area.

Ordinarily the negative opinion of an ally about a country's decisions is regrettable but not tragic. In this case, however, the Eisenhower administration's determination that 'in these circumstances perhaps we cannot be bound by our traditional alliances' was catastrophic for Britain.[20] Britain depended on the United States in 1956 for surplus food and for the military equipment it used in the Suez invasion. If Middle Eastern oil supplies were cut off, the United States would have to make up the difference. Finally, if British reserves proved insufficient to support sterling, the only country which could make up the shortfall would be the United States.

The strain on sterling had started as soon as Nasser had nationalized the Canal. Indeed, one of the reasons for Britain placing economic sanctions on Egypt was to prevent Egypt from withdrawing its sterling from London.[21] Ironically these measures hurt Britain more than they hurt Egypt. By August Britain's balance of payments position had clearly suffered. As both public officials and private investors considered trade deficit figures an important indication of the position of sterling such a deterioration boded ill for the pound's future.

The British government might have taken various preliminary steps such as obtaining a drawing from the International Monetary Fund or a loan from the United States. But British officials found themselves caught in a bind. Any such measures would advertise the weakness of sterling and could tend to encourage holders to sell sterling. These sales would exacerbate the drain of reserves a drawing or other action was designed to prevent. Of course the British government could have suspended the progress which had been made towards convertibility. But officials rejected this option for several reasons. The first was the ever greater importance which the British placed on the sterling area and the position of the pound. Indeed, one Bank of England official said that the British should forcibly intervene in the Suez affair in order to safeguard sterling and the sterling area.[22] Furthermore, with other European countries groping towards convertibility and with the West German economy increasingly challenging that of Britain, the British government feared that its still pre-eminent financial position in Europe would be sacrificed if it permitted any regression from convertibility.

During November 1956 the British government's obsession with the position of sterling enabled the Eisenhower administration to force Eden's government to agree to an Anglo–French withdrawal from Egypt.[23] After the United States supported a United Nations resolution condemning the invasion, the British cabinet, notwithstanding the fact that a majority of ministers believed that a forceful capture of the Suez Canal was a vital national interest, agreed on 6 November to a cease-fire. But having misread American intentions throughout the crisis, Eden and his colleagues misunderstood the American position once again. They thought that their agreeing to a cease-fire would lead to immediate American aid to Britain. However, the Eisenhower administration insisted than an actual Anglo–French troop withdrawal from Egypt remain the prerequisite for any American assistance. The American government had no intention of permitting a *sub rosa* victory for its erstwhile ally.

By the middle of November British reserves had declined by $200 million dollars. Such a drain ensured that, even if no further losses during the month occurred, British reserves by 1 December would be below $2,000 million, the minimum amount considered acceptable for sterling. Both the British and American governments realized that the second half of the month would be decisive.

The only country with sufficient resources to help Britain was the United States. Washington controlled both the World Bank and the International Monetary Fund. The New York capital markets would bow to the administration's wishes and other markets were in their infancy or non-existent. Communist sources were obviously unavailable. Yet United States officials for a time refused even to see the British ambassador. As Lord Harcourt, the Economic Minister at the British embassy in Washington informed London: 'We meet a blank wall at every turn with the administration.'[24] American officials remained furious over the British 'betrayal'. They also believed that the Suez invasion had presented the United States with a unique opportunity to free itself of guilt by association with the colonialist powers and forge links with the Arab world. The Eisenhower administration, then, determined not to aid Britain until it agreed that Anglo–French forces would be withdrawn from Egypt.

Consequently, Britain was left to twist slowly in the wind. An announcement of the British reserves was due on 4 December. If it showed a decline below the $2,000 million mark, the British government feared that a real run on the pound might develop, forcing Britain to devalue sterling. Investors agreed with this gloomy forecast; 20 and 21 November proved the worst days yet, with the Bank of England losing a total of $48 million.[25] Finally, on 27 November, United States secretary of the treasury George Humphrey agreed to discuss substantive proposals to aid the British once France and Britain withdrew their troops from Egypt. Anglo–American discussions continued up to the deadline. On 3 December the British government finally committed itself to a troop withdrawal in a fashion which satisfied Eisenhower that the British and French governments 'had gone adequately to meet the requirements'.[26] Therefore, on the next day when Chancellor of the Exchequer Harold Macmillan revealed in the House of Commons that British reserves stood at $1,965 million, he was also able to announce that the American government had promised massive financial support; a loan from the United States Export-Import Bank, American support for a British drawing from the International Monetary Fund, and favorable consideration of a British request for a waiver of payments under the

Anglo–American loan agreement of 1945. This assistance allowed the British government to retain the pound at £1 = \$2.80. Thereafter the British government struggled through a series of financial crises which regularly threatened the position of sterling. Devaluation finally came in 1967 and with it the end of the sterling area.

Eden had insisted that the Suez invasion was necessary to protect Britain's vital interests. Yet he and his ministers agreed to sacrifice their plans in order to save the sterling parity and the sterling area. Why did British leaders place so much emphasis on monetary considerations? The answer is twofold. First, the British have always had a strong attachment to a high exchange rate. The strength of the pound was historically of great benefit to important sectors of the British economy, especially the financial activities of the City of London. However, as time went on the preference for a high exchange rate became more generalized and certainly helped blind policy-makers to the advantage of other choices. This attitude is especially striking because the experience of the 1930s with a floating exchange rate had been so positive. Yet a quarter of a century later the knowledge so dramatically revealed during the 1930s had been virtually forgotten.

Other nations, however, take a different view. In Germany, the rate of inflation during the twentieth century has been the most important financial indicator. The hyper-inflation of the 1920s having burnt itself into the German memory, any increase in the inflation rate sends shock waves throughout the economy. Furthermore, post-war German governments preferred a low exchange rate in order to stimulate exports.

Second, the increased economic linkage between Britain and its Empire and the Commonwealth during the post-war period provided a further reason for the increased emphasis during the 1950s on the position of the pound. Of equal importance was the spiraling growth of the sterling area as a substitute for the more tangible evidence of strength the British lacked. An ostensible victor in the Second World War, Britain clearly could no longer compete with the United States and the Soviet Union. But when followers of Halford Mackinder began to push for stronger imperial ties in order to compensate for the greater land mass of the United States or the Soviet Union, they never envisioned such a tremendous emphasis on the position of sterling. As time went on, rather than serving to bind Britain to its Empire and the Commonwealth, the pound became a millstone around Britain's neck. Encouraging so many foreigners to hold sterling made it a hostage to their fortunes and thus left the British economy subject to the vagaries of both its own and other economies. The result was the disastrous 'stop-go' or 'zig-zag' economy which plagued Britain for the three decades after the Second World War.

There were options; Britain could have gone to a floating rate pound or lowered the exchange rate to a more reasonable level.[27] But the British government had been warned by Commonwealth central bankers that either scheme would mean the end of the sterling area.[28] At a time when British strength was eroding in so many other ways, British policy-makers simply could not view such a policy change as an alternative to be pursued.

These historical examples, from 1931 and 1956, demonstrate two different British responses to the same problem — a currency which was overvalued held by a country which was overextended. What relevance, if any, do these examples hold for the United States of the 1990s? The answer is that in their own way, each example can help illuminate a depressing worst-case scenario facing the American people during the next decade.

The example of Britain's decision in 1931 to leave the gold standard has several things to offer policy-makers. Historians point to the chaos of the inter-war era, to which Britain contributed as much as anyone else, as an example of what happens to the world monetary system if there is no clear leader willing to be the lender of last resort.[29] Britain fulfilled this function prior to 1914, the United States after the Second World War. However, just as Britain was unable to continue its traditional role in the wake of the First World War and the United States was unwilling to step into the void, thus crippling the world economy in the 1920s and 1930s, so the United States can no longer fulfil this function today. Japan, the country which now possesses sufficient financial resources to play such a role, is not ready to assume these responsibilities. Furthermore, just as the Bank of England wanted to retain global financial leadership, so the United States is not ready to renounce its power.

The financial crisis which hit Britain during the summer of 1931 had both an international and a domestic component: the foreign element was the collapse of the Central European banking system; the domestic component was the massive (for its time) British budgetary deficit. Both these aspects are present today. Ever larger Third World debts have continued to strain the international banking system. Notwithstanding significant attempts to ameliorate the situation, American banks (and with them the American economy) remain at risk from the massive amount of overdue Third World loans. The American savings and loans system is in crisis. Another shock such as higher American interest rates could wreck the precarious balance.[30] Furthermore, a series of open foreign defaults might even bring down the American and world financial systems in the same way as the failure of the Creditanstalt destroyed the inter-war financial order.

The domestic element of the British crisis — a very large budget deficit — is also present today. Indeed Alan Greenspan, Chairman of the Federal Reserve Board, has said that the health of the American economy is imperiled by the deficit.[31] Among other things, the deficit crowds out private borrowers and also increases American dependence on foreigners. In 1931 the need to borrow money from abroad forced the Labour government to accept the values of its lenders which in this particular case meant a slashing of unemployment benefits. Because banks have made adherence to an IMF austerity program a prerequisite to refinancings and new money loans, Third World countries during the 1980s have been repeatedly forced to learn this lesson. Now the United States may be forced to swallow the same medicine.

The British government and the Bank of England ultimately liberated themselves from the incubus of the gold standard. However, it seems very doubtful that the United States could follow the same route today and opt out of the world monetary system. First of all, there is no substitute such as the sterling area which buoyed the British economy after 1931. Indeed, with the coming 1992 European integration, the United States will find itself increasingly needing to woo other massive blocs which soon may need the United States less than it needs them. The Common Market's evolution provides another reason for mounting American problems: no longer will the United States and the Soviet Union alone possess the advantages of a large land mass and vast internal markets without interfering national borders.[32]

Further, given the structure of the American economy, it seems highly unlikely than an autarkic policy would be feasible. As the world economy has grown more interdependent in general, the United States's economy in particular has become integrally linked with those of other nations. Forgetting such items as consumer goods and Japanese cars, the American economy is dependent on foreign suppliers. Undoubtedly a separation would throw the American economy into recession, at the very least.

Britain's experiences during the Suez crisis of 1956 are even more directly relevant to the United States. While the American public is not as psychologically bound up with the American exchange rate as was the British, other factors make the two situations similar. Britain's policy choices were circumscribed by its lack of economic resources. Financial dependency on the United States brought political vassalage. Furthermore, because the British government did not feel able to break from the United States, both countries understood after 1956 that the British position was behind and never in front of the United States.

Today the United States is facing a similar situation. As of 1987 foreigners held one-tenth of America's national debt, an amount that has continuously increased. Lest that sum seem inconsequential, it should be recalled that the Securities and Exchange Commission considers 5 per cent ownership to be significant enough to require reporting and observation. Foreign investment in the United States has climbed from $196 billion in 1974 to $1.5 trillion in 1987.[33] Suppose that Japanese, German and British investors, to name some of the biggest, decide to sell dollars until the American government followed a policy of their choosing? We have already seen examples when Japan's reluctance to purchase United States Treasury bills has sent the American government into a panic.[34] Suppose at a future auction, that the Japanese government, either alone or in concert with European nations, suggests that it might refuse to purchase new Treasury bills unless Washington undertook certain actions? While a United States administration would probably find it relatively easy to cope with outright pressure, less subtle suggestions concerning a possible alteration in American policy might be more difficult to fend off.

To be sure, the British examples under discussion provide a worst-case scenario. But even if the results from the changes in the American financial position are less dramatic, the ever mounting American reliance on foreign money will surely circumscribe the political and economic freedom of action to which this country has become accustomed during the last seventy-five years. Foreigners are increasingly trading in their American IOUs for hard assets. It is not without significance that Japanese investors own large chunks of Honolulu, 30 per cent of the real estate of Los Angeles and perhaps the ultimate symbol of the 'American Century' the Rockefeller Center.

The growth in American dependence on foreign and foreign-owned plants cuts across the board but has an especially serious effect on weapons procurement. Many commentators who dispute the seriousness of the deficit point to American military strength as a decisive difference between the American and British cases. But they fail to consider adequately the effect of America's financial troubles on its military position. Budget restraints and constraints make it difficult to develop and purchase new weapons systems. Such systems which are developed increasingly depend on foreign technology for component parts. Most importantly, the American deficit has caused the Reagan and Bush administrations increasingly to emphasize burden-sharing, which translates into a determination to push Japan and West Germany into picking up ever greater shares of the cost of military defense. Forcing its allies to 'do their part' may play well during election campaigns but policy-makers will soon be forced to face the fact that these nations will rightly demand a far greater say in the way their money and manpower is allocated. Furthermore, at a time of great change in the international system, the possible disturbing implications of a rapidly rearming West Germany (now a united Germany) and Japan are clear.

Equally ominously, the American finance and service sector, which was meant to lead the nation triumphantly into the twenty-first century, is finding itself overwhelmed by foreign, especially Japanese, competition. The disparity in financial resources is striking. For example, in the two years since the crash of October 1987, American banks have raised $5.7 billion in equity while in the same period eight major Japanese banks raised over $22 billion.[35] A country which is dominant in neither industry nor finance cannot retain its position as the leading country in the world. Clearly the American-led world monetary system will be transformed in major ways over the next decades. Perhaps this evolution is inevitable; perhaps it will prove beneficial to world order. But Americans have grown accustomed to making economic and policy choices for themselves and for others. The United States position of independence and leadership has certainly been diluted if not lost entirely. American policy-makers undoubtedly will be coping with the consequences for the next decades.

Notes

1. Florence Nightingale, *Letters From Egypt: A Journey on the Nile, 1849–1850* (New York, 1987), p. 74.
2. Leonard Silk, 'The US and the World Economy', *Foreign Affairs: America and the World*, **65**, 3, 1987, pp. 458–76.
3. Benjamin M. Freidman, *Day of Reckoning* (New York, 1988), p. 19.
4. R. Heilbroner and P. Bernstein, *The Debt and the Deficit: False Alarms/Real Possibilities* (New York, 1988). See also Jonathan Rauch, 'Is the Deficit Really so Bad?', *The Atlantic*, **263**, 2, February 1989, pp. 36–42; and Milton Freidman, 'Why the Twin Deficits are a Blessing', *Wall Street Journal*, 14 December 1988.
5. R. G. Hawtrey, 'The Cost of War', 12 Aug 1921, Public Record Office (PRO), London, T208/41.
6. For example, by 1918, privately held British debt in the United States amounted to $1,027.3 million.
7. Britain actually officially remained on the gold standard through the war, only going off it in 1919. In fact, however, foreign exchange trading was prohibited throughout the conflict.
8. Cunliffe Committee, 'First Interim Report', 15 Aug 1918, para. 47, PRO, T208/17.
9. The post-war gold standard differed from its pre-war counterpart in that it was a gold bullion standard. Gold coins no longer circulated in Britain.
10. It also remains one of the most notorious examples of such cooperation. Many, both at the time and subsequently, have blamed the later Wall Street boom and crash on this decision. President Herbert Hoover, for one, condemned Strong as a 'mental annex' of Europe (*The Memoirs of Herbert Hoover; The Great Depression*, New York, 1952, p. 10).
11. J. M. Keynes, *The Collected Writings of John Maynard Keynes*, Vol. XX, *Activities 1929–1931* (Cambridge, 1981), p. 1.
12. Report of the Committee on Finance and Industry, July 1931 (London HMSO), Cmd 3897.
13. The story of this fight may be found in Diane B. Kunz, *The Battle for Britain's Gold Standard in 1931* (London, 1987).
14. For the story of the Anglo–American loan agreement of 1945, see, e.g., Richard Gardner, *Sterling–Dollar Diplomacy* (New York, 1969); and Robert Hathaway, *Ambiguous Partnership* (New York, 1983).
15. As Bernard Potter writes: 'Just before the war the empire had accounted for 39.5% of Britain's imports and 49% of her exports. After the war the imperial proportion of what trade she still had left was even greater. 1945–49: imports: 48%, exports: 57.5%; 1950–54: imports: 49%, exports 54%' (*The Lion's Share: A Short History of British Imperialism 1850–1983*, London, 2nd ed, 1984, p. 320.
16. George C. Peden, 'The Political Economy of Britain's Decline 1951–57', unpublished paper, p. 11.
17. These factors included Eden's belief that Nasser was seeking to expunge British influence from the Middle East, Eden's personal loathing of Nasser and the effect of domestic political pressures on Eden.
18. The French government's desire to go to war against Nasser stemmed from the fact that it blamed the Egyptian leader for instigating and supporting the rebellion in Algeria. Israel sought to use this opportunity to try to crush Egyptian power which had been seriously augmented by communist arms sales in September 1955.

19. Israeli troops launched an attack on Egypt on 29 October 1956. Using the pretext that their goal was to separate the combatants, British and French airborne forces landed in Egypt on 5 November. The remainder of their forces landed the next day.
20. Memorandum of Conference with the President, 29 October 1956, John Foster Dulles Papers, Princeton University, Princeton, New Jersey, John Foster Dulles Papers in the Dwight D. Eisenhower Library, WHM Box 4.
21. Both the United States and Britain had placed economic sanctions on Egypt; the British ones were far more sweeping and included the blocking of both governmental and private Egyptian accounts.
22. G. Bolton, 'Sterling and the Suez Canal Situation', 1 Aug 1956, Bank of England, G 1/124.
23. A full account of the American government's pressure on Britain may be found in my *The Economic Diplomacy of the Suez Crisis* (forthcoming).
24. W. Harcourt to Sir Leslie Brown, 19 Nov 1956, B/E, G 1/124.
25. Sir Robert Makins to Harold Macmillan, 22 and 23 Nov 1956, PRO T236/4190.
26. Memorandum of Telephone Conversation with President, 3 Dec 1956, Telephone Conversations Box 5, Dulles Papers, JFD/DDE.
27. The one serious discussion of a floating rate for the pound was the 1952 'ROBOT' scheme. Determined opposition by the Commonwealth countries, which would have seen the value of their sterling balances decline yet again, helped torpedo this plan. See Alec Cairncross, *Years of Recovery: British Economic Policy 1945–51* (Oxford, 1985).
28. C. F. Cobbold to Treasury, 19 Nov 1956, B/E, G1/124.
29. Leading exponent of this view is Charles Kindleberger whose book, *The World in Depression* (Berkeley, 1973) is a classic in monetary history.
30. As these debts are mainly dominated in dollars they are very sensitive to changes in the American economy, especially alterations in American interest rates. For an excellent account of the international debt problem, see Jeffry Frieden, *Banking on the World* (New York, 1987).
31. *New York Times*, 18 November 1988.
32. The Japanese and West German economic miracles would also seem to suggest that the advantages of a large land mass are overrated.
33. Martin and Susan Tolchin, *Buying into America* (New York, 1988), p. 6.
34. Tolchin and Tolchin, pp. 10–11.
35. *New York Times*, 27 October 1989, p. D2.

8 The United States and inter-war money and finance: lessons for Japan's future from America's past*

Jeffry Frieden

Japan is the world's largest international creditor. Its investors finance much of the US government's deficit, and their purchases of American private assets are both economically and politically visible. What private finance is available to the developing world is largely from Japanese lenders. Japanese banks dominate the world financial markets, its securities firms dominate global stock exchanges, and its enormous pool of funds drives interest and exchange rates around the world. Perhaps more than in any other area of the international economy — and perhaps as a reflection of things to come — Japan rules the commanding heights of international finance.

Japan's preponderant international financial position has not been matched by Japanese government involvement in managing the world's monetary and financial system. This parallels Japan's relative invisibility in trade negotiations, outside of bilateral disputes due to its large current account surpluses. From some quarters, indeed, there has been a drumbeat of criticism accusing the Japanese of enjoying the benefits of a stable international economic order while paying few of the costs of preserving that stability. Others argue that the Japanese either should not or cannot do more than they are.

Whatever policy position one prefers in the debate over Japan's 'international responsibilities', it is important to have a reasonable analysis of what these responsibilities are and what determines Japanese policies toward them. This analysis might take many forms, from pure theory to a minutely detailed examination of the Japanese political economy. Or one can take a different tack and look at an analogous historical experience, that of the United States in the inter-war period.

The position of the United States after the First World War, indeed, was similar to that of Japan today in many ways. The United States was the

* The author acknowledges the financial assistance of the German Marshall Fund of the United States and of the Social Science Research Council for research related to this study.

world's leading international lender and investor, its banks and corporations fueling economies around the world. However, the United States refused to accept many of the sorts of 'international responsibilities' that are now being urged on Japan (not least by Americans). There is a widespread belief that this refusal played a major part in precipitating or exacerbating the Great Depression. To analyze inter-war America is to help understand the relationship between a nation's international economic position and its role in managing or stabilizing the international economy — that is to say, whether and why an international economic power takes on some of the duties of international leadership. From there one can consider the implications for the current and future role of Japan, and for international economic cooperation.

The importance of the problem

The moral overtone of debates over 'responsibilities' to the world economy unfortunately charges with emotional content a problem that is more analytical and practical than normative. The issue is how best to ensure that mutually beneficial exchange can be carried out in a world wrought with uncertainty.

Economic activity raises politically controversial problems of two general types, those involving distribution and those involving coordination. The first category is straightforward: no matter how much one believes in the magic of the marketplace, there is no doubt that markets are not always good for everyone. The marketplace can work to savage the wealth of some even while it multiplies that of others. This gives rise to familiar and generally politicized distributional problems of how, or whether, to tax the winners and compensate the losers. Nothing can eliminate the differential distributional effects of the market. The problems they give rise to are important, but for the purposes of this essay they will be ignored.

Another set of issues has to do with coordinating activities that actors agree should be carried out. This might be something as trivial as standardized weights, or something as significant as property rights. Without certain assurances, exchange that might be mutually beneficial will not take place: lenders will not lend unless they expect to be repaid, buyers will not buy unless they expect delivery. There is a range of activity for which coordination is desirable, and this essay focusses on the problem of coordination raised within this range.[1]

International economic interaction gives rise to many coordination problems. Even cross-border economic transactions agreed to be of mutual benefit cannot take place without coordinated efforts to make them feasible. Some way of measuring international payments — gold, national currencies, SDRs — reduces the costs of cross-border transactions to all parties. Security of cross-border contracts encourages international trade and lending, to the advantage presumably of both buyers and sellers, lenders and borrowers. In this sense, it is appropriate to focus on the benefits reaped if leading economic powers cooperate to provide for a stable international environment, as opposed to the costs associated with international economic predation and turmoil. It is reasonable to stipulate that coordination is better than conflict.[2]

To apply this directly to international monetary and financial relations depends to a large extent on cooperation among the nation-states whose citizens play a major role in international trade and payments. Without agreement on an international monetary regime — what will be considered money, and how its value will be determined — cross-border trade and payments are extremely difficult. Without agreement on enforcement of contracts across borders — what constitutes compliance, and how disputes will be mediated — international lending and investment is severely limited.[3]

The biggest problem faced by attempts to cooperate is cheating on agreements, generally known as the problem of 'free riding'. Participants in any coordinated agreement can cheat — an individual can steal property, break contracts, or run red lights. Such individuals presumably do not intend, nor would they support, bringing down the system of private property rights or abolishing traffic laws, but if everyone acts in those ways this would be the inevitable result. Just as cheating occurs domestically, so participants in international coordination can cheat: a country whose currency is used in international payments can inflate, imposing an inflation tax on foreigners holding the currency. And, just as is the case domestically, free riding internationally will undermine the system — even if each member might wish the system to persist.

In the international economy, there may be quite a few such public or collective goods whose provision improves international welfare, but which are subject to the problem of free riding. How many such collective goods there are, and what they are, is controversial. One influential list includes maintaining open goods markets, providing long-term loans in times of economic contraction, supplying short-term loans in times of crisis, stabilizing the exchange rate system, and coordinating domestic monetary policies.[4] For our purposes, the exact composition of the public goods is less important than the more general point that some such goods exist and that their provision is crucial to fruitful international economic exchanges.

It is in this sense that a country's 'responsibilities' toward the international economy can be discussed. Inasmuch as a nation's investors, traders and others benefit from international monetary and financial predictability, it is reasonable to expect them to contribute toward maintaining it. Otherwise the country would be free riding on existing cooperative agreements, taking advantage of them without helping preserve or pay for them. Japan's critics, for example want Japan to play a greater role in monitoring and enforcing international contracts, perhaps bankrolling new debt agreements with Latin America. They also want Japan to take on explicit obligations toward international currency markets, whether by internationalizing its financial system or by intervening to stabilize foreign exchanges. These demands parallel those made upon the United States in the inter-war period. What motivates a country to shoulder its responsibilities, then, is an important analytical question.

Analytical alternatives

National policy towards international economic 'responsibilities' is a subset of foreign policy more generally, for the analysis of which there are many contending approaches. One may focus, however, on two potential explanations, which are clearly within the social-scientific camp that assumes that actors are rational maximizers; the use of them here emphasizes economic utility as the focus of this optimizing behavior. The two positions, international and domestic, are not mutually exclusive, although much of the literature regards them as such.[5]

The first approach emphasizes a world made up of nation-states, and thinks about how these units interact. In this view, each unitary rational state calculates the costs and benefits associated with possible policies, and chooses the policy that maximises the state's returns. International collective action problems — overcoming the temptation to free ride on the cooperation of others — are central to this approach.

To focus on international monetary and financial policies along the lines discussed above, each state will look at what it would gain, in a world of predictable currencies and contracts, from the benefits of international coordination in this issue area. It will then weigh the price it would have to pay toward the provision of this coordination — perhaps its contribution to an intervention fund, or to a contract monitoring and enforcement mechanism. An important part of the state's calculation will be the expected effects of free riding; the more free riding reduces the benefits of coordination, the less tempted the state will be to free ride. If, despite the state's failure to contribute, the agreement holds and the state is able to benefit from it, there is little incentive to contribute. If, on the other hand, the state's failure to contribute causes the agreement to collapse, or leads to the state's exclusion from its benefits, there is a strong incentive to contribute.

In a simple sense, the focus here is on expected 'backwash' effects of failing to cooperate. If a state's cheating on its international agreements creates a massive backwash whose effects outweigh the gains from cheating, the state is likely to maintain its commitments. If, for example, one nation-state's failure to honor its debts led, with certainty, to a collapse of international financial and trading relations, and this collapse was deemed to impose greater losses on the nation-state than the gains from debt default, the rational state would honor its debts. If, on the other hand, one nation's debt default created no generalized backwash, no fallout for world trade and payments, then the nation would not take these considerations into account and would, other things being equal, be more likely to default.[6]

This framework leads to relatively straightforward predictions of national policies toward international monetary and financial cooperation. A country's willingness to contribute to this cooperation will increase as its benefits from cooperation increase, presumably as its exposure to international monetary and financial trends increases. The more a country trades, invests and lends, the more it will value international cooperation in this field and the more willing it will be to pay for it. On the other hand, the higher the cost of cooperating, the less likely the country will be to do so. Finally, the greater the extent to which the country can free ride, that is, avoid the costs of cooperation while enjoying the benefits, the less likely it will be to participate in cooperative ventures. This last situation is a function of a country's importance to international money and finance: cheating by an inconsequential actor will have little impact on the system as a whole, while cheating by one of the great financial powers might bring the system down. Thus, the greater the negative backwash effects of cheating on the cheater, the less likely it will be to cheat.

A perspective that views states as unitary actors in the international monetary and financial systems gives rise to simple predictions about state action. The more integrated a country is into international financial markets, the more likely it will be to contribute to cooperative endeavors. The larger a player the country is in global financial markets, the more likely it will be to contribute to cooperation (instead of free riding). It should be noted that these two are not necessarily related: small countries can be highly integrated into global markets, while large players can be relatively insulated. But the more integrated, the more cooperative, controlling for size; the larger, the more cooperative, controlling for level of integration.[7]

The second analytical approach rejects the assumption that states are unitary actors, and focuses on the domestic level of analysis. In this view, national policy is not made by rational calculation of the national interest, but rather by pressure brought to bear by self-interested socio-economic groups. Such groups prevail upon politicians to undertake policies that may be bad for the country as a whole, but good for some groups. The challenge is to show the interests at play and their effect — what the demands of the various groups will be, and how they will be weighed in the political process.

In the realm of international monetary and financial policy, the interests of domestic groups can be discussed along lines similar to those used to project national interests. Domestic groups for whom international trade and investment is important and beneficial will be inclined to pressure their government to support their overseas activities, including participation in international cooperative ventures. This set of actors includes, most prominently, exporters and those banks and corporations with foreign investments and loans. Groups, on the other hand, who are uninvolved in international trade and investment or who are threatened by them will be indifferent or hostile to attempts to use public funds for international efforts they regard as irrelevant or harmful. The indifferent are those in non-traded goods and services and without overseas investments and markets; the hostile are those industries harmed by foreign competition that would be reduced if international trade and payments were curtailed.

This domestic approach to foreign economic policy expects coalitions to form on the basis of the economic interests at stake. Those who gain most from higher levels of international financial and monetary cooperation will battle for national contributions to this cause; those who do not gain much or who lose from increased international financial activity will oppose such contributions. The outcome will be the result of conflict and bargaining among these economic interest groups, factored through national political institutions.

If the international explanation of foreign policy is correct, then large countries and those more integrated into international finance will play a greater role in international monetary and financial cooperation. If the domestic explanation is correct, then coalitional battles of indeterminate outcome will occur, but their lines will be drawn on the basis of the economic interest of sub-national groups. As will be shown below, the American case does not fit the former explanation well. The United States was roughly as large, and roughly as financially integrated with the rest of the world, after the First World War as it was after the Second World War. Yet it played little part in attempts to stabilize international financial and monetary relations in the former instance, while it took nearly complete control in doing so in the latter case. What had changed were not the characteristics of the nation-state as a unit, but the configuration of coalitional interests within the country and their influence on policy.

America abdicates

The United States dominated international lending and investment in the years after the First World War. Its position of economic leadership was essentially unchallenged, although British acceptance of this position was sometimes grudging. American finance and direct investment drove economic trends in Europe, Latin America and even parts of the colonial world. However, the official attitude of the US government was at best detached, at worst openly hostile to attempts to forge international cooperative agreements in the monetary and financial realms.[8]

By the end of the First World War the United States stood practically alone in international finance. The wartime allies were deeply in debt to the US government, and private American bankers were virtually the only source of foreign capital for the reconstruction and reorganization of European economies. American trade and investment had displaced that of Great Britain in Latin America, and threatened to supplant that of other metropolitan powers in their colonies and protectorates.

The United States was at least as important an actor in the international financial system in the 1920s as it has been over the past forty years. By 1929 the United States accounted for 31 per cent of the stock of all international loans and investments outstanding, the United Kingdom for another 38 per cent.[9] A more accurate measure of relative importance is capital flows, in which the American position was overwhelming. While reliable figures are not available, the United States accounted for well over half of all new international loans and investments in the 1920s. Whether on a stock or a flow basis, the American share of international capital movements was proportionally far greater after the First World War than it has been since the Second World War.

Just as the United States after the First World War dominated international capital flows, so international finance and investment were of relatively great importance to the US economy. Foreign bonds floated on Wall Street averaged over a billion dollars a year in the 1920s, equivalent to more than one-sixth of annual corporate bond flotations. Foreign direct investment averaged over a half-billion dollars a year. In 1922 the stock of overseas loans and direct investments totaled $9.1 billion, equivalent to 12 per cent of the American Gross National Product (GNP). By 1929 they were $15.2 billion, equal to 15 per cent of GNP. In comparison, in 1970 America's overseas loans and direct investments of $119 billion were 12 per cent of GNP, and the 1980 level of $517 billion was 19 per cent. If the latter figures were corrected for peculiarities of modern banking markets, the 1970 figures would fall to $97 billion and 10 per cent, the 1980 figures to $396 billion and 15 per cent.[10] In any event, by any measure foreign lending and investment was at least as important to the United States in the 1920s as it has been in the period since 1945.

The absolute centrality of US loans and investment to the international economy in the 1920s was perfectly clear to contemporaries, as it has been to subsequent observers. American private capital flows were crucial to the post-war reconstruction of Europe, financing one-sixth of all investment in Germany and similar proportions in other Central and Southern European nations. American private bankers arranged and financed stabilization programs that reorganized the economies of Germany, Poland, Rumania, Italy, Belgium, and other nations. In Latin America, an orgy of American private lending and direct investment fed an economic euphoria that came to be knows as 'the dance of the millions'. Princeton economics professor Edwin Kemmerer — the 'money doctor', as he was called — roamed from country to country to supervise national economic policies and certify their reliability to American investors.[11] American oilmen displaced the British and Dutch in Latin America, and moved in on their protected reserves in the Middle East.[12]

Despite the extraordinary prominence of American banks and corporations in the world economy of the 1920s, American public officials were notably absent from most discussions of international economic cooperation. At the Versailles Conference in 1919, the United States under Woodrow Wilson presented elaborate designs for the post-war political and economic order, and the other conferees largely accepted the American plans. However, after Wilson was unable to obtain Congressional approval for American membership in the League of Nations, the United States government essentially deserted the international scene. American official involvement in international economic negotiations was foreclosed by the political predominance, within the United States, of isolationist sentiment. After the League went down to defeat, supporters of a greater role for the US government were unable to prevail in domestic debates over foreign policy. The isolationists dominated the political arena, and there was little that their opponents could do about that.

The deep division over the proper role for US foreign economic policy in the 1920s had its origins in the divergent interests of the country's major economic interest groups.[13] 'Internationalism' was rooted in the new overseas activities of the country's major money-center banks, and its major multinational corporations; it also found support among export-oriented farmers and a few industries with important foreign markets. Internationally oriented bankers and industrialists belonged primarily to the internationalist wing of the Republican Party, or were Wilsonian Democrats; export agriculture was important to the Democratic Party in the South. For these groups, the world economy had come to be significant. They had a clear and present belief that the government should act firmly and aggressively to lead in the stabilization of international economic relations.

First and foremost, the economic internationalists believed that the government should reduce or forgive European war debts to the United States. 'Those debts should be cancelled', J. P. Morgan, Jr. told the *New York Times* in 1922.[14] The allies owed the US government ten billion dollars, and so long as the United States insisted on payment it introduced an element of instability into European financial and monetary affairs. War debts complicated economic policy-making in the former allied countries. They encouraged the French and Belgian governments to press demands for a high level of German reparations, and they reduced the ability of the indebted nations to borrow on private financial markets. All in all, the economic internationalists saw war debts reduction or cancellation as a crucial step that the US government should take to contribute to European economic recovery and international monetary stability. More generally, they believed that the United States government needed to be actively involved in stabilizing and reconstructing European economies and currencies.

Internationally oriented business groups also believed in the need for the United States to reduce its trade barriers. Long a bastion of protection, the United States had begun to liberalize in 1913, but after the First World War protectionist barriers were raised again. Bankers with major overseas loans needed the American market to be open to their debtors, as investment banker Otto Kahn explained: 'Having become a creditor nation we have got now to fit ourselves into the role of a creditor nation. We shall have to make up our minds to be more hospitable to imports.'[15] American exporters feared that continued protection would lead foreigners to close their markets to American products. On both grounds, trade liberalization was desirable.

However, at virtually every step of the way the policy preferences of the economic internationalists were thwarted by the overwhelming opposition of the politically dominant economic isolationists. The socio-economic bases of the isolationist forces lay in those portions of the US economy that remained unconnected to the foreign sector. The rapid expansion of the country's overseas investment and trade was narrowly concentrated in a few economic sectors. The majority of the country's manufacturing industries, and even much of its agriculture, faced serious import competition and had no desire to open the economy any further.[16]

The economic isolationists were adamantly opposed to any trade liberalization, since they feared competitive pressure from abroad. By the same token, they had no desire to see the US government spend taxpayers' money to stabilize or otherwise assist their European competitors. Inasmuch as war debt forgiveness would make European economies more competitive with the United States, it was undesirable; inasmuch as it would reduce the US Treasury income and perhaps require tax increases, it would depress domestic economic activity. On all counts, then, the economic isolationists opposed the positions of the country's internationally integrated banks and corporations.

The isolationists were hardly a fringe group. For all intents and purposes they controlled Congress and most Cabinet positions in the Republican administrations that held office from 1921 to 1933. Economic internationalists were more successful at influencing governmental or quasi-governmental agencies out of the public eye. Foremost among these was the Federal Reserve Bank of New York, which was sympathetic to the interests of the money-center banks. The State Department, too, tended to sympathize with the international businessmen. In both cases, however, participation in attempts at international economic cooperation had to be carried out surreptitiously, for Congress would block whatever it knew was going on.

American official participation in efforts to coordinate national policies toward the international monetary and financial system was severely limited by the political dominance of the economic isolationists at home. The limitations placed on the US government by domestic isolationism made it impossible for official American delegations to be openly involved in the most important international economic negotiations of the period. For example, the all-important stabilization of the German economy, carried out first under the Dawes and then under the Young Plans, required American support, but the US government could not be involved. While the other parties to the agreements were represented by their central banks, the American delegation was composed of partners and friends of J.P. Morgan and Company, which provided the bulk of the original German stabilization loan. When, as part of the Young Plan, the Bank for International Settlements was established in 1930, partly to oversee German finances and partly to provide a framework for international monetary and financial cooperation, again the members were the European central banks and Morgan and Company.

In trade policy, protectionists within the United States generally prevailed. The trend toward liberalization begun under Wilson was reversed by the Republican protectionists, and tariffs were raised in 1921 and 1922. In 1930, the Smoot–Hawley Act raised American tariffs to extremely high levels, and may have contributed to the trade wars that characterized the 1930s.

The inability of the internationalists to get the US government to commit to international cooperative ventures seriously undermined the strength of those ventures. There was something fundamentally unstable about European stabilization programs that were financed by American private bankers with the support of European governments but without the support of the US government. It was also difficult to square the dramatic increases in US overseas lending with the progressive closure of the US market to foreigners, for the dollars to service these debts would directly or indirectly have to be earned by selling in the US market. The refusal of the US government to involve itself in international economic negotiations, and its studied unwillingness to take into account the international consequences of its economic policies, probably contributed to the collapse of the already fragile international monetary, financial and trading orders during the first years of the Depression.

The contrast with American government policy after the Second World War is stark. The evolution of US policy away from economic isolationism probably began with Franklin Roosevelt's inauguration in 1933, although the change was halting and gradual. In 1934 the Reciprocal Trade Agreements Act indicated a willingness to consider commercial liberalization, although trade barriers were reduced only slowly. In 1936 the United States, Great Britain, and France — later joined by Belgium, the Netherlands and Switzerland — negotiated a monetary agreement to stabilize exchange rates. However, it was not until the Second World War itself that the United States began to take firm leadership of international economic organization.

American planning for the post-war economic order began almost immediately after the outbreak of the Second World War. Principles of commercial liberalization were written into such wartime Anglo–American accords as the Atlantic Charter and the Lend-Lease Agreement. The Bretton Woods Agreements completed in 1944 were largely American-inspired, and committed the United States and the world to systematic monetary and financial coordination. The Bretton Woods institutions did not evolve as their architects had planned; one of them — the International Trade Organization — was not approved and was replaced by the General Agreement on Tariffs and Trade. However, they were led by the US government, they were firmly rooted in the economic internationalism of the 1920s, and they clearly involved American leadership for international economic cooperation. And they oversaw a thorough-going liberalization of international trade and payments, in the context of general economic expansion. Despite a similar position in the international monetary and financial system, then, the United States played strikingly different roles in the aftermaths of the First and Second World Wars.

Explaining American abdication

American policies toward the international economy generally, and the international monetary and financial system specifically, were of great importance after both the First and Second World Wars. In the first instance, although American private lenders and investors dominated international capital movements, the government was simply uninvolved in efforts to supervise, coordinate, or otherwise stabilize international monetary and financial affairs. US government inaction almost certainly contributed to the monetary, financial and general economic instability that characterized the inter-war years. In the second period, however, the United States took on major international responsibilities, providing the reserve currency for international trade and payments, and founding and financing international institutions for monetary and financial cooperation. It is probable that this American role contributed to the relatively cooperative character of economic relations among Western countries since the Second World War, and perhaps even to post-war economic growth. This, and fears about future international economic cooperation, makes it important to explain why the United States acted as it did in those two periods. Thus one returns to the two analytical frameworks, at the international level and at the domestic level, to see how they perform.

The fundamental difference between US monetary and financial policy in the years after the two World Wars cannot credibly be ascribed to a fundamental difference in the position of the United States in international finance and investment. Although the world of 1950 was very different from the world of 1920, as was the position of the United States, the differences are not sufficient to explain such divergent policy outcomes. The United States in the 1920s was the world's predominant financial and investment power. The fact that its predominance in 1950 was even clearer does not explain why the government was so supremely uninterested in monetary and financial matters in the fifteen years after the First World War. To return to the backwash theme, it cannot convincingly be argued that the backwash from American isolationism was so much less damaging to the United States in the 1920s than in the 1950s that it was justified in the former period but not in the latter.

It might be argued that American policy-makers were simply poorly informed about the consequences of their action or inaction. In this sense, American policy might have been the result of inadequate recognition of the new realities, of insufficient appreciation of the size of the backwash. This notion is difficult to maintain, for virtually every member of what would eventually become known as the Eastern Establishment agreed on the need for the United States to play a leading international economic role. Wall Streeters were fully aware of the implications of American isolationism, and they included such foreign policy leaders as Dean Acheson, John Foster Dulles, James Forrestal, W. Averell Harriman, Robert Lovett, and John McCloy. These men and their ilk, who ran American foreign economic policy in the 1940s and 1950s were ready and willing to run it in the inter-war years, in very similar ways.[17]

When the Smoot–Hawley Act was before President Hoover in 1930, virtually every major economist in the country signed an open letter arguing persuasively that a significant tariff increase was a bad idea in all senses. The tariff was raised nonetheless. Although virtually every internationally oriented business leader and economist agreed on the need for purposive American policies toward international money and finance in the 1920s and 1930s, such policies were not forthcoming. It was not for lack of information that American inter-war policy-makers 'ignored their international responsibilities'.

It might be argued that American economic leadership materialized in the 1940s due to the Soviet–American antagonism that developed after the Second World War. The problems with this argument are many. First, Woodrow Wilson also justified much of his internationalist program for American leadership on the basis of the Bolshevik threat, but was unable to win support for it. Second, at the time of the evolution of the new American policies (1939–43), the bipolar nature of post-war Europe was far from clear; many American planners expected the British to be far stronger and the Soviets to be far weaker. Third, the United States might have interpreted post-war bipolarity as a license to design a managed or coercive sub-system, as the Soviet Union did. There would seem to be little inevitability about bipolarity breeding economic openness at one of the poles and closure at the other. Where the Cold War probably mattered most was in strengthening the domestic political position of supporters of an American commitment to global economic and political supremacy. The alleged Soviet threat was invoked to convince those who would otherwise have been antagonistic to American international involvement that such involvement was necessary to stop the spread of communism.[18]

The difference between American policy in the 1920s and after the Second World War was due primarily to a different domestic political line-up. The proximate cause was that the economic nationalists lost a series of domestic political battles over the course of the late 1930s and 1940s. The Democrats were traditionally associated with international economic openness — Roosevelt's secretary of state, Cordell Hull, was a committed free-trader — and they dominated the American political scene from 1933 on. Within the Democratic Party, economic nationalism had some supporters, but they were a distinct minority.

Although it seems clear that American policy-makers required domestic political support for this leadership, this leaves open the question of why the internationalists were able to prevail at the domestic level. The 1930s may have produced an ideological association of economic nationalism with conflict and war in the public mind, which dampened enthusiasm for isolationism. But Republicans committed to traditional protection had no difficulty garnering support from heartland industries for economic nationalism. And, after all, the Republicans swept the House and Senate in 1946. A more plausible explanation is that the Second World War largely eliminated the foreign competitors of many of the economic interests that traditionally had been highly nationalistic. By the middle of the war it was clear that the European powers were not going to survive the conflict with their industrial plant intact. By the end of the war the level of destruction was so great that the possibility of significant post-war European competition was nearly out of the question. This changed the market position of many American industries, and dampened their opposition to international economic involvement by the US government. Indeed, the improved competitive position of previously import-competing American firms gave them a new incentive to support American government attempts to stabilize international trade and payments. They now had high hopes of selling to a devastated Europe. A plausible argument would thus be that the Second World War improved the real or potential market position of American economic groups, leading them to drop their opposition to economic internationalism or even to become supporters of it. This helped shift the balance decisively toward support of American international activism.

Whether the specifics of this interpretation are correct or not, the more general implication is that national-interest calculations of the effects of foreign economic policy play relatively little role in determining national policies. No matter how large the expected backwash may be for the country as a whole, if the domestic interests that dominate the policy process are unconcerned about them policy will ignore them. Logically plausible arguments about the putative relationship between size and level of integration in the international financial and monetary systems, on the one hand, and national responsibilities to maintain the systems, on the other, seem to have played little role in the inter-war American case. Domestic distributional divisions, predictable on the basis of the economic situation of the various interest groups involved, seem to have had a much greater impact on policy outcomes.

It is impossible to generalize on the basis of one case. However, this was an important case, with broad international and domestic implications. Similar phenomena seem to be observable in many other parallel situations, in which sub-national distributional interests have a greater effect on foreign economic policy than does some logically derived 'national interest' pursued by the state.[19]

The two analytical approaches are not necessarily mutually exclusive. They might be combined by imputing the sorts of strategic calculations ascribed in the international framework, not to a unitary rational nation-state, but rather to the sub-national interest groups themselves. In this way, for example, the size of the United States in the international monetary and financial system would enter not into calculations by policy-makers trying to maximize national welfare, but rather into calculations by American overseas lenders with a direct interest in the international financial order. The greater the importance of the United States government to international monetary cooperation, the more those groups interested in such cooperation will lobby the US government to provide it. By the same token, the level of integration of the nation-state into the international monetary and financial order would affect calculations about the attractiveness of international economic cooperation not because of policy-makers' attention to national costs and benefits, but because a higher level of integration tends to produce more economic interests that stand to benefit from cooperative national policies. In other words, the strategic components of the international-level approach may be valid, but should be applied not to the nation-state as a whole but to the relevant interest groups affecting state policy.

Conclusions and implications

American inter-war policies toward the international monetary and financial systems were driven primarily by domestic conflicts between those for whom more cooperative foreign economic policies were valuable, and those relatively unconcerned about or opposed to those policies. The latter groups, the economic nationalists and their allies, were politically predominant throughout most of the inter-war period. Although the balance of political power began to shift toward the more internationally oriented groups with the election of Franklin Roosevelt, it was not really until the Second World War that American government policy shifted definitively toward direct leadership of international money and finance. Changing patterns of national economic position played relatively little role. The United States was more or less as important a player in international lending and investment after the First World War as it was after the Second World War; overseas loans and investments were roughly as important to the United States in both periods. Changes in American international economic relations did not affect government policy directly, but rather as they were factored through the particularistic interests of private groups who battled out their differences in the domestic political arena.

The parallel with contemporary Japan is instructive. If the American comparison is valid, it suggests that Japan's new international economic position will affect Japanese foreign economic policy as this position is filtered through the country's domestic socio-economic and political interest groups. Japan is likely to shoulder more of its 'responsibilities' toward international money and finance if and only if there is support from powerful interest groups for this change in policy. The most likely candidates as supporters are, of course, the Japanese banks and corporations that are increasingly important actors in world markets. Inasmuch as they are interested in more active Japanese government policy, and inasmuch as they are able to prevail over domestic groups who oppose this activism, Japanese policy can be expected to evolve in the direction of more international monetary and financial leadership. But this evolution is not inevitable, as the American experience shows.

If the parallel holds, a number of lessons of relevance to those interested in contemporary Japan — either as analysts or as policy-makers — might be drawn. One clear implication is that attempts to force or browbeat Japan into paying more of the costs of international monetary and financial stability may be misguided. Japan's political leaders are hamstrung by domestic socio-economic and political forces, and foreign pressure may be unable to change this balance of forces. Indeed, foreign threats may backfire, for they run the risk of inflaming opposition to Japanese international involvement rather than stimulating support for it. Japanese foreign economic policy is more susceptible to domestic pressures than American or European policy-makers may wish it to be. Just as foreign demands for American international involvement in the 1920s were powerless to alter the domestic American political balance, so the ability of foreigners to change Japanese domestic political conditions is limited.

On the other hand, if the analogies are accurate, such foreign pressures on Japan may be superfluous. Japan has become more integrated into international money and finance, and as the foreign interests of its major banks and corporations have grown, domestic support for a 'more responsible' Japanese international economic role has also risen. Recent changes in Japanese domestic regulations and international monetary and financial policies indicate a willingness to play a larger part in international monetary and financial affairs, and these changes have largely been a result of changes in domestic political conditions and interest-group pressures.[20]

More generally, the domestic focus of this analysis leads to relatively optimistic predictions about future international economic cooperation. To be sure, the international variant would leave little room for hope. If national policy toward the international economy were in fact dominated by rational unitary calculations of the costs and benefits of cheating on existing cooperative agreements, the prospects for cooperation would seem very dim. The structure of the international financial and monetary system has, in the international analytical framework, become less favorable to cooperation, for the number of relevant actors has increased dramatically over time. In the 1920s, international financial flows went essentially from the United States and Great Britain to the rest of the world. With only two creditor countries to speak of, the international financial and monetary system was essentially defined by the policies of those two countries. After the Second World War, it was essentially defined by American policies alone. In the period since 1960, however, virtually all developed countries have become major overseas investors. The proliferation of actors should, in a world of unitary rational nation-states, make cooperation more difficult. The evidence might be read in a number of ways, but it is doubtful that it would support this view. Cooperation among many financial centers was far easier in the 1980s than it was among the two major financial powers in the inter-war period.

The domestic analytical framework, unlike the international, emphasized the interests of domestic socio-economic groups, and here there is little question about the contemporary depth and breadth of those interests in the international economy, and in providing political support for international economic cooperation. In the 1920s, only in Great Britain were internationally oriented economic groups powerful, and even there the strength of the Empire lobby, a proxy for economic nationalism, was very great. Everywhere else, whether in Central Europe, France, the United States, Japan, or Latin America, there were major splits among socio-economic groups on international economic policy, and internationally oriented sectors were relatively weak.

Today, holdings of overseas assets have become far more common within developed nations. In addition, as adjustment and restructuring have taken place in many sectors, and as the mobility of capital has increased dramatically, business-community opposition to international economic integration has declined substantially. Even in the largest countries, including the United States, the process of financial, commercial and productive integration has altered the material position of most of the major segments of the American economy. Most large businesses, and most major investors, hold internationally diversified portfolios, and support generally cooperative international economic policies. Of course, some portions of the business community and the labor movement remain geographically, and often sectorally, immobile, and some domestic conflict on these issues is bound to continue. The implication is that future domestic debates on American foreign economic policy are unlikely to divide the business community so fiercely as they did in the inter-war years, and that there is likely to be much more support for national policies committed to a high level of international economic openness and cooperation. As indicated above, a similar argument could be made for the Japan of the 1990s: its business community is now international enough that it will exert pressure on the Japanese government to sustain or increase its efforts at international economic cooperation.

In any case, the more general analytical point to be made is that international conditions affect national economic policy-makers *through* domestic socio-economic and political groups. This framework allows for a more nuanced, and more accurate, analysis of the American inter-war experience, and of other experiences as well. It also provides for more optimistic predictions about the future of the international monetary and financial order than models in which unitary nation-states seek to maximize their 'national interest'. In this instance, happily, the theory provides both accurate explanations of the past and optimistic predictions of the future.

Notes

1. It should be emphasized that many coordinating 'solutions' have significant distributional consequences: the enforcement of property rights may be good for economic growth in the long run, but very bad for members of traditional villages who find themselves stripped of free access to formerly communal property. This is also true of the international economy: the workings of the global economy may have differential consequences for groups or whole nations, as with oil price increases, a collapse in the copper market, or a world-wide run-up in interest rates. It is artificial to pretend that international coordination problems do not raise international distributional concerns. Credit contract enforcement can amount to forcible despoilment of recalcitrant debtors, even unto gunboat diplomacy. Cooperation for the purpose of contractual predictability tends to reinforce the status quo, and may have domestic or international distributional consequences that are undesirable on normative or other grounds.
2. Readers will recognize here traditional descriptions and extensions of public goods. International economic cooperation is certainly not a pure public good, but certain aspects of it come reasonably close. Cross-border contract enforcement and international monetary stability — analogous to property rights and a non-inflationary environment domestically — are certainly 'rival in consumption' (that is, their consumption by one precludes consumption by another) and excludable, and thus are not pure public goods. The distributional consequences of the provision of these goods can be significant. It might be analytically more accurate to think of them as club goods in which the club is the universe of those most interested in cross-border investment and international payments. This distinction is not important to the discussion in this chapter. On related issues see Joanne Gowa, 'Public Goods and Political Institutions: Trade and Monetary Policy Processes in the United States', *International Organization*, **42**, 1, Winter 1988, pp. 15–32.
3. The similarities to much of the neo-Realist literature in International Relations are obvious. The far-reaching conclusions drawn by much of this literature — such as in the so-called Theory of Hegemonic Stability — do not, however, follow. The claims here are much more limited, and more directly related to Charles Kindleberger's original work on the Great Depression that sparked much subsequent discussion in the hegemonic stability tradition. See Charles Kindleberger, *The World in Depression* (Berkeley: University of California Press, 1973), pp. 291–308.
4. This list is that of Charles Kindleberger, 'Dominance and Leadership in the International Economy: Exploitation, Public Goods, and Free Rides', *International Studies Quarterly*, **25**, 2, June 1981, p. 247.
5. For another summary of the positions, and a more detailed extension to the issues at hand, see my 'Capital Politics: Creditors and the International Political Economy', *Journal of Public Policy*, **8**, 3/4, July–December 1988, pp. 265–86.

6. Of course, default may lead to country-specific penalties on the defaulter. These are for present purposes presumed to be constant, so that they do not vary with the nation-state's ability to bring the world financial system crashing down.

7. This largely ignores the effects of time horizons. For example, a borrower, even a large one strongly integrated into global finance, might fail to service its debts because it determines that the short-term benefits of default outweigh the discounted long-term costs of the financial disruption that might ensue. However, the notion that discount rates might vary among countries is itself not fully consistent with the assumption that states differ only in their size or power, which is fundamental to most versions of the unitary rational state approach.

8. The discussion here draws on my *Banking on the World: The Politics of American International Finance* (New York: Harper and Row, 1987), pp. 25–78; and my 'Sectoral Conflict and US Foreign Economic Policy, 1914–1940', *International Organization*, **42**, 1, Winter 1988, pp. 59–90. Only where information is not taken from these publications will exact citations be given. A parallel story involves the evolution of American domestic economic-policy institutions in response to changes in the international position of the US economy. For one treatment see Lawrence Broz, 'Wresting the Scepter from London: The International Political Economy of the Founding of the Federal Reserve', Ph.D. dissertation, UCLA, forthcoming.

9. Calculated from Eugene Staley, *War and the Private Investor* (Garden City, New York: Doubleday, Doran and Company, 1935), pp. 523–38.

10. Figures are from the *Economic Report of the President*, various issues. GNP for 1922 is actually Net National Product plus 10 per cent, the average difference for this historical period. The correction referred to is to net out overseas liabilities of US banks from their overseas assets. Since most of the liabilities in question are to the banks' own branches, they should in fact be subtracted from the banks' overseas asset position. In the figures presented, this is the only consideration of net assets. Of course, given the peculiarities of American economic policies in the 1980s, the American net overseas asset position is now strongly negative.

11. Paul Drake, *The Money Doctor in the Andes* (Durham, North Carolina: Duke University Press, 1989).

12. See, for example, my 'Oil and the Evolution of US Policy toward the Developing Areas, 1890–1950: An Essay in Interpretation', in *Oil and the Twentieth Century World Economy*, R.W. Ferrier and A. Fursenko, eds (London: Routledge, 1989).

13. See especially my 'Sectoral Conflict'.

14. John Douglas Forbes, *J. P. Morgan, Jr.* (Charlottesville: University Press of Virginia, 1981), p. 125.

15. Mary Jane Maltz, *The Many Lives of Otto Kahn* (New York: Macmillan, 1963), pp. 204–5.

16. Barry Eichengreen, 'The Political Economy of the Smoot–Hawley Tariff', *Research in Economic History*, **12**, pp. 1–43. He discusses the competitive position of American industrial and agricultural sectors in the 1920s.

17. For evidence of the pre-Second World War origins of most post-war policies, and the widespread recognition of their desirability on the part of major business leaders, see my *Banking on the World*, pp. 57–9.

18. ibid, pp. 65–74.

19. See my 'Capital Politics' for this point in more detail; as applied to Latin American debtors, see my 'Classes, Sectors and Foreign Debt in Latin America', *Comparative Politics*, **21**, 1, October 1988, pp. 1–20; and my 'Winners and Losers in the Latin American Debt Crisis: The Political Implications', in *Debt and Democracy in Latin American*, Robert Kaufman and Barbara Stallings, eds (Boulder: Westview Press, 1989), pp. 23–37.

20. For one such argument, see David Dollar and Jeffry Frieden, 'The Political Economy of Financial Deregulation in the United States and Japan', in *Structural Change in the American Financial System*, Giacomo Luciani, ed. (Rome: Fondazione Olivetti, 1990).

9 *The politics of empire: a theory with an application to the Soviet case*
Jack Snyder

Paul Kennedy's book, *The Rise and Fall of the Great Powers*, has reminded a wide readership of the value of historical perspectives in understanding current problems of grand strategy. Kennedy notes that geopolitical overextension has been the self-inflicted fate of imperial powers, and draws cautionary lessons for the contemporary superpowers. Kennedy is less explicit, however, in tracing the causes of this penchant for overextension, and thus leaves one uncertain about the required antidotes.[1]

It is argued here that the sources of Kennedy's 'imperial overstretch' lie in the domestic politics of the great powers. Though all of these powers have shown a penchant for overextension, some have been much more extreme in this regard than others. A review of the experience of five great powers suggests that overextension has been greatest when the political system has been dominated by logrolling among groups having a parochial interest in empire. Imperial Germany and Japan are such cases. Expansion has been more moderate when such imperialist cartels have been controlled either from above, by a strong unitary oligarchy, or from below, by a democratic electorate. The Soviet Union exemplifies the former pattern; the United States and Britain, the latter. Only the Soviet case is examined here.[2] The argument is that the Soviets have been most expansionist when Soviet politics was most dominated by the logrolling of military and ideological interest groups. Mikhail Gorbachev is attempting to regain control over these groups by strengthening both the center and the grassroots *vis-à-vis* these imperialist cartels. If he succeeds, the Soviet expansionist impetus should diminish.

Introduction

Great powers in the industrial age have shown a striking proclivity for self-inflicted wounds. Highly advanced societies with a great deal to lose have sacrificed their blood and treasure, sometimes risking the survival of

156

their state, as a consequence of their overly aggressive foreign policies. Two states, Germany and Japan, proved so self-destructive that they wound up in receivership. Most of the other great powers, including the United States and the Soviet Union, have exhibited similar tendencies from time to time, but they were better able to learn from the adverse reaction that their aggressive behavior provoked. The great industrial powers have punished themselves in two related ways: self-encirclement by provoking an overwhelming opposing coalition, and imperial overextension, that is, persistent expansion into the hinterland beyond the point where rising costs begin to outstrip declining benefits. Both forms of self-punishment have common roots, and will often be referred to here as overexpansion.

A basic principle of the balance of power is that the most aggressive states make the most enemies.[3] Self-encirclement is what results when an indiscriminately aggressive power threatens so many of its neighbors that they all coalesce against it. When this occurs, those powers that are least capable of self-evaluation may embark on 'preventive' war to break the ring of encirclement. But if the balance of power works as it normally does, this attempted breakout will entail high risks and a low probability of success. Indeed, the more the aggressor succeeds, the more he will find overwhelming power ranged against him. For example, at the outset of war in 1914, Britain, France and Russia enjoyed a three-to-two advantage over Germany and Austria in most indicators of industrial capacity. Though Germany succeeded in knocking Russia out of the war, that ratio climbed to five-to-two once the United States joined in.[4] Likewise, in the Second World War, Germany, Japan and Italy provoked an opposing coalition that was by 1943 outstripping them three-to-one in armaments production.[5]

States that are better learners may provoke encirclement, but then shy away from war or even begin to appease some of their enemies. Britain, for the most part, has been a good learner and an astute appeaser, which explains, in Paul Kennedy's phrase, 'why the British Empire lasted so long'.[6] Though Lord Palmerston flirted with the idea of expanding the Crimean War into a European war to extinguish Russian power permanently, when neutral powers and Palmerston's own allies objected, the British cabinet forced him to sign a compromise peace.[7] Likewise, Britain's aggressive colonial expansion in the scramble for Africa left her at odds with every major European power by the turn of the century. Calculating the disastrous erosion of the naval balance that this could cause, Britain quickly ended her 'splendid isolation', settling disputes with Japan, France and Russia, and thereby strengthening her hand in the competition with Germany.

Despite this astute interlude, Britain did not remain immune from the lure of overextension. One of the reasons that Neville Chamberlain had to appease Hitler at Munich was that so much of Britain's strength was frittered away throughout a far-flung empire.[8] So pervasive is the phenomenon of overextension that even arch-appeasers and arch-retrenchers suffer from it.

Another state with a mixed record of overassertiveness, but quick learning is the Soviet Union. Belligerent behavior in the Berlin crises, the Korean War, and the Sino–Soviet rift provoked an array of potential enemies that outnumbered the Warsaw Pact by more than three-to-one in national income.[9] The Soviets have been good learners in the short run, however, following each of their counterproductive militant phases with attempts to defuse opposition through self-restraint and overtures toward *détente*[10]

The handmaiden of self-encirclement is often imperial overextension. Aggressors get into trouble not only because they provoke balancing coalitions of other great powers, but also because they get stuck in quagmires in the hinterland. Up to a point, imperial expansion may be a paying proposition for a strong power. Sometimes resources and markets can be gained more cheaply and more reliably by military than by economic means. The historical experience of all empires shows, however, that at some point the costs of additional expansion begin to outstrip its benefits.[11] Easy, nearby targets that yield a high return are exhausted. Logistical burdens of further expansion rise, making it easier for an opposing coalition to impose heavy costs by resisting expansion.

All of the industrial great powers have expanded past the point where marginal costs equal marginal revenue. Even Britain had its Boer War and its repeated forays into Afghanistan, in the face of repeated lessons that this remote land was beyond the perimeter of Britain's sustainable power. Britain, however, was an explicit calculator of the marginal costs and revenues of expansion and almost always learned to retrench in the face of negative feedback.[12] Similarly, the Vietnam War touched off over a decade of inflation, starved America's regular military forces of funds, demobilized domestic support for America's global role, sowed dissention in NATO, and encouraged Soviet geopolitical assertiveness in the 1970s. Thus, the war caused most of the outcomes that it was designed to forestall. As a consequence, Americans fairly quickly learned that Vietnam, and many other places in the Third World, were beyond America's sustainable perimeter of empire.[13]

Though Britain and America were good learners, Japan learned its lessons about overextension backwards. Japan strove to conquer China in order to have an autarkic military–industrial base. But already by 1937, the China quagmire was in fact eating up Japan's industrial base, diverting expenditures from industrial investment into current military consumption.[14] But unlike Britain, Japan did not appease and retrench. Instead, she gambled on still more expansion to cut off supplies to China and to conquer resources even further afield, in South East Asia. As a consequence, Japan wound up both in a hinterland quagmire in China and with an overwhelming great power, the United States, ranged against her.

In short, two basic dynamics of international politics — the balance of power and the diminishing returns of expansion — exact harsh penalties on overly aggressive states. All of the great powers of the industrial era, to one extent or another, have acted in defiance of those equilibrating forces. Some of them — Britain, the Soviet Union and the United States — have been relatively quick to liquidate self-defeating overexpansion. Others — Germany and Japan — provoked encirclement by belligerence and then sought security through still further aggression.

Explaining overexpansion

Three explanations for this endemic proclivity towards self-punishing aggressiveness and for variations in its intensity exist: international anarchy, cognitive processes, and coalition politics and ideology. Each of them has different implications for how to control the aggressive inclinations of states and how to stabilize international politics.

The first explanation, called Realism by its adherents, argues that the costs and risks of aggression are unavoidable in an anarchical international environment that forces states to use warlike means to guarantee their own security. The more vulnerable states are to the depredations of others, the more aggressive states must become, if only in self-defense.[15] But this explanation founders on the Realists' own argument that states typically form balancing alliances to resist aggressors. Therefore, at least in the long run, the balance of power that arises out of international anarchy punishes aggression; it does not reward it.

Many statesmen, however, have accepted the view that security requires aggressiveness and expansion. Seeing the world as a place in which the balance of power fails to operate, they envision falling dominoes, neutrals jumping on the bandwagon with a rising aggressor, and paper-tiger enemies collapsing when attacked but becoming strong and voracious when appeased.[16] Such views, for the most part erroneous, have been endemic among the great powers. They have been most extreme among the most aggressive and self-defeating great powers, Germany and Japan.

Two alternative explanations, challenging traditional Realism's assertion that aggressiveness is a necessary response to anarchy, contend that the belief in security through aggressiveness is based on misperceptions. They disagree, however, about the source of these misperceptions. A cognitive explanation suggests that paper-tiger images of opponents and misconceptions of the balance of power are caused by inherent biases in the information that is most readily available to statesmen, or by biases in the lessons and analogies that come to mind most readily in interpreting this information.[17] One can argue, however, that the main sources of bias in tasks like the gathering of information about the enemy or the selection of lessons to be drawn from the past are social and political, not cognitive.

Another explanation contends that strategic misconceptions are propagated by interest groups that benefit disproportionately from expansionism or militarism. By justifying their parochial interests in terms of national security, they seek to pass the costs of aggressive policies onto society as a whole. The more powerful and persuasive such groups are, the more the state will be inclined toward self-defeating aggression.[18]

Herein lies a paradox, however. Very powerful interests, such as 'the ruling class', have a major stake in the long-run health of the society as a whole, and thus have only a limited incentive to milk society for short-run parochial gain. Conversely, groups with very narrow interests lack the power or authority to harness the state's resources for their own ends. Thus, the role of propaganda, especially the selling of strategic myths like the domino theory, is indispensable for explaining how parochial interests hijack national policy. Even this may be problematic, however, since interest-group propaganda is often transparent and suspect.

In fact, parochial interests gain control over national policy not simply through their separate propaganda efforts, but by joining in coalitions. Through logrolling, each group gets what it wants most, and cost are diffused to society through taxes imposed by the state. Logrolling by its nature pays off concentrated groups' interests and ignores diffuse interests, like taxpayer interests, which are hard to organize.[19] Since interests in expansion and militarism are typically more concentrated than interests opposed to them, expansionism that rewards interest groups, but hurts society, is more likely whenever ruling coalitions are formed by logrolling. Overexpansion has been more extreme than that preferred by any individual group, due to the compounding of separate imperial programs through the logrolling process.

Strategic mythmaking plays a role in the making of imperial coalitions, as a result of jockeying for advantage by interest groups comprising the coalition or as a result of the coalition leader's attempts to justify the overcommitments that are endemic to the logrolling process. Indeed, the selling of myths is easier for coalition leaders than for individual interest groups because the instruments and credibility of the state can be harnessed to the task, and because self-serving strategic arguments are less traceable to the parochial interests that benefit from them.

Logrolling is a feature of most political systems, but when it is the dominant feature, self-defeating expansion is more extreme. This was the case in Germany and Japan, where the social consequences of late industrialization gave rise to logrolling among narrow-interest groups, producing overcommitted expansionist policies and extreme imperialist ideologies.[20] In contrast, the democratic systems of early industrializers like the United States and Britain strengthened diffuse interests opposed to overexpansion.[21]

The comparatively unitary political system of the Soviet Union, the origins of which lay in the dynamics of 'late, late' industrialization, strengthens the encompassing perspective of the top leadership, which has an incentive to counteract parochial views of the costs and benefits of empire. The Soviet case suggests that this unitary check on expansionist logrolling and mythmaking works fairly well when the political system is dominated by a unitary oligarchy having broad interests across a variety of economic or bureaucratic sectors, for example, the Whig aristocracy in Britain and the Soviet Politburo. It works poorly in cases where unitary power is held by a single man, whose idiosyncratic strategic ideas and choices are unchecked by any second opinion, for example, Stalin and Hitler. In short, in both democratic and unitary–oligarchical systems, self-defeating aggressiveness has been more limited and strategic myths have been less extreme than in systems dominated by logrolling among cartels.

The Soviet case

The Soviet Union has been a moderately expansionist power, occasionally provoking the formation of balancing coalitions, but learning to retrench in the face of effective opposition. Since its early days, Bolshevik foreign policy has taken a militant stance toward the capitalist great powers, believing that the revolution in Russia could be secure only with the triumph of revolution in the more advanced countries. Thus, Soviet Russia was born believing in security through expansion. Xenophobic security fears were subsequently exacerbated by Stalin's rhetoric linking internal and external threats as a motivating tactic in the campaigns to collectivize agriculture, industrialize at breakneck speed, and purge 'spies, enemies and wreckers'.

Despite this, Soviet foreign policy in the 1920s and 1930s remained quite moderate. Despite the revolutionary rhetoric of the Comintern, escalated in 1928 to coincide with the militant domestic rhetoric of the First Five-Year Plan, actual foreign policy followed the defensive principles of 'socialism in one country'. Stalin, like Lenin before him, counted on intense rivalries among the capitalist states to buy time for the development of Soviet power. As early as 1925, Stalin held the view that if war came 'we shall have to take action, but we shall be the last to do so in order to throw the decisive weight into the scales'.[22] The Soviet Union could avoid early embroilment in a conflict by building up a military deterrent and by avoiding provocations that could give a pretext for an attack. *Vis-à-vis* both Germany and Japan, Stalin tried for the most part to be both militarily strong and diplomatically conciliatory. Thus, Stalin exploited the incentives for buckpassing in a multipolar balance-of-power system, adopting a hedgehog posture in order to deflect conflict in other directions.[23]

After the Second World War, Soviet foreign policy showed a greater tendency toward overexpansion, though it retained an ability to learn well from its failures. Three times — Stalin's intensification of the Cold War, Nikita Khrushchev's missile diplomacy, and Leonid Brezhnev's Third World expansionism — aggressive Soviet actions unified the opposing camp, provoked it to intensify its military preparations, alienated neutrals and socialist allies, and wasted scarce Soviet economic resources. Three times the Soviets learned at least temporarily to retrench from their aggressive stance in order to demobilize the opposing forces that their actions had conjured up. And in the third of these episodes of learning, it seems that Gorbachev and his supporters may have learned a deeper, perhaps more permanent lesson about the counter-productiveness of militancy and expansionism.

Consequently, what needs to be explained about Soviet behavior is (1) the lack of significant overexpansion before the Second World War, and Stalin's adoption of a hedgehog strategy, (2) the three periods of moderate overextension after 1945, (3) the relative effectiveness with which the Soviets learned to retrench from these bouts of overextension and self-encirclement, and (4) initial signs of the qualitatively different character of Soviet strategic learning in the Gorbachev period.

Changes over time in Soviet strategic concepts correlate with the degree of inclination toward overexpansion. Stalin's pre-war hedgehog strategy was based on the assumption of a hostile West, but few opportunities to pursue this zero-sum competition through offensive action. In contrast, post-war overexpansion was fueled first by Andrei Zhdanov's notions of a hostile West and many offensive opportunities, and subsequently by Khrushchev's and Brezhnev's concept of offensive *détente*. In this latter view, the West was a paper tiger, aggressive but also susceptible to being lulled or overawed into surrendering its positions of strength in the global competition. Finally, interludes of retrenchment, above all the Gorbachev period, coincided with the rise in the belief that Western hostility is contingent on Soviet provocations, and that offensive opportunities are scarce.

International–systemic explanations help account for Stalin's pre-war balance-of-power strategy and for post-war periods of retrenchment. The more expansionist periods, however, are harder to explain in terms of rational adaptation to the incentives posed by the international system. Even in the periods in which Soviet policy was astute, it is worthwhile asking what domestic political conditions allowed this relatively clear-sighted strategy.

The most popular cognitive theory explaining Soviet overexpansion and subsequent retrenchment is the 'Bolshevik operational code', a particular brand of offensive tactics ostensibly inculcated by Bolshevism's formative experiences.[24] But this theory fits poorly with the actual practice of Soviet grand strategy up to the first Berlin crisis. The Bolshevik operational code makes its first clear-cut appearance in fact thirty years after the events that supposedly caused it, at a time when almost all of the old Bolsheviks except Stalin were already dead.

Domestic political structure offers a more satisfactory explanation of both the general moderation of Soviet expansionism and its more assertive episodes. Russia's pattern of 'late, late' development was different in kind, not just in degree, from German 'late' development.[25] Russia was so backward that its old social structure was largely swept away under the pressure of war and revolution triggered by competition with more advanced societies. The Bolshevik revolution and Stalin's subsequent 'revolution from above' replaced it with the strong, centralized political institutions needed to force through the social, economic and military development that could make Russia a viable competitor in the international system. Whereas 'late' development, characterized by industrial cartels financed by bank capital and an atavistic military–agricultural élite unintegrated into the industrial economy, produced a cartelized political system, Russia's 'late, late' development produced a unified political system, dominated by a relatively unified Bolshevik political oligarchy capped by a personal dictator.

Unlike the particularistic logrolling of élite cartels in the 'late' system, élites in the 'late, late', unitary polity had relatively encompassing foreign-policy interests. It is true that the Bolshevik élite as a whole had a parochial interest in the inflation of foreign threats and the glorification of world-wide revolutionary aims, which helped to legitimate their power. But the ruling élite in a unitary system had a strong incentive to distinguish clearly in their own minds between these rhetorical appeals and excessively expansionist behavior, which might provoke foreign intervention that would threaten their survival. To the extent that the 'late, late' polity was a unitary system dominated by an élite group with relatively encompassing interests, there was little incentive for overexpansion and little opportunity for imperialistic or militaristic cartels to hijack national policy.

However, after the Second World War and especially after the death of Stalin, the party, and industrial and military institutions created by Stalin's revolution from above increasingly acted as interest groups, using the militant, mobilizing rhetoric of the First Five-Year Plan to advance their own, parochial policy agendas. The ruling coalition that was created within the Politburo increasingly had to take into account the need to logroll these interests, which were often militaristic and expansionist, and also to integrate them into the less militant perspectives of another rising constituency, the cultural and technical intelligentsia. Khrushchev's and Brezhnev's concepts of offensive détente, which worked at home but not abroad, were ideologies that tried to reconcile proponents of three sets of irreconcilable interests: (1) party ideologues, who wanted support for 'progressive change' around the world, (2) the military, who wanted an arms build-up, and (3) the intelligentsia, who wanted a thawing of tensions internationally and domestically. Even before Stalin's death, Soviet aggressiveness in the late 1940s may have been caused in part by Stalin's attempt to manage the emergence of these proto-interest groups.

Periods of Soviet retrenchment before Gorbachev were mere interludes during which discredited imperial coalitions regrouped on a slightly modified basis. This oscillation between expansion and retrenchment reflected the tension between the cartelized aspects of the post-Stalin political system, which promoted overexpansion, and the residual unitary role of a Politburo élite with encompassing interests. Gorbachev, responding to the economic necessity of creating new institutional arrangements, may be breaking this pattern by increasing the power of both the center and the grass roots *vis-à-vis* ossified military, industrial and party bureaucracies. If so, the political impetus that spurred Khrushchev's and Brezhnev's overexpansion might be permanently curtailed.[26]

Soviet strategic concepts

Like British debates on grand strategy, Soviet strategic thinking has been quite diverse, with as many as four conceptually distinctive schools of thought active at any given time, and with considerable variation in the relative strength of the contending schools over time. For the sake of analytical convenience, these outlooks can be divided along two dimensions: first, whether imperialist hostility toward socialism is conditional or unconditional, and second, whether offense is the best defense in international politics. This yields the following four permutations (see also Figure 9.1).[27]

1. Molotov: Western hostility is unconditional; the defense has the advantage

Viacheslav Molotov, Foreign Minister in the mid-1950s, argued that Soviet efforts to relax tensions with the West would not reduce the imperialists' hostility, but would only reduce vigilance within the socialist camp. However, he saw very few opportunities to exploit imperialist vulnerabilities through offensive action, arguing against Khrushchev for example that the Third World and Yugoslavia were inextricably tied to the opposing camp. Attempts to woo them by reforming Russia's Stalinist image would only lead to unrest in Eastern Europe, he accurately predicted. Consequently, the Soviet Union should adopt a hedgehog strategy of autarky, internal repression, and the forced-draft development of Russia's military–industrial base.[28] In short, Stalinists

	Defense has the advantage	Offense has the advantage
Western hostility is unconditional	Molotov	Zhdanov
Western hostility is conditional	Malenkov Gorbachev	Khrushchev Brezhnev

Figure 9.1 Schools of strategic thought

like Molotov and Lazar Kaganovich, weaned on Stalin's strategy of 'socialism in one country', saw a militant defense as the best way to secure the revolution. As Stalin himself had put it, 'Of course, the Fascists are not asleep. But it is to our advantage to let them attack first; that will rally the working class around the communists.'[29]

2. *Zhdanov: Western hostility is unconditional; offense has the advantage*

Andrei Zhdanov represented a different brand of militancy. Like Molotov, he believed that Soviet concessions would not diminish the aggressiveness of the West, but he was distinctive in arguing that a political offensive was the best defense against imperialism's hostile onslaught. As part of his militant Cominform strategy, for example, Zhdanov promoted the use of violent strikes by Western communist parties as a means to prevent the implementation of the Marshall Plan, which Zhdanov saw as the groundwork for an American policy of rollback in Eastern Europe.[30]

3. *Malenkov: Western hostility is conditional; the defense has the advantage*

Georgii Malenkov, Premier from 1953 to 1955, in contrast, believed that Western aggressiveness could be defused by Soviet self-restraint, and that defensive advantages dominated the international system. Malenkov's views dovetailed with the arguments of Eugene Varga, the prominent Soviet economist, who contended that institutional changes in the American state during the Second World War had made it a stronger but less aggressive international competitor, more able to control the heedlessly aggressive impulses of the monopoly capitalists.[31] Malenkov argued that the imperialists had become realistic and sane enough to be deterred by a minimum atomic force, so that defense budgets could be safely cut and the heavy-industrial priority reversed.[32] Moreover, he argued, Soviet political concessions in Europe would demobilize and split the West, leading to a new Rapallo-like era. There is evidence that Malenkov warned on similar grounds against invading South Korea.[33]

4. *Khrushchev and Brezhnev: Western hostility is conditional; offense has the advantage*

Khrushchev and Brezhnev shared the Malenkov–Varga thesis that 'realists' in the West made possible a relaxation of international tension, but they coupled this with a belief in offensive advantages in international politics. Imperialists could behave in a heedlessly aggressive manner, they believed, but prudent forces within the capitalist camp, especially the bourgeois state and public opinion, could restrain the most reckless of the monopoly capitalists. Soviet policy could strengthen the influence of such realists in two ways: first, Soviet efforts to shift the world correlation of forces, including the military balance, to the advantage of socialism would cause realists increasingly to shun the dangers of direct confrontation; second, Soviet projection of an image of restraint in the methods by which it pursued its expansionist goals would lull the West. These two elements would reinforce each other, according to Khrushchev and Brezhnev. The increased strength of the socialist camp would leave the imperialists little choice but to accept *détente* on terms favorable to socialism. *Détente* in turn would weaken imperialism by hindering its counter-revolutionary interventions in the Third World. The success of the strategy depended, in their view, on active measures to improve the Soviet position at the expense of the West, not simply on the passive acceptance of a stalemate or balance.[34] As Khrushchev put it: 'Peace cannot be begged for. It can be safeguarded only by an active purposeful struggle.'[35]

In short, any explanation of the Soviets' moderate proclivity towards overexpansion should be able to account for (1) the secular evolution from hedgehog to offensive *détente* to Malenkovite dominant strategies, (2) the post-1945 cyclical oscillation between more and less militant strategies, and, if possible, (3) the disagreements among proponents of the four strategic orientations at any given time. That explanation does not lie, for the most part, in either international–systemic factors or cognitive processes, but in domestic politics.

Domestic politics: atavisms of the revolution from above

The political consequences of 'late, late' industrialization help to explain all of the variations in Soviet foreign policy — Stalin's *realpolitik*, post-war periods of overextension, differences in the strategic conceptions of different political leaders, and Gorbachev's strategic retrenchment. The Soviet 'late, late' pattern was like a flat-out version of German late industrialization: rapid, concentrated in large-scale heavy industry, centrally financed, and shaped by state intervention.[36] But this difference in degree was so great that it constituted a difference in kind. To carry out this revolution from above, old social groups had to be broken and political power concentrated in the hands of a unitary 'organizational weapon', to use Philip Selznick's term for the Communist Party.[37] The resulting political and economic structures were so concentrated that, rather than being bases for interest-group logrolling as in the German case, they could be dominated from the unitary focal point of the totalitarian dictator.

These characteristics of the "late, late" pattern affected foreign policy outcomes. The superconcentrated, almost monistic political structure meant that the interests motivating policy-makers at the apex of the structure tended to be 'encompassing' rather than parochial. By limiting the role of vested interests and coalition logrolling in generating strategic ideologies, this promoted balance-of-power realism in the foreign policy of the totalitarian pre-war period. Though a militant ideology and exaggeration of foreign threats were needed to forge an organizational weapon to carry out the revolution from above and to justify the hardships and repression it would bring, the unitary political structure made it possible to insulate actual foreign policy from the blowback effects of this ideological rhetoric. More generally, the unitary character of the Soviet political system helps to explain the Politburo's continuing ability to correct the worst of its mistakes.

After the revolutionary stage of the industrial transformation was completed, the institutions and ideas that it created lived on for decades as atavisms. The military–industrial complex and the mobilizing 'combat party' played a key role in the formation of domestic political coalitions, driving foreign and security policies in a militant, expansionist direction. Recently, however, Gorbachev and his allies have been attacking these old institutions and ideas, identifying them as self-serving holdovers from the out-moded tasks of 'extensive' economic development — that is, the administrative mobilization of underutilized human and material resources. Instead, argue the reformers, the Soviet Union needs to break the power of these old institutions and dogmas in order to create new institutions which will be better suited to the needs of 'intensive' economic development — that is, the efficient allocation of resources in response to demand.[38] Given the nature of this task, they argue, these new institutional forms must allow a greater role for markets and grass-roots political participation. By breaking the power of imperialist interests and by creating stronger incentives for *détente* and participation in the world market, these developments may be harbingers of the waning of Soviet militarism and expansionism.[39]

Institutions and ideas of the revolution from above

Stalinist institutions were marked by their origins, that is the attempts of an autocrat to whip a backward society to modernize in the face of foreign competition. In this process, international pressure provided both the motive and the opportunity to smash obsolete institutions and replace them with more efficient, centrally controlled ones.[40] 'Old Russia . . . was ceaselessly beaten for her backwardness,' Stalin warned at the height of the First Five-Year Plan. 'We are fifty or a hundred years behind the advanced countries. We must make good this lag in ten years. Either we do it or they crush us.'[41]

The tsars, too, had tried to spur revolution from above for much the same reason. However, Stalin explained, 'none of the old classes . . . could solve the problem of overcoming the backwardness of the country'.[42] Instead, they were barriers to the needed transformation. But all of these old urban and élite classes, including the old working class, had been swept away between 1917 and 1921 by the combination of war, revolution, foreign intervention, and civil war. The Bolsheviks were not yet strong enough in the early 1920s to break the peasantry and mobilize the material and labor surpluses needed for rapid industrialization.

During the 1920s, however, they were able to forge a spearhead for completing the social transformation from the ranks of the new, *tabula rasa* working class, which was younger and less tainted with reformist trade-unionism than the old working class had been.[43]

This revolution had institutional and intellectual consequences. Institutionally, its implementation required a more militant mobilizing party, the strengthening of repressive police institutions, and a more centralized authoritarian economic structure to overcome bottlenecks and to assert the priority of military-related heavy-industrial production. Through upward mobility from the new working class, it also created by the late 1930s a politically dependent, hothouse technical élite — what Stalin called 'a new Soviet intelligentsia, firmly linked with the people and ready en masse to give it true and faithful service'.[44] This was the Brezhnev generation, for which the Great Purges cleared the way.

Intellectually, these institutions and personnel were motivated and tempered through the inculcation of an ideology of political combat and the exaggeration of internal and external threats. This mobilized energies when pecuniary rewards were lacking, justified repression, and legitimated the priority of resource allocations for the military–industrial complex. According to the definitive study of the enlistment of workers in the campaign to collectivize agriculture:

> The recruitment drive took place within the context of the First Five-Year Plan mobilization atmosphere. The Stalin leadership manipulated and played upon popular fear of military intervention and memories of civil war famine, rekindled by the 1927 war scare and the grain crisis of the late 1920s. The dominant motifs of the First Five-Year Plan revolution were military and the imagery was that of the Russian civil war. The working class was called upon to sacrifice for the good of the cause and the preservation of the nation. The state sought to deflect working class grievances away from systemic problems and toward the 'external' and the 'internal' enemies — that is, the 'kulak,' the 'bourgeois' specialist, the Nepmen, and the political opposition (inside the Party) all said to be in league with the agents of international imperialism.[45]

Though this paranoid, pressure-cooker atmosphere was largely fomented from above by Stalin and his allies, recent studies have stressed that it was readily internalized and exploited by the upwardly mobile militants that were Stalin's shock troops. During the collectivization campaign and the later purges, these young radicals exaggerated the threat of foreign subversion to push campaigns to extremes and to sweep away the older bureaucratic élite that was blocking their path to social advancement.[46]

Stalinist atavisms and the politics of expansion

After the period of rapid social mobilization, these institutions and ideas lived on as atavisms. By the late 1940s, the institutional instruments of mobilization were turning into self-interested cartels. The intellectual instruments were turning into tools for justifying these institutional interests, especially the role of orthodox ideology in shaping society, the allocative priority of the military–industrial complex, and petty interference by party bureaucrats in day-to-day economic administration.

Foreign policy ideas played an important role in rationalizing and reconciling group interests. By the late 1940s and 1950s, the four schools of thought in Soviet grand strategy discussed above had emerged, each supported by a distinctive constituency. Molotov's hedgehog strategy gained adherents among Stalin's old henchmen and the military–industrial complex. The Zhdanovite strategy appealed to party militants, while Malenkov sought adherents for a domestic and international relaxation of tensions among the intelligentsia. The fourth school of thought, offensive *détente*, resulted from the efforts of political entrepreneurs like Khrushchev and Brezhnev to form coalitions among the other three. It was this fourth school that held the reins of policy for most of the 1950s, 1960s and 1970s. The preferences and power of individual interest groups are necessary, but not sufficient, to explain this outcome. Only by adding the dynamics of logrolling and strategic mythmaking by coalition leaders can Soviet overextension in this period be fully explained.

Molotov, the military and the hedgehog strategy

Molotov, at least by the time of Stalin's death, was promoting a strategy of 'fortress Russia', shunning adventurism but stressing high levels of vigilance against socialism's enemies at home and abroad. Since Molotov's prestige and legitimacy hinged on being Stalin's chief lieutenant, especially in foreign affairs, his interests as well as his habits were served by being the guardian of orthodoxy.

A more enduring constituency for this hedgehog strategy lay among the military–industrial interests. When Khrushchev, for example, moved to limit military spending and simultaneously to provoke foreign conflicts, Frol Kozlov became a powerful leader of the opposition. His political base was rooted in Leningrad's military-oriented economy.[47] In Kozlov's view, which became so prominent in the Brezhnev era, the methodical development of Soviet military strength was the prerequisite for successful dealings with the West.

The professional military itself inclined to this view, which served as a justification for high levels of expenditure on military forces and the heavy-industrial sectors that supplied them. The strategy was also congenial to the military, because it warned against foreign showdowns for which the military felt unprepared. Western scholarship on the 'pacifist realism' of military professionals would expect such an outlook.[48] This view was prevalent under Khrushchev. During this period, the strategic ideology of the Soviet military stressed straightforward threat inflation, denying that there were any 'realists' in the West who could be partners in arms control, or, for that matter, who could be intimidated by

Khrushchev's brinkmanship into accepting *détente* on Soviet terms.[49]

However, in the Brezhnev era, increased Soviet capabilities made the top brass much more willing to advocate military intervention abroad and to brandish Soviet military power to deter American intervention against Soviet Third World clients.[50] For example, seeing off the Egyptian War Minister at Moscow airport on the eve of the June 1967 war, Marshal Andrei Grechko advised: 'Stand up to them! The moment they attack you, or if the Americans make any move, you will find our troops at your side.'[51] Later, during the war of attrition, when Aleksei Kosygin, of the Politburo, was telling the Egyptians to 'cool the situation' and avoid 'anything that can be taken advantage of by the Israeli warmongers', Grechko was urging the opposite:

> You should be more daring . . . why are you afraid? The Soviet navy in the Mediterranean is following the American Sixth Fleet like a shadow. They can't do anything. If the Americans put their marines into Israel we are ready to land our troops in your territories. And then I should like to see who would win![52]

Finally, in June 1972, Grechko told the Politburo, in the presence of the Egyptian Chief of Staff that, contrary to established Soviet policy of restraining the Arabs by limiting arms supplies, 'Egypt must be supplied with the weapons to ensure victory'.[53]

These anecdotes show not only that the Soviet military leadership came to abandon the hedgehog strategy for a more assertive stance, but also that the military adopted arguments reminiscent of the logic of offensive *détente*, extended to provide a theory of escalation control in limited conflicts. Soviet military capabilities would constrain American escalation, even while a Soviet client used Soviet-supplied arms to achieve 'victory' over an American ally. This logic was also applied in preparing for a limited conventional war in Europe. The Soviet Army would strive for a decisive victory using conventional forces only; realists in NATO would be deterred from retaliating with nuclear weapons by the threat of Soviet escalation. Flush with increased capabilities, the Soviet military was weaned from the hedgehog strategy and coopted into a coalition favoring the more assertive strategy of offensive *détente*.[54]

The military's interest in such a strategy is not difficult to imagine, since it produced a demanding task that would justify open-ended expenditures on conventional forces. Why the military was politically worth coopting into a ruling coalition is a less straightforward question. Surely the political power of the military does not stem from any fear that it will mount a coup against a leader it dislikes. Rather, the military's power over policy stems from its virtual monopoly of information and analytical expertise in many aspects of the national security debate.[55] Its value to a ruling coalition, and the political danger it poses to potential enemies, stem from the same source. The military can enhance the political credibility of leaders that if favors by endorsing their national security strategies on technical grounds. Similarly, it can undercut the credibility of leaders that it opposes. This power to persuade cannot be used to dictate to a unified leadership, but it can be used to good effect when civilian leaders are jockeying against each other, as was the case during much of the post-Stalin period.

Zhdanov, the militant party and progressive change abroad

The essence of the Zhdanovite strategy was the militant use of party instruments to promote 'progressive' political change abroad. Its constituency was the Communist Party bureaucracy and its orthodox ideologues, who needed a strategic ideology to use as a weapon in struggles against a competing faction led by Malenkov. As early as 1941, Malenkov was attempting to promote the professional interests of the new technical élite against meddling party bureaucrats. He descried the 'know-nothings' and 'windbags' in the party bureaucracy who exercised 'petty tutelage' over industrial experts, rejected sound technical advice, and spouted empty quotations about 'putting the pressure on'.[56] Because the war greatly increased the autonomy of technical experts, Stalin, by 1945, needed to use Zhdanov to promote a 'party revival' to redress the institutional balance of power.

Zhdanov used foreign policy ideas as a weapon in this struggle. He inflated the threat of ideological subversion from abroad in order to justify the priority of ideological orthodoxy at home. He argued for the thorough communization of Eastern Europe, including East Germany, relying heavily on the mobilizing skills of the party to carry it out.[57] And he emphasized the strategic value of communist fifth columns in the West.

Though interest-group politics clearly influenced the Zhdanovite strategic ideology, it is less clear that this militant view prevailed in Soviet policy after 1947 because of the power of this particular group. Stalin may have backed this viewpoint after the adoption of the Marshall Plan because international conditions seemed to require such a militant approach. Some authors, however, suggest that Stalin had to inflate the foreign threat in this period as a means to reassert social controls that had been relaxed during the war. In addition, they note that Stalin maintained his own power in part by playing off his lieutenants and their institutional constituencies against each other. In promoting the 'party revival' as a counterweight to Malenkov and Lavrenty Beria, Deputy Prime Minister and directing internal affairs, Stalin may have found it tactically expedient to support the militant Cominform strategy that the Zhdanovites preferred. Some sources note that Stalin was often ill during this period, that he made virtually no speeches to assert publically his own policy preferences, and that he both feared Beria and was unsure how to control him. Other sources assert that the Berlin Crisis and the Korean attack were strictly Stalin's own ideas. They also note his phone conversations directing Zhdanov's strategy at the founding meeting of the Cominform and his personal role in reversing Zhdanov's pro-Yugoslav policy. On balance, domestic political explanations for the militant Soviet strategy after 1947 are neither clearly proved nor refuted.

Upon Zhdanov's death in 1948, the heir to his strategy and position in the Central Committee Secretariat was Mikhail Suslov. He defended the Zhdanov line against Malenkov's criticism that it had served only to unify and militarize the West.[58] Suslov, until his death in 1982, served as the proponent of militant and ideologically orthodox means for promoting progressive change abroad and as the enforcer of the party's corporate interests in the domestic coalition-making process.[59]

Malenkov, the intelligentsia and the relaxation of tensions

Malenkov argued for a relaxation of tensions in Soviet policy at home and abroad, echoing Eugene Varga's arguments that the strengthened capitalist state was better able to control the aggressive monopoly capitalists. Consequently, the increasingly realistic imperialists could be deterred with a small nuclear force, whereas a more menacing military and diplomatic stance would only play into the hands of the military–industrial complex in the West.

Malenkov sought a constituency for these views among the urban middle class and the cultural and technical intelligentsia. The charges leveled by Zhdanovite inquisitors against Varga's book read like a sociological profile of Malenkov's would-be constituency: 'technical' and 'apolitical', suffering from 'empiricism', 'bourgeois objectivism', and a 'non-party' outlook.[60] Malenkov's conception of international politics served the interests of the intelligentsia by removing the major justification for oppressive petty tutelage over them by party ideologues and bureaucrats, for the economic priorities that impoverished their living standard, and for a renewal of the purges.[61]

This strategy failed, however, because the class that Malenkov hoped to recruit was subject to counter-pressures. Many of them worked in the military–industrial complex; others had benefited from Stalin's 'Big Deal' with the new intelligentsia, receiving some of the minimal trappings of petty bourgeois status and life-style in exchange for absolute political loyalty to the orthodox regime.[62] Even a decade later, Kosygin still found that this stratum constituted an inadequate social base for a similar strategic ideology.[63]

The Khrushchev and Brezhnev synthesis

The strategies articulated by Molotov, Zhdanov and Malenkov were each associated with one of the key constituencies that formed around the institutions left over from the First Five-Year Plan. That is why each of them failed. None of these strategic ideologies had a sufficiently broad-based appeal to prevail in Soviet politics. Khrushchev and Brezhnev succeeded because they used the concept of offensive *détente* to achieve that broader synthesis.

In promoting offensive *détente*, Khrushchev and Brezhnev were acting as political entrepreneurs, cementing a broad political coalition with a strategic ideology that promised something for everyone: progressive change for Suslov and the ideologues; military modernization and enhanced national security for the military–industrial constituencies; *détente* and increased foreign trade for the cultural and technical intelligentsia. The problem was that this political formula worked at home but not abroad. In practice, it led to overcommitted, contradictory policies that provoked the hostility of the West, revealing (as Gorbachev has put it) that its strategic vision was 'a world of illusions'.[64]

This process played itself out somewhat differently under Khrushchev and Brezhnev, reflecting the different political uses to which the two leaders put the strategy of offensive *détente*. In the early Khrushchev period, offensive *détente* was a strategic ideology that served to legitimate the outcome of political logrolling. This was also how Brezhnev used the strategy. But in the period between 1958 and 1962, Khrushchev tried to use offensive *détente* as a tool to escape the contraints of his logrolled coalition, provoking the worst of the Cold War crises as a consequence.

Khrushchev's version of the strategy of offensive *détente* hinged on nuclear technology and especially the ICBM. They were to serve as a cheap cure-all, changing the correlation of forces and leading to *détente* with the West, a favorable political settlement in Europe, low-cost security, and the freeing of resources for a rise in Soviet living standards.[65] Such arguments were an attractive element in Khrushchev's political platform during the succession struggle.[66] They had the further advantage that they could not fully be tested until the ICBM was actually produced. By 1958, Khrushchev had his ICBM and was eager to move on to the next phase of his domestic game plan, capping military expenditures and increasing investment in chemicals and other sectors that would benefit agricultural and consumer production.[67] However, the West refused to play its part in the script. Instead of becoming more 'realistic', the Americans rejected pleas for a summit, refused to move toward recognition of the German Democratic Republic, and seemed headed toward the nuclearization of the Bundeswehr.[68]

Khrushchev sought to push on with his budgetary reversal despite this, but several Politburo members balked. 'Until the aggressive circles of the imperialist powers reject the policy of the arms race and preparations for a new war, we must still further strengthen the defenses of our country', said Suslov. This had been 'the general line of our party . . . in the period 1954–1957', and implicitly it had been Khrushchev's own personal pledge during the succession struggle. Thus, Suslov called on Khrushchev to 'honestly fulfil (the Party's) duties and promises before the Soviet people'.[69] The Berlin crisis offered Khrushchev a way out of this impasse. Using it as a lever to gain a summit, the recognition of the GDR, and progress on the test ban treaty, Khrushchev hoped to demonstrate that the correlation of forces had already changed enough to achieve *détente* on favorable terms, allowing radical cuts in conventional forces and a leveling off of nuclear expenditures.[70]

This attempt to use offensive *détente* to escape from the constraints of political promises helped put Khrushchev on the slippery slope that led to his replacement in 1964 by the team of Brezhnev and Kosygin. Brezhnev learned from this that offensive *détente* could not be used to escape the strictures of coalition politics, but he did not learn that offensive *détente* was an inherently self-defeating policy. Indeed, the story of his own coalition-building strategy suggests that he thought that the distribution of political power in the 1960s still made offensive *détente* an indispensable tool in domestic politics.[71]

At first, Brezhnev maneuvered to create a coalition on the moderate left. As part of this tactic he attracted ideologues and the moderate military with a foreign policy which stressed support for 'progressive' Third World states, notably the Arabs, and a military policy that emphasized a huge conventional buildup, while opening the door to nuclear arms control. This isolated Kosygin and Nikolai Podgorny, of the Politburo, on the right, who were vulnerable because of their insistence on reduced defense spending, and A.N. Shelepin, of the Politburo, on the extreme left, who apparently hoped to use a platform of even more reckless Third World adventures and domestic economic reform to attract a social-imperialist coalition.[72] But soon a flaw appeared in Brezhnev's policy of moderate appeasement of the cartels of the left. The strategy was extremely expensive, making him vulnerable to Kosygin's charge that it was wrecking the economy and scuttling indispensable reforms.

To parry this charge, Brezhnev developed a revised version of the 'correlation of forces' theory and the strategy of offensive *détente*. The improved military balance and the liberation of progressive forces in the Third World would encourage realism in the West, leading to *détente*, arms control and technology transfers that would solve the Soviet Union's economic problems without Kosygin's structural reforms. The memoirs of defector Arkady Shevchenko show graphically how these pie-in-the-sky arguments were crafted to appeal to the delegates to the 1971 Party Congress, which ratified the strategy and for the first time gave Brezhnev a commanding political advantage over his rivals.[73]

Despite this political victory, Brezhnev was nonetheless stuck with a strategy that was too costly and overcommitted. Through the mid-1970s, he fought a running battle with Marshal Grechko and the military over the budgetary implications of *détente* in general and SALT in particular. Only after 1976, with Grechko's death and the installation of a civilian defense minister, did strategic force procurement flatten out and nuclear warfighting doctrines wane.[74] The battle revived, however, as a result of the Reagan defense buildup, with Chief of the General Staff Nikolai Ogarkov insisting that it would be a 'serious error' not to increase military outlays. In the wake of the Polish crisis, however, the civilians were more worried about the danger of cutting social programs, and Ogarkov was dismissed.[75]

Signs of growing skepticism about backing radical Third World regimes also began to surface in 1976,[76] but could not proceed very far until

Suslov's death in 1982. A year later, even Yuri Andropov, head of the KGB, was stressing the need to limit the cost of Soviet counterinsurgency wars in support of pseudo-Marxist regimes, noting that 'it is one thing to proclaim socialism, but another to build it'.[77] Thus, through the failure of Brezhnev's strategy of offensive *détente*, some of the intellectual and political precursors to Gorbachev's new thinking were already in place.

In sum, Soviet expansionist behavior and strategic concepts have had their roots in the institutional and intellectual legacy of Stalin's revolution from above. Atavistic interests with a stake in military–industrial budget priorities and militant promotion of 'progressive change' abroad have exploited the ideological baggage of Stalinism to legitimate the continuation of their dominant social role. When Malenkov tried to change this, pushing forward new ideas and a new social constituency, Stalin was quoted to justify his removal from office: 'In face of capitalist encirclement . . . "to slacken the pace means to lag behind. And those who lag behind are beaten."'[78] To gain power, an innovator like Khrushchev had to distort his policies to try to attract or outflank the atavistic interests and ideas, leading to contradictions and overcommitment at home and abroad.

The Gorbachev revolution

Under Khrushchev and Brezhnev, Soviet politics became less unitary and increasingly cartelized, but the Gorbachev reforms may succeed in breaking this mold. If so, logrolled coalitions, cemented by an ideology of offensive *détente*, will no longer be the prevailing pattern in Soviet politics and foreign policy. If Gorbachev's domestic strategy works, the Soviet system will become less cartelized, more unitary (through a strong presidency), and at the same time more democratic, as the reformist élite tries to enlist market forces and grassroots political participation in its struggle against entrenched interests.[79]

Several factors make such a development feasible, if not inevitable. These include the requirements of the intensive stage of economic development, the discrediting of the old institutions by the stagnation and foreign policy failures of the late Brezhnev period, and the increasing size and importance of the intelligentsia as a result of the natural processes of modernization. Ironically, a final factor favoring the Gorbachev reforms is the Stalinist legacy of centralized institutions suited to the task of social transformation from above.

Gorbachev realizes, however, that the needed reforms cannot simply be forced through in the tsarist and Stalinist 'top-down' manner, using administrative coercion and exaggeration of foreign threats to whip the population to greater efficiency. Intensive economic development will require economic decentralization, initiative from below, increased production for the consumer sector to provide incentives, and probably a fuller integration into the world market.[80] In its foreign policy component, such a reform strategy would require not just a short respite from heavy military expenditures, but a durable, long-term *détente*. Unlike his predecessors, Gorbachev understands that 'changes in the correlation of forces in the favor of socialism' hinder *détente*, rather than promote it, because they provoke balancing reactions from the West. Soviet military build-ups serve only to provoke a high-technology arms race that starves Soviet civilian sectors of scarce resources and heightens Western vigilance against technology transfers to the East.[81] To reduce West Europe's sense of a prevailing threat from Soviet military capabilities, Gorbachev has consistently proposed a restructuring of both military blocs to de-emphasize offensive types of forces, which were the hallmark of the Brezhnev era.

It remains to be seen whether Gorbachev will succeed in breaking the pattern of cartelized politics which dominated the Khrushchev and especially the Brezhnev years. And even if he does succeed in breaking the cartels, it is still uncertain that he will establish a stable system of government based on a strong Presidency and grassroots democracy. But if he does succeed, and if the theory developed here is correct, increasing the power of the unitary leadership and the democratic grassroots will have a moderating effect on Soviet militarism and expansionism. If this new domestic pattern prevails, Gorbachev's *détente* will not go the way of Khrushchev's or Brezhnev's offensive *détente*.

Conclusions

The Soviet Union has three times flirted with overexpansion: in the early Cold War period, during Khrushchev's missile diplomacy, and during Brezhnev's overextension in the Third World. But each time the Soviet leadership has learned to retrench before major damage was done. Apart from these three interludes, Soviet grand strategy has been realistic and moderate.

The moderate periods, the effective learning, and even the overly aggressive behavior during the fluid period immediately after 1945, can all be plausibly explained as rational responses to prevailing international circumstances. Khrushchev's and Brezhnev's wishful attempts to reconcile *détente* and expansionism cannot. Cognitive explanations, such as the Bolshevik operational code, fare even worse, despite their current popularity. These explanations are either non-falsifiable, or, in their falsifiable versions, they posit a largely mythical Bolshevik intellectual legacy. The offensive behavior depicted in the operational code becomes a hallmark of Soviet diplomacy in 1947–8, not in 1917. Moreover, even after Khrushchev ostensibly revised the philosophical basis of the operational code in 1956, Soviet behavior remained offensive. Finally, Gorbachev's successful learning about the realities of grand strategy may be the result of a cognitive process, but why he has had more success in implementing a new strategy than previous learners, like Malenkov and Kosygin, is a domestic political question.

The Soviet Union's domestic political character as a 'late, late' industrializer provides the most complete explanation both for periods of overextension and moderation. Stalin's *realpolitik* and, more generally, the Politburo's ability to learn from its mistakes is due to the encompassing interests of the élite dominating the top of the unitary polity, which was created by the 'late, late' pattern of development. The three periods of moderate post-war overextension can be explained as the result of the increasing cartelization of the political system, due to the ossification of the institutions and ideas of Stalin's revolution from above. Of these three, the Khrushchev and Brezhnev periods are clear cases, while the Zhdanov period is at least plausible. Finally, Gorbachev's more moderate foreign policy is made possible by his mobilization of centralized and grassroots power to hamstring atavistic cartels.

Simple interest-group theories of overexpansion, without the logrolling element, explain little of this. In the Khrushchev and Brezhnev cases in particular, the logrolling dynamic was crucial to the outcome of overextension. Moreover, strategic mythmaking played a role in each period of overextension. Coalitionmakers succeeded by espousing a strategic ideology that convinced several groups that their conflicting interests could be simultaneously achieved.

Though domestic coalition politics offers the single best explanation for variations over time in Soviet expansionism, this does not mean that the international system was irrelevant to Soviet behavior. On the contrary, the international system shaped Soviet behavior in several ways. First, the international environment helped create the structure of the 'late, late' polity by smashing the old domestic order in the First World War and by providing the competitive environment that spurred Stalin's revolution from above. Second, during periods of relatively unitary politics, Soviet policy was closely shaped by the incentives of the balance-of-power system. Finally, even during relatively cartelized periods, international conditions helped make or break strategic ideologies. Most episodes of Soviet belligerence or expansionism have had international triggers — the Marshall Plan, the rearming of West Germany, the U-2 affair, or the Jackson–Vanik Amendment and the post-Vietnam syndrome — that made the strategic arguments of some Soviet factions more plausible than those of other factions.[82] According to Herbert Dinerstein, Malenkov was undermined by Dulles's massive retaliation speech.[83] Kosygin's attempt to promote a low-profile foreign policy was made more difficult by the escalation of the Vietnam War.

Conversely, Western balancing reactions have at other times served to discredit expansionist strategies. The huge American military buildup in response to the Korean attack gave Malenkov an opportunity to press his conciliatory line in foreign affairs. America's stiff response to Khrushchev's Cuban gambit, followed by President Kennedy's conciliatory American University speech, convinced Khrushchev to shift to a less offensive brand of *détente*. NATO's successful deployment of Pershing missiles undercut Brezhnev's notion that a one-sided military buildup was compatible with *détente* in Europe.

Obviously, international events influence the viability of strategic arguments in Soviet domestic politics. What is less clear is which Western policies help the Malenkovs and the Gorbachevs and which help their foes. Two hypotheses might be advanced in this regard.

First, hard-line or highly competitive Western policies help Soviet soft-liners only when Soviet hard-liners are in power. American firmness after the Korean attack, the Cuban missile adventure, and the late Brezhnev imperialist binge helped Soviet doves, because the American action was clearly provoked by the Soviets' own assertiveness. America's deployment of B-29 bombers in Britain in response to the Berlin blockade, for example, allowed Malenkov's faction to argue persuasively that Soviet militant foreign policy had placed atomic-capable aircraft within range of the Soviet homeland for the first time.[84] Conversely, hard-line American positions simply discredit Soviet doves when they are in power. This is the lesson of America's grudging response to Malenkov's thaw in 1953.

A second hypothesis is that Western firmness has a harmful effect on the credibility of Soviet doves when defensively motivated moves are indistinguishable from offensive ones. The Marshall Plan undercut Varga's position in the Soviet policy debate because the economic instruments that were needed to shore up France and West Germany were indistinguishable from the means to lure Eastern Europe and create an American *place d'armes* on the continent.

In short, Soviet expansion and its waning under Gorbachev are best explained as the result of Soviet domestic political structure. This does not mean that Western actions are irrelevant to Soviet behavior. Rather, it means that their effects are filtered through the medium of Soviet coalition politics.

Notes

1. Paul Kennedy, *The Rise and Fall of the Great Powers* (New York: Random House, 1987).
2. It draws on Jack Snyder, *Myths of Empire: Domestic Politics and Strategic Ideology* (Ithaca: Cornell University Press, forthcoming, 1991).
3. Realist theory has been ambiguous about whether states balance against the most powerful state or the most threatening state, taking into account both power and intentions. Stephen Walt, *The Origins of Alliance* (Ithaca: Cornell University Press, 1987), argues for the latter view unambiguously and persuasively.
4. Paul Kennedy, 'The First World War and the International Power System', *International Security*, **9**, 1, Summer 1984, pp. 7–40, reprinted in Steven Miller, ed., *Military Strategy and the Origins of the First World War* (Princeton: Princeton University Press, 1985), pp. 21, 25.
5. Paul Kennedy, *The Rise and Fall of the Great Powers*, chapter 7.
6. Paul Kennedy, *Strategy and Diplomacy: 1870–1945* (London: Fontana, 1984), chapter 8.

7. This is argued most vigorously by Winfried Baumgart, *The Peace of Paris, 1856* (Santa Barbara: ABC-Clio, 1981).

8. On British strength and deployments, see Brian Bond, *British Military Policy between the Two World Wars* (Oxford: The Clarendon Press, 1980). On British overextension more generally, see Miles Kahler, *Decolonization in Britain and France* (Princeton: Princeton University Press, 1984).

9. Stephen Walt, 'Alliance Formation and the Balance of World Power', *International Security*, **9**, 4, Spring 1985, pp. 42–3.

10. On Soviet learning, see Marshall Shulman, *Stalin's Foreign Policy Reappraised* (New York: Atheneum, 1969). On Soviet defusing tactics, see Deborah Welch Larson, 'Crisis Prevention and the Austrian State Treaty', *International Organization*, **41**, 1, Winter 1989, pp. 27–60.

11. Robert Gilpin, *War and Change in World Politics* (Cambridge: Cambridge University Press, 1981). When I use the terms 'empire' or 'imperial', I mean any expansionist great power.

12. Examples of such calculations may be found in Malcolm Yapp, *Strategies of British India, 1798–1850* (Oxford The Clarendon Press, 1980), pp. 335, 341–3.

13. This was apparent in former Defense Secretary Caspar Weinberger's exclusionary criteria for the use of American military forces abroad (*FY87 DOD Annual Report*, pp. 78–9).

14. Michael A. Barnhart, *Japan Prepares for Total War: The Search for Economic Security, 1919–1941* (Ithaca: Cornell University Press, 1987), pp. 95–6, 103.

15. In addition to Walt, see Robert Jervis, 'Cooperation under the Security Dilemma', *World Politics*, **30**, 2, January 1978, pp. 167–214.

16. See Stephen Van Evera, 'Causes of War', Ph.D. dissertation, UC Berkeley, 1984.

17. Scholars are just beginning to explore this particular application of cognitive theory. I have tried to pull together a cognitive explanation for strategic misperceptions based on hypotheses in Richard Nisbett and Lee Ross, *Human Inference* (Englewood Cliffs: Prentice-Hall, 1980); Robert Jervis, *Perception and Misperception in International Politics* (Princeton: Princeton University Press, 1976); and Deborah Larson, *The Origins of Containment* (Princeton: Princeton University Press, 1985).

18. The progenitor of this line of argument was J. A. Hobson, in his work on imperialism. Closer to my own formulation of it is Van Evera, 'Causes of War'. My use of the terminology of rent-seeking cartels to describe imperialist interest groups derives from Mancur Olson, *The Rise and Fall of Nations* (New Haven: Yale University Press 1982).

19. For a brief overview of the dynamics of logrolling, see Dennis Mueller, *Public Choice* (Cambridge: Cambridge University Press, 1979), pp. 49–58. See also the discussion of 'distributive issue areas' by Theodore Lowi, 'American Business, Public Policy, Case Studies, and Political Theory', *World Politics*, **16**, 4, July 1964, pp. 677–715.

20. On the differences between early, late and 'late, late' industrializers, see Alexander Gerschenkron, *Economic Backwardness in Historical Perspective* (Cambridge: Belknap, 1962). The classic statement on logrolling among expansionist interest groups in Wilhelmine Germany is Eckart Kehr, *Economic Interest, Militarism, and Foreign Policy* (Berkeley: University of California Press, 1977).

21. The theoretical basis for this argument is derived from Anthony Downs, *An Economic Theory of Democracy* (New York: Harper, 1957), which is summarized, qualified and contrasted with logrolling by Norman Frohlich and Joe

Oppenheimer, *Modern Political Economy* (Englewood Cliffs: Prentice-Hall, 1978), pp. 127–30.

22. Louis Fischer, *Russia's Road from Peace to War* (New York: Harper and Row, 1969), p 304; on Lenin, pp. 48–51.

23. Even the exception proves the rule. Foreign Minister Maxim Litvinov's collective security policy can easily be explained as an attempt to lure France into a direct fight on her own border with Germany, while the Soviet Union would be insulated from significant involvement by the barrier of Polish territory. The most insightful analyses of this situation are Telford Taylor, *Munich* (Garden City: Doubleday, 1979), pp. 452–6; and Barry Posen, 'Competing Images of the Soviet Union', *World Politics*, **39**, 4, July 1987, pp. 579–604.

24. Nathan Leites, *A Study of Bolshevism* (Glencoe: Free Press, 1953); Alexander George, 'The "Operational Code": A Neglected Approach to the Study of Political Leaders and Decisionmaking', *International Studies Quarterly*, **13**, 2, June 1969, pp. 190–222.

25. In this analysis, I draw mainly on Gerschenkron, *Economic Backwardness in Historical Perspective*.

26. Detailed support for this analysis may be found in Jack Snyder, 'The Gorbachev Revolution: A Waning of Soviet Expansionism?', *International Security*, **12**, 3, Winter 1987–88, pp. 93–131.

27. These four strategies are a variation on the four images discussed in Franklyn Griffiths, 'The Sources of American Conduct: Soviet Perspectives and Their Policy Implications', *International Security*, **9**, 2, Fall 1984, pp. 3–50. The most important difference is that I split Griffiths's first image into two strategies, those of Molotov and of Zhdanov.

28. David J. Dallin, *Soviet Foreign Policy after Stalin* (Philadelphia: Lippincott, 1961), esp. pp. 229, 332–3; Mohamed Heikal, *Sphinx and Commissar* (London: Collins, 1978), pp. 90–2; and Uri Ra'anan, *The USSR Arms the Third World* (Cambridge: MIT Press, 1969), chapter 4.

29. E. H. Carr, *Twilight of the Comintern, 1930–35* (New York: Pantheon, 1982), p. 27.

30. Gavriel Ra'anan, *International Policy Formation in the USSR: Factional 'Debates' during the Zhdanovshchina* (Hamden, CT: Archon, 1983). Werner Hahn, *Postwar Soviet Politics* (Ithaca: Cornell University Press, 1982), sees Zhdanov as relatively moderate, especially in comparison with the party militants that succeeded him, like Suslov. In fact, Zhdanov's constituencies did lead him to be 'moderate' on some foreign and security issues at least some of the time — e.g., limits on defense spending (to undercut Malenkov's heavy-industrial base), opportunities for foreign trade (a Leningrad interest), and communization of Eastern Europe by political (not police) methods. But the suggestion that Zhdanov was actually opposed to the Cominform policy that he implemented so vigorously is certainly at odds with the memoirs of the European communists who lived through it. See Jerry Hough, 'Debates about the Postwar World', in Susan J. Linz, ed., *The Impact of World War II on the Soviet Union* (Totowa, NJ: Rowman and Allenhead, 1985), p. 275; Eugenio Reale, *Avec Jacques Duclos au Banc des Accuses* (Paris: Plon, n.d.), pp. 10–11 and *passim*. Zhdanov's Cominform speech is reprinted in Myron Rush, *The International Situation and Soviet Foreign Policy* (Columbus: Merrill, 1969).

31. G. Ra'anan, pp. 64, 68–70; Hough in Linz, pp. 268–74; Marshall Shulman, *Stalin's Foreign Policy Reappraised* (New York: Atheneum, 1969), pp. 32–4, 111–17; Bruce Parrott, *Politics and Technology in the Soviet Union* (Cambridge: MIT

Press, 1985), pp. 82–91; and Ronald Letteney, 'Foreign Policy Factionalism under Stalin, 1949–50', Ph.D. dissertation, Johns Hopkins University, School of Advanced International Studies, 1971, pp. 61–2, 65.

32. Herbert Dinerstein, *War and the Soviet Union* (New York: Praeger, 1959), chapter 4.

33. Letteney, p. 330. Letteney also provides indirect, but voluminous evidence that Malenkov and his allies criticized the 1948 Berlin policy as having justified the formation of NATO and the deployment of American nuclear forces within striking distance of the Soviet Union (pp. 56, 77, 82–3, quoting *Izvestiia*, 12 February 1949; 19 March 1949; and 22 July 1949). Note also that Zhdanov appointees ran Soviet policy in Germany until the lifting of the blockade in 1949, when they were replaced by Malenkov–Beria men. (Ann Phillips, *Soviet Policy Toward East Germany Reconsidered: The Postwar Decade* (Westport, CT: Greenwood, 1986), p. 34). Authors like Dunmore who portray Malenkov as a belligerent cold warrior during this period present virtually no evidence to support their view. It is likely, however, that Malenkov supported the military buildup at this time, because it led to the return to power of his wartime heavy-industry cronies. (Jeremy Azrael, *Managerial Power and Soviet Politics* (Cambridge: Harvard University Press, 1966), chapter 5). I am indebted to Dr Azrael for a helpful discussion of these issues.

34. Griffiths, 'Sources', pp. 3–50, and Raymond Garthoff, *Détente and Confrontation* (Washington: Brookings, 1985), pp. 36–68, elaborate on and qualify these basic themes.

35. Quoted by Adomeit, p. 224.

36. Gerschenkron, *Economic Backwardness*.

37. See P. Selznick, *The Organizational Weapon* (Glencoe: Free Press, 1960), and *Leadership in Administration* (New York: Harper and Row, 1957), p. 125.

38. When I use the term institution, I mean not only bureaucratic organizations, but also established ways of organizing social relationships, such as the institution of central planning or of the market.

39. Valerii Karabaev, Doctor of Economic Sciences, makes explicit the connection between many of these concepts in 'Our Debts', *Literaturnaia gazeta*, 21 October 1987, p. 4, translated in Foreign Broadcast Information Service, Daily Report, Soviet Union, 29 October 1987.

40. In addition to Gerschenkron, for a state-building perspective on the Bolshevik revolution, see Theda Skocpol, *States and Social Revolutions* (Cambridge: Cambridge University Press, 1979).

41. Quoted in Isaac Deutscher, Stalin (New York: Oxford University Press, 1949), p. 328.

42. Deutscher, p. 321.

43. Sheila Fitzpatrick, 'The Russian Revolution and Social Mobility', *Politics and Society*, **13**, 2, 1984, 124–6.

44. Speech to the March 1939 Party Congress, quoted in Sheila Fitzpatrick, 'Stalin and the Making of a New Elite, 1928–1939', *Slavic Review*, **38**, 3, 1979, pp. 377–402.

45. Lynne Viola, 'The Campaign of the 25,000ers: A Study of the Collectivization of Soviet Agriculture, 1929–1931', Ph.D. dissertation, Princeton University, October 1984, p. 59, also available as *Best Sons of the Fatherland: Workers in the Vanguard of Collectivization* (New York: Oxford University Press, 1986). For Stalin's speeches showing the manipulation of the 1927 war scare for factional and mobilizational purposes, see Jane Degras, *Soviet Documents on Foreign Policy*, II, 1925–1932, (London: Oxford University Press, 1952), pp. 233–7, 301–2.

While Stalin was trumpeting the threat in public, a briefing to the Politburo from Foreign Minister Chicherin argued flatly that the idea of an imminent danger of war was utter nonsense (Michal Reiman, *Die Geburt des Stalinismus*, Frankfurt: Europaische, 1979, p. 37).

46. Viola, 'The Campaign', p. 29; and J. Arch Getty, *Origins of the Great Purges* (Cambridge: Cambridge University Press, 1985). For a debate on the new social history of the Stalin period, see the essays by Fitzpatrick, Stephen Cohen and other commentators in *Russia Review*, **45**, 4, October 1986. Wolfgang Leonhard recounts that the new intelligentsia was so steeped in the militant ideology of revolution from above that, when given access to the foreign press, 'we could hardly summon up any interest' in viewpoints couched in 'expressions which were so entirely meaningless to us'. Only Trotskyite publications were dangerous, he explains, because they 'wrote in our own language' (*Child of the Revolution*, Chicago: Regnery, 1958, p. 235).

47. On the political economy of Kozlov's Leningrad, see Blair Ruble, *Leningrad: Shaping the Face of a Soviet City* (forthcoming), p. 33 and *passim*. On the budgetary and foreign policy stance of Kozlov and other military–industrial figures in the late Khrushchev period, see Carl Linden, *Khrushchev and the Soviet Leadership* (Baltimore: Johns Hopkins University Press, 1966), pp. 50–54 and *passim*; Sidney Ploss, *Conflict and Decision-Making in Soviet Russia* (Princeton: Princeton University Press, 1965), pp. 216–34; Christer Jonsson, *Soviet Bargaining Behavior: The Nuclear Test Ban Case* (New York: Columbia University Press, 1979), pp. 133–208; and Michel Tatu, *Power in the Kremlin* (New York: Viking, 1970). Hannes Adomeit, *Soviet Risk-Taking and Crisis Behavior* (London: Allen and Unwin, 1982), p. 262, points out that Kozlov was apparently not a risk-taker.

48. Samuel Huntington, *The Soldier and the State* (New York: Random House Vintage edn, 1957), pp. 62–79; and Richard Betts, *Soldiers, Statesmen, and Cold War Crises* (Cambridge: Harvard University Press, 1977). Note the fundamental amendments to this thesis proposed by Van Evera, *Causes of War*.

49. Jonsson, chapters 11–13.

50. On the Soviet military's role in the decision to invade Afghanistan, see F. Stephen Larrabee, 'Gorbachev and the Soviet Military', *Foreign Affairs*, **66**, 5, Summer 1988, pp. 1002–26, esp. p. 1006; also, Kimberley Martin Zisk, 'Soviet Civil–Military Relations and the Decision to Use Force Abroad', paper presented at a conference at the Rand Corporation, Santa Monica, April 1988.

51. Heikal, *Sphinx and Commissar*, p. 28.

52. Heikal, pp. 194–5. This is corroborated in general terms by analysis of the Soviet press reported in Ilana Kass, *Soviet Involvement in the Middle East* (Boulder: Westview Press, 1978); and Dina Spechler, *Domestic Influences on Soviet Foreign Policy* (Washington: University Press of America, 1978).

53. Lt. General Saad el-Shazly, *The Crossing of the Suez* (San Francisco: American Mideast Research, 1980), p. 161.

54. For more details in support of this interpretation, see Snyder, 'Gorbachev Revolution', pp. 123–4, and for background on the strategy itself, see Michael MccGwire, *Military Objectives in Soviet Foreign Policy* (Washington: Brookings Institute, 1987).

55. Condoleezza Rice, 'The Party, the Military and Decision Authority in the Soviet Union', *World Politics*, **40**, 1, October 1987, pp. 66–71, and Stephen Meyer, 'Civilian and Military Influence in Managing the Arms Race in the U.S.S.R.', in Robert Art *et al.*, eds, *Reorganizing America's Defense*

(Washington: Pergamon Brassey's, 1985), pp. 37–61, make this argument.

56. William McCagg, *Stalin Embattled* (Detroit: Wayne State University Press, 1978), p. 117, for this quotation; *passim* for the interpretation on which this paragraph is based.

57. On this point see also Timothy Dunmore, *Soviet Politics, 1945–1953* (New York: St. Martin's, 1984), pp. 116–17, and Radomir Luza, 'Czechoslovakia between Democracy and Communism, 1945–1948', in Charles S. Maier, ed., *The Origins of the Cold War and Contemporary Europe* (New York: New Viewpoints, 1978), pp. 73–106.

58. Ronald Letteney, 'Foreign Policy Factionalism under Stalin, 1949–1950', Ph.D. dissertation, Johns Hopkins University, SAIS, 1971, *passim* but esp. p. 197, quoting a Suslov speech in *Pravda*, 29 November 1949. See also Marshall Shulman, *Stalin's Foreign Policy Reappraised* (New York: Atheneum, 1969), pp. 118–20.

59. On Suslov and the International Department ideologues, see Roy Medvedev, *All Stalin's Men* (Garden City, NY: Anchor, 1984), chapter 3; Arkady Shevchenko, *Breaking with Moscow* (New York: Knopf, 1985), pp. 180, 190–1, 220, 262; and Bruce Parrott, *Politics and Technology in the Soviet Union* (Cambridge: MIT Press, 1985), pp. 193–8. See also the works cited above by Gelman, Tatu, Linden, and Ploss.

60. Franklyn Griffiths, 'Images, Politics and Learning in Soviet Behavior toward the United States', Ph.D. dissertation, Columbia University, 1972, pp. 40–1.

61. Ploss, p. 68; Boris Nicolaevsky, *Power and the Soviet Elite* (NY: Praeger, 1965), chapter 3, esp. p. 153; and Roger Pethybridge, *A Key to Soviet Politics* (London: Allen and Unwin, 1962), pp. 30–6.

62. Vera Dunham, *In Stalin's Time: Middleclass Values in Soviet Fiction* (Cambridge: Cambridge University Press, 1976).

63. Parrott, pp. 182–6, 190, 197; Gelman, p. 85 and *passim*; and Heikal, p. 194.

64. My interpretation closely parallels that of James Richter, 'Action and Reaction in Soviet Foreign Policy', Ph.D. dissertation, UC Berkeley, 1989). Richter's very important dissertation, based on exhaustive research in primary sources, is in some respects an application to foreign policy of George Breslauer's authority-building argument, which *inter alia* showed how the Soviet coalition-making process leads to overcommitted, 'taut' policy platforms (*Khrushchev and Brezhnev as Leaders*, London: Allen and Unwin, 1982, esp. p. 288).

65. Richter, adding nuances, develops a similar argument from an analysis of leadership speeches, which can be corroborated from a variety of other kinds of sources. See Arnold Horelick and Myron Rush, *Strategic Power and Soviet Foreign Policy* (Chicago: University of Chicago, 1966) on nuclear diplomacy; Parrott, pp. 131, 158–63, and 171–2, on the political role of nuclear and other high technology policies; Parrott, p. 137, for Khrushchev's ideas about 'the social significance of the ICBM'; and Heikal, pp. 97–8, 128–9, for an exposition to Nasser of Khrushchev's strategic theory.

66. As early as 1954, Khrushchev had used nuclear strategy as a successful political weapon against Malenkov and, in a passage from a speech that his colleagues excised from the *Pravda* version, Khrushchev bragged that 'we were even quicker than the capitalist camp and invented the hydrogen bomb before they had it; we, the Party and the working class, we know the importance of this bomb' (Wolfgang Leonhard, *The Kremlin without Stalin*, Westport, CT: Greenwood, 1975, p. 88).

67. For some minor qualifications, see Breslauer, pp. 67–71.

68. Jack Schick, *The Berlin Crisis, 1958–1962* (Philadelphia: University of Pennsylvania Press, 1971).
69. *Pravda*, 12 March 1958. Richter alerted me to this speech.
70. Linden advanced the hypothesis that, in some general way, a victory in Berlin would give Khrushchev the prestige he needed to check his domestic opponents and push on with his economic program. Richter, however, is the first to clarify this argument conceptually and to show in convincing detail how it worked.
71. The following reconstruction draws on Gelman, Parrott and Richter.
72. For Shelepin's probable stance, in addition to sources cited by Gelman and Parrott, see Joan Barth Urban, 'Contemporary Soviet Perspectives on Revolution in the West', *Orbis*, **19**, 4, 1976, pp. 1359–1402, esp. p. 1379. On his support for economic reform, see Christian Duevel, 'The Political Credo of N. G. Yegorychev', Radio Liberty Research Paper No. 17, 1967, and Richard Anderson, 'Competitive Politics and Soviet Global Policy: Authority Building and Bargaining in the Politburo, 1964–1972', Ph.D. dissertation, UC Berkeley, 1989.
73. Shevchenko, pp. 211–12.
74. Bruce Parrott, *The Soviet Union and Ballistic Missile Defense* (Boulder: Westview Press, 1987), pp. 27–39, on resource allocation debates in the mid-1970s; Michael McGwire, *Military Objectives*, pp. 61–2, 108–12; and Richard F. Kaufman, 'Causes of the Slowdown in Soviet Defense', *Soviet Economy*, **1**, 1, January–March 1985, pp. 9–32, on military policy changes in 1976–7.
75. Parrott, *BMD*, pp. 46–7; see also Garthoff, p. 1018, fn. 21.
76. Elizabeth Valkenier, 'Revolutionary Change in the Third World: Recent Soviet Assessments', *World Politics*, **38**, 3, April 1986, pp. 415–34.
77. *Pravda*, 16 June 1983; CDSP, 35:25, p. 8.
78. *Pravda*, 24 January 1955; CDSP, 6:52, p. 6.
79. For elaboration on the arguments presented in this section, see Snyder, 'Gorbachev Revolution'.
80. The *New York Times*, 4 December 1987, quotes Gorbachev's economic adviser, Abel Aganbegyan, as saying: 'we have set ourselves a task to make our ruble convertible. But to do that we have to change our pricing system to bring it closer to the outside. We will be conducting price reform in 1989 and 1990.'
81. The CIA estimated in a 1986 report that by the early 1990s, when the Soviets would need to retool for a new generation of weapons, there would be a zero-sum trade-off between the use of scarce high-technology resources for current military production and for investment in the long-run modernization of the civilian economy (US Central Intelligence Agency and Defense Intelligence Agency, 'The Soviet Economy under a New Leader', paper prepared jointly by the Central Intelligence Agency and the Defense Intelligence Agency for the Subcommittee on Economic Resources, Competitiveness, and Security Economics of the Joint Economic Committee, US Congress, 19 March 1986, esp. pp. 20–4).
82. The clearest cases are perhaps the U-2 (Tatu, part one) and Jackson–Vanik (Gelman, p. 161; Urban, p. 1379). On the effect of the international setting on domestic coalitions and foreign policy debates, see Jack Snyder, 'International Leverage on Domestic Political Change', *World Politics*, **42**, 1 October 1989, pp. 1–30.
83. H. Dinerstein, *War and the Soviet Union* (New York: Praeger, 1962 ed), chapter 4.
84. Letteney, p. 77, citing V. Matveyev in *Izvestiia*, 22 July 1949.

10 *The power of historical analogies: Soviet interventions in Eastern Europe and US interventions in Central America*
Dwain Mefford

Analogical reasoning and the structure of decisions

In foreign policy, as in everyday life, analogies are used to understand the present in terms of the past. The practice is ubiquitous and serves the purpose of reducing a new and possibly threatening situation to a variation of something familiar. For better or worse, what is known or believed is often transferred wholesale to new contexts. While the parallels drawn might be apt in some cases in some respects, the overall resemblance may well be superficial, with differences and discrepancies overwhelming similarities. As a consequence, analogies are simultaneously powerful mechanisms for orienting policy and sources of grave misperception and error. Much of the research on human judgment, by, for example, Daniel Kahneman and Adam Tversky, stresses the detrimental character of drawing explicit or implicit analogies. But recent work by a number of psychologists interested in problem-solving and processes of attribution emphasizes the more positive aspects by which analogies provide an initial understanding of the situation or problem.[1] Without this understanding, human action in a complex world would hardly be possible. Some linguists and theorists concerned with the formal and computer replication of human reason and the use of natural language take a more radical position. Not only is the use of analogies seen as a recurrent strategy for guiding inference, but analogies are recognized as among the most powerful mechanisms devised by the human mind for coping with complex and ambiguous information.[2]

In the study of political decisions, historians and political scientists have documented the costs of the uncritical use of analogies, in particular regarding judgments that have precipitated military action. These

185

treatments are generally anecdotal in nature. The historical record, in particular the memoir material, is searched for instances in which policy is determined by the likeness a decision-maker sees between one case and another. A classic example is President Truman's initial reaction to the aggression by North Korea. He claimed to have seen immediate and profound parallels between the challenge posed by the communists in North East Asia in 1950 and the German reoccupation of the Rhineland in 1936.[3] Some of the most insightful accounts of the inner workings of policy-making and problem-solving characteristics of administrations or key individuals have focused upon the repertory of historical examples that are repeatedly invoked.[4]

Whereas the psychological and historical literature provides a surfeit of examples of individuals using analogies to choose among options and solve problems, efforts in these fields to provide a systematic conception of how the process operates remain rudimentary. The work with human problem-solving in Cognitive Science and Artificial Intelligence recognizes the importance of analogy and metaphor but, to date, has produced little general theory that is immediately relevant to political analysis. One can report merely that while the work with concept attainment is suggestive, by, for example, R. Michalski, Jaime Carbonell, T. M. Mitchell and Patrick Winston, it has been confined to specialized data structures and their manipulation. The attempts to extract rules from examples and induce correspondences between problems, by, for example, Jaime Carbonell and Allan Newell, is intriguing but ultimately sheds but faint light on the type of judgment and reasoning that appears to be at work when decision-makers draw historical analogies.

A simple but effective conception of analogical reasoning involves the matching of sequences of symbols in a computer model. There are, however, more sophisticated and realistic forms of analogical reasoning that use complex script-like structures in place of simple event sequences. These conceptual structures capture more effectively the argument and reasoning inherent in the formulation of policy. The construction of policy options involves assembling plans. Elements of these plans are extracted from historical experience through the use of analogies. A second model of foreign policy-making combines the general notion of plan construction with the process of extracting plans or plan fragments from historical cases. There are, however, two critical issues that must be faced in any effort to study analogical reasoning in political settings. The first concerns the collective, competitive and game-like process by which analogies are posed and adjudicated as arguments are brought for and against their relevance to a particular situation. The second relates to the acquisition and reinterpretation of analogies. This is the issue of how historical 'lessons' are extracted from events.

Shifting the focus of analysis: from events and outcomes to cognitive process

In an important article on the utility of case studies as building blocks for theory, Alexander George attempted to merge the skills of the historian and the political scientist.[5] He called for an analytic strategy that was a cross between the broad, but shallow, statistical study of events and the detailed, but confined, recounting of single cases. His objective was to create a 'differentiated' theory of foreign policy behaviour that was reliable, that is, informed by a significant number of instances, and was at the same time sophisticated and 'focused' in terms of the questions it asked. It might seem that in wanting the best of what the political scientist and historian have to offer, he was proposing to square the circle. But his strategy was based on the sound proposition that systematic comparison is dependent upon the deliberate manner in which each case is described using a common set of categories, and not upon the number of cases. In short, the number of cases can be small and highly selective, yet still constitute an adequate base for extracting and validating historical insights.[6]

Concentrating on the craft of disciplined comparison as it is practiced in the historical sciences, George sweeps aside the statistician's cardinal concern with sampling from a population under a distribution. He implicitly justifies this in terms of the utility of the results. The findings that emerge are expressed in a language sufficiently rich and pertinent as to be of use to the policy-maker. George's lack of concern with the foundations of confirmatory statistics can be justified on more theoretical grounds. It is frequently the case in political analysis, for example, in the study of war termination or of the relative effectiveness of compulsion or compellence, that the universe of events is small enough that the cases selected constitute a sizeable portion, if not the whole of the relevant population.[7] As a consequence, the question of sampling from a distribution has no meaning. The set of cases used in this essay is a case in point. There are only a handful of crises in Eastern Europe in the period from February 1948 to January 1983 that meet the criteria for inclusion, namely situations that posed a vital threat to Soviet control. In general, if the criteria for inclusion are sufficiently restricted — a condition George rightly assumes is often the case in political analysis — then it is feasible to collect the entire universe of events. When this is the case, the size of the N is literally neither 'large' nor 'small'; sampling theory does not apply. Though George does not make this explicit in his discussion, the first step of his procedure, that of carefully constraining the domain under investigation, helps to ensure that the data tend to constitute a population rather than a sample. It follows that the statistical procedures that might be applied to this population are entirely exploratory and descriptive in the sense that the notion of an 'exploratory mode' has been contrasted with a 'confirmatory mode' in current thinking about the statistician's craft.

The virtue of George's approach lies in the sophisticated hypotheses it generates. As he points out, these are 'cast in the form of contingent generalizations [that have] the capability for more discriminating explanations'. To illustrate the desirability of this type of proposition over that which is typical of much of the work in quantitative international relations, George juxtaposes 'a general explanatory theory such as war is the result of miscalculations with a richer, more differentiated theory comprised of contingent generalizations that identify the different conditions under which different types of miscalculations lead to different types of war outbreaks'. As he claims, 'the second type of differentiated theory not only has greater explanatory power, it also has far greater practical value for policy makers because it enables them to make more discriminating diagnoses of emerging situations in which some kind of miscalculation might lead to an outbreak of violence'[8].

There are obvious advantages in pursuing explanations that are rich in information, but questions arise concerning the cost and feasibility of the data analysis required to induce such elaborated conditional findings. If the explanation is, in effect, known in advance and the task is simple to check its validity, then the research problem is clear and easily managed. But if the richly conditioned or contingent proposition is not known in advance, or is only dimly intuited, then the research problem becomes more difficult and may verge on the impossible due to the size of the space of hypotheses that must be searched. It may well be that the number of possible or interesting combinations of values across the variables, i.e. hypotheses to be investigated, propagates at a rate that outraces the researcher's unaided capacity to investigate. George does not expressly address this question. Perhaps his research strategy is intended to apply only to small populations of cases described in terms of no more than a score of variables or attributes. The work that he and his collaborators have pursued to date is roughly of this order. While restricting the complexity of the research problem does allow the analyst to proceed efficiently, much depends on whether it is possible in principle to tackle larger sets of more richly described cases. The problem of how to extend the program of systematic comparative analysis may ultimately decide the question of whether it is capable of sustaining cumulative theory.

Extending and generalizing 'structured, focused comparison'

A technique does exists for implementing the type of data analysis George envisions, which also compliments his research program by fashioning a question that radically shifts the focus of comparison. In addition to events and the attributes of actors, one can add the actor's cognitive processes including how the actor compares events and attributes. This involves a 'doubling up' of the phenomena under investigation. Where the issue of comparison is generally approached as a question of method, as in George's discussion, it is considered here as part of the object of research itself. The actor's cognitive process of searching for patterns among cases is an essential part of the decision-making process that must ultimately be described and explained. Stepping from comparative case analysis to the study of how cases are compared *by decision-makers* effectively transforms a question of method into a question of substance. It constitutes a bridge between conventional data analysis and cognitive modeling. Figure 10.1 illustrates the point.

A COGNITIVE ANALYSIS OF FOREIGN POLICY

STANDARD ANALYSIS OF FOREIGN POLICY

Researcher's task: identify and compare the process by which decision makers extract and rework patterns.

Researcher's task: extract and report patterns.

Data object: set of cases e.g., crises in Eastern Europe which threaten Soviet control.

Data object: the actor's cognitive processes including how the actor extracts patterns from cases.

Typical Questions for the Researcher Working in the Inner Box
1. On what criteria are cases to be included/excluded?
2. How are the cases to be described?

Typical Questions for the Researcher Working in the Outer Box
1'. What criteria does the decision-maker impose in selecting prior cases as relevant to a current decision problem?
2'. What is deemed salient about these cases, ie., how are they perceived or described by the decision-maker?
3'. What debate or conflict ensues from differences in how cases are selected and interpreted?

Figure 10.1 A cognitive analysis of foreign policy

Analogical reasoning in foreign policy: the Soviet case

The use of analogies is as commonplace in foreign policy as it is in everyday life. A theory of policy formation, and of decision-making more generally, must take this form of reasoning as part of its theoretical objective. To accomplish this requires a conception of the process at work. In drawing an analogy one case is used to inform the interpretation of another on the basis of parallels and discrepancies. Historical analogies are so familiar, and sometimes so subtle, in political debate that they go unnoticed. For example, in the case of Czechoslovakia in 1968, *Pravda* and *Izvestia* articles of July and early August are laced with explicit and coded references to the Polish and Hungarian precedents. Personal accounts by participants or witnesses to the internal debates within the Czech and Soviet communist parties and government bodies are also filled with examples in which historical parallels are drawn. A pair of analogies that recur in the Czech and Soviet deliberations, as well as in subsequent commentary and analysis, involve matching the situation in Czechoslovakia in mid-August 1968 to that of Hungary and Poland in October 1956. Although the decision problem was an extremely complex one for the Soviet leadership, it seems that the decision to use military force in Czechoslovakia largely hinged on the judgments of Soviet, Polish and East German leaders as to whether that country was another Poland or another Hungary.[9]

Other precedents are mentioned, including that of the ejection of Tito's Yugoslavia from the Cominform in 1948 and the Soviet use of troops to re-establish order following the Berlin uprising in 1953, but the studied attention gravitates to the crises in Poland and Hungary in October and November 1956. There is abundant evidence for this interpretation in the memoirs and personal accounts by individuals who witnessed the internal debates. An example is a diary entry made by an arms control specialist of the Soviet Central Committee, Mikhail Voslensky, in his summary of a conversation on the situation in Czechoslovakia with V. V. Zagladin, Boris Ponomarev's deputy. In response to the report Voslensky made on his return from Prague in the first week of April, Zagladin captured the Soviet problem in terms of factors that distinguished the Czechoslovakian situation from that of Hungary. To him the parallels with Poland were overriding:

> It is certainly possible that with some turn of events antisocialist forces may appear, but these will be isolated individuals, and are not to be compared with Hungary. [Regarding Dubcek, it should be remembered that] there were panicky voices in 1956 and 1957 when Gomulka was named party head, and yet nothing happened.[10]

In short, analogies recur repeatedly in the published media, transcripts, communiqués and, if we believe firsthand reports, in the conversations and thinking of the political figures closest to crucial decisions. They also figure prominently in the analyst's effort, after the fact, to describe and explain what transpired. The parallels and discrepancies between cases are seized upon to explain the twists and turns of events. The analogy or juxtaposition is not simply a turn of phrase, but is integral to the analysis.

Analogies are not only used to focus the description of events, but serve as a basis for exploring what might have been the case had certain factors or accidents not intruded. Jiri Valenta's post-mortem on Alexander Dubcek's strategic errors is an example. By contrasting Dubcek to Tito, and to a lesser extent to Gomulka, Valenta concludes that Dubcek failed to learn the cardinal lesson of effective resistance to Soviet military intervention: a small state must maintain the credible possibility that force will be resisted by force. At an early point in the course of events Dubcek denied himself this option by offering up General V. Prchlik in an effort to placate Warsaw Pact criticism. Analogies are used by decision-makers, and by analysts attempting to understand the decision-makers' reading of their situation and options. More than this, analogies are not simply rhetorical devices, but play a commanding role in shaping decisions by imposing certain options while masking others.

The situation that confronted the Soviet leadership as of the second week of August 1968 was the product of a chain of events that had unfolded since the spring of that year. The task for the analyst seeking to reconstruct the Soviet decision is to generate a set of strategies or courses of action that emerged from that situation. In structuring the decision problem, each of these strategies is to be evaluated in terms of the costs and risks entailed, with the result that options are criticized and ranked as they might be analyzed in a planning document or briefing book. In effect, the purpose is to replicate the way in which the decision problem takes on structure and definition, that is, the way in which options are created and deemed realistic and worth entertaining. This process is to a significant extent driven by the explicit or intuitive matching of features of the current situation against those of other situations, real or imagined. The dynamism and complexity of this process can be captured in the form of a programmable procedure. When applied to a situation and equipped with a memory containing some set of case histories, the task for the computer program is to piece together one or more strategies, each of which is constructed on the basis of what the historical record and received opinion hold to be the result of pursuing similar strategies in similar contexts.

Using the history of Soviet responses to crises in its East European bloc as a laboratory, the object of the program is to re-create strategies that the Soviet leadership may have entertained at particular points in time. Of special interest are those turning points at which the Soviet Union weighed the prospect of outright military intervention. In approaching this problem the program exploits the role of historical analogies as they are used in identifying and choosing among hypothetical courses of action. Sequences of events representing past cases are fed into memory. The program matches the current situation, for example, the events of July and August 1968, against these prior cases. Once precedents have been found, they are assembled into a composite graph representing courses of action leading from the current situation into possible futures. These paths are then inspected for costs and risks, and an analysis is printed out which contains recommendations as to how the Soviet Union should proceed and why.

A language of events and actions for the Soviet case

Before it is possible to compare histories and construct contingency plans, the histories must be described in some uniform way. Much of the systematic comparative work on crisis behavior encodes cases as lists of values on variables without regard for an ordering across the variables. That is, crucial information inherent in the temporal ordering of events is ignored. This accounts for the static character of much of the social science research that studies foreign policy within the framework of analysis of variance. There is a body of work expressly concerned with the temporal ordering and dynamics of events, for example studies of the phases or stages of crises.[11] The model described here treats historical cases as sequences of situations or events chained together by, at a minimum, an ordering in time. Recognizing that it is artificial to suppress the varieties of causal and intentional relations that transform mere chronology into interpreted history, for the purposes of this simple sequence-based model it is sufficient to restrict the relationships among events to the simplest imaginable, that of temporal succession. The empirical data therefore take the form of a mere skeleton of a chronicle. In the range of historical accounts, the data structure assumed in this study most closely resembles those simple chronicle-like entries reposited in such yearbooks as *Kessing's Contemporary Archives*.

To facilitate the manipulations used to extract patterns and to construct strategies, the events are recorded using a standardized set of phrases. These, in turn, are given simple labels to speed the process of matching so as to reveal more clearly patterns and regularities. This process of encoding can be illustrated using a fragment of the Czechoslovakian case. First, a raw précis is needed. Starting the case history with Antonin Novotony's appeal to Leonid Brezhnev, an abbreviated account of the course of events is extracted from case analyses.[12] In the effort to standardize and encode the case of the Soviet involvement in Czechoslovakia, the account is partitioned into paragraphs or propositions, each expressing an action from a predefined list. These propositions are then rewritten in a stylized form for the convenience of translating them into an internal representation to be used by a program. Without loss of information, these propositions are further encoded by assigning unique symbols to each.[13]

A coding scheme of this type is devised with two basic purposes in mind. One concerns the fullness of the description it permits, and the other involves the effectiveness with which the descriptions can be searched for patterns and parallels. By generalizing the conventional notion of a coding scheme to the related but more encompassing concept of a formal language, both objectives can be met. The primitives of the language, its basic vocabulary, and the organization of the language reflect the purpose of the investigation, that is, Soviet strategic planning as it applies to Eastern Europe. The language devised must be capable of adequately expressing those factors that are likely to affect Soviet calculations. More than this, the language must be designed in such a way that the process of drawing analogies can be replicated, along with the subsequent activity of piecing together the options and contingency plans informed by such analogies.

The lexicon used by the system consists of an inventory of predicates that, taken together, make up a rudimentary language for describing political events of concern to the Soviet Union in Eastern Europe. This language can easily be expanded to embrace a wider domain of events. Moreover, because the procedures for searching the case histories are independent of the way in which the cases are encoded, the language of description can be altered as desired. The lexicon, although limited and inelegant, serves the present purpose. The bulk of the terms denote political actions exerted by one regime or political faction against another. These actions are sorted into four groupings by agent, for example, the Soviet Union, East European communist parties, and so on.[14] A fragment of the lexicon is displayed in the form of a tree in Figure 10.2. Once encoded on the basis of this lexicon, a case is expressed compactly as a sequence of symbols. With the case histories in this form it is possible to proceed to the issues of search, comparison and manipulation intrinsic to the creation of historical analogies.

Matching, splicing and rewriting histories

The procedure described enables the researcher to represent cases as sequences of discrete symbols. At this point the problem of capturing the type of comparison and inference involved in the use of historical analogies becomes formally identical to a type of problem that is of central concern to a number of fields. Though there are important variations, the general task involves finding that subset from a sequence that best matches a given sequential pattern. In the example of Czechoslovakia in 1968, the sequential pattern to be matched is the encoded set of events preceding the Politburo decision of 17 August 1968. This sequence is to be compared against seven historical cases that, like the situation, have been rendered as sequences of symbols in accordance with the coding instrument described in the previous section. The cases include:

1. Czechoslovakia 1948 (culminating in the bloodless coup of February 25, 1948 in which the Communist Party takes over control from Eduard Benes's coalition government).
2. Yugoslavia 1948 (the tension in Soviet–Yugoslav relations resulting in the expulsion of Tito's Yugoslavia from the Cominform).
3. East Germany 1953 (triggered by the Berlin uprising in June 1953).
4. Poland 1956 (the Natolin faction surrenders power to Gomulka, and Marshal Rokossovsky is recalled to the Soviet Union).

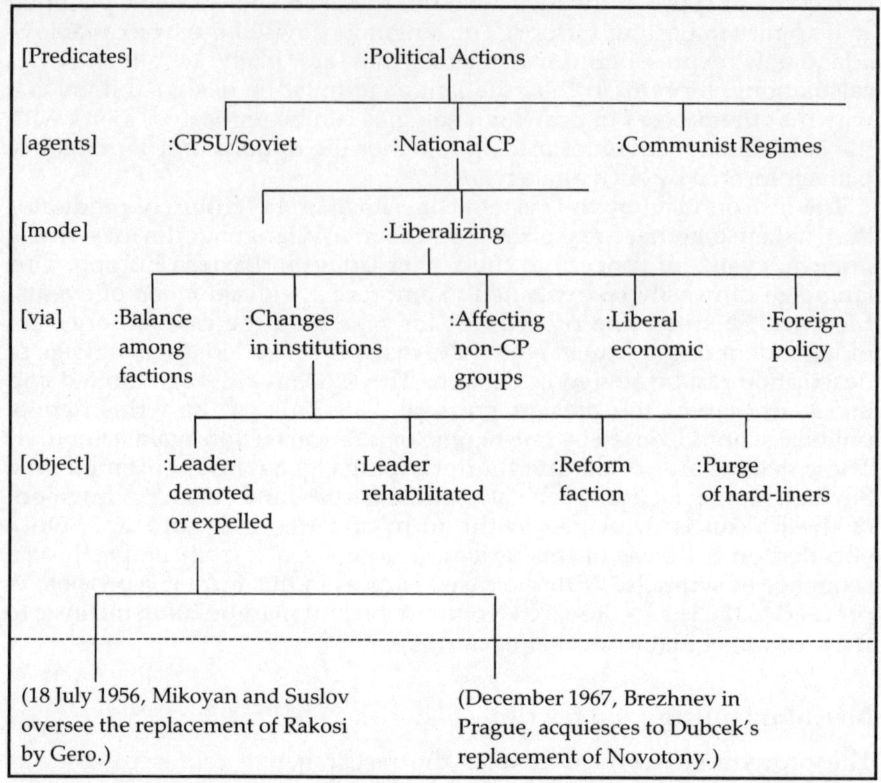

Figure 10.2 The structure of the political lexicon. The line across the base of the tree represents the step from the historically unique event to its description in terms of progressively more general categories.

5. Hungary 1956 (Nagy's reform movement erupts into anti-Soviet rebellion).
6. Albania 1960 (a function of the Sino–Soviet rift and Soviet *rapprochement* with Yugoslavia).
7. Rumania 1964–8 (over questions of Rumanian sovereignty in matters of CMEA policy and the stationing of WTO forces on Rumanian territory).

Measures of discrepancy and deformation

Although the essential task is conceptually straightforward, sequence comparison in rich domains encounters a number of complications. These stem from the problem of evaluating partial matches, when the notion of resemblance is ill defined. Much of the current work in this area derives from a strategy developed in the theory of error-correcting codes and parsers.[15] V. I. Levenshtein defines a general measure of difference between two sequences in terms of the number of insertions, deletions and substitutions required to transform the one into the other. Each of these operations is assigned a cost function; the 'distance' between two sequences is set equal to the minimum cost set of transformations required to convert the one into the other. If the weights are properly chosen such that the conditions of positive definiteness, symmetry and the triangle inequality hold, then the measure so defined is a true metric.

The essential idea of Levenshtein's procedure can be conveyed using a parlor game where the object is to change one word into another by successively altering letters. In his example, Joseph Kruskal converts 'WATER' into 'WINE', whereas Ju. A. Schreider uses the Russian terms for 'BLACK' and 'WHITE'. An illustration is useful because it conveys not only the basis for indexing the similarity of two sequences, but introduces a notation that has several uses. Following Kruskal, a succession of letter-by-letter changes (that happen to be minimal) can be displayed using the 'listing' depicted in Figure 10.3.

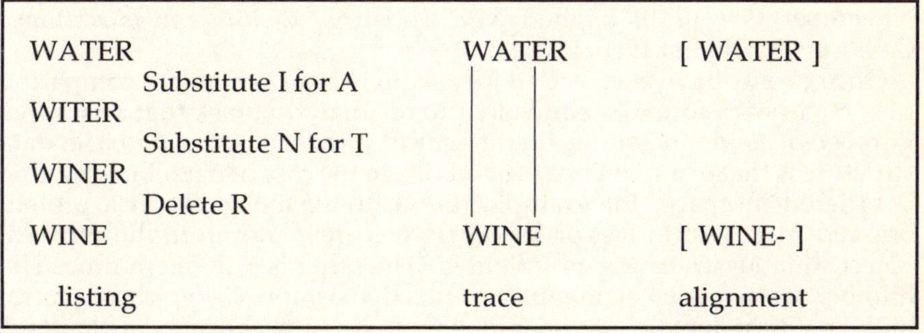

Figure 10.3 Three representations of the transformation used to match sequences of symbols

Each representation has its uses. The listing, while more cumbersome, is sometimes of theoretical interest because, as in computer science and microbiology, it can be construed as recording a sequence of physical processes and their intermediate products. It can be conceived as a process model where the individual transformations correspond to physical or computational transformations that are realized in some substantive domain.

The more compact notational forms of the trace and alignment can serve to describe the procedure used to render the comparative process at work in the construction of historical analogies. In fashioning its recommendation for Soviet policy in the Czechoslovakian crisis in the summer of 1968, the system finds partial matches between the situation it is given and sequences of events within the East German, Polish, Rumanian, and Hungarian cases. The closeness of the resemblance varies, however. The events in Hungary following 24 October 1956 most closely approximate the Czech case. The match found between the Czech case prior to invasion and the Hungarian case can be conveniently expressed as an alignment in which the symbols in the respective sequences represent actions and events as encoded by the lexicon described earlier. A 'D', for example, stands for a diplomatic action.

Hungary   (29 Oct. – 2 Nov. 1956)   [D M F P F C]
Czech.   (4 Aug. – 14 Aug. 1968)   [D' — F' — — C'][16]

With the costs associated with insertions, deletions and substitutions each set to 1, the system determines that the best match aligns the events on the eve of the Soviet invasion of Czechoslovakia with events just prior to the Soviet invasion of Hungary. The event-by-event match between the two sequences identifies the publication of the 'New Chart' in the Hungarian case [D] with the Bratislava Declaration [D']; the Soviet decision to cancel the evacuation of troops from Hungary on 30 October 1956 [F] is matched with the announcement of troop maneuvers on the Czech frontier on 11 August 1968, [F']; and the warnings in *Pravda* on 2 November 1956 [C] is aligned with the shrill warnings in *Literaturaya Gazata* on 14 August 1968, [C'].

Once events have been coded into sequences of symbols,[17] comparing case histories is formally equivalent to an analytical task that arises in a number of fields including mathematical microbiology. The basic data structure is that of a sequence of symbols. In the case of microbiology, one is ordered in space, for example, the array of molecules in a protein ordered from first to last or left to right corresponding to the physical object suitably stretched and oriented. The other is ordered in time. The number of articulated elements or events that comprise a typical sequence in the political domain is similar in magnitude to the number of elements in matching problems typical in genetics and other fields.[18] The programmed procedure initially used to search the case descriptions for matching subsequences of events is based on work with error-correcting parsers.[19] The current version of the program uses a computationally cheaper procedure based on an algorithm developed by R. A. Wagner and M. J. Fischer and by Peter Sellers.[20]

Analogies in action: The Soviet strategy on the eve of the invasion

The theoretical problem in the study of foreign policy differs from that confronting the mathematical microbiologist. The political analyst is interested not only in identifying and comparing patterns, but also in using them to fashion strategies. This adds an additional step to the analysis, as becomes apparent in the study of Soviet policy in Eastern Europe. The object is to reconstruct political deliberation and a decision that results in an action. In reconstructing Soviet policy on the eve of the 1968 invasion of Czechoslovakia, the model, in the form of a computer program, devised a stratagem that, though historically incorrect, appears superior to actual Soviet action in several respects. Effectively freezing the stream of events that preceded the Politburo session of 17 August 1968 — the date on which the fateful decision to invade was reached — the program is set the task of reconstructing the strategies that Leonid Brezhnev, Mikhail Suslov and other key Soviet officials may have individually or collectively raised or dismissed on that date. After identifying several feasible actions and discarding them on grounds of cost or risk, the program fixed upon a strategy of steadily incrementing the Warsaw Pact troop level of the forces than engaged in 'staff maneuvers' on Czechoslovak territory. The recommendation was that this force be increased until it equalled the number of armored divisions that had been assembled on Hungarian territory in the first week of November 1956. While this preferred strategy is historically wrong, since the Soviets in fact chose to invade in dramatic fashion with a force twice that used in Hungary twelve years earlier, the system's solution to the strategic problem is arguably superior to the actual Soviet decision for a number of political reasons. It is equally ruthless, yet more subtle, not incurring many of the costs and risks incumbent in a massive military action. The program in effect rediscovers Michel Tatu's criticism of the Politburo's suboptimal decision. Rather than applying force in the dramatic and politically costly form of an outright invasion,

> One can argue that a steady reinforcement of [the contingent introduced at the end of May] similar to what took place in Hungary on October 30 to November 1, 1956, might have been another course of action. The maneuvers could have evolved into a creeping invasion of the country with the same outcome as the August intervention but with less dramatic overtones.[21]

Constructing analogies is only one cognitive process among many within the overall task of creating and evaluating possible courses of action. Although analogies act to focus the imagination, their relation to the actual process of decision in most cases is an indirect one. Although on occasion they may exert such control on imagination and debate that they effectively exclude all other possibilities and, thereby, dictate policy by default, normally the analyst or policy-maker entertains several analogies that vie for consideration. This exercise of the imagination is clearly at work as decision-makers structure and refine the options before them. Analogical reasoning demarcates the landscape or world of possibilities, which, subsequently, is examined in a reasoned and articulated way.

As John Steinbruner and others have argued, this preliminary structuring of the imagination or effort to manage the 'structural' uncertainty of the decision problem is woefully understudied. Yet it may be intrinsically more important as a determinate of outcomes than other steps in the decision process, including those of applying optimal or satisficing decision rules. Analogical reasoning is neglected by decision analysts perhaps because the process goes largely unnoticed by the decision-makers themselves. The initial way in which a problem is conceived and explored is often relegated to the realm of intuition and *Fingerspitzengefuhl*. Nevertheless, the activity of evoking analogies may be a prime determinant of how the strategic problem in question comes to be defined.

Composite analogies

To this point we have concentrated on the procedure by which the historical record or memory might be searched in the effort to extract analogies. The question arises as to how these historical parallels, each loaded with different semantic content and judged to be of varying relevance, as indexed by the metric imposed, are utilized to define and evaluate options. How are analogies, once retrieved, refined and reworked, used as part of the critical process of constructing a policy? In the example cited earlier, Vadim Zagladin's reasoning illustrates this activity. He explicitly imposes a pair of analogies, the Hungarian and Polish precedents, juxtaposing the Czechoslovakian situation against the factors and risks identified with the two prior experiences.[22]

Because both the situation and the case histories can be presented as sequences of events and actions, a multitude of cases can be represented simultaneously as a directed graph in computer memory. If we assume a composite graph of this form, constructed on the basis of fragments of the past (and possibly other scenarios supplied by ideology or professional training), then the decision problem amounts to exploring and evaluating the sometimes overlapping and cross-cutting event sequences in the graph. This suggests how analogies, though rooted in unique events, can stimulate the creation of strategies that are relatively unprecedented. Such innovative strategies are informed by analogy, but represent an inventive variation that takes into consideration other analogies and factors particular to the situation at hand. The resulting scenario or contingency plan is, thus, an amalgam. The hypothetical Soviet strategy of incremental pressure generated by the computer program is an example. Although based on five historical cases, it is not a slavish copy of any one. In short, the analogies serve to define the problem space; they only indirectly determine the set of strategies that emerge from the exploration and inspection of this space of possibilities.

In solving a problem a program searches a 'problem space' seeking a sequence of actions (or a least costly sequence of actions) that leads from a state described in terms of a set of initial conditions to a state that is defined as within the solution or goal set. The problem space consists of all permitted combinations of the actions available to the program and, in general, is of such size that it cannot be exhaustively inspected. Hence the need for heuristic strategies for paring down the search space. In a certain sense the use of historical analogies to structure a decision problem can be construed as the imposition of heuristics. The better interpretation, however, is to view the pattern-matching procedures as a method for constructing a highly constrained problem space. In this fashion the computational task of searching for viable political strategies is kept in bounds.

Going beyond the technical issue, the process by which this problem is constructed can be construed as a partial theory of the problem-solving processes actually engaged in by decision-makers and analysts. There is, therefore, both a computational and theoretical payoff. As in the modeling of weak methods, a solution is defined as a path, i.e. a sequence of actions, that traverses the graph. In keeping with worst case analysis, a strategic solution to the problem posed by a situation is defined in essentially negative terms. It must traverse the graph without entering into a prohibited event (or into the neighborhood of a prohibited event). In the present example two events are considered prohibited due to their negative impact on Soviet interests: a national Communist Party's decision to share power, i.e. to default on its role as the leading political force; and the outbreak of a bloody, anti-Soviet rebellion. In the search for a viable strategy, if the system encounters either of these events, it discards its current plan and backs up a safe distance from the disturbing event. In addition, it reports out the failed strategy, citing the likelihood or possibility of encountering such an eventuality as grounds for dismissing the strategy under consideration. The system as written is risk-averse: if at all possible it searches for a course of action that safely avoids such outcomes.

In summary, this sequence-based model of analogical reasoning generates an initial decision tree on the basis of commanding parallels between the crisis situation and the best analogy it can draw from the historical cases. In this description particularly adverse events are flagged as presenting dangers to be avoided. Dismissing courses of action that lead to such negative outcomes, the system attempts to piece together a path or contingency plan that leads from the description of the current situation to a terminal point. In the Czechoslovakian example, the strategy devised approximates that which Michel Tatu called 'creeping invasion'. It is modeled after the Hungarian precedent, but contains a unique twist not present in the case histories. It is both historically informed and innovative like the best foreign policy problem-solving it is intended to explain.

A more realistic model of analogical reasoning: the United States and Guatemala

If the plausibility of the strategies generated is the measure of performance, then the sequence-based model performs adequately. But if we demand more from the model, that it construct strategies in a way that resembles the deliberations of a policy-making group, then the model fails. It lacks verisimilitude at the process level. An alternative conceptual approach that cuts deeper into the subject matter of foreign policy would

utilize more complex cognitive structures like the script-like structures
that are so prevalent in political argument. Policy papers, confidential
memoranda, the newspaper pieces of syndicated columnists, are all laced
with references to types of situations, prior events and chains of
consequences. Because structures of this sort are ubiquitous both in
speech and writing, it is easy to conclude that the same or similar
structures are in fact integral to the reasoning which these structures
convey. Even if this is not the case and there is a sharp difference between
inference as it appears in public and inference as it takes place in the mind
of the individual, these narrative and plan-like structures would
nevertheless figure in a theory of foreign policy because they are part of
the discourse through which the policy is communicated. Unlike the
cognitive theorist who can argue over the reality of these structures, the
political theorist must treat them as real because they are instrumental to
the collective cognitive process of politics. The question is not whether
they are to be included, but what specific form they are to take and how
they are to be incorporated into a process model of foreign policy-
making.

To strengthen the case for script-like structures, one should consider
the properties of the ideas and arguments that are typically used in
formulating policy. One example is the exchange of memoranda in which
options were posed from which emerged the plan to use covert means to
overthrow the President of Guatemala. In the first months of the
Eisenhower administration, in a document titled 'the Guatemalan
Problem in Central America', Adolf Berle, a Latin American expert and
well connected in the region, sketched a plan for the Jackson Committee,
ie. the International Information Activities Committee, under C. D.
Jackson. In justifying the plan he identified the following possibilities.

(1) American armed intervention —like that of 1915. This is here ruled out
    except as an extremely bad last resort, because of the immense
    complications which it would raise all over the hemisphere.
(2) Organizing a counter-movement, capable of using force if necessary,
    based in a cooperative neighboring republic. In practice this would
    mean Nicaragua. It could hardly be done from Mexico, and neither
    Salvador nor Honduras appears strong enough, though they might
    help.[23]

This fragment of an option paper is narrative or script-like, both in its
parts and in the overall message it conveys. It makes cryptic references to
past events and policies, indicating that it is partly constructed out of
images of past episodes. At the same time it projects the feasibility of
possible futures in terms of their political and material requirements.
Since this memorandum is typical of many that can be found in the
documents, unless strong arguments to the contrary can be mustered, it
would seem that a theory of the policy process would identify narrative
structures like these and trace out how they are formulated and reworked
over time. The basic structure involves not simply sequences of events as

assumed in the first model, but goal-oriented structures, including plans and fragments of plans.

The dynamics of analogical reasoning

An alternative to the notion of analogical reasoning as a rule-based, sequence-matching process is a conception that views political reasoning in terms of the acquisition and reworking of prototypical cases. A case-based or exemplar-based system offers advantages on a number of fronts, both conceptual and technical. Such a design effectively dispenses with the construction of rules. This, in turn, solves the nagging problem of how to justify the assertion that rules must reside somehow in individual memory or must underlie, in some shape or form, the discursive process by which policy is formulated. If experience, or experience transformed into stylized or myth-like episodes, is used directly in interpreting situations and projecting futures, then the question of what the rules are and where they reside becomes irrelevant. A memory-based system that reasons in this fashion has been programmed.[24] Presented with a partial description of an object or concept, it uses parallel search to retrieve from a large memory those examples that are most like the object; the properties of the retrieved object(s) are then used to infer unknown properties of the original object via comparisons by superimposition. Stanfill and Waltz claim that though their approach resembles the work with case-based reasoning of, for example, Roger Schank and Janet Kolodner, memory-based reasoning differs in that it uses memory match exclusively as its means of inference, rather than using memory search as an extension or supplement to a domain model of reasoning.

Foreign policy is pieced together out of proposals and arguments, each of which is plan-like in structure. The overall process can be characterized, therefore, as one that assembles and aggregates plans. It is incremental, incomplete and, in general, inconsistent. This is the case because the collective process is the activity of human beings who are all of these things, and who, moreover, are linked together though lines of control and communication that are often noisy and structurally ambiguous. To make matters worse, this whole activity happens in real time in the face of events that continually overturn assumptions and render arguments and strategies irrelevant. As was argued in the context of the first model, one of the principal qualitative mechanisms at work in the formulation of policy involves the use of past cases to guide the understanding of new situations. Somehow, prior cases are retrieved and matched. They are added to the cluttered tabletop of assumptions and intuitions which inform arguments. This process of reasoning about the present on the basis of experience or incidents in the past is the defining issue of the work in 'case-based' and 'memory-based' reasoning.[25] Reasoning on the basis of prior cases, which in the previous model was approached through the notion of 'anaology', is the principal form of structural inference at work in the formulation of foreign policy, as it is in contingency planning more generally. But to retrieve, adapt and apply previous cases requires that there be a stock of cases plus the means to identify and access them. Much of the research in case-based reasoning, particularly models of legal reasoning, by, for example Kevin Ashley and Edwina Rissland, assumes the prior existence of a body of well-structured cases. In foreign policy this assumption is much more problematic than it is in law. One is forced to consider the question of how the stock of cases is acquired and organized in the first place. This in turn raises perplexing questions of what it is that might be stored and in what form — fundamental issues in the study of human memory, and questions that have led researchers in Artificial Intelligence seriously to rethink their representations. A case in point is Roger Schank's radical revision of the Schank–Abelson notion of 'script'.[26]

The second model of analogical reasoning in foreign policy is motivated by the question of how cases or structures in memory are acquired. It treats the use of cases in problem-solving tasks and the acquisition of cases as elements of a single process. That process basically involves constructing, manipulating and collapsing plans. This reduction or truncation is best thought of as a process not separable from, but interleaved with, the act of planning. The complementarity of these cognitive tasks is characteristic of all human problem-solving in which memory plays a role, which means that it is intrinsic to all problem-solving as it has been conceived since the work of George Polya. The concern here is not with the duality of learning and applying what is learned in general, but with how it operates within the context of foreign policy, where it is manifest in the extraction of 'lessons'. To draw out the double nature of the planning activity, i.e. the reorganization of memory entailed in its very use, requires a working model supported by actual examples.

Converting plans to lessons

In a cabinet meeting in February 1954, John Foster Dulles, Eisenhower's secretary of state, outlined what the primary US objective would be at the tenth Inter-American Conference to be held in Caracas the following month. The goal for the American delegation would be 'to secure a strong anti-Communist resolution which would recognize Communism as an international conspiracy instead of regarding it merely as an indigenous movement'.[27] This diplomatic objective was instrumental in a plan of action that figured prominently among the options that the Eisenhower administration was then considering as a possible response to the threat it saw in Guatemala. The task that the administration had set for itself was to rid the hemisphere of the communist menace that President Arbenz was believed to represent. The plan, or at least one of the plans, that this diplomatic initiative would serve, appears to be modeled on the Korean intervention that had been concluded just the year before. With the political backing of an international organization, and under the legal authority of a treaty, the United States would conduct a military intervention in the guise of a multilateral action. Such an action would not only solve the immediate problem in Guatemala, but would achieve the larger purpose of proving that the United States could meet the challenge of world communism with strength and resolve.

Whether Dulles in fact contemplated seriously such a plan cannot be demonstrated conclusively, but there is ample evidence that he may have explored the argument. Minutes of cabinet meetings, cryptic references in the logs of phone conversations, and other documents support such a contention.[28] At a minimum, it is plausible to assert that Dulles, and probably a number of other high officials charged with formulating US policy, may have been reminded of the Korean experience and considered reusing the combination of diplomacy and force that had succeeded in that earlier case.

This, in essence, is what the second model of analogical reasoning constructs as it searches for cases in memory. The proximity of the Korean case, its magnitude on several political dimensions, and the fact that it shares with the Guatemalan situation the high-level goal of defeating world communism, are sufficient grounds for retrieving it and treating it as a possible model. The process of retrieval and projection of previous cases serves as the principal adductive mechanism for inventing options. It is central to the planning system in which the learning process is embedded. The learning or acquisition of 'lessons', or something similar, must occur if they are to be subsequently applied in the construction of plans. Somehow, from the welter of information that surrounds a real event, a record is extracted that takes a form that can be easily retrieved and projected onto new situations. If what is retained of past episodes is to be instrumental in the construction of new plans, then it is reasonable to assume that these structures in memory are plan-like in their own right. As a working hypothesis, we suggest that what is retained are, essentially, truncated copies of the planning activity associated with prior experience. If this is the case, then the act of planning on the basis of previous experience amounts to piecing together new plans out of old ones. On the question of the invention or the creation of 'new' possibilities, the imaginative act essentially involves deforming and recombining elements of past experience.

Policy is a goal structure and the set of plans that serve those goals. There is no requirement that the plans be consistent with each other — they may be predicated on different sets of facts or versions of facts. There is also no requirement that plans be even self-consistent, though one would expect that, if nothing else, the adversarial process that pits one plan against another, would impose something approaching local consistency. Because plans are basically nested structures, with higher-order plans spawning lower-order ones, identifying the extent of a plan can be problematic. Dulles's strategy for the Caracas meetings is a case in point. It can be treated as a plan in its own right, or, with equal justification, as a subplan, instrumental to the more inclusive objective of overthrowing the regime in Guatemala. That, in turn, may be a part of something larger. Basic to any historical interpretation is the choice of level that is to be treated as prime. For example, reading Dulles's actions with the benefit of hindsight, it is relatively easy to interpret the strategy at Caracas as a feint to draw attention away from the primary strategy, which was what later became a covert action. The point is that reality is inevitably more complex and need not be reduced to a unique ordering of goals and strategies. The action at Caracas can be viewed as an end in its own right, or as instrumental for one or more encompassing strategies. In reality it was probably both. In any event, recognizing that the policy plate, at any one time, has a great number of things on it, and that plans overlap and fold into each other, one can, nevertheless, focus on individual structures. A window thrown up by the system does this in a quite literal way. Figure 10.4 is an example in which a piece of Dulles's strategy is displayed.

The window is a tree on its side. The nodes in the tree are propositions, generally in the form of a predicate followed by arguments. For example, the expression 'multilateral_action(oas,us)' stands for the proposition that the United States pursues multilateral action through the auspices of the Organization of American States. The order of the predicate and its objects or arguments, the use of underscores, and the fact that everything is in lower case, are all unfortunate artefacts of the computer language in which the system is written.[29] What is of real importance in the figure is the relationship among the propositions. The dependency among the statements is represented by their proximity and by the depth of indentation. If one isolates the first two lines in the figure, they can be read as asserting the implication that: if legal basis for some action is true or exists, then multilateral action is also true. In short, the reason, support or warrant for a proposition is to be found on the lines immediately below it and at a deeper level of indentation. This corresponds to the standard tree representation in which the branching structure replicates the logical dependency among propositions.

The structure of propositions in Figure 10.4 can be interpreted as a plan in its own right, or as a subplan of something larger that extends beyond the limits of the window. This is what the window in the figure represents. It is a partial view of a collection of plan-like structures which, taken together, constitute a policy at a particular moment in time. Though this structure may be large, its basic composition is simple. Propositions are linked chainlike with simple implications via a branching structure that signals a conjunction of propositions. The pair of propositions on which Dulles's call for multilateral action depends is an example of such a conjunction. Conjunctions can be read off a figure like that in Figure 10.4 by matching up depth of indentation. Thus:

> 'multilateral_action(oas,us)'   depends upon
>   'find_legal_basis_for_action(oas)' and
>   'marshal_political_support(oas,us)'.

This says that, for multilateral action to succeed, it must be the case both

```
┌──────────────── WINDOW–15.MARCH.1954 ────────────────┐

  multilateral_action(oas,us):-
        find_formal_basis_for_action(oas):-
              exists_operational_clause(oas,rio_pact):-
              look_up_clause(rio_pact,clause_6).
        marshal_political_support(oas,us):-
              propose_resolution(us),
              adopts_resolution(oas),
              not blocking_action(oas,Opposition):-
                 blocking_action(oas,panama_et_al
                    offers_parallel_resolution(Oppos).

└──────────────────────────────────────────────────────┘
```

Figure 10.4 A window on a segment of a planning structure

that there is a legal basis for the action (in the sense, perhaps, of a treaty provision), and that sufficient political support for the action can be marshaled. In Dulles's case it turns out, historically, that the first condition was satisfied (or at least can be stipulated as arguably true given clauses in the Rio Pact), but that sufficient political support was absent because key Latin American states resisted the prospect of armed US intervention in the region.[30]

Extracting lessons from cases

Extracting a lesson amounts to truncating a tree structure, like the one in Figure 10.4. The structure is collapsed, that is, a number of the propositions, paths or entire subtrees are discarded. What remains is then committed to memory, that is, it is added to the stock of working cases that may be later retrieved and applied in subsequent situations. In general, what is saved of the original tree is its goal structure and those aspects of the plan which are deemed 'problematic', i.e. those aspects that warrant special attention. By defining 'problematic' in different ways, one gets different heuristics for extracting lessons. Some of the more intuitive formulations yield the most plausible results.

If one treats as 'problematic' only those steps in a plan which are frustrated by events, then, in the Dulles example, the subplan for determining whether formal legal authority exists is suppressed. This step in the plan did not present a critical problem, either because the Rio Treaty authorized such actions or, more likely, the question was never seriously raised because the plan failed for other reasons before the matter came to a head at the OAS. Because the second requirement of the plan, namely the existence of political backing from Latin American countries, was lacking, that branch is labeled 'problematic; and remembered. It failed because Latin American sensitivity to the question of US military intervention effectively frustrated Dulles's design for opposing communism in the Western hemisphere. Because it was a major source of doubt, it degraded the plan as a means for achieving stated goals. Defining 'problematic' as a source of plan failure, a possible heuristic for extracting lessons would collapse the plan in Figure 10.4 (reproduced at the top of Figure 10.5) into the lesson contained in the window in the bottom of Figure 10.5. Because there are arbitrarily many ways to operationalize what counts as 'problematic', in principle there are as many potential heuristics for extracting lessons. But there may in fact be only a small number that reflect how failure propagates through plans.

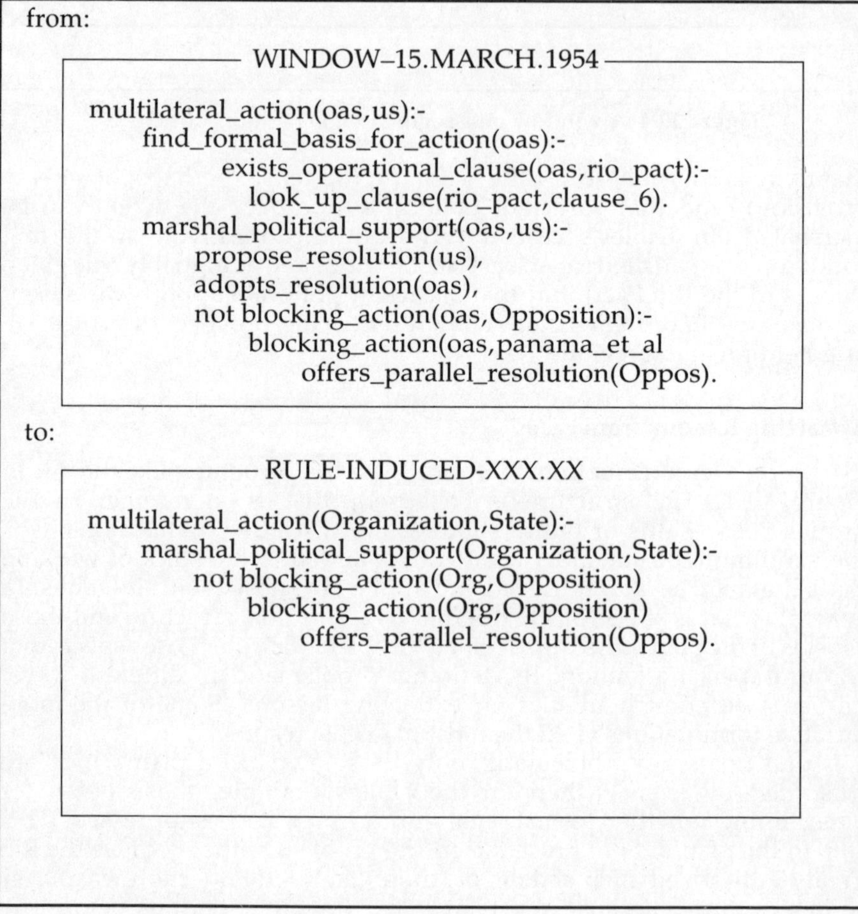

Figure 10.5 Extracting a 'lesson' from a plan

Because foreign policy is the resultant of the perspectives and arguments of different individuals, each equipped with different beliefs and different styles, it is likely that there will be variation in the heuristics they apply as they extract lessons from cases. It is interesting to consider what the aggregate effect is, or can be, as the mix or distribution of heuristics is varied. What the mix in fact is at a given point in times is, of course, an empirical question. But what difference changes in the mix might make in the conduct of policy is a question that can be posed and investigated in the spirit of monte carlo design or perturbation theory. The purpose of introducing this issue here is to point to the type of question that arises when one shifts the focus from the single individual to that of a collection of individuals. Shifting from planing as an individual activity to planning as a distributed activity raises a wholly new set of questions, comparable to those that emerge in the shift from rational choice to social choice. In the immediate context of how lessons are extracted, or the broader question of what structures are retained in memory, the step to the collective level corresponds to some familiar problems in politics. Using even the simple heuristic described here, different individuals are likely to treat different aspects of a plan as 'problematic'. As a result they may remember and subsequently use different versions of what transpired. Examples in foreign policy are legion, the retrospective treatments of Vietnam being a case in point. The different lessons that are drawn from what is nominally the same event can be jarringly contradictory. These differences clearly impact on policy.

Foreign policy viewed as a workspace of partial plans

Dulles's strategy at the OAS meetings, which was boiled down in the previous example, was only one branch of a many-branched policy. There were other strategies under active consideration. These included proposals that circulated among the members of the Jackson Committee, in particular the ideas in Berle's memoranda which C. D. Jackson passed directly to Eisenhower in late March 1953. While this might have been the first articulated plan for handling Guatemala, other plans were put forward at about the same time, including one that originated with President Somoza. The eventual decision to use covert action contained elements of several of these earlier plans, but added new features, which, it can be argued were taken directly from the operation to overthrow Mohammed Musaddiq in Iran in August that year.

In explaining foreign policy, one needs to reconstruct the rolling process by which options, like these, are recognized, sorted and reworked over time. As a step in this direction strategies and proposals can be represented in a common plan-like form. Some of these are well structured and include operational dimensions, but others are vague and disconnected. At any one point in time, there is a working set of plans. Viewed across time, this set changes because ideas are added and deleted, and because the proposals themselves mutate as they are extended, chopped, compared, merged, and otherwise revised. The space in which these plans are located is a 'blackboard' because it functions much like the blackboards used in production systems. Policy at an instant in time is a forest of plans in such a space. When it is explicitly represented it looks and functions, in fact, virtually like a blackboard.

One must not only inspect the contents and arrangement of the blackboard, but also watch it as its contents change across time. One can take the notion of change one step further by stipulating that the blackboard itself, which corresponds in effect to an organization of people, is continually assembled and reorganized over time as individuals are added or removed, or as their access or links are altered. This is an idealization, but it has some degree of verisimilitude. Consider the exit of Cyrus Vance, the Secretary of State, from the Carter administration. Vance's resignation constituted a genuine change not only in policy but in the very space of possibilities for policy. The metaphor of a team of individuals working at a blackboard in their collective effort to solve problems matches fairly well some common intuitions as to what actually transpires on a daily basis within the inner sanctums of administrations. The justification for using this particular metaphor is that it brings together, in an immediate way, an actual political system and a well-developed class of system designs that can be implemented on a computer. The objective is to move in a natural way from one to the other.

Tracing policy through time

One of the plans or subplans on the blackboard as of 31 March 1953 was the one advanced by Berle. Twelve months later, very little of Berle's plan remains. It is superseded by others, in particular by the idea of covert action that gains momentum in the summer and fall of 1953. For the study of the dynamics of policy formation, it is interesting to re-create the rise and demise of Berle's proposal. That resulted partly from the impact of events, namely the failure of diplomatic threats, and partly from competition with other plans that were posted in mid-1953, including one modeled on the operation in Iran. The evolution of US policy toward Guatemala in the first year of the Eisenhower administration can be pictured as a series of time-stamped blackboards — or snapshots of the same blackboard at different points in time. To see how a progression like this is actualized in the computer model requires examining the contents of the blackboards. The Berle plan appears to dominate initially, but quickly loses ground.

On taking office in January 1953, Eisenhower established the International Information Activities Committee, and made C. D. Jackson, a former *Time* executive, and a central figure in the draft-Eisenhower movement, its director. Within the first month of the new administration, Eisenhower charged the committee with producing a 'dynamic plan' to 'push the Russians back'.[31] Jackson solicited ideas from Berle. Berle's response, as recorded in his diary and in his biography, was to rework an argument that he had presented the previous month at a workshop conducted by the Council on Foreign Relations. The result was a memorandum titled 'Outline of Political Counterattack against Soviet Aggression', in which he reversed the standard Cold War scenario, and argued that the communist challenge was more likely to test US vigilance in the Western hemisphere, rather than in Europe or Asia. '[The] primary target (not secondary as commonly thought) will be the disorganization and seizure of portions of the Western Hemisphere.'[32] On 31 March, Berle submitted a longer memorandum on Guatemala that outlined possible courses of action. These included the use of military force 'like that of 1915', which Berle recommended against because of the political costs in the region. In addition to the unilateral use of force, Berle considered the possibility of creating what he termed a 'countermovement'. This raised the question of whether it should be based in a neighboring country, or should be independent of other states in the area. At all costs, according to Berle, the United States should avoid conspiring with Somoza, who would be 'anxious' to assist. The political liability of using this 'symbol of corruption' would be too great. Should the plan fail, Somoza's regime might be jeopardized. Third in Berle's list of options, and the one he most preferred, would be concerted regional action backed up by a US declaration and US economic pressure. In Berle's scenario this 'moral intervention' would either force Arbenz to get rid of the communists in his government, or it would force him to resign in favor of a political moderate.

Using Berle's own outline, and quoting verbatim where possible, as an example of the type of structure that would be posted on a blackboard, Berle's proposal can be rendered as a plan, which can be manipulated by the procedures in a computer model (Figure 10.6). To make the encoding transparent, the steps in his argument can be assembled into an outline and coded in a propositional form like that introduced in the Dulles example. Once a plan is in this form, it can be modified and extended through a process of political debate.[33] This argumentative process is informed by analogies. The product of the debate and planning that surrounds policy, in turn, becomes a source of analogies to be drawn upon in subsequent cases. In this fashion a dynamic cycle of policy-making and historical reasoning is set in motion. This second model of analogical reasoning captures — if in an artificial way — the process by which political lessons are extracted from situations, only to be reworked and reused in the envisioning of future courses of action.

Goal:counter communist penetration of the Western hemisphere.
Goal: counter communist penetration of Guatemala.
Goal: 'how to clear out the Communists'.
Via: 'armed intervention like that of 1915.'
But: 'This is here ruled out except as an extremely bad last resort, because of the immense complications it would raise all over the hemisphere.'

Via: 'organized countermovement, capable of using force'
Either: based in a neighboring country.
Such as: Mexico
But: that is politically unrealistic.
or: Somoza's Nicaragua,
But: that would identify the United States with that 'symbol of corruption'.
or: . . .

Via: 'moral intervention', which amounts to
Organizing a Central American 'Political Action Group'
Which includes only non-Somoza Nicaraguans.
appointing a US ambassador as 'theater commander'
and issuing
Declarations by the regional countries.
Declaration by the United States.
and this heightened by economic pressure.
Meanwhile US agents would
stir up dissent.
make overtures to the Guatemalan military.

Figure 10.6 The plan in Adolf Berle's memorandum to C.D. Jackson

Notes

1. See, for example, Herbert A. Simon, 'Artificial Intelligence Systems that Understand', *Proceedings, International Joint Conference on Artificial Intelligence* (1977), pp. 1059–73, and Robert J. Sternberg, *Intelligence, Information Processing and Analogical Reasoning: The Computational Analysis of Human Abilities* (Hillsdale, NJ: Lawrence Erlbaum, 1977).
2. Andrew Ortony, ed., *Metaphor and Thought* (New York: Cambridge University Press, 1979); David Rumelhart and Andrew Ortony, 'The Representation of Knowledge in Memory', in Richard C. Anders *et al.*, eds, *Schooling and the Acquisition of Knowledge* (Hillsdale, NJ: Lawrence Erlbaum, 1977); George Lakoff and Mark Johnson, *Metaphors We Live By* (Chicago: University of Chicago Press, 1980); Wendy G. Lahnert and Martin H. Ringle, eds, *Strategies for*

Natural Language Processing (Hillsdale, NJ: Lawrence Erlbaum, 1982); and George Lakoff, *Women, Fire and Dangerous Things: What Categories Reveal About the Mind* (Chicago: University of Chicago Press, 1987).

3. Harry S. Truman, *Memoirs*, II (Garden City, NY: Doubleday, 1956), p. 333. See also Ernest R. May, *Lessons of the Past: The Use and Misuse of History in American Foreign Policy* (New York: Oxford University Press, 1973), and Thomas G. Paterson, J. Garry Clifford and Kenneth T. Hagan, *American Foreign Policy*, I, (Lexington, MA: D. C. Heath, 1983), pp. 472ff.

4. Lloyd Gardner, *Architects of Illusion* (Chicago: Quadrangle Books, 1970); and David S. McLellan, *Dean Acheson: The State Department Years* (New York: Dodd, Mead and Co, 1976).

5. Alexander L. George, 'Case Studies and Theory Development: The Method of Structured, Focused Comparison', in Paul G. Lauren, ed., *Diplomacy: New Approaches in History, Theory and Policy* (New York: The Free Press, 1979), pp. 43–68.

6. Alexander L. George and Richard Smoke, 'Deterrence and Foreign Policy', *World Politics*, **61**, 2, 1989, pp. 170–82.

7. Alexander L. George, David K. Hall and William E. Simons, *The Limits of Coercive Diplomacy: Laos, Cuba, Vietnam* (Boston: Little, Brown and Company, 1971); and Alexander L. George and Richard Smoke, *Deterrence in American Foreign Policy: Theory and Practice* (New York: Columbia University Press, 1974). See also William Sewell, 'Marc Bloch and the Logic of Comparative History', *History and Theory*, **6**, 1967, pp. 208–18.

8. George, 'Case Studies and Theory Development', p. 59, and George, Hall and Simons, *Limits of Coercive Diplomacy*, p. 511.

9. Christian Schmidt-Hauer and Adolf Muller, *Viva Dubcek: Reform und Okkupation in der CSSR* (Koln, Kiepeneaer and Wutsche, 1968); Fritz Ermath, 'Internationalism, Security and Legitimacy: The Challenge to Soviet Interests in East Europe, 1964–1968' (RM-5909-PR, Santa Monica, CA: The RAND Corporation); Philip Windsor and Adam Roberts, *Czechoslovakia 1968, Reform and Resistance* (New York: Columbia University Press, 1969); Jiri Pelikan, *Ein Fruhlung, der nie zu Endegeht: Erinnerungen eines Prager Kommunisten* (Frankfurt: Fischer, 1976); Jiri Valenta, *Soviet Intervention in Czechslovakia, 1968: Anatomy of a Decision* (Baltimore: The Johns Hopkins Press, 1979); and Michel Tatu, 'Intervention in Eastern Europe', in Stephen S. Kaplan *et al.*, eds, *Diplomacy of Power: Soviet Forces as a Political Instrument* (Washington, DC: The Brookings Institution, 1981).

10. 'Freilich können bei einem Umschwung auch antisozialistische Kräfte auftauchen, aber das sind Einzelpersonen, mit Ungarn ist das nicht zu vergleichen. Im Zusammenhang mit der Ernennung von Gomulka . . . gab es 1956/57 auch panische Stimmungen, und es ist doch nichts passiert.' M. Woslenski, 'Das wird nur den Amerikanern helfen', Tagebuch-Notizen des sowjetischen Funktionars Michael Woslenski uber die Hintegrunde der Prag-Invasion [That Will only Help the Americans', The Diary of the Soviet Functionary, Michael Woslenski, regarding the Background of the Prague Invasion.] *Der Spiegel* 32. Jahrgang, 21 August, 1978, p. 126.

11. Lincoln P. Bloomfield and Amelia C. Liess, *Controlling Small Wars: A Strategy for the 1970s* (New York: Alfred A. Knopf, 1969); Richard E. Barringer, *War Patterns of Conflict* (Cambridge, MA: MIT Press, 1972); and Lee Farris, Hayward R. Alker, Kathleen Carley and Frank L. Sherman, 'Phase/Actor Disaggregated Butterworth-Scranton Codebook', Project Working Paper (Cambridge, MA: Center for International Studies, MIT, 1980).

12. See note 9.

13. A case in narrative form is reduced to a list of events and rewritten as a sequence of stylized propositions. A coded symbol is assigned to each of these. For example, 'December 1967: The Stalinist head of the Czechoslovak Communist Party, Antonin Novotony, calls on Brezhnev to support him against the challenge to his leadership posed by the reform-minded opposition within the party; Brezhnev travels to Prague but adopts a "hands off" policy.' This is rendered as a pair of propositions in which a predicate is followed by a list of qualifiers.

> K42 [NATIONAL CP/GOVERNMENT ACTION:INVOLVING THE S.U.
> :APPEALS
> :FOR SUPPORT AGAINST CHALLENGE WITHIN THE PARTY]
>
> D22 [CPSU/SOVIET ACTION:BETWEEN S.U. AND BLOC MEMBER(S)
> CONCILIATORY:NEGOTIATIONS WITH NATIONAL CP LEADER(S)
>
> POLITBURO:LEADING TO CHANGE IN NATIONAL CP LEADERSHIP
> :SOVIETS ACQUIESCE TO THE RISE OF A NEW LEADER]

14. Those actions indicative of the Soviet Union or its leadershp are grouped under one heading, as are those actions initiated by individual Eastern European communist parties and those involving the collective participation of several communist regimes operating formally or informally under the guise of the Warsaw Pact Treaty Organization or the Council for Mutual Economic Assistance. A final group involves actors within socialist societies which are neither affiliated with the Community Party nor identified with other states. Examples include unions, spontaneous mob violence, public pressure, and the like. Several difficult-to-categorize actions are also included in this set, e.g., economic crisis. The division into these four groupings is a matter of convenience and does not signify a serious nomenclature. We have experimented with more differentiated lexicons patterned after case grammars, but a relatively simple inventory of political actions suffices as a base for the present study. See Eugene Charnick, and Yurick Wilks, *Computational Semantics* (New York: North Holland, 1976).

15. V. I Levenshtein, 'Binary Codes Capable of Correcting Deletions, Insertions and Reversals', *Cybernetics and Control Theory*, **10**, 8, 1966, pp. 707–10 (Russian original in *Doklady Akademii Nauk SSR*, **163**, 4, 1965, pp. 845–8); and 'Binary Codes Capable of Correcting Spurious Insertions and Deletions of Ones', *Problems of Information Transmission*, **1**, 1966, pp. 8–17 (Russian original in *Problemy Peredachi Informatssi*, **1**, 1, 1965, pp. 12–25; S. M. Ulam, 'Some Combinatorial Problem Studies Experimentally on Computing Machines', in S. K. Zaremba, ed., *Applications of Number Theory to Numerical Analysis* (New York: Academic Press, 1972), pp. 1–3; and K. S. Fu, *Syntactic Pattern Recognition and Applications* (Englewood Cliffs, NJ: Prentice-Hall, 1982), pp. 246–75.

16. The alignment reveals several of the complications that typically arise in this type of matching problem. One involves the difference in the number of symbols in the two sequences. With historical data, as with data encountered in other domains, it would be highly restrictive to permit only correspondences between sequences of exactly the same length. In working with political histories, it is likely that one account may be richer in detail than another and yet the two may be deemed to be structurally quite similar. The

problem is to construct a matching procedure that is insensitive to minor differences in the detail of the reportage. In the continuous case this issue is called 'time-warping' and arises in many areas of research, particularly that of speech recognition. The technical problem of constructing the best alignment(s), given an initial sequential pattern and a set of sequences to be inspected, is solved using a dynamic programming strategy. See, for example, Bruce W. Erickson and Peter H. Sellers, 'Recognition of Pattern in Genetic Sequences', in David Sankoff and Joseph Kruskah, eds, *Time Warps, String Edits and Macromolecules: The Theory and Practice of Sequence Comparison* (Reading, MA: Addison-Wesley, 1983), pp. 55–91. This work is motivated by the problem typical of the comparison of RNA, DNA and protein sequences in microbiology. See, for example, T. F. Smith and M. S. Waterman, 'New Stratigraphic Correlation Techniques', *Journal of Geology*, **88** 1980, pp. 451–7; and their 'Identification of Common Molecular Subsequences', *Journal of Molecular Biology*, **147**, 1981, pp. 195–7; and Peter Friedland and Lawrence H. Kedes 'Discovering the Secrets of DNA', *Communications of the ACM*, **28**, 1985, pp. 1164–86.
17. The program reported here uses a subset of the 255 distinct bit strings used to encode the ASCII character set, but this choice is arbitrary, dictated solely by the desire efficiently to compare and manipulate the cases once encoded.
18. In the study of proteins and nucleotides, the vocabulary consists of either four or twenty terms; there are roughly thirty distinct terms in the political lexicon employed in this case study. The length of the typical sequence in the work in molecular biology ranges from less than one hundred molecules to thousands in the case of RNA, and to millions in the case of DNA. A typical political history may include one hundred or more events or actions. In short, at an abstract level, the isomorphism between the essential features of the two research problems suggests that the formalism and procedures that have proven effective in the one may hold out promise for the other.
19. Alfred V. Aho, D. S. Hirschberg and John D. Ullman, 'Bounds of the Complexity of the Longest Common Sequence Problem', *Journal of the Association for Computing Machinery*, **23**, 1974, pp. 1–12; Aho, John E. Hopscroft and Ullman, *The Design and Analysis of Computer Algorithms* (Reading, MA: Addison-Wesley, 1974); E. Tanaka and K.S. Fu, 'Error-Correcting Parsers for Formal Languages', *IEEE Trans Comput*, 1978, C-27, pp. 605–16; and K. S. Fu, *Syntactic Pattern Recognition and Applications* (Englewood Cliffs, NJ: Prentice-Hall, 1982).
20. R. A Wagner and M. J. Fischer, 'The String-to-String Correction Problem', *Journal of the Association for Computing Machinery*, **21**, 1974, pp. 168–73; Peter H. Sellers, 'An Algorithm for the Distance Between Two Finite Sequences', *Journal of Combinator Theory*, 1974, A16, pp. 253–8; and his 'On the Theory and Computation of Evolutionary Distances',. *SIAM Journal of Applied Mathematics*, **26**, 1974, pp. 787–93.
21. Tatu, 'Intervention in Eastern Europe', p. 224.
22. Woslenski, 'Das wird nur den Amerikanern helfen', pp. 126–9.
23. Blanche W. Cook, *The Declassified Eisenhower: A Divided Legacy* (Garden City, NY: Doubleday, 1981), p. 234.
24. See Craig Stanfill and David Waltz, 'Toward Memory-Based Reasoning', *Communications of the ACM*, **29**, 12, 1986, pp. 1213–28.
25. See Dwain Mefford, 'Case-Based Reasoning, Legal Reasoning, and the Study of Politics', *Political Behaviour*, **12**, 2, 1990, pp. 125–58; and 'Steps Toward Artificial Intelligence: Rule-Based, Case-Based and Explanation-Based

Models of Politics', in Valerie M. Hudson, ed., *Artificial Intelligence and International Politics* (Boulder, CO: Westview Press, 1990).

26. Roger C. Schank and Robert P. Abelson, *Scripts, Plans, Goals, and Understanding: An Inquiry into Human Knowledge Structures* (Hillsdale, NJ: Lawrence Erlbaum, 1977); Schank, *Dynamic Memory; A Theory of Reminding and Learning in Computers and People* (New York: Cambridge University Press, 1982); and Schank, 'Language and Memory', *Cognitive Science*, **4**, 3, 1983 pp. 243–84.

27. Minutes of cabinet meeting, 26 Feb 1954, cited in Richard H. Immerman, *The CIA in Guatemala: The Foreign Policy of Intervention* (Austin: University of Texas Press, 1982), p. 145.

28. See references and reconstructions in Immerman, *The CIA in Guatemala*; Immerman, 'Eisenhower and Dulles: Who Made the Decisions?' *Political Psychology*, **1**, 2, Autumn 1979, pp. 3–20; Cook, *The Declassified Eisenhower*; and Stephen Schlesinger and Stephen Kinzer, *Bitter Fruit: The Untold Story of the American Coup in Guatemala* (Garden City, NY: Anchor Press/Doubleday, 1982).

29. On the Xerox 1108, the version of these programs was equiped with a simple parser that converted the program's output to a more pleasing form, but the present system is written for the IBM-PC, and the interface is a luxury that limitations on memory precluded.

30. See Cole Blasier, *The Hovering Giant: US Responses to Revolutionary Change in Latin America* (Pittsburg: University of Pittsburg Press, 1976); Immerman, *The CIA in Guatemala*, and 'Eisenhower and Dulles'; and Walter Lefeber, *Inevitable Revolutions: The United States in Central Amerca* (New York: W. W. Norton, 1984).

31. Immerman, *The CIA in Guatemala*, p. 130.

32. ibid. See also Beatrice B. Berle and T. B. Jacobs, *Navigating the Rapids, 1918–1971, from the Papers of Adolf A. Berle* (New York: Harcourt, Brace, Jovanovich, 1973).

33. Dwain Mefford, 'Changes in Foreign Policy Across Time: The Logical Analysis of a Succession of Decision Problems Using Logic Programming', in Urs Luterbacher and Michael D. Ward, eds, *Dynamic Models of International Conflict* (Boulder, CO: Lynne Reinner Publishers, 1985), pp. 401–23; Mefford, The Policy Process and the Evolution of Argument: Casting Theory in the Form of a Series of Computer Programs', unpublished paper presented at the International Studies Association conference, Washington, DC, April 1987; and Mefford, Analogical Reasoning and the Definition of the Situation: Back to Snyder for Concepts and Forward to Artificial Intelligence for Method', in Charles F. Hermann, Charles W. Kegley and James N. Rosenau, eds, *New Directions in the Study of Foreign Policy* (Boston: Allen and Unwin, 1987), pp. 221–44.

11 *Learning and reasoning by analogy*
Alex Hybel

Introduction

We are captives of the past. Whether as individuals who must cope with mundane problems or as foreign policy-makers who need to defuse the latest international crisis, our decisions are anchored to lessons inferred from previous experiences. How we interpret the past, however, can vary significantly even when our lives are affected by the same event. Just as two drivers caught in the same gridlock might deduce different lessons from their common experience, so might two foreign policy-makers absorbed by the demands of the same international political crisis reach different conclusions regarding the nature of the problem.

Decision-making is a process that involves the identification and definition of problems and the ordering and choosing among alternatives.[1] Most decision analysts have channeled their efforts to the second task. They define the problem in advance and then identify a hierarchy of available options by referring to the values of the decision-makers.[2] Recently, however, analysts have argued that the initial formulation of a problem can have a decisive effect on the decision actually reached.[3] They have proposed that the solution to a problem is not simply the function of a set of values ordered hierarchically, but is also the result of the way in which the problem itself is interpreted.

Contextual factors associated with past events impose interpretations on new issues.[4] This relationship has been acknowledged by several students of foreign policy. Richard Neustadt and Ernest May, Deborah Larson, Richard Ned Lebow and Robert Jervis, for example, have argued that foreign policy leaders use historical examples to define problems, to formulate options, or to oppose proposed policies. Some of them have viewed the use of historical analogies critically, as a source of illusion and error in the decision-making process. As explained by Robert Jervis, analogies tend to 'obscure aspects of the present case that are different from the past one'.[5]

The claim is justified. History is filled with instances in which leaders sought to resolve new problems by resorting to solutions used in earlier times, quite ignorant of the fact that the differences between the cases stretched far beyond the variance in time. In the early 1980s it was not unusual to suggest that the lessons of Vietnam should be studied before concluding that it was imperative to send troops into Nicaragua to topple the newly established Sandinista regime. Too often these arguments were voiced without recognizing that the two problems were decidedly different. Likewise, twenty years earlier, John F. Kennedy, convinced apparently that Barbara Tuchman's book, *The Guns of August*, articulated some important lessons about the First World War, used some of them to design the way he would respond to the Soviet deployment of nuclear missiles in Cuba. Although another major world war was averted, careful analysis of the two problems would have revealed that their differences outweighed their similarities. And finally, little historical insight is required to recognize the inappropriateness of President Harry Truman's reference in 1950 to the Munich débâcle to define the problem posed by the invasion of South Korea by its northern counterpart.

Analogies can be sources of error and illusion in decision-making processes, but they are also the means most commonly used for defining problems which, in turn, influence the way alternatives are abstracted and choices made. As linguists and theorists who focus on the formal and computer replication of human reason have noted, analogies are among the most powerful mechanisms devised by the human mind for coping with uncertainty and value complexity.[6] It is necessary to derive an analogical theory of foreign policy-making that moves beyond the two-step proposition typically advanced by some students of foreign policy. Their basic contention has been that behavior is the function of lessons inferred from past events.[7] Analogical reasoning is a process significantly more complex than the one just described.

This essay will focus on and link two approaches to the analysis of analogies. It will start with Robert Sternberg's theory of analogical reasoning in which he proposes a mechanism to map out logically the component mental operations that sustain a series of related information-processing tasks and 'to discover the organization of these component operations in terms of their relationships both to each other and to a higher-order constellation of mental abilities'.[8] Based on the assumption that limitations exist on the human ability to process vast amounts of information, Sternberg proposes that the behavior of a human cognitive system can be depicted as a mechanism designed to delineate the nature of a problem as it surfaces, sort out the information needed to address it, and structure the type of inferences that are derived from the information gathered. For Sternberg, reasoning by analogy in the form of 'A is to B as C is to D', in which the first pair relationship is discovered and then mapped according to a particular rule to outline a second identical structural relationship, is such a type of mechanism.

The addressing of a problem involes more than reasoning. As an individual is confronted with a new situation, he will seek to define the problem in some familiar context. Thus, reasoning by analogy in the form 'A is to B as C is to D' may or may not remain constant. Jaime Carbonell has proposed that learning by analogy is the most common learning mechanism and that it involves solving problems incrementally as the analyst derives generalizations from the discovery of commonalties among previous and present situations. Past behavior, however, is not incorporated automatically into the current problem, but is adapted to meet its special demands. Responses to earlier problems, in other words, bring about the formation of what Carbonell refers to as 'familiar problem space'.[9]

The two theories approach analogy from significantly different perspectives. More importantly, they do not capture individually the overall process involved in problem structuring. Sternberg's theory proposes a sophisticated mechanism for describing the inference, mapping an application of a hierarchical relationship between four or more concepts, some of which symbolize inferences derived from the information processed. The model, however, is static. Each process is presented as if it were a new beginning, as if each had been structured outside its historical context. Carbonell's theory, on the other hand, while unable to explain how an initial structure is inferred, mapped and linked in a hierarchical relationship, helps explain by the concept of 'familiar problem space' how a past problem structure is transformed to fit the criteria of the new problem.

This essay combines Carbonell's and Sternberg's theories in order to create one that explains the dynamic, differentiated process of foreign-policy-making. Referring to analogy as the similarity of relationships, this theory explains how policy-makers initially structure the relationships between several ideas, and how they subsequently infer new relationships from the existing structures. These new relationships entail the selection of alternatives and the means to implement them. The successful solution to a problem leads to the creation of a 'problem space'. This concept provides the theory with a dynamic context and, as a result, the means to assess the extent to which policy-makers refer to the 'problem space' when a similar problem arises at a later time.

Proposing a theory involves more than creating a conceptual framework. It is indispensable, as a second task, to delineate the manner in which it can be tested empirically. To capture the nature of the decision-making process, it is imperative to find an appropriate unit of analysis. In this case, the unit of analysis will be the scenario.

In its simplest form, the construction of a scenario consists of the narration of a story as it unfolds over time. Analysis of the sequence of past events must consider not only the decisions that were made but also what problems were being addressed and how objectives and alternatives were evaluated and ordered at different points in time. Each identified event in a scenario, therefore, is designed to capture information that ranges from the identification of the policy implemented, to the description of the specific content of the policy, to the specification of the objectives sought by different parties, and finally to the characterization of how each major party rationalized its choice. By systematically comparing this information within one case across time, a pattern is likely to emerge. This pattern, in turn, can be compared with the patterns that might have emerged from other cases. From this comparison, it will be possible to structure the different forms that reasoning and learning assume and how they are linked across time.

Learning and reasoning by analogy

The role of reason in human affairs has been the subject of some of the most intensive philosophical debates in Western civilization. Socrates, Aristotle, the Stoics, and the Epicurians were among the first to propose that with perfect knowledge humans would do the correct and moral thing which, in turn, would lead to happiness and the good life. Within the boundaries of this general idea Adam Smith promoted the notion of 'efficiency', and Jeremy Bentham the concept of 'utility'.

Adam Smith in *The Wealth of Nations* proposed that society is well served by a man who seeks to act out of self-interest, for his action promotes efficiency. Bentham, one of the foremost utilitarians in the nineteenth century, sought to reconcile self-interest and social interest by proposing that an individual acts in the general good because it is in his self-interest to avoid social recrimination and eternal punishment upon death. Although great thinkers of past ages often promoted rationality, rarely did they think that the action of the common man was based on reason. The rational man, the merchant, for instance, capable of seeing his own best economic interests and acting on them dispassionately, was not a precise depiction of the real individual but an 'ideal' useful for bounding certain of man's decisions for theoretical purposes in economics.[10]

It was this type of 'ideal' rational man that captured the interest of foreign policy analysts. Since the end of the Second World War, the study of foreign policy has been dominated by one school of thought —political realism. Adherents to political realism have been among the most vehement supporters of the view that rationality is an assumption intrinsic to foreign policy. Decision-makers comprising the official, bureaucratic manifestation of the state are assumed to act as a unitary actor and to formulate external policies based on rational calculations of costs and benefits. Political realism, however, is not a precise replica of rational models of decision-making. In decision theory, the rational individual is one who, when confronted with a problem, makes the choice that has the best chance of bringing about a consequence that is highly desired by him. That same consequence, however, might not be as attractive to an individual with a different rank-order of preferences. In the realist paradigm, it is assumed that all states have as their most valued objective the protection or augmentation of power. States seek power — both the ability to influence others and the resources that can be used to exercise influence — by rationally calculating their interests in terms of power.[11] The connection between power and rationality was explained by Hans Morgenthau when he noted that to give meaning to the raw material of foreign policy, i.e. power, political reality must be approached with a rational outline.[12]

The realist perspective has been challenged widely since Morgenthau first attempted to give it a theoretical form. Scholars became troubled by the pleasing logic and simplicity of an argument that placed so much emphasis on the assumption of rationality. That a decision-maker would want to fulfil his most wanted objective remained incontestable. But doubts arose about the decision-maker's commitment to gather information beyond that level at which existing expectations are simply reaffirmed, or his willingness to process information that led to contradictory inferences. Moreover, there was little assurance that the decision-maker would have a clear idea of his values, and would know how to differentiate and rank them. And finally, concern also existed regarding the decision-maker's devotion to the detailed analysis of a broad range of alternatives that must precede the selection of the optimal policy.[13] These doubts and concerns were not compartmentalized by any specific field. Social psychologists had for many years questioned the relevance of the 'rational man' as a useful assumption and posited alternative theories that sought to capture the individual's approach to solving problems. In response to this concern, they suggested a variety of theories that adopt competing perspectives on how the individual approaches and resolves a problem. One of them is scheme theory.

Schema theory has its philosophical roots in the distant past. It was the Alexandrian school of grammarians in Ancient Greece that first used analogy as a mathematical and logical term for 'equality of ratios', as in a:b = c:d. Grammarians several centuries before and after Christ were concerned with prescribing 'good' grammar. They did this by establishing rules for their similarities and differences in inflection. When first applied to inflectional paradigms, the term 'analogy' was used to reflect regularities that appeared in grammar as mathematical proportions between individual forms of individual words. This view was eventually contested by the Stoics, who proposed that the formation of an analogy was not founded on logical considerations, but was the product of usage, and that it did not always reflect 'equality of ratios' but 'similarity of ratios'.[14]

These two conceptions have survived all subsequent challenges and have been used to explain how individuals approach problem- solving. Under the rubric of schema theory, the individual is viewed as a decision-maker overwhelmed by sensations and information who, in an attempt to define and resolve a problem, will resort to shortcuts. Rather than following quasi-scientific rules and procedures when making inferences and decisions, the individual searches for a generic concept stored in the memory that might seem appropriate to the problem at hand. In other words, to understand the world, the problem-solver tries to match 'what he is experiencing to past incidents stored in memory . . . he searches until he has found a schema that summarizes and categorizes one or more similar stimulus configurations in the past'.[15]

Attempts to explicate the matching process between concepts have been approached from at least two perspectives: the information-processing approach and the componential approach.[16] The information-processing view of human cognition maintains that in order to understand the behavior of a human cognitive system as it focuses on a problem, one must discover the processes used to solve it and to identify the plan that integrates specific processes into a functional package that produces the desired results.[17] The central weakness of models that rely on an information-processing perspective is that they lack a 'mapping' operation that helps, on the one hand, to identify the analogy between the pair terms in the first group and the pair terms in the second group and, on the other hand, to communicate the established solution.[18] This shortcoming can be remedied by using a componential approach. The general purpose of this approach is to identify the mental operations underlying a series of information-processing tasks and to discover the organization of these operations in terms of their relationships to each other and to higher-order mental functions. The relationship and significance of these two approaches require discussion.

H. Shalom and I. M Schlesinger, seeking to extend the theory of analogical reasoning designed by C. Spearman in 1923, define an analogy item as a relationship between one or more ordered pairs. Each relationship, they add, is structured by a 'domain' and a 'range'.[19] For instance, let us assume that many of the impressions derived about Latin American regimes by the US government are functions of how those regimes treat US companies investing in their respective countries. In a relationship specifying actions initiated by the host country toward US companies investing abroad and inferences derived by US administrations about these actions, the domain could consist of stricter labor laws (sll), expropriation (e), or preferential tax treatment (ptt); while the range could include two inferences made by the United States: the host government is anti-US (hgaUS), or the host government is pro-US (hgpUS).

The Cartesian product in a relationship consists of all possible sets of ordered pairs between the domain and the range. If the actions just proposed describe the universe of possible steps by the host country and inferences derived from these actions by the United States, then the Cartesian product would have the following format: {(sll,hgaUS), (sll,hgpUS), (e,hgaUS) (e,hgpUS), (ptt,hgaUS), (ptt,hgpUS)}.

As presented, the Cartesian product describes all possible sets of ordered pairs without identifying the relationships that are pertinent to analogical reasoning. In analogical reasoning it is critical to distinguish between the rule that refers to the logical relationship among analogical terms, and the rule that refers to the particular formula used by the analyst to understand the analogy. The first rule is generally referred to as the selection rule (SR), while the second rule is commonly identified as the connection formula (CF). The selection rule and the connection formula need not be the same. Moreover, to the extent that politics is not always animated by logic, stipulation of the selection rule might not be a requirement. For all practical purposes, therefore, explaining an analogy in politics involves forming a connection formula and applying it. Since relationships in politics cannot be assumed to remain constant, the connection formula used to explain an analogy at one point in time need not be the same subsequently. Going back to the earlier example, it could be suggested that whenever a host government in Latin America begins either to enforce stricter labor laws on US companies or to engage in a policy of expropriation, a US administration is likely to label such a government as anti-US. From this connection formula, the following relationships can be inferred:

sll:hgaUS :: e:hgaUS
sll:hgaUS :: ptt:hgpUS
e:hgaUS :: ptt:hgpUS

The difference between the above format and the Cartesian product is that in the latter the modes of action by the host government are not paired with all possible modes of inference by the US government but only with those established by the connection formula. Moreover, the rule of relations in the second pair of the analogy, i.e. e:hgaUS, corresponds to an inference of the rule relating the two elements of the first half of the analogy. Whether this relationship remains constant or is replaced by a different one depends on whether the US government introduces a different connection formula. The introduction of a different connection formula could be the function of a new lesson learned from a new experience, or it could reflect the presence of a new administration in Washington.

It should be noted that although the information-processing model of analogical reasoning proposed by Shalom and Schlesinger is very detailed, it does not include an explanation of how the pair terms in the first and second group are identified and the solution communicated. This problem, Robert Sternberg proposes, can be dealt with by creating a mechanism that identifies the mental operations, delineates their relationship to one another, and 'maps' a higher-order relation of equivalence between two lower-order relationships.[20]

Sternberg defines analogy as a hierarchy of relationships that takes the form 'A is to B as C is to D'. The terms 'domain' and 'range' are also part of Sternberg's componential theory of analogical reasoning, but they are used differently from the way they are used in the theory proposed by Shalom and Schlesinger. In the new theory the 'domain' refers to the terms A and B, while the 'range' pertains to C and D. Thus:

A:B :: C:D
Domain   Range

For Sternberg, 'an analogy exists when there is a rule, Y, that maps a domain rule, X, into a range rule, Z'.[21] In other words, the first lower-order relationship is discovered in the domain of the analogy, which is then mapped to the range of the analogy through the formation of an isomorphic relationship, that is, an identical structural relationship. However, the relationships within the domain and the range are not the products of independent instances but are linked to the higher-order relationships that are not time bound. There are three critical components in Sternberg's componential theory of analogical reasoning: attribute identification, attribute comparison and control.[22] The first step in the analogical process is the translation of the stimulus into some type of mental representation from which additional mental inferences can be subsequently carried out. The mental representation is stored in the working memory and has a value component. The attribute process is referred to as 'encoding'. Placed in terms of the example discussed earlier, encoding could consist of comprehending and storing in memory the following analogical terms: sll, e, ptt, hgaUS, and hgpUS.

At the attribute comparison stage, four steps are generally executed. The first step is the 'inference' by which a rule, X, that related the terms in the domain is discovered. The outcome of this inference is then stored in the decision-maker's memory. In the example analogy, inference could be represented as the discovery of the relationship between sll (stricter labor laws) and hgaUS (host government is anti-US). The required second step in the attribute comparison is referred to as 'mapping', and it involves the discovery of a higher-order rule, Y, that maps the domain of the analogy into the range. In other words, mapping requires discovery of a rule that relates the first term of the domain to the first term of the range.[23] In the example analogy, mapping could be represented as the discovery of the relationship between sll (stricter labor laws) and e (expropriation). The higher-order rule that addresses the relationship between the first terms of the domain and the range is also stored in memory. 'Application' is the third step in the attribute comparison, and it calls for the generation of a rule, Z, that forms a second term for the range that is an expression of the correct answer. In the example analogy, application is the creation of a rule that enables the decision-maker to decide that hgaUS (host government is anti-US) correctly completes the relationship between the domain and the range. The fourth and final step, 'justification', is optional. This process is required only in those instances in which none of the terms available is an exact expression of the correct answer and, thus, is necessary in order to find an option which can be justified as the closest to the initially visualized answer.

'Control', the third and final component in Sternberg's componential theory of analogical reasoning, involves primarily the translation of the solution of the problem into a response. The response in the example analogy could entail a reduction in financial aid by the United States to the country that expropriated US companies. A schematic representation of this process is presented in Figure 11.1. In addition, Table 11.1 offers a summary of the key elements of the componential model of analogical reasoning.

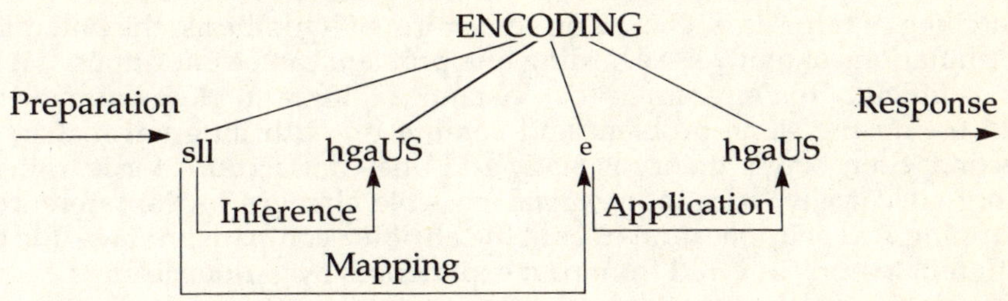

Figure 11.1 Schematic representation of analogical reasoning theory*

*Derived from Sternberg's own schematic representation.

Table 11.1 Components of analogical reasoning theory

PARAMETER	PROCESS	DESCRIPTION
1. Attribute identification	1. Encoding	1. Attributes and value of terms in problem identified
2. Attribute comparison	2. Inference	2. Rule X, relating two terms in domain identified
	3. Mapping	3. Rule Y, relating first two terms in domain and range generated
	4. Application	4. Rule Z, to form the second term in the range generated
3. Control	5. Response	5. Solution in attribute comparison translated into response

Sternberg's componential theory is useful in the sense that all major processes are explicitly stated in their relationships to each other. Moreover, it is specific in its description of the operations of the three critical components: attribute identification, attribute comparison, and control. Finally, the theory achieves a considerable degree of parsimony by specifying all operations with a minimum number of components.

The putative importance of analogy in problem-solving, however, must transcend the issue of reasoning. First, the theory must attempt to explicate how the rule X, which relates the terms in the domain, is discovered. Or, as pointed out by Mark Keane, Sternberg's type of theory does not explain how the terms in the domain are initially identified as being related to one another. Solving this problem is critical, for if the matching of terms is not based on some form of hypothesis, the potential permutations of matches regarding one problem can be enormous.[24] It is not difficult to envision, for instance, different decision-makers addressing the same problem and coming up with different matches. Second, Sternberg's theory is static and does not account for learning. More specifically, it cannot explain possible changes in the inference, mapping and/or application rules at the attribute comparison stage due to different lessons inferred from past experiences by various leaders.

Analogies are the functions of purposes. Different individuals arrive at different interpretations of the same problem, depending on their current goals.[25] Similarly, different individuals with different goals, drawing analogies as they confront a common problem, will be inclined to select different matching terms for the domain, even in instances in which they refer to the same past experience. Sternberg's componential theoretical framework can be extended by adding two aspects to it: purpose and learning. Purpose, as Mark Keane suggests, can be defined in terms of an individual's goal or subgoal at the time he is addressing a problem.[26] Purpose, however, does not exist entirely independently of learning. Past experiences can alter not only the way in which individuals attempt to solve new problems, but also their goals and subgoals.[27]

According to Jaime Carbonell, experience in problem-solving is gained incrementally.[28] A decision-maker, when encountering a new problem situation, is reminded of past situations at different levels of abstraction that resemble the present problem. The problem-solver derives a generalization from the discovery of commonalties among previous and current situations and the successful application of policies to solve those problems. The derivation of a generalization, however, is flexible enough that past behavior is not incorporated automatically into the current situation, but adapted to meet its special demands. Moreover, if in a new situation the problem-solver performs an action that proves to be inappropriate, discovery of the error that brought about the unintended results could trigger a discrimination process that would help delineate the range of applicability of the generalization from which the initial action had been derived.

Critical to Carbonell's theory on learning by analogy is the concept of 'familiar problem space'. Invariably, an individual will solve a familiar problem faster and with more self-assurance than he will an unfamiliar one. What makes a present problem space familiar is the memory of similar past problems and their corresponding solutions. At this point, however, it is important to differentiate between two processes: remembering and reasoning. Rumelhart and Abrahamson propose that the retrieval of specific information stored in the memory involves remembering, while the retrieval of the structure of one or more relationships among concepts is referred to as reasoning.[29] Although Carbonell does not specifically differentiate between remembering and reasoning, it is evident that he is concerned with the latter process when he notes that the best method of computing similarities among episodic memories is by comparing their structures based on a 'relative invariance hierarchy'.[30]

The first step in analogical reasoning, notes Carbonell, is the retrieval of a structure defining the relationships among one or more concepts. To decide what structure to retrieve from the memory, the decision-maker remembers an experience in which he was fulfilling similar goals. Hence a comparison of the structures of goals is a crucial component for modeling a reasoning process. Having retrieved a structure that was applicable to the solution of an old situation, the decision-maker must transform the structure to fit the criteria for the new problem. In so far as the structure was retrieved because the goals addressed in past and present situations were similar, the decision-maker must assess the extent to which the structure must be altered to meet the new goals.

The critical factor in Carbonell's theory of learning by analogy is that the transformation process requires only that present and past problems be structurally similar, rather than identical. A decision-maker, therefore, can learn by simply storing solutions to new problems. Moreover, if one type of problem recurs with frequency, the decision-maker might formulate a generalized plan for dealing with future occurrences of that problem. At this stage, the decision-maker would no longer be engaged in analogical reasoning, for he would not be reasoning from a particular member of a cluster of similar experiences.[31]

The theories proposed by Sternberg and Carbonell approach analogies from significantly different perspectives. Sternberg's theory is static in the sense that although it can describe the process involving the inference, mapping and application of a hierarchical relationship between four concepts, it cannot explain why a particular structure was selected over another, nor how a structure retrieved from a past situation is transformed when applied to a new one. Carbonell's theory, on the other hand, takes the position that learning by analogy is a dynamic process involving the retrieval and transformation of structures from one problem to another. But this theory omits from its framework the different stages in the structure generation process. To develop a rich and differentiated analogical theory of foreign policy, the two processes just described must be incorporated into a single framework.

A theoretical framework of reasoning and learning by analogy

The first phase in the analysis of a foreign policy is to recreate the process by which policy-makers define a problem. Analogy, the similarity of relations, is a good starting point.[32] In the case of the United States, for instance, let us assume that its leaders believe that a useful measure of a foreign government's ideological predilection is its treatment of US companies in the country it rules. A government that engages in expropriation (e) is described as being dominated or influenced by communists (hgc), while one that grants preferential tax treatments (ptt) is identified as being anti-communist (hgnc).[33] These relationships can be structured in the following analogical format:

e:hgc :: ptt:hgnc

This analogical format does not delineate the full structure of the problem. The next step in the process is to identify the types of inferences, if any, that a US administration dervies from each relationship. One of the practices of US governments since 1945 has been to infer that control of a government by communists enhances the Soviet Union's ability to dominate the affected state and other bordering states. Conversely, to the extent that a government shows signs of supporting a capitalist economic system, the assumption in Washington has generally been that the Soviet's capacity to impose its will on that state will be measurably constrained. We can define the two additional concepts as the presence and absence of Soviet control, respectively, and symbolize them as follows: presence of Soviet control = PSC, and absence of Soviet control = ASC. The new relationship can be structured in the following analogical format:

hgc:PSS :: hgnc:ASC

The two-pair relationships thus delineate the boundaries of United States actions. But actions must be placed in the context of purposes. To minimise the chances that the continued presence of a government that shared the Soviet Union's ideological preferences might provide the latter with opportunities to expand its power, the United States has often concluded that its only option was to overthrow that government. At the same time, US administrations have been adept at supporting governments that favor a capitalist economy. Decision-makers in Washington have assumed in many instances that one of the most effective ways of containing the Soviet Union was to help capitalist economies flourish. The two new concepts just introduced can be symbolized as follows: overthrow = o, support = s. Thus:

hgc:o :: hgnc:s

The last step in the structuring of the problem requires the determination of how to implement the alternatives selected. Two of the most common practices of US administrations have been to rely on a covert paramilitary operation to overthrow a regime that was believed to be communist, and to provide economic aid to a government that supports the continued development of a capitalist economy. The selection of the first policy instrument has been driven generally by the need to fulfil two subgoals. On the one hand, there has been the sense that it was imperative for the United States to ensure that no communist regime be able to remain in power in Latin America and that its leaders recognize this commitment. On the other hand, US governments have on occasion believed that it was critical not to promote the belief among Latin Americans that the United States was an interventionist power unconcerned about violating the sovereign rights of states. The second policy instrument, in turn, has often been used as a means to strengthen the governing capabiity of regimes friendly to the United States. The two new concepts can be symbolized as follows: covert paramilitary invasion = cpi, economic aid = ea. Thus:

o:cpi :: s:ea

The problem just described is represented by four two-pair analogical relationships structured in a hierarchical mode. The domain and range of each pair relationship can be divided into independent pairs in such a way that the pairs defining each domain can be linked in order to structure one case, while the pairs defining each range can be linked in order to structure a diametrically opposite case. The reasoning process in Washington prior to the invasion of Guatemala in 1954, for instance, could be described by the first pair relationships linked among themselves in the form of conditions, as follows:

If (hg) does (e),
then (hg) is (hgc).
If (hg) is (hgc)
then the likelihood of (PSC) increases.
To avert (PSC)
then (o).
If (o),
then (cpi).

In 1954, the United States toppled Guatemala's government. This success could have convinced policy-makers in Washington that it was justifiable to store in their memory the structure that defined the relationships among the different concepts relevant to the problem. The composition of the structure defining the problem in 1954 is what Carbonell refers to as the 'problem space'. It is at this stage that the application of analogical reasoning to the analysis of foreign policy moves away from the consideration of what types of pair relationships are inferred by decision-makers to the comparison of problem structures. Having stored in memory the relationships between different concepts, the decision-maker no longer needs to recreate the same process. Instead, as a new situation develops, he must decide whether the conditions defining it are compatible with the conditions defining the old problem. In addition, the decision-maker must determine whether the respective goals correspond. In 1961, for instance, policy-makers seem to have retrieved the problem structure they had stored in memory seven years earlier and used it as a guide to attempt to topple a new regime — the Castro government. A definitive answer, however, cannot be proposed without a detailed analysis of the decision-making process in Washington at that time.

The analysis of foreign policies in the context of scenarios

Every decision-making activity in foreign policy involves, in some form or another, problem formulation and the ordering of and selection among alternatives. To understand the nature of this dynamic process, it is imperative that an analytical structure be set up. As already noted, the appropriate unit of analysis to deal with this process is the 'historical narrative' or 'scenario'.

The scenario is a historical case which consists of a sequence of events interconnected in time. By observing how the interacting parties define the problem and how they order and select their respective alternatives, and by systematically comparing the evolutions of these different policies in time, it is possible to identify the patterns that different forms of reasoning and learning assume.

To compare scenarios, it is necessary to identify the sequence of events in terms of generalized components. Each event is, in effect, a package that answers questions at two levels. Questions at one level refer to the interactions between states. At a second level, they assume that states are not monolithic actors, but rather are composed of individuals and groups capable of imposing differing interpretations on situations. Thus, at the intrastate level, questions refer to the interactions among principal decision-makers. The questions addressed at the interstate level are:

(i)   What action was initiated?
(ii) Who initiated the action?
(iii) Who were the principal intended targets of the action?
(iv) What was the extent of the action?
(v)   When was the action initiated?

The questions addressed at the intrastate level are:

(i)   What were the alternatives considered?
(ii) Who were the principal proposers of these alternatives?
(iii) What objective(s) did each principal proposer believe had to be achieved?
(iv) How did each proposer rationalize his choice of alternative?

In sum, both sets of questions help fulfil different analytical objectives. For instance, in June 1960 the United States cut the Cuban sugar quota by 95 per cent. The record of this event at the interstate level reads as follows:

WHAT:	Trade sanction
WHO:	United States government
INTENDED TARGET:	Cuba
WHEN:	June 1960
EXTENT:	95 per cent reduction in sugar quota

The description of the event is incomplete. To understand the reasoning process in Washington that led to the reduction in the sugar quota, it is necessary to look at the decision-making process. The initial narrative, therefore, must be expanded. In June 1960, the White House, believing that it was necessary to damage Cuba's economy in order to get rid of Fidel Castro, ordered a 95 per cent reduction in the sugar quota. This decision was much harsher than the action proposed by the US ambassador to Cuba, Philip Bonsal. The ambassador, convinced that the proposed action would strengthen Castro's hand in Cuba and draw him closer to the Soviets, suggested that the United States either warn Cuba that the balance of the sugar quota would be reduced, or simply reduce the quota less drastically. This description tells a richer story. It is built on the assumptions that actions have purposes and that decision-makers in an administration do not always agree as to how they should be realized. The record of this event at the intrastate level reads as follows:

ALTERNATIVES: Major versus limited reduction in sugar quota
PROPOSERS: White House versus US ambassador to Cuba
OBJECTIVES: Undermine Castro's power
RATIONALIZATION: Major reduction in sugar quota would
                   undermine Castro's power, versus major
                   reduction in sugar quota would strengthen
                   Castro's power and draw him closer to the
                   Soviets.

The described event represents the action of the United States and the process that led to the selection of an alternative at one point in time in the overall scenario structure that defines the US government's interactions with the Castro regime. As presented, the story is static and ahistorical. The side-by-side examination of two distinct but not-fully-unfolded scenarios should help clarify the context in which cases can be compared (Tables 11.2 and 11.3).

Table 11.2 Comparison of two not-fully-unfolded scenarios*

	US–Guatemala 1952–1954	US–Cuba 1959–1960
WHAT:	Passage of agrarian reform law and expropriation	Passage of agrarian reform law and expropriation
WHO:	Arbenz government	Castro government
TARGET:	United Fruit	Oil refineries and other US-controlled companies
WHEN:	June'52–Feb. '53	July '59–Oct. '60

EXTENT:	234,000 acres of land owned by United Fruit	Texaco, Esso, Royal Dutch, and agricultural land
PROPOSERS:	President Arbenz	Fidel Castro, Raul Castro, Ernesto Guevara
OBJECTIVES:	Eradicate dependency on US investors	Eradicate dependency on US investors
RATIONALIZATION:	Independence could be achieved only by breaking all ties with foreign investors	Independence could be achieved only by breaking all ties with foreign investors
WHAT:	Intervention plans ordered	Intervention plans ordered
WHO:	Eisenhower administration	Eisenhower administration
TARGET:	Arbenz government	Castro government
WHEN:	Mid-1953	Early 1960
EXTENT:	President Eisenhower orders CIA to draft plans for paramilitary intervention	President Eisenhower orders CIA to draft plans for paramilitary intervention
ALTERNATIVES:	1. Draft plans for paramilitary intervention	1. Draft plans for paramilitary intervention
	2. Pressure Central American states to exert economic and political pressure on Guatemala	2. Use economic sanctions
		3. Do nothing
PROPOSERS:	1. Eisenhower, John Foster Dulles, and Allan Dulles	1. Eisenhower, Richard Bissell, and Richard Nixon
	2. C.D. Jackson and Adolf Berle	2. C.D. Jackson and Adolf Berle
		3. Philip Bonsal

OBJECTIVES:	Clear the communists out of Guatemala	Clear the communists out of Cuba
RATIONALIZATION:	1. Political and economic pressure had failed	1. Political and economic pressure would not be enough to topple Castro regime. Force might prove to be only alternative
		2. Paramilitary activity was too risky
		3. Economic pressure or military force would only help strengthen Castro regime
WHAT:	Paramilitary invasion begins	Paramilitary invasion begins
WHO:	Eisenhower administration	Kennedy administration
TARGET:	Arbenz government	Castro government
WHEN:	18 June 1954	17 April 1961
EXTENT:	Small number of Guatemalan nationals financed by CIA enter Guatemala	1400 Cuban nationals financed by CIA land at Bay of Pigs in Cuba
ALTERNATIVES:	Launch invasion	Launch invasion
PROPOSERS:	Eisenhower and Allan Dulles	Kennedy and Allan Dulles
OBJECTIVES:	Eliminate communist influence in Guatemala	Eliminate communist influence in Cuba
RATIONALIZATION:	Only by overthrowing Arbenz would the US be able to eliminate communism in Guatemala	Only by overthrowing Castro would the US be able to eliminate communism in Cuba

*The comparison is incomplete. It excludes many important events that transpired between the dates identified, such as the decision arrived at in June 1960 in Washington to impose a 95 per cent reduction in Cuba's sugar quota.

Table 11.3 Comparison of partial reasoning processes in two not-fully-unfolded scenarios

	US–Guatemala: 1952–1954	US–Cuba 1959–1961
	Guatemala–US	*Cuba–US*
Alternative 1	To achieve full independence from foreign control, Guatemala must expropriate foreign companies	To achieve full independence from foreign control, Cuba must expropriate foreign companies
Policy	Foreign companies expropriated	Foreign companies expropriated
	US–Guatemala	*US–Cuba*
Assumption 1	If Arbenz government expropriates US companies, then Arbenz government is communist	If Castro government expropriates US companies, then Castro government is communist
Assumption 2	If Arbenz government is communist, then US national interest is threatened	If Castro government is communist, then US national interest is threatened
Alternative 1	To protect US national interest, Arbenz government must be overthrown by a covert paramilitary invasion	To protect US national interest, Castro government must be overthrown by a covert paramilitary invasion
Alternative 2	To protect US national interest, Arbenz government can be pressured to resign by exerting economic and political pressure jointly with American states	To protect US national interest, Castro regime can be undermined by exerting economic and political pressure
Policy	Covert paramilitary intervention initiated	Covert paramilitary intervention initiated

The limited time-reach of the Guatemalan and Cuban scenarios and the simplicity of their preliminary representation make it difficult to grasp fully the implications of this type of analysis. But even with these constraints, it is possible to imagine the types of comparisons that this method of analysis facilitates. With more fully developed scenarios it would be feasible to delineate how decision-makers reasoned, whether they made references to past events, and, if they did, how they structured such events in order to confront the new problem.

The use of the scenario, moreover, facilitates the task of assessing the impact that beliefs have on decision-making. With a few exceptions, most efforts to assess the role of a decision-maker's beliefs in his decision-making have been somewhat impressionistic and of a tentative nature.[34] This should not be surprising. As Holsti noted:

> Unlike the analyst who can index his variables with such measures as GNP per capita, arms budgets, trade figures, votes in the UN General Assembly, or public opinion, those interested in the beliefs of decision makers have no yearbook to which they can turn for comparable evidence, much less quantitative data presented in standard units.[35]

A thorough analysis of the potential relationship between beliefs and decisions requires detailed data, amassed from documents, public statements made by the decision-makers, open-ended interviews, and inferences made by participant observers. This task is not insurmountable if the subject involves just a few decision-makers, focusing on the same problem, for a very short period of time.[36] A complete analysis, on the other hand, is almost beyond reach if the focus is on numerous US administrations, responding to problems emanating from a large number of countries, across several decades. Considering these difficulties, a study should make certain that there is sufficient information to describe the *dominant* beliefs of the foreign policy actors most involved in defining the various problems and selecting solutions for them.[37]

One of two techniques is generally used to evaluate the effect that beliefs have on decisional choices: the 'congruence' procedure or the 'process-tracing' procedure.[38] The first procedure relies on a nomothetic–deductive mode of explanation for the purpose of assessing whether congruence exists between the content of certain beliefs and the content of certain decisions. The analyst establishes the decision-maker's beliefs on the basis of data from his earlier life-history and considers whether they are congruent with his policy preferences and decisions. The determination of congruency is arrived at deductively. To show that the inferences derived are justified, the analyst must demonstrate that congruency between beliefs and decisions is genuine, not spurious, and that the decisional output would have been different under a dissimilar set of beliefs.[39]

The process-tracing procedure approach requires more information than the congruence procedure with regard to how the actual policy was made. This approach is similar to the one used in historical analysis. Rather than relying on a deductive argument to contend that beliefs affect decisions, the process-tracing procedure seeks to establish the potentially broad influence that beliefs have on foreign policy by outlining their effect on the actor's receptivity to and assessment of incoming information regarding a particular problem, his definition of the problem, his identification and evaluation of alternatives, and his choice of policy and policy instruments.[40] In other words, this approach must also rely on extensive sources to depict the decision-maker's beliefs; but then, rather than by-passing what goes on inside the black-box, it tries to schematize the effect that beliefs have at different stages of the decision-making process.

Conclusion

By the mid 1970s the study of foreign policy had experienced what at that time might have seemed a critical metamorphosis. Scholars such as Robert Axelrod, Matthew Bonham, Alexander George, Robert Jervis, Michael Shapiro, John Steinbruner, and many others, made powerful arguments for analyzing foreign policy not from the perspective of an objective reality ready to be grasped in its true context by decision-makers, but from the perspective of the cognitions of the decision-makers. Their arguments, at least initially, did not fall on deaf ears. Many scholars, excited by the theoretical implications of the new focus, responded to the challenge. The excitement, however, was short-lived. It was soon recognized that attempts to engage in sophisticated empirical analyses were bound to be frustrated by the presence of psychological theories that conflicted with one another significantly, and by the unavailability of reliable data.[41] Thus, in the 1980s, the number of foreign policy studies that focused on the cognitive processes of decision-makers began to diminish, and less cumbersome approaches were introduced.

This change in direction signified that parsimony was king once again. But at what cost? Without reference to domestic and international structures, it is impossible to explain the nature of outcomes. However, to understand why one outcome resulted instead of another, it is essential to investigate the extent to which the different obstacles imposed by the structures were accounted for by the policy from which the various consequences followed.

In a world in which information is rarely available in the quantity necessary to eliminate all risks, evaluating the effectiveness of a policy in overcoming the various barriers contained by the different structures requires understanding of how leaders reason. For years analysts used, in some form or another, a conception of the decision process derived from rational choice models. The concept of rationality, like the concept of power, has not been easy to displace from the realm of foreign policy analysis, although its theoretical relevance has long been acknowledged to be meager. Most troubling about this is the fact that scholars have tended to accept assumptions about human nature proposed by individuals who have rarely sought to understand human nature —

economists and mathematicians.

One need not be cautious in deploring this blind commitment to the assumption of rationality. The concept, since it was first conceived, was promoted as an ideal. Ideals, as generally understood, can be sought, but never achieved. This dividing line, which philosophers throughout the centuries had little difficulty in drawing, began to lose its hue with the advent of modern science in the early seventeenth century. Convinced that man had the intellectual tools to explain the universe that surrounded him, analysts imposed the assumption of rationality on the study of a broad variety of subjects, including economics. It did not take long for this conception to move into the realm of politics. The association between politics and rationality has taken various forms throughout the centuries, and this is not the place to describe it. Suffice to say, as suggested earlier, the study of foreign policy has been an obvious victim of this association. Scholars have become so attached to the notion that rationality is the cure to all major ills that they have great difficulty accepting that the 'mind of man, for all its marvels is a limited instrument',[42] and that, as a consequence, foreign policy-making is unlikely ever to become the product of a rational process. In addition, we seem to have forgotten George Orwell's warning that politics, more than any other field of human interaction, is less an instrument for expressing thought than a means for 'preventing thought'.[43] When Orwell delivered his criticism, he had in mind the debasement of language. Indirectly, however, he was reminding us that since language reflects our thoughts, the absence of careful thought as we make political decisions, either as voters or as foreign policy-makers, signifies in no small measure the absence of rationality.

Discarding the rationality assumption could be interpreted as an attempt to promote the idea that we should lower our theoretical expectations as foreign policy analysts. Nothing could be further from the goal that drives this argument. When scientists decided to investigate the behavior of the atom, they did not expect to derive a theory as parsimonious as that postulated to explain and predict the trajectory of a falling apple. But at the same time, they realized that existing arguments could not capture the more complex behavior of the atom. A similar view underlies the suggestion here. Foreign policy is concerned with acts generally initiated by a small group of complex individuals, with a variety of interests and beliefs, that affect an array of human targets. To provide useful explanations of this process we must learn to theorize about how these individuals reason, and we must do so without being afraid to be burdened by the presence of complexity.[44]

The theory proposed here does not attempt to run away from complexity, nor does it promote it for its own sake. Analogical thinking is not an easy process to structure, particularly in its linkage with an individual's beliefs. Although the association of both concepts complicates the nature of the explanation and the theory, the end result justifies the loss of parsimony. The obstacles to the conduct of solid empirical analysis are unlikely to become less cumbersome with time. The likelihood of greater complexity, however, rather than pulling us away from the analysis of the cognitive processes of decision-makers, ought to push us closer to it.

The field of social psychology is in a constant state of flux, with no single theory being able to act as the sole dominant force. How much we benefit from it depends on our willingness to look seriously at the various theories and test their explanatory reach across a range of cases. This endeavor is bound to bring significant benefits, along with some high costs, but we must take the risk. As we ponder the potential costs of future failures, it might help to keep in mind Socrates' dictum that if we believe 'that we must try to find out what is not known, we should be better, braver, and less idle . . .'.

Notes

1. Dwain Mefford, 'Combining Historical Narrative and Game Theory in a Rule Based System', paper delivered at the Annual Meeting of the Western International Studies Association, Los Angeles, CA, October 1985, p. 3.
2. Ralph L, Keeney and Howard Raiffa, *Decisions with Multiple Objectives: Preferences and Value Tradeoffs* (New York: John Wiley and Sons, 1976); and Howard Raiffa, *Decision Analysis: Introductory Lectures on Choices Under Uncertainy* (Reading, MA: Addison-Wesley, 1968).
3. Amos Tversky, and Daniel Kahneman, 'The Framing of Decisions and the Psychology of Choice', *Science*, **211**, 4481, January 1981, pp. 453–8.
4. Jaime G. Carbonell, 'Learning by Analogy; Formulating and Generalizing Plans from Past Experience', in Ryszarol S. Michalski, Jaime G. Carbonell and Tom M Mitchells, eds, *Machine Learning: An Artificial Intelligence Approach* (Palo Alto, CA: Tioga Publishing Company, 1983); Herbert A. Simon with John R. Hayes, 'The Understanding Process: Problem Isomorphs', in Herbert A. Simon, ed, *Models of Thought* (New Haven, CT: Yale University Press, 1979); and George Polya, *Mathematics and Plausible Reasoning: Patterns of Plausible Inference*, Vol. II (Princeton: Princeton University Press, 1954).
5. Robert Jervis, *Perception and Misperception in International Politics* (Princeton: Princeton Univeristy Press, 1976), p. 220.
6. George Lakoff and Mark Johnson, *Metaphors We Live By* (Chicago: Chicago Univeristy Press, 1980); and Wendy Lehnert and Martin Gingle, eds, *Strategies for Natural Language Processing* (Hillsdale, NJ: Lawrence Erlbaum, 1982).
7. Here I am referring principally to the works by Richard E. Neustadt and Ernest R. May, *Thinking in Time: The Uses of History for Decision Makers* (New York: The Free Press, 1986); Jervis, op. cit.; and Ernest R. May, *'Lessons' of the past: The Use and Misuse of History in American Foreign Policy* (New York: Oxford University Press, 1973). These works have been extremely informative and helpful but have, for the most part, misapplied the concept of analogy.
8. Robert Sternberg, *Intelligence, Information Processing and Analogical Reasoning* (Hillsdale, NJ: Lawrence Erlbaum, 1977), p. 65.
9. Carbonell, op. cit.
10. Not being able to distinguish the merit of one man's demand for pleasure

from that of any other man, Bentham argued that all the pleasures of all men must be treated as equally valuable, and that the maximization of these pleasures was the only rational standard of political right. See W. L. Davidson, *Political Thought in England: The Utilitarians from Bentham to J. S. Mill* (New York: Holt, Reinhart and Winston, 1916); J. Bentham, *Deontology*, arranged and edited by J. Bowring, Vols. I and II (London: Longman, 1934); and A. Marshall, *Principles of Economics*, 8th edn, (London: Macmillan, 1920).

11. See Robert Keohane, 'Theory of World Politics: Structural Realism and Beyond', in Ada W. Finifter, ed., *Political Science: The State of the Discipline* (Washington, DC: The American Political Science Association, 1983), p. 508; and B. Bueno de Mesquita, *The War Trap* (New Haven: Yale University Press, 1981), pp. 29–33.

12. Hans M. Morgenthau, *Politics Among Nations* (New York: Alfred A. Knopf, 1983), p. 5.

13. See Herbert A. Simon, *Models of Man* (New York: John Wiley and Sons, 1957).

14. E. A. Esper, *Analogy and Association in Linguistics and Psychology* (Athens: University of Georgia Press, 1973), pp. 1–2.

15. Deborah Larson, *Origins of Containment* (Princeton: Princeton University Press, 1985), p. 52.

16. See Sternberg, op. cit., chapters 3 and 4.

17. Rober Kail and James W. Pellegrino, *Human Intelligence: Perspectives and Prospects* (New York: W. H. Freeman and Co, 1985), pp. 52–3.

18. Sternberg, op. cit., p. 112.

19. H. Shalom and I. M. Schlesinger, 'Analogical Thinking: A Conceptual Analysis of Analogical Tests', in R. Reurstein, I. M Schlesinger, H. Shalom and H. Narrol, eds, *Studies in Cognitive Modifiability*, Report 1, Vol. II (Jerusalem: Haddasah Wizo, Canada Research Institute, 1972).

20. Sternberg, op. cit., p. 112.

21. ibid.

22. ibid., p. 135.

23. ibid., p. 136.

24. Mark Keane, 'On Drawing Analogies When Solving Problems: A Theory and Test of Solution Generation in an Analogical Problem-Solving Test', *British Journal of Psychology*, **76**, 1985, p. 450.

25. G. B. Madison, *Understanding: A Phenomenological-Pragmatic Analysis* (London: Greenwood Press, 1982); and Roger C. Schank, *Dynamic Memory: A Theory of Reminding and Learning in Computers and People* (Cambridge: Cambridge Univerisity Press, 1982).

26. Keane, op. cit., p. 450.

27. March implicitly infers these changes when he contends that goals cannot be assumed to remain constant through time. See James March, 'Bounded Rationality, Ambiguity and the Engineering of Choice', paper presented at Carnegie-Mellon Univeristy, October 1977.

28. Carbonell, op. cit., p. 137.

29. D. E. Rumelhart and A. A. Abrahamson, 'A Model for Analogical Reasoning', *Cognitive Psychology*, **5**, 1, 1973, pp. 1–28.

30. Carbonell, op. cit., pp. 151–2.

31. ibid., p. 152.

32. 'Analogy' will be referred to as 'the similarity of relations', since it is difficult to assess the ratios between foreign policy concepts.

33. To many analysts these similarities of relations will seem simple-minded.

Whether they are or not is not important for the time being. The sole purpose of presenting the relations in such simple forms is to facilitate the understanding behind analogical reasoning.

34. Some of the exceptions have been the works by Stephen Walker, 'The Interface Between Beliefs and Behavior: Henry A. Kissinger's Operational Code and the Vietnam War', *Journal of Conflict Resolution*, **21**, 1, March 1977, pp. 129–68; Steven W. Hoagland and Stephen G. Walker, 'Operational Codes and Crisis Outcomes', in Lawrence S. Falkowski, ed., *Psychological Models in International Politics* (Boulder, CO: Westview Press, 1979); and Larson, op. cit.

35. Ole Holsti, 'Foreign Policy Formation Viewed Cognitively', in Robert Axelrod, ed., *Structure of Decision* (Princeton: Princeton University Press, 1976), p. 35.

36. Here I am using Larson's study of four US foreign policy-makers as my principal criterion.

37. One of the basic ideas behind the operational code is that in the analysis of the relationship between beliefs and decisions that pertain to foreign policy the only beliefs that are important are the political.

38. See Alexander L. George, 'Case Studies and Theory Development: The Method of Structured, Focused Comparison', in Paul G. Lauren, ed., *Diplomacy: New Approaches in History, Theory and Policy* (New York: The Free Press, 1979), p. 105.

39. George, op. cit., pp. 105–9.

40. ibid., p. 113.

41. See Holsti, op. cit., pp. 39–52.

42. Steinbruner, 1974, p. 13. For an excellent critique of rational choice theory see the January 1989 issue of *World Politics*.

43. George Orwell, 'Politics and the English Language', in Orwell, *Selected Essays* (Harmondsworth: Penguin, 1957), p. 157.

44. Complexity is automatically increased as we attempt to understand where the frame of reference for the actors' thinking comes from, but this process is critical. As Richard Ned Lebow and Janice Gross Stein contend, the most important determinant of decisions is not 'the process of choosing among options, but the prior definition and the construction of the problem to be decided'. See Richard Ned Lebow and Janice Gross Stein, 'Rational Deterrence Theory: I Think, Therefore I Deter', *World Politics*, **XLI**, 2, January 1989, p. 214. See also Herbert A. Simon, 'Human Nature in Politics: The Dialogue of Psychology with Political Science', *American Political Science Review*, **79**, 2, June 1985, p. 295.

Conclusion
Alan Henrikson

The premise of this book is that historical knowledge, in its various forms, is one of the principal intellectual resources of statesmen. Inescapably, statesmen themselves are 'historians of a kind,' as Michael Fry suggests in his introductory essay, in that they habitually, though sometimes naïvely, inexpertly and misleadingly 'use' history in the crafting of policy. The underlying assumption of such a view of the utility of history is that it can be regarded objectively — that is, with sufficient detachment to be able to *decide* to refer to it, to *choose* to be influenced by it, to *want* to become a part of it. Historical memory, in this theory, is somewhat optional, and recollection of particular events, therefore, selective. Such objectification of the past is a necessary precondition of consciously using it, making it an instrument of policy. For without such detachment man is himself an object of history, caught up within structures and forces which, whatever his innate strengths, he cannot manipulate because he does not, subjectively, perceive them as external to him.

Although the instrumental idea of history is as old as Thucydides, the idea of 'using' history as a source of specific policy guidance may seem typically American.[1] In its extreme 'American' form, the notion of using history implies a faith in mankind's ability to transcend its past, to rise above history's ruins perhaps with the aid of recycled building blocks taken from previous periods. The debt to the past, however, is minimal. As Louis J. Hartz has shown, Americans did not have a feudal past — castles and cathedrals — to destroy, and thus grew up liberally.[2] Historical ideology, in particular, has not greatly concerned most of them. Daniel J. Boorstin contends that 'the peculiar strengths of American life have saved us from the European preoccupation with political dogmas and have left us inept and uninterested in political theory'.[3] The mentality of Americans, including their attitude toward history, has been pragmatic.

The contrary idea — let us term it, not merely for convenience, the 'European' notion — holds that the function of history is, scientifically, to describe the past 'as it actually happened' — *Zeigen wie es eigentlich gewesen ist*, in Leopold von Ranke's famous expression. The events of history, in this view, become objects of contemplation rather than devices for use — artefacts, as it were, rather than tools. The past is a kind of monolith in relation to which present and future, though not entirely seamless or without fissures, are essentially continuous extensions. Lapidary practical 'lessons' cannot be hewn from this massive structure without regard to the context, or deeper organization, of the succession of events and situations through time. History 'teaches' little that is both useful and important, according to this view. It simply is. Historical facts should be learned, so that man may know who he is, and how he and his circumstances may be changing. But history cannot be made to serve. The historical spirit, Clio, cannot — like a genie from a bottle — be summoned to help man perform great deeds. Human progress, to the extent that it occurs, is achievable only slowly in 'European' history. Revolutions, or even true reforms, are rare; moreover, they can be reversed, turned back into counter-revolutions. Historical developments thus may be cyclical as well as linear. Common recurrences over time become enduring patterns, and these become more or less permanent structures. The conservative spirit of such historiography is thoroughly embodied in the words of the great French historian of material civilization, Fernand Braudel. 'The event is, or is taken to be, unique; the everyday happening is repeated, and the more often it is repeated the more likely it is to become a generality or rather a structure,' writes Braudel. 'It pervades society at all levels, and characterises ways of being and behaving which are perpetuated through endless ages.'[4]

The relatively pragmatic, future-oriented 'American' sense of history is especially well expressed by that quintessentially American philosopher, John Dewey. The word history has a double sense, Dewey noted. It means 'that which happened in the past' and also, more interestingly, 'the intellectual reconstruction of these happenings at a subsequent time'. The idea that history, in the second sense, somehow 'reinstates' the past 'as it actually happened' seemed 'incredibly naive.' The past is simply not so strongly insistent as that, Dewey believed. Nothing about it is inexorable; nor is anything in it even immutable. It is subject to the present, in fact: 'For historical inquiry is an affair (1) of selection and arrangement, and (2) is controlled by the dominant problems and conceptions of the culture of the period in which it is written.' In using the past, Dewey contended, people 'are compelled to modify it', to meet their own present needs. 'History cannot escape its own process. It will, therefore, always be rewritten.' As a new present arises, the past becomes 'the past of a different present' — in a sense, a new past. Dewey's instrumentalist conception of history was clear: 'Intelligent understanding of past history is to some extent a lever for moving the present into a certain kind of future.'[5]

The German historian Friedrich Meinecke, though a writer on Machiavellism, expressed an opposing view. He could not deny the interest of more present-minded scholars than he in using history to comprehend and, perhaps, practically to influence the flow of current affairs. 'The desire to derive lessons, examples, or admonitions from history belongs among the ineradicable basic motives which have always led to historical writing,' he acknowledged. But he deplored the tendency. 'From this come the greatest dangers to its scientific character — tendentious distortion, idealization, or misrepresentation.' Meinecke humanly conceded that 'we indeed wish to learn something for our own lives from history'. The study of ordinary causalities in history 'yields practical lessons in abundance,' he allowed. 'Whatever has occurred in history due to general, typical, and recurring causes can also recur in the present and can be handled in the light of the experience of bygone times.' To be sure, Hegel had denied that governments and peoples had ever learned anything from history, or more precisely had ever acted in light of the lessons to be drawn from it, Meinecke noted. But the statesman Bismarck believed history to be very useful. 'For me history is above all something to be learned from,' the German Chancellor declared. 'If events themselves do not recur, situations and characters do, and the observations and study of these can stimulate and shape one's mind.'

Even 'the individual, inimitable, and irreplaceable in history', though offering no 'practical utility', could sometimes be effective, Meinecke understood, as 'a spiritual content, as ideal model' for persons or societies possessed of 'a related and receptive individuality'. The obvious danger in such reliance, however, was 'epigonal dependency', that is, surrendering inwardly to 'spirits of the past'. Models should not become masters. The very 'finest and highest instruction' that history could give, Meinecke concluded, is that which springs, unsought, from 'the pure appreciation of historical individualities as such' — a contemplative absorption in, rather than a coercive adaptation of, the most remarkable occurrences of the past.

> It is then history's own value which becomes valuable to us. It consists in nothing else than the corroboration of the infinitely creative power of the spirit, which although it does not guarantee us rectilinear progress, yet promises an eternally new birth of valuable historical individualities within the bounds of nature.[6]

These two very different approaches to 'using' history — the essentially pragmatic (or 'American') and the essentially scientific (or 'European') — are here fundamentally distinguished in order to establish a philosophical and historiographical basis for considering a problem — the role of 'lessons' of the past in the process of policy-making — that has received new attention in recent years. Part of the explanation of this interest is the sense of historical 'decline' that has afflicted, in particular, the United States — although Great Britain and the Soviet Union have been affected even more dramatically.[7] As with Gibbon's *Decline and Fall of the Roman Empire*, the downward trajectories of the American, British and Soviet 'empires' since their heydays — in the US case, the generation or so after the Second World War — have become generally accepted truths. Those involved in those stylized stories, statesmen as well as scholars, wish better to understand the process of declination in order to counteract and, perhaps, even to reverse it. There is a contrary view of the current trend of history: that a 'new world order' is being born. As will be discussed further, part of the reason for the widespread interest in history is the desire to learn how the present historical moment, seen to be filled with promise, can be realized in new forms of international cooperation.

In the sections that follow, I shall, first of all, consider the most basic questions regarding the relationship of historical reasoning to policy-making that are varyingly posed and in different ways answered in the preceding chapters of this book. Three questions in particular will be addressed: is historically based thinking *rational* — that is, consistent with logical and empirical policy analysis, necessarily focused on current problems? Is it *compelling* — that is, actually influential in policy-making discussions, perhaps relative to other kinds of expertise and advice? And, most important, is it *valid* — that is, productive of correct conclusions and appropriate recommendations, leading to sound decisions for future policy?

In the succeeding section, I attempt to apply the above-stated questions together with some of the answers to them offered by the book's other contributors, as well as myself, to history-related issues of current American foreign policy. That is, I shall examine the historical thinking evident in the Bush administration's foreign policy-making to date. In the final section, I will identify briefly certain improvements that might be made in the methods and the processes involved in bringing historical knowledge to bear on present policy.

The contributors to this book do not assert that the study of history is the only way of reducing uncertainty about the future. It is not the master key to the problems of statesmanship — 'the only true policy science,' as Henry Kissinger, reminiscently of Bismarck, is said to have said.[8] Still less do the present writers propound 'historicist' doctrines, grand explanatory theories according to which the element of uncertainty actually is removed from history through subsumption of events under 'laws' that make historical developments predictable or destined.[9] What the authors do, however, is to make a very strong case, as articulated by Michael Fry at the beginning, that history in its several 'forms' — history learned, history observed, and history experienced — helps statesmen to 'cope', that is, to meet the future on more or less even terms.

There are, as indicated above, difficulties in this argument. One is a persistent question concerning historical thinking's 'rationality'. Can reflective thinking be entirely reasonable? A number of authors, including Fry himself, have pointed out that rationality itself is an 'idealization' — a standard by which human thinking is abstractly judged rather than an accurate characterization of it in life. Jonathan Haslam, identifying a deeply 'irrational' element in Soviet policy-making toward Japan, owing to the traumatic defeat suffered by Russia in its 1904–5 war with Japan, suggests that the very idea of the rational decision-maker is a necessity of theory-building, rather than a product of the empirical scholar. Alex Hybel, too, emphasizes that the rational man is an 'ideal', useful to theorists, particularly economists, for bounding certain of man's decisions. In politics, the school of 'realism', positing that decision-makers rationally calculate their interests in terms of maximization of power, surely simplifies human motivation in order to achieve explanatory consistency and predictability. Following Herbert A. Simon, Hybel questions whether, in fact, real-world decision-makers do have clear conceptions of their values, and actually can differentiate among or rank-order them. Persons in power, or anywhere else, just do not seem to think that way. He doubts as well the reality of decision-makers' devotion to option-choosing, the detailed analysis of a broad range of alternatives that, ideally, should precede the selection of the optimal policy — as distinct from a merely 'satisficing' one.[10] As a result, he implies, political choices tend to be suboptimal — that is, if judged by the unrealistic standards of rationality. His own advice is to discard 'the rationality assumption' altogether, even if this means accepting, unparsimoniously, far greater complexity in our conception of how the human brain works, and what makes policy-makers tick.

Even if, in the unlikely event, individual decision-makers could be shown to act rationally, as 'maximizers' of their perfectly understood and efficiently pursued goals, the fact that, as Hybel and others point out, foreign policy is made by *groups* of persons, having a variety of interests and beliefs, undermines a major premise of political realism: the assumption of the unitary rational state, conceived of as a single actor. Jeffry Frieden, seeking to understand why the United States did not accept its economic 'international responsibilities' in the inter-war period but did do so later, looks not for careful calculations of 'national interest'. He concentrates instead on the varying pressures brought to bear on governments by 'self-interested socio-economic groups'. The interplay of these groups and their demands upon the state, and not the state itself, were what determined so-called national policy. When American exporters and those American banks and corporations making overseas loans and investments became more dominant, in competition for control over policy with more domestically oriented groups, US foreign economic policy became more 'internationalist'. This result was not a function of centrally chosen 'internationalism', rationally decided upon.

Jack Snyder, performing a similar analysis of the Soviet Union's foreign expansionism through time, finds that 'logrolling' among groups within the Soviet Union having an interest in extended empire in part accounts for the aggressiveness of Soviet international behavior in certain periods. Contrary to widespread belief, he finds Soviet foreign policy has tended to be more moderate when controlled by one man, even the idiosyncratic Joseph Stalin and, at present, the virtuosic Mikhail Gorbachev who seems to rely on his own sense of direction and the prospect of all-Union, mass-democratic support. The competing bureaucratic interests inherited from the Khrushchev and Brezhnev periods thereby can be kept in check. Without such an explanatory model, Soviet foreign-policy offensives of the past would be inexplicable, because they were, as quickly became evident, counterproductive, given the constraints imposed by the international system, ie, the operation of the balance of power. During this century Japan and Germany similarly have seemed to act irrationally (that is, self-destructively), whereas Great Britain and the United States have been relatively good learners (that is, long-term self-preservers), having wisely 'appeased' other, rising powers and 'retrenched' from overextended positions when difficulties arose from their activities abroad.

Snyder's explanation of this pattern, on which predictions tentatively can be based, is seen by him to lie mainly in the composition of a country's internal political system. Not fundamentally challenging human rationality as such, he emphasizes the special reasoning of interest groups, who 'hijack' national policy, and also broad strategic rationalizations, such as the fear-of-encirclement myth, which strong parochial interests foist off upon a credulous public. In the British and the American systems, in contrast, foreign policy is more moderate and self-regulating. It is successful because there are more internal counterchecks on adventurism — that is, many more domestic 'second opinions' to be heard. The key to Snyder's explanation, however, is not the inherent rationality of the masses but the logic of coalitional politics, and its effects in the realm of ideology.

If statesmen do not decide upon their policies rationally, then it would seem to follow that the composite reasoning used in national policy-making, including arguments based on history, are not rational either. Dwain Mefford, however, defends historical thinking, including analogizing, against this line of criticism. His own reservations about the use of historical analogies, and the way these analogies so far have been studied, concern mainly the failure of both analogizers and their critics to set the topic in the frame of reference of a comprehensive theory of learning. Historical cases often are cited too anecdotally. Historical reasoning is not merely episodic remembering; it is truly systemic thinking, of a fundamentally important kind.

What Mefford and also Hybel especially emphasize is the role of analogical thinking at the *initial* stages of any individual or group reasoning process aimed at future action or policy choice. Michael Fry, too, points out that statesmen use analogies to interpret situations and to formulate and frame problems, in addressing them prior to determining how to resolve them. Historical comparison helps to restrict the universe of choice and to narrow down the range of alternatives that deserve consideration. It assists in differentiating between what is intellectually imaginable and what is politically feasible, Fry observes, somewhat wistful about the loss of imaginative range and creative possibility entailed by this simplification.

Is there also a loss of reason in this constriction? Mefford thinks not. He argues that analogical thinking is not the mere imposition of simple event-sequences upon a current problem but, rather, a much more flexible mental procedure in which, in game-like fashion, many analogies are posed and adjudicated as *further* arguments and facts for-and-against their relevance to a particular immediate situation are adduced. The process naturally is complex, especially when the deliberation becomes collective, but the schemata inherent in analogies help to make it controllable.[11] Analogies are akin to "plans", which, when used in the future-oriented construction of policy options, are assembled, rearranged, and sometimes also collapsed, if and when changes in objectives or circumstances occur that make the analogies inappropriate.

Mefford might even quarrel with Fry's point about the loss of creativity. In the use of analogies by policy analysts, the parallels and discrepancies between past and present cases are seized upon to explain the twists and turns of events. An element of play is involved. However, the analogy or juxtaposition is not simply a turn of phrase, he insists, but integral to the analysis, which is open-ended and can be progressive. Analogies are used not only to 'focus' the description of events but also to serve as a basis for 'exploring' what might have been had certain factors not emerged or certain accidents not intruded. Whether such mental exploration of past contingencies, at the margins of a present situation, genuinely amounts to creative imagination — producing alternative visions, not merely alternative strategies and tactics — remains, however, a serious question. In sum, historical reasoning, though rational, is not perfectly so.

Whatever the scope of analogical thinking's constriction, it surely is a mistake, in Alex Hybel's phrase, to believe that we are 'captives of the past' — as if we must look toward the future in a rearview mirror. Hybel himself, though skeptical of historical thinking's rationality, believes that the initial formulation of a problem can have a 'decisive' effect on the decision eventually reached, and that this effect, though potentially misleading, is far from valueless.

Is historical reasoning in fact compelling, or genuinely influential in policy-making and in the debate that precedes and in the discourse that expresses it? Is it, in truth, decisive? Or is it only comparatively compelling? How pervasive, and therefore inescapable in the sphere of rhetorical disputation, is history-based reference and deduction? Basically, is such argumentation resistible, and why and how?

Fry has commented, in his introduction, on the special *gravitas* of history, on how a group's 'historian' can dominate a debate, on the invocation of precedent as a means of gaining 'legitimation' or 'justification', and also on the 'surprise' that historians experience when political leaders and government officials seem to take their work so seriously. Perhaps this is because, as he amusingly speculates, historians, 'impressive and disinterested', seem to compare well with shifty lawyers, urgent scientists, and eager strategists.[12] There is no reason a priori, he emphasises, why being historically knowledgeable, whether as a scholar or a statesman, should discourage the search for 'information', i.e. current facts about the problem at hand. Nonetheless, historical knowledge does seem in some way to be privileged.[13]

It has weight, as Condoleezza Rice indicates in discussing the thinking of the Soviet general staff. As Diane Kunz shows in her comparative-historical analysis of national banking policies, the sterling era and strength of the pound were, in British minds, major 'psychological' factors in offsetting the difference between Britain's declining power and the rising power of the United States and the Soviet Union in the 1950s.' 'This history-engendered fixation, which she calls an 'obsession', contributed to Britain's vulnerability when, during the 1956 Suez crisis, the Eisenhower administration delayed support for the Eden cabinet's effort to maintain the value of sterling until British and French forces withdrew from Egypt. Other nations, too, have had long-lasting attitudes toward economic matters that were formed in the past. Germany is one case. The hyperinflation of the 1920s had 'burnt itself' into the German memory, as Kunz notes. Any increase in the inflation rate even today sends shock waves through the German economy. She alludes to painful American memories that have influenced current economic policy as well. In commenting on the trade surplus that Japan now has accumulated with the United States, she remarks that it is 'not without significance' that the Japanese today own large chunks of Honolulu. Protection of property is thus, via the trauma of Pearl Harbor, associated with the defense of territory. It might be remarked, in passing, that such examples of especially powerful, policy-shaping historical memories do not exert their influence rationally, through the formal canons of analogy. Such history is not used, in the pragmatic sense, but rather felt, emotionally. These feelings are compelling, in part because they are *not* examined logically.

Many of the contributors to this book, Diane Kunz included, accept, as a parallelism that is almost irresistible, what seems to be the unique comparability of the previous international experience of Great Britain as a world leader, or 'hegemon', and the contemporary international leadership experience of the United States. Especially in assessing America's current 'decline' from its post-war zenith, the British precedent asserts itself. David Lake, focusing analytically on the theory of 'hegomonic stability', follows others in regarding Britain's relative decline after 1870 as the closest historical analogue to the disintegration in the US-led world order during the post-1945 era, and as a fruitful source of lessons for present American policy. He cites this as a case of history-based theory, and not just a historical sequence or narrative having an effect on public consciousness and perhaps also public policy.[14] In systematically questioning, point-by-point, the accuracy of this UK–US comparison, noting particularly the greater size of the American domestic market and the greater availability to the United States of great-power allies, Lake nonetheless, in effect, revalidates the British analogy's authority — as a framework for analysis, if not so much as a fount of practical wisdom.[15] Other contributors find greater utility in the history they examine.

Comparing the acquisition of political knowledge, including national strategies, to the evolution of strategy in the game of chess, Dwain Mefford shows how past-derived 'lessons', on many levels, can inform present and future conduct. He takes as a particular case the rich example of the 1962 Cuban missile crisis. With fascinating precision and in exquisite detail, Mefford demonstrates that the lessons that initially were drawn from that unforgettable experience — including the American conclusion that the favorable outcome of the crisis is 'perhaps the pre-eminent example of the successful use of a compellent threat', in Thomas Schelling's term — were drawn very tendentiously.[16] Alternative explanations — particularly the view that the peaceful outcome was achieved through 'a private deal' by which the United States agreed to remove its Jupiter missiles from Turkey in exchange for the Soviet Union's immediate withdrawal of its missiles from Cuba — were more or less suppressed, in part in order to protect the Kennedy administration from a possible right-wing political reaction at home and also to minimize objections from America's allies (including Turkey, a NATO member). Despite contemporary public and literary misrepresentations of the event, however, the actual story was not forgotten by participants; and, in recent meetings, American and Soviet veterans of the crisis have come together to reconstruct a narrative of the episode that does greater justice to the experience of both sides, and also perhaps more closely approximates scientific historical truth.[17] A shared belief in the distinctiveness and importance of the missile crisis warrants the extraordinary attention given to it.

Out of this process and other, similar joint deliberations, Mefford suggests, the perfection of an informal code, or set of rules amounting to a 'regime', for US–Soviet conduct can be advanced. Such rules consist in part of summaries of previous Washington–Moscow interchanges, i.e. their common diplomatic history. The past, therefore, is integral to any program of political learning through re-examined historical experience, resulting perhaps in international bonding.

How obligatory will the rule-like 'lessons' of such a mutual teaching process based on the missile-crisis experience prove to be? The power of the past, as Dewey suggested, depends on how relevant it remains or, more accurately, on how pertinent its reconstruction makes it continue to be. Some of the American participants in the original event themselves came to think, by the late 1980s, that 'the crisis holds no significant lessons for today'. This was principally so because the Soviet Union by then had achieved nuclear parity with the United States, and it therefore could not be compelled to retreat from an otherwise exposed position. Because of this changed circumstance, the missile crisis seemed 'no more (or less) relevant to present concerns than, say, the Peloponnesian Wars'. If the event were seen as being mainly about diplomatic bargaining rather than about military power or political will, however, it could remain highly pertinent, and perhaps practically instructive. The very retrospective malleability of the October 1962 story, however, somewhat detracts, as Meinecke might have noted, from the 'finest and highest instruction' it could offer: the marvelousness of its historical individuality. In sum, history may be more compelling when it is contemplated than when it is construed.

What can be said about the validity, or correctness and appropriateness, of the political lessons derived from history in the crafting of policy? When Meinecke noted that Hegel had denied that peoples or governments ever had learned anything from history, or its lessons, he added wryly: 'It is probably more correct to say that they have seldom learned the things the observer might wish to see them learn.'[18] In other words, what the actual lessons of history are, and which of these should be carried out in the conduct of policy, is in the last analysis a matter of honest individual judgment, related to the perspective afforded by one's seat of judgement or vantage.

Dwain Mefford refers to 'the fine art' of drawing historical lessons. The way a problem is conceived initially often is thought of as a matter of 'intuition and *Fingerspitzengefühl*,' he writes.[19] One is reminded that Meinecke himself confessed that, in intellectually striking a balance among competing causal imprints in explaining an event in history, an 'indefinable finesse' in exercising judgment, more artistic-intuitive than natural-scientific, was required.[20]

One can be more definite than this, however. To a considerable degree, the deriving of historical lessons is a function of *position* and also a function of *purpose*. Both of these vary, from person to person, group to group, country to country. In brief, the validity of historical lessons is relative. Alex Hybel is right in noting that, just as two drivers caught in the same gridlock might deduce different lessons from their common experience, so also might two foreign policy-makers, engaged in the same international crisis, reach different conclusions regarding the nature of their problem, what should be done about it, and, afterward, how they escaped it if they did. The drivers, or policy-makers, have different locations and also different destinations. Thus they have different experiences to interpret. The lessons they draw, although derived from the same context, also are likely to be different.

It is perhaps only the historian, one like Meinecke having little current-policy interest, who has a chance of explaining an international traffic jam with something like synoptic objectivity.[21] A rare historian-diplomat who did so, with a remarkable political detachment and moral dispassion, was the US State Department official, Louis J. Halle, in his book *The Cold War as History* (1967). Following the Cambridge historian Herbert Butterfield, who discerned in the great conflicts of mankind 'a terrible human predicament', Halle characterizes the Soviet–US Cold War struggle situationally. It was not 'a case of the wicked against the virtuous' but rather 'the case of the scorpion and the tarantula in the bottle'.[22] It emphasizes the point being made here to note that Halle wrote this book when in retirement from government service and living in Switzerland, neutral and intermediate between East and West.[23] Not every statesman or scholar can expect to achieve such distance and equipoise.

Apart from the possible misinterpreting of the Cuban missile crisis, as being resolved in fact by an American missiles-for-Russian missiles trade, the greatest alleged historical distortion discussed in the present volume concerns 'the Arab–Israeli conflict', alternatively defined as 'the Palestine problem'. Rashid Khalidi, in recounting this dramatic case of the importance of the initial conceptualization of a problem, contends that 'the power to name' actually can carry control over the political process. That is to say, the definition of the historical challenge of settling both Jews and Arabs in the territory of Palestine has partially determined the basic direction of the international search for a solution. He laments that the course of Western, particularly American, diplomacy has been one of dealing with the Arab states, rather than the Palestinian people themselves, as the relevant protagonists (or antagonists) in the situation. The Palestinians were not considered a real 'party' but rather were thought of as 'refugees', to be resettled somewhere. The whole problem, which actually has a Palestinian core' from Khalidi's perspective, was recast by US policy-makers as one of mutually acceptable and secure 'frontiers' between Israel and its neighbors, rather than as one of sovereign control over territory, over a homeland.

Part of the explanation of the still-prevailing misrepresentation of this historically evolved situation, Khalidi explains, has been preoccupation of the United States, at least until recently, with its global contest against an expansionist Soviet Union. The 'imperatives of the local situation', as he terms the necessitous position of the Palestinian community, have tended throughout the post-war period to be played down in favor of 'inputs from elsewhere'. Besides the preoccupation of American policy-makers with the Soviet Union, these factors included relations with America's European allies, the situation of Jewish refugees in Europe, and domestic political considerations related to the American Jewish community, generally favoring Israel.

Had 'the history' — both the genesis of the Palestine problem and Britain's previous experience of it — intellectually been acquired by the US government, Khalidi proposes counterfactually, the evolution of the region would have been different. But, instead, an 'alternative narrative' of events, based largely on the official Israeli position, has dominated American understanding. Its substantive elements include 'mythical' beliefs about the weakness of Palestinian nationalism, the capability of the Jordanian state, and the lack of wider Arab world sympathy for the Palestinians. Only within the institutional memory of the foreign-policy bureaucracy, Khalidi suggests, are elements of the 'real story' perhaps preserved.

Furthermore, owing in part to its misunderstanding of the present situation and the related earlier history, the United States, in its diplomacy, has ignored evidence, compiled by violent events in 1948, 1956 and 1967, of the 'futility' of attempting to achieve a Middle Eastern settlement on any basis other than 'a comprehensive one' — that is involving all questions and all concerned parties, regional and also extraregional. This is an important proposition which, if historically valid, should interest governments today.[24] 'Multilateral diplomacy,' Khalidi goes on to explain, does not necessarily mean bringing all the parties together but, rather, taking them all seriously and dealing with every one.[25] The lessons taught by the past experience of attempting to deal with the problem bilaterally, in direct talks between Israel and its individual Arab neighbors, have been mostly negative — from the Arab point of view. This is partly because, as Khalidi revealingly notes, the Arab countries' interlocutors have been subjected to debilitating domestic, Palestinian, and other Arab 'pressures'. A more comprehensive, international peace process, conceivably, would alleviate these threats and demands.

Although the practical lessons drawn by Khalidi are, manifestly, as partisan as those of devotees of the 'alternative narrative', they are seriously intended. The relativity of historical lesson-drawing for policy-making makes it necessary, however, to strive for a greater objectivity. To some extent this can be reached, as Hegel suggests, by looking at history 'from a higher vantage point'.[26] More than sheer perspective, however, is needed. As Herbert Butterfield emphasizes, historical science also gives depth. It 'leads us to place a different construction on the whole human drama, since it uncovers the tragic element in human conflict. In historical perspective we learn to be a little more sorry for both parties than they knew how to be for one another.'[27] Such human sympathy is a lesson for diplomacy, and a corrective against facile lesson-drawing from the experience of the past.

Can the findings of this book, though on balance more theoretical than practical, help to inform the history-based intellectual processes of current American foreign policy-making? Before venturing a response to this question, which seems a fair test of the work, I shall offer, for factual reference, a brief account of the 'history' — the events and actions themselves and also the historical explanations and interpretations being placed on them — of the Bush administration in world affairs.

Implicit in this task is the question of whether the history that one is living through, whether as academic observer or as political participant, can be considered with enough detachment, affording the possibility of objectivity, to be 'used'. Has enough time passed for even a Deweyite 'reconstruction' of recent events to occur, for the purpose of pragmatic history? Surely there is not enough such temporal distance for 'the pure appreciation' of history's great individualities which Meinecke personally sought, to achieve a truly scientific understanding of the past. An historian, nonetheless, perhaps should be emboldened by Butterfield's advice at an earlier time of international crisis, the onset of the Cold War:

> Politicians, in the hurry of affairs and in the stress of conflict, may hardly have an opportunity to cover the problem in an all-embracing survey, for we must regard them as generally acting under great pressures. We in universities, however — and especially those of us who study history —

have a duty to think in longer terms and seize upon the problem precisely where the difficulties are most challenging.

Contemporary history — that of the present — should be written with 'prayer and fasting', however.[28]

The very historic quality of the present — the widespread feeling, shared by many political leaders, that the world faces a choice between order and chaos — invites immediate assessment. One may be reminded of the grandly philosophical way that President Bush gave his perspective on the trend of world affairs in his inaugural address on 20 January 1989. A 'new breeze' is blowing, he said, in that message. A world 'refreshed by freedom seems reborn.' In man's heart, if not yet in fact, 'the day of the dictator is over,' he declared. 'The totalitarian era is passing, its old ideas blown away like leaves from an ancient, lifeless tree.'[29]

A State Department planning officer, Francis Fukuyama, then went so far as to proclaim 'The End of History' (with history being conceived as a Hegelian dialectical process). 'What we may be witnessing,' wrote Fukuyama, 'is not just the end of the Cold War, or the passing of a particular period of postwar history, but the end of history as such: that is, the end point of mankind's ideological evolution and the universalization of Western liberal democracy as the final form of human government.'[30] Although the actual influence of Fukuyama's historical speculation on administration policy no doubt then was exaggerated, the attitude toward the past that he expressed — heralding a triumph of Western idealism — was pervasive.

How was this triumph accounted for by the administration, and how should it be explained? In the answers to this question one may find keys to understanding the history-based political logic of the subsequent policy of the Bush administration. The major explanation, offered by the President himself in an address at Texas A & M University, was simply: 'Containment worked.' He elaborated: 'Containment worked because our democratic principles, institutions, and values are sound and always have been. It worked because our alliances were and are strong; and because the superiority of free societies and free markets over stagnant socialism is undeniable.'

The actual mechanism of containment's success, the President suggested with an allusion to George F. Kennan's original conception of that strategy, was the internal dynamic of the Soviet system itself. This had been put under external pressure by the West's 'adroit and vigilant application of counter-force', in Kennan's formulation.[31] As Bush noted, Kennan and the other 'wise men' who had crafted the strategy of containment 'believed that the Soviet Union, denied the easy course of expansion, would turn inward and address the contradictions of its inefficient, repressive, and inhumane system. And they were right'. The Soviet Union was having to confront 'hard reality'.[32]

Other factors that President Bush mentioned at that time, notably

America's 'principles, institutions, and values' or ideological influence, also need to be factored into the equation of world change. These are not so easily mediated by active statesmanship but tend to work through a demonstration effect, and resulting emulation by others — an 'emanation' of power, so to speak.[33] Stated differently, America is seen as being effective internationally less because of what it *does* than because of what it *is*. However, there still may be, as Fry notes in his introductory essay, an element of intellectual coercion in any such adoption by other countries of a great power's (that is, American) attitudes and policies. The actual net effect of physical and intellectual containment may not in fact have been what is usually assumed. The historical effect may have been, on balance, to increase the Soviet Union's 'glacial isolation'.[34]

An alternative model of world change needs to be considered in accounting for present prospects of a new world ordering. Less obligatory than either containment or emanation, it is what Fry terms mutually reciprocal, transnational learning. In part this refers simply to the now virtually frontierless international flow of information. The material basis of this circulatory process is economic interdependence, which the chapters by Lake, Kunz and Frieden describe. It is now evident that vast amounts of modern information have long penetrated even the Iron Curtain, and quietly have altered mass thinking behind that supposed barrier. This makes the events of the revolutions of 1989 seem, in retrospect, almost inevitable, unforced, natural, not a product of American policy.

Using the intriguing metaphor of a 'conversation', a non-coercive communicative process in which a participant is nonetheless more the led than leader, Dwain Mefford describes a somewhat narrower, more focused international dialogue — of which the James Baker–Eduard Shevardnadze relationship might be considered a new prototype —of statesman on opposite sides finding possible new forms of cooperation through regular interchange.[35] More than just 'keeping in touch', such a process of high-level diplomatic communication, not negotiation *stricto sensu*, involves mutual exploration of past histories, basic needs, current positions, strategy and tactics, norms and rules, and perhaps also visions of a common future. Essential to the formation of a joint 'regime', it also could become the basis of an even wider international order.

These bright hopes, however caused, suddenly were dashed when, on 2 August 1990, the military forces of Iraq, under the leadership of President Saddam Hussein, invaded Kuwait. Subsequently, Iraq formally annexed Kuwait, making it one of its provinces. To date, the conflict has been presented largely in military terms, as a question of 'aggression' forcibly to be resisted. 'Where does American stand?', President Bush rhetorically asked in a speech at the Pentagon. 'I answer: America stands where it always has — against aggression.'[36] In an address to the Veterans of Foreign Wars, he made clearer the historical meaning of this commitment by citing the military antecedents, particularly the Second World War in which he himself had served as a young Navy pilot. This was the master experience forming his own political generation.[37] 'History experienced,' as Fry terms it, can be collective as well as individual — a bond between men rather than a barrier dividing them. 'Think back with me to World War II, when together allies confronted a horror which embodied hell on Earth. Or Korea, where UN forces opposed totalitarianism,' Bush said. He even briefly mentioned Vietnam, although that experience, even less filled with victories than the Korean conflict, was somewhat finessed in the speech.

'Throughout history,' the President declared, 'we have learned that we must stand up to aggression.' The 'first lesson' of that history, 'as vivid as the memories of Normandy, Khe Sanh, Pork Chop Hill', is that 'aggression must and will be checked — or, better, prevented'. 'Half a century ago,' he said in closing, 'the world had a chance to stop a ruthless aggressor and missed it. I pledge to you: We will not make that mistake again.'[38] It is worthy of note, again, that the whole Vietnam experience — the quagmire image, the entrapment — was glossed over. The awkward 1960s were, in a sense, bypassed in order to get to the more conveniently instructive 1930s Here is a case of deliberate selectivity, made easier when the events identified are fairly remote.

The precise name of the mistake made in the 1930s was, as President Bush and other members of his administration noted (without defining it well), 'appeasement'. As the President said in his first important televised address on 8 August, following the Iraqi invasion, 'if history teaches us anything, it is that we must resist aggression or it will destroy our freedoms. Appeasement does not work. As was the case in the 1930s, we see in Saddam Hussein an aggressive dictator threatening his neighbors.'[39] This initial, history-based characterisation of the Iraqi challenge determined much of the subsequent discussion.

Secretary of State James Baker also evoked the experience of the 1930s. Intent upon the possibilities of constructing a post-Cold War world, he stated in testimony before the House Foreign Affairs Committee that 'America's role in this sea of change in world politics is straightforward: We must leave behind not only the Cold War but also the conflicts that preceded it'. He saw Saddam Hussein and his aggression as an unwelcome throwback to an earlier age:

> The line in the sands of Arabia is also a line in time. By crossing into Kuwait, Saddam Hussein took a dangerous step back in history. Maybe he thought the world would consider Kuwait expendable, that we would think of it as just a small, faraway country of which we knew and cared little. Possibly he remembered the 1930s when the League of Nations failed to respond effectively to Mussolini's aggression against Abyssinia, what is today Ethiopia.[40]

Perhaps Saddam Hussein had 'learned' dangerously false 'lessons' from the 1930s.

A more specifically intended reference to the 1930s was Baker's invocation of that fearful, cynical decade so as to defeat the idea of a compromise territorial settlement, or 'partial solution', which would leave Iraq in possession of all of the Rumaila oil field and Kuwait's Warbah and Bubiyan islands near the mouth of the Shatt al Arab. Here the most pertinent comparison is with Czechoslovakia in September 1938. Its marginal but strategically important Sudetenland was demanded by Nazi Germany at the Munich conference and then received. The United States looked on as Britain and France helped dismember Czechoslovakia. 'We made this mistake in the 30's,' Baker said. 'We did not stand up in opposition to unprovoked aggression. And we remember what happened in Europe when we refused to take a principled stand.'[41] Much the same argument was used by Baker against 'linkage' — relating the Kuwait invasion to the Palestinian problem, with Saddam Hussein trading off his occupation of Kuwait for an Israeli removal of its forces from the West Bank. That would make him appear to be a liberator.[42] In the view of the US government, dictators must have no rewards for aggression, even indirect ones.

These references to the 1930s became controversial when the President personalized the challenge by comparing Saddam Hussein with Adolf Hitler. The policy implication, probably not wholly intended, was that the United States government was augmenting Bush's original 'four simple principles' — Iraqi withdrawal from Kuwait, restoration of the legitimate Kuwaiti government, security for the Persian Gulf, and protection of American citizens abroad — with a further, more 'offensive' purpose: removal of Saddam Hussein from the leadership of Iraq and, perhaps also, reduction of Iraq's present and future capacity to make war.[43]

Early in the crisis the President also made it clear the he would hold Saddam Hussein 'accountable' for any harm down to Americans in territories under his control. Reports of the mistreatment of the Kuwaiti population by Iraqi forces led the President to call the actions 'Hitler revisited', and to add: 'But remember, when Hitler's war ended there were Nuremberg trials' — thus warning of future war-crimes prosecutions of Saddam and his comrades in arms.[44] Here he invoked legal-historical precedent — using history as law. His point connoted as well a denunciation of the Iraqi military's use of poison gas, against Iranians during their recent war and also against Iraq's own Kurdish minority. When the Saudi Arabian defense minister, Prince Sultan, seemed to suggest ceding Baghdad some disputed territory as part of an arrangement to induce Iraqi troops to leave Kuwait, President Bush cited the Iraqi army's 'crimes against humanity'. Blandishments were no way to treat atrocities. 'I'm reading a book and it's a book of history, a great, big thick history of World War II,' he said in a speech in Burlington, Vermont, 'and there's a parallel between what Hitler did to Poland and what Saddam Hussein has done to Kuwait.'[45] The implication was that it would be both dangerous and immoral to bargain with Iraq.

Here is a case of what Fry terms 'history learned', augmenting history directly experienced. President Bush's own personal exposure to the Second World War postdated the American entry after Pearl Harbor and was centered on the Pacific theater. The European theater of operations was something he had only observed from afar or experienced remotely. Poland's travails were not known to him in detail. After ravaging that country, Bush might have learned from the 'great, big thick history', the German dictator egregiously had proffered his hand in peace, evidently believing that it could be accepted. It was bloodied, and it could not be.[46] Neither, by extension, could Saddam Hussein's.

Subsequently, in Mashpee, Massachusetts, President Bush, now plainly engaged in the conscious 'reconstruction' of history for pragmatic purposes, suggested that Saddam Hussein actually was worse then Hitler in that he deliberately had placed hostages, including some Americans, as 'human shields' at potential military targets, thus forcing upon the US government the dilemma of possibly having to attack its own citizens. Bush had not examined in detail what Hitler had done, so the comparison was tendentious and one-sided. Responding to questions about how the Iraqi leader could be worse than the man responsible for the Holocaust, the President shifted his ground — to the legal issue of the status of foreign embassies in occupied territory. Saddam Hussein had more conspicuously interfered with foreign embassies, including the American embassy in Kuwait City, than even Hitler appeared to have done. It would not be tolerated. 'I believe that the embassy should remain open because I don't believe a dictator should violate international law by starving out or isolating another person's embassy,' said President Bush, a former ambassador himself. 'I think there's a fundamental principle involved in that.'[47] The whole system of diplomatic privilege and immunity arguably was at stake.

In a Thanksgiving Day talk at a US Marine outpost in Saudi Arabia, the President epitomized United States policy in a way that was heavily dependent on history. He declared that 'our diplomats and our citizens held hostage must be freed'. It was time for 'Saddam, the invader', to 'stop toying' with American hostages and to 'stop trying to starve out our little beleaguered embassy in Kuwait City'. It was time to 'put an end to this cruel hostage bazaar', bartering human beings as in 'the days of the slave trade'.[48] Thus he stirred American memories of the Civil War as well as prejudices against an ancient Middle Eastern social custom. Some Americans might have remembered the Barbary Wars, when hostages were used to extort tribute from the United States.[49]

There are times, President Bush also said in his Thanksgiving Day speech, when 'any nation that values its own freedom must confront aggression'. The people of Czechoslovakia, from which he and his wife, Barbara, had just come, 'know first-hand about the folly of appeasement,' he said. Here he alluded not only to the consequences of the surrender of territory made to Hitler's Germany but also perhaps to the encouragement given to Hitler by pro-German fringe groups in Czechoslovakia itself. The parable may have served to fortify the members of the international coalition ranged against Iraq. Germany took control of all of Czechoslovakia in March 1939. 'They know about the tyranny of dictatorial conquests,' Bush said of the Czech people. 'And in the World War that followed, the world paid dearly for appeasing an aggressor who should and could have been stopped. We're not going to make that mistake again', he declared syllogistically. 'We will not appease this aggressor.'[50]

Why was this decade — the 1930s — chosen? As I have suggested in introducing this concluding essay, history really only can be said to be 'used' when it is viewed with a degree of objectivity, which permits some choice in historical reference. The basic reason for the selection of the 1930s, surely, was an honest perception by Bush of a similarity, accompanied by a belief that the public would accept his authoritatively drawn parallels. The history of the 1930s and the resulting world war has, in Michael Fry's term, a special gravitas. The Bush administration's probable desire to preclude another critical re-examination of the more rancorous Vietnam experience also has been noted.

A further partial explanation for the Bush administration characterizing the crisis this way — as resistance to unexpected and unprovoked 'aggression' — was perhaps to cover up for the inadequacy of US policy in the immediately preceding period, prior to the 2 August Iraqi invasion.[51] This phase of policy, an obvious failure, has been characterized by Senator Claiborne Pell, chairman of the Senate Foreign Relations Committee, as one of 'wishful thinking, appeasement, and greed'. A press commentator interpreted Pell's criticisms as follows: 'wishful thinking' meant hoping that an all-carrot-no-stick approach would bring Saddam Hussein to moderation; 'appeasement' meant tolerating the Iraqi leader's use of poison gas, military-equipment smuggling, and violent threats against Israel; and 'greed' meant America's large agricultural sales to Iraq, not to mention substantial oil purchases from Iraq.[52]

Whatever the motivations that actually lay behind this characterization, the US government's handling of the relationship with Iraq throughout the 1980s was at best ineffective, and possibly counterproductive.[53] There is a just historical balance to be made between an 'aggression' theory of the Gulf crisis and an 'appeasement' explanation of it. We must decide between these competing causal imprints, in Meinecke's sense. Yet, in part as we do not know for certain of Saddam Hussein's inner reactions to American diplomats' pre-crisis assuagings, the 'aggression' version will have the upper hand, which in any case it probably in fact deserves. By emphasizing the completely 'unprovoked' (and, by implication, totally 'uninvited') Iraqi invasion, and labelling it 'aggression', the Bush administration, however, has virtually assured that there will be no fundamental reassignment of causal and moral responsibility. The very way the 'aggression' and 'appeasement' models rhetorically are presented makes them mutually exclusive. That is, if President Bush is a 'Churchill', he cannot be a 'Chamberlain'. Should this become the consensus, history will have served Bush's purpose. There is a shadow over the whole debate, however, of imitativeness — of what

Meinecke called 'epigonal' dependency.'

A noteworthy aspect of the Bush administration's anti-appeasement campaign after Iraq's invasion was its collective spirit — a marked contrast with the unilateral internationalism of the Reagan administration before it. The approach taken was not so much Wilsonian, although some observers believed they saw Wilson-like elements in it, as it was Rooseveltian. It was reminiscent of the great-power diplomacy of Franklin Delano Roosevelt, and even carried suggestions of Tehran and Yalta — that is, what later came to be called 'condominium'.

'In particular,' noted Secretary Baker in testimony before Congress early in September, 'the Soviet Union has proven a responsible partner, suggesting new possibilities for active superpower cooperation in resolving regional conflicts.' Accordingly, as he noted, President Bush would meet President Gorbachev in Helsinki further to strengthen 'our ties of partnership'. He commented on how different the current conflict in the Gulf would look if the 'old-style zero-sum thinking' still were driving Soviet policy in the region.[54]

President Bush, too, emphasized the centrality of the new Washington–Moscow relationship in United States policy. Following his meeting with his Soviet counterpart in the Finnish capital on 9 September, he reported to Congress: 'We stand today at a unique and extraordinary moment. The crisis in the Gulf, as grave as it is, also offers a rare opportunity to move toward a historic period of cooperation.' Out of these troubled times, he said, 'our fifth objective', could emerge (beside his previously stated four goals related directly to the Gulf situation): 'a new world order'.

This would be 'a new era — freer from the threat of terror, stronger in the pursuit of justice, and more secure in the quest for peace, an era in which the nations of the world, East and West, North and South, can prosper and live in harmony,' Bush said. He had shared this 'vision' in Helsinki with President Gorbachev who, along with other leaders around the world, understands that 'how we manage this crisis today could shape the future for generations to come'.[55]

This 'vision' would seem to a lengthy historical one, but is it more than a sensation of the moment — in Butterfield's words, a product of 'acting under great pressures'? What is the objective evidence for such a prospect, and for the judgement that the Gulf crisis is 'one of the defining moments of this new era', in Baker's formulation?[56] Is the Secretary's and the President's subjective sense of being located at a turning point between two eras — Cold War bipolar conflict and post-Cold War multilateral cooperation — wilful self-delusion? Is it largely a means — an instrumental use of history — of winning greater domestic and international support for a particular military and diplomatic strategy? Or is it actually a valid historical reading — the deeper objective truth — of the trend of the times? Is it possible for statesmen, who are subjectively at one with a historical period and who are actively engaged in its affairs, to have sufficient detachment from their own circumstances, and from themselves within those circumstances, to grasp history in a scientific and not merely a pragmatic way? If not can the historian, also a contemporary, do any better?

A historical opinion may be ventured. In a sense, the regional Gulf crisis is a sub-Cold War struggle, subordinate chronologically as well as logically to the US–Soviet bipolar relationship. Secretary Baker, in speaking about the 'sea of change' in world politics, stated that we must leave behind not only the Cold War 'but also the conflicts that preceded it', within which he included the Iraqi invasion of Kuwait.[57] Through intimate cooperation with the Soviet Union — the Cold War bipolar American rivalry with the Soviet Union turned inside out, making the Soviet Union a collaborator rather then a competitor — he could keep 'the past' firmly in the past, under control. As if to defend the Fukuyama thesis declaring 'The End of History', Baker struggled mightily, intellectually as well as diplomatically, to keep the Old World — that is, ideological and history-based conflict — from being reborn. Superpower control (mainly American 'leadership') was to be the predominant factor in maintaining this situation. Such *dirigiste* diplomacy, however, might not be sufficient. Individual statesmanship, no matter how brilliant, needs to be supplemented by 'fail-safe' or reinsurance systems.[58] It needs to be institutionalized — in effect, to be made independent of leadership. A truly new world order would be a collective one.

To interpret the present Gulf crisis as a test, or 'defining moment', of the new era, therefore, may be backward-looking or reactionary rather than forward-looking or genuinely progressive. To an extent, the Bush administration's vision of the future is a mirror image — an inverted picture — of the failed bipolar, Cold War international order. The true, more deeply systemic sources of the shape of the future may be arising in other regions and in other domains of activity, well beyond the issue of containing aggression.

At the start of this essay it is posited that statesmen, in order to 'use' history, must have sufficient detachment from it so as to be able consciously, and accurately, to employ it. The preceding examination of the Bush administration's thinking about foreign-policy questions may serve to make evident both the powerful effect of history in its various forms — learned, observed and experienced — and some of the pluses and minuses of its effect. Both the President, who continues to read historical works, and his Secretary of State, who studied classics, are keenly interested in history and are plainly conscious of their role in it; and wish to play it well. For them history is a guide but also, as Michael Fry points out, a judge.

Their applications of historical data and knowledge for the purposes of practical statesmanship are, in terms of Meinecke's warning, scarcely free of elements of 'tendentiousness', 'idealization,' and 'misrepresentation'. Probably this is inevitable, given man's lack of Olympian perspective, that of the gods. Nonetheless, the tendancy can and should humanly be resisted, and an attempt made to make contemporaneous pragmatic history as scientific as it can be. 'How, exactly?', a reader will ask.

A first suggestion is pedestrian, but perhaps the most important: getting the facts, learning the story, mastering the brief — 'getting it right', in Fry's irreducible phrase. '*Having* it right', a statesman might retort, for there is a premium in international politics on getting it right the first time, that is, correctly interpreting a foreign situation from the outset. The correct 'intuition' into a situation was considered by Henry Kissinger to be his greatest strength, as indeed it perhaps was.[59] For the less intuitive, instruction is needed, and this ordinarily comes from institutions, from academies and also governments themselves.

The problems of continuity of historical knowledge through administrative transitions are, in the US government, particularly 'horrendous', as Fry suggests. Although Rashid Khalidi writes optimistically of the institutional knowledge of the US State Department regarding the Middle East, he does not perhaps sufficiently take into account the effects of regular personnel rotation, movement in and out of government, and the inadequate recording and retrieval systems for information. The historical 'memory well' of the State Department is hardly empty. It is full. But it is murky, and not good for the extracting of pertinent facts and policy-relevant precepts. Valiant attempts by the State Department Historical Office to gain needed support and funding for the more rapid production of the documentary *Foreign Relations of the United States* series and for the conduct of comprehensive oral-histories — the debriefing of returning or retiring officers for the guidance of their successors — have met with only limited success.[60] This situation must be rectified. One difficulty, an attitudinal problem, is that the typical American Foreign Service Officer, as a former State Department historian once sharply remarked, considers himself or herself 'a great historian', his or her *own* great historian.[61] Arguably, that is just what these officers ought to be, or to try to be — while remaining ever-mindful of the inherent limitations of simultaneous, participant history. Statesmen are, unavoidably, 'historians of a kind', as Michael Fry has acknowledged.

Academic scholarship of foreign affairs, like the conduct of foreign policy itself, also depends critically on having the complete and accurate record of previous diplomatic proceedings. A number of authors in this volume have emphasized the centrality of the 'data' problem, not only for verifying substantive interpretations of particular events — such as the Cuban missile crisis — but also for being able to entertain certain basic *kinds* of historical explanation. As Alex Hybel has noted, this problem is particularly serious, perhaps inescapably so, in examining the 'rationality' of decision-making and more complex cognitive models of statesmanly behavior which involve the precise tracing of the thought paths of leaders. Such persons, highly active, tend to be inaccessible, sometimes even to themselves. Other types of information may be more attainable. Statistical data, such as required by the authors in this book working on economic history and in international political economy, are

perhaps easier to accumulate. But they may be even harder to manage —
that is, to analyze and interpret correctly.

This brings me to a second suggestion: more ventures in international,
comparative history. The most remarkable demonstration so far is the
mutually reciprocal, transnational learning that has occurred, through
retrospective joint note-comparing by official participants as well as
academic experts, following the 'Cuban missile' or 'Caribbean' crisis. As
this slight but meaningful difference in nomenclature indicates, the
American and Soviet sides did not even picture this episode in quite the
same way. The American name highlights the functional, or military-
strategic, significance of the event, whose physical proximity and military
importance were taken almost as given. The Soviet name highlights its
distant geographical location, and the difficulty of protecting a
symbolically important ally in an exotic and remote place.[62]

By comparing and perhaps concerting divergent perspectives, the
opposed participants in past crises (and, in some cases, perhaps in
continuing conflicts) can build common historical premises for future
decision-making, possibly more coordinated if not actually joint.
Together, they may find better ways out of the dilemmas they face. A
shared view of history provides both a degree of homogeneity and, as Fry
notes, a basis for consensus that is 'more authentic' than that fashioned
by the psychological pressures of group debate or, one might add, the
apparent imperatives of crisis diplomacy, such as the Persian Gulf
showdown. Besides further Soviet–American cases of conflict that might
retrospectively be examined are many, including those suggested in this
book, involving other partners to historic controversy: the Arab–
Palestinian–Israeli disputants (Khalidi), Russia and Japan (Haslam), and
even the United States and Great Britain (Lake, Kunz, and Frieden).
Relations between the United States and the Soviet Union, on the one
hand, and the smaller countries regarded historically as lying within their
respective spheres of influence, on the other, also merit binational study
(Snyder, Mefford and Hybel chapters). Such retrospective examinations,
almost unavoidably, are related to present phases of international
controversies and problems. Historical re-examination thus verges on
what has been called 'Track Two' diplomacy, or the unofficial exploration
of potential official positions, to be taken up sooner or later, on 'Track
One', by those now in authority.[63]

A third counsel is more philosophical and, by its very nature, less
useful in the pragmatic 'American' sense. That is the wisdom, also
recommended by Meinecke, of respecting the pastness of the past — of
recognizing and conceding to the 'individuality' or singularity of previous
events and historical patterns. The repeatable, practical, lesson-teaching
occurrences of history, such as the processes of everyday life
recapitulated by materially-oriented historians including Fernand
Braudel, generally are not the events — economic cataclysms, social
upheavals, foreign wars — that most concern statesmen who often face
situations that are largely unprecedented. These occurrences are history's

greatest 'individualities'. Sometimes they even are turning points in world history, such as the present conjuncture of remarkable events around the globe, in time, might turn out to be. History does not foreshadow the future, but its study does help statesmen knowingly to meet it.

Notes

1. The pioneering work of this kind is Ernest R. May, *'Lessons' of the Past: The Use and Misuse of History in American Foreign Policy* (New York: Oxford University Press, 1973). Its 'American' approach was remarked upon by a British reviewer in 'Poor Clio', *The Economist*, **250**, 6810, 2 March 1974, pp. 108–9. See also Richard E. Neustadt and Ernest R. May, *Thinking in Time: The Uses of History for Decision Makers* (New York: The Free Press, 1986).
2. Louis J. Hartz, *The Liberal Tradition in America: An Interpretation of American Political Thought Since the Revolution* (New York: Harcourt, Brace and World, 1955).
3. Daniel J. Boorstin, *The Genius of American Politics* (Chicago: Phoenix Books, 1953), p. 4.
4. Fernand Braudel, *The Structures of Everyday Life: The Limits of the Possible*, vol. I of *Civilization and Capitalism: 15th–18th Century*, trans. Siân Reynolds (New York: Harper and Row, 1979–84), I, p. 29.
5. John Dewey, 'Historical Judgments', in Hans Meyerhoff (ed.), *The Philosophy of History in Our Time* (Garden City, New York: Doubleday and Company, 1959), pp. 169, 172.
6. Friedrich Meinecke, 'Values and Causalities in History', in Fritz Stern (ed.), *The Varieties of History: From Voltaire to the Present* (New York: Meridian Books, 1956), pp. 269–70, 283–4, 411n. Alan K. Henrikson, 'Thinking Historically', *The Fletcher Forum of World Affairs*, **2**, 2, May 1978, pp. 225–32, uses the similar word 'singularity' of great events. Hegel's remark about statesmen and nations not learning from history was based on a belief that they *should* not do so. 'Each age and each nation finds itself in such peculiar circumstances, in such a unique situation,' he argued, 'that it can and must make decisions with reference to itself alone (and only the great individual can decide what the right course is).' Georg Wilhelm Friedrich Hegel, *Lectures on the Philosophy of World History*, trans. H. B. Nisbet (Cambridge: Cambridge University Press, 1975), p. 21.
7. The historian Paul Kennedy, in the work which crystallized the debate about American 'decline', observes that 'it simply has not been given to any one society to remain *permanently* ahead of all the others, because that would imply a freezing of the differentiated pattern of growth rates, technological advance, and military developments which has existed since time immemorial'. Paul Kennedy, *The Rise and Fall of the Great Powers: Economic Change and Military Conflict from 1500 to 2000* (New York: Random House, 1987). p. 533. That the United States nonetheless remains *relatively* in a strong position is emphasized by Joseph S. Nye, Jr., in *Bound to Lead: The Changing Nature of American Power* (New York: Basic Books, 1990).
8. A comment to the author by a former US State Department historian. The degree of conscious parallelism between Kissinger and his presumed German model can be surmised from Henry A. Kissinger, 'The White Revolutionary:

Reflections on Bismarck', in D. A Rustow ed., *Philosophers and Kings: Studies in Leadership* (New York: George Braziller, 1970), pp. 317–53. For an insightful critique of Kissinger's historical thinking, see Robert L. Beisner, 'History and Henry Kissinger', *Diplomatic History*, **14**, 4, Fall 1990, pp. 511–27.

9. The modern classic critique of deterministic historical philosophy is Karl R. Popper, *The Poverty of Historicism* (London: Routledge and Kegan Paul, 1957).

10. Herbert A. Simon, *Models of Man: Social and Rational* (New York: John Wiley and Sons, 1957), pp. 204–5. Simon defines his term 'satisficing' as 'finding a course of action that is "good enough"'.

11. Mefford does not sufficiently distinguish between *historical* analogies and other political analogies, even political metaphors and verbal figures, which might be suggestive. Such an approach to history seems highly pragmatic. Going beyond Dewey's belief in the 'reconstruction' of past events to make them more relevant and useful, Mefford's analysis suggests that memories of complex historical occurrences can be, and often are, *de*constructed — into simpler, script-like bits — for their suggestiveness in current policy-making.

12. Ernest May, himself a historian, states: 'It is not my contention that historians are especially well qualified as advisers on what to do. Like other humans, some may be and some may not.' Arthur Schlesinger, Jr., he comments, 'appears to have been valued by Kennedy,, and on occasion his usefulness was related to his background as a history professor'. For example, when in 1961 President Kennedy was considering a settlement in Laos involving a coalition government and was warned that such a government would be taken over by its communist members as had happened earlier in Czechoslovakia, Schlesinger was able to counter that this had not always happened — France, Italy and Latin America offered counterexamples (May, *'Lessons' of the Past*, p. 173). On the reverse relationship — the effect of policy-making experience on the crafting of history — see Arthur M. Schlesinger, Jr., 'The Historian as Participant', *Daedalus*, **100**, 2, Spring 1971, pp. 339–58.

13. Hegel emphatically disagrees. Every situation in the past or the present is unique, and can teach nothing specific, he contended 'Amid the pressure of great events, a general principle is no help, and it is not enough to look back on similar situations (in the past); for pale recollections are powerless before the stress of the moment, and impotent before the life and freedom of the present' (Hegel, *Lectures on the Philosophy of World History*, p. 21).

14. 'Policymakers tend to think either in sequential or systemic terms — which is to say, as either historians or political scientists — but rarely both,' comments John Lewis Gaddis, 'Expanding the Data Base', *International Security*, **12**, 1, Summer 1987, p. 20.

15. For another demonstration that the British analogy is a continuing historical force to be reckoned with, see David P. Calleo, *Beyond American Hegemony: The Future of the Western Alliance* (New York: Basic Books, 1987), chapter 8, 'The *Pax Americana* and the *Pax Britannica*'.

16. Compellence is defined simply by Schelling as the capacity 'to make an adversary do something' — as distinct from deterrence, the ability 'to keep him from starting something' (Thomas C. Schelling, *Arms and Influence*, New Haven: Yale University Press, 1966, p. 69).

17. James G. Blight and David A. Welch, *On the Brink: Americans and Soviets Re-examine the Cuban Missile Crisis* (New York: Hill and Wang, 1989).

18. Meinecke, 'Values and Causalities', 411n.

19. US Deputy Secretary of State Lawrence S. Eagleburger, when working on

Park Avenue with Kissinger Associates, explained what the consulting firm offered its clients. What they get, said Eagleburger, is 'Henry's *fingerspitzengefühl*'. 'Fingerspitzengefühl', *Time*, **127**, 7, 17 February 1986), p. 29.

20. Meinecke, 'Values and Causalities', p. 270.

21. His friend Ernst Troeltsch regarded 'the comprehension of the present as the final goal of all historical study'. Meinecke considered this 'surely a legitimate and necessary goal, but neither the only nor the highest one'. Troeltsch reproached him for a 'tendency to break loose into objective and pure contemplation' (ibid., 411n).

22. Louis J. Halle, *The Cold War as History* (New York: Harper and Row, 1967), pp. xii–xiii. In his work *History and Human Relations* (London: Collins, 1951), pp. 16–17, Herbert Butterfield had written: 'Behind the great conflicts of mankind is a terrible human predicament which lies at the heart of the story; and sooner or later the historian will base the very structure of his narrative upon it. Contemporaries fail to see the predicament or refuse to recognise its genuineness, so that our knowledge of it comes from later analysis — it is only with the progress of historical science on a particular subject that men come really to recognize that there was a terrible knot almost beyond the ingenuity of man to untie.'

23. Halle then was a professor at the Graduate Institute of International Studies in Geneva.

24. William Quandt in a passage, 'Rediscovering the International Conference', describes previous American government interest in this idea, involving even the direct participation of the Soviet Union. See his US Policy Toward the Arab–Israeli Conflict', in William B. Quandt, ed, The Middle East: Ten Years After Camp David, (Washington, DC: The Brookings Institution, 1988), pp. 357–86. 'A whole mythology had grown up in Washington about the horrors of the October 1, 1977, joint communique issued by the two superpowers [printed in the book as appendix B],' he comments critically (p. 373). 'The best thing said about it was that it was so appalling that it had driven Sadat to Jerusalem to avoid dealing with the Soviets.'

25. A scenario for this purpose is offered by former US Assistant Secretary of State for Near Eastern and South Asian Affairs Harold H. Saunders, in his, 'Reconstituting the Arab–Israeli Peace Process', ibid., pp. 413–41.

26. Hegel, *Lectures on the Philosophy of World History*, p. 26.

27. Butterfield, *History and Human Relations*, p. 17.

28. ibid., p. 36.

29. President Bush, inaugural address, 20 January 1989, *Department of State Bulletin*, **89**, 2154, April 1989, pp. 1–3. For a critical review of the Bush administration's foreign policy during most of its first year, see Alan K. Henrikson, 'A "New Breeze" or the Winds of Old? The Foreign Policy of the Bush Administration', *Revista Española de Estudios Norteamericanos* (Centro de Estudios Norteamericanos, Universidad de Alcalá de Henares), no. 2, Otoño de 1989, pp. 29–82.

30. Francis Fukuyama, 'The End of History', *The National Interest*, no. 16, Summer 1989, pp. 3–18.

31. George F. Kennan, *American Diplomacy, 1900–1950* (New York: Mentor Books, 1951), 'The Sources of Soviet Conduct', p. 99. On p. 105, Kennan argued that it would be 'an exaggeration' to say that American behaviour 'unassisted and alone' could bring about 'the early fall of Soviet power in Russia', but he nonetheless posited that the United States did have the power 'to increase

enormously the strains' under which Soviet policy operated, in this way promoting 'tendencies which must eventually find their outlet in either the break-up or the gradual mellowing of Soviet power'.

32. President Bush, 'Change in the Soviet Union', address at Texas A & M University, College Station, Texas, 12 May 1990, *Department of State Bulletin*, **89**, 2148, July 1989, pp. 16–17.

33. Alan K. Henrikson, 'The Emanation of Power', *International Security*, **6**, 1, Summer 1981, pp. 152–64.

34. This is the heterodox suggestion of Anders Stephanson, *Kennan and the Art of Foreign Policy* (Cambridge, Mass.: Harvard University Press, 1989), p. 106.

35. For a list of their numerous encounters, see 'Chronology: Baker–Shevardnadze Meetings', *US Department of State Dispatch*, **1**, 7, 15 October 1990, pp. 188–9.

36. President Bush, 'Against Aggression in the Persian Gulf', address to employees at the Pentagon, 15 August 1990, *US Department of State Dispatch*, **1**, 1, 3 September 1990, pp. 54–5.

37. Bush's closest associates in the administration belong to younger-age cohorts, with somewhat different generational experiences that surely condition their general international outlooks, and even their specific views of the Persian Gulf situation. For example, the President's top assistant for national security affairs, retired Air Force Lieutenant General Brent Scowcroft, experienced war first in Korea and, partly as a result, tends toward more modest military objectives. Implying that the United States in the Gulf situation ought not to exceed its initially stated objectives, which generally are assented to by a supportive international coalition, Scowcroft makes an argument for moderation on the basis of the consequences of the Korean War decision to drive beyond the 38th parallel toward the Yalu River, causing China to intervene. 'The Yalu River is a case where it looked like a great thing to do, but in fact it caused us enormous problems,' he reflects pointedly. 'And therefore, while it would be nice to do some other things than what we specifically started out to do,' he notes of the Gulf crisis, 'what I'm saying is we would consider it a signal victory to accomplish what we said we need to do.' (Andrew Rosenthal, 'Bush's Modulator of the Gulf Policy, And of What Not to Do or Say Now', *New York Times*, 3 October 1990.) It was the war in Vietnam, however, that formed the strategic perspectives of both General Colin M. Powell, chairman of the Joint Chiefs of Staff, and General H. Norman Schwarzkopf, commander of Operation Desert Shield. Both of them spent two tours with infantry battalions there. Official indications are that, if war starts, it will not proceed in 'step-by-step escalation', but with a 'full-blown attack by air, sea and ground forces, all at once', against both Kuwait and Iraq. 'The reason for the all-out strategy can be summed up in one word: Vietnam' (Fred Kaplan, 'Applying Vietnam's Lessons', *Boston Globe*, 12 November 1990). Two worthy studies of the generation-relatedness of attitudes toward foreign policy are: Michael Roskin, 'From Pearl Harbor to Vietnam: Shifting Generational Paradigms and Foreign Policy', *Political Science Quarterly*, **89**, 3, Fall 1974, pp. 563–88, and Ole R. Holsti and James N. Rosenau, 'Does Where You Stand Depend on When You Were Born? The Impact of Generation on Post-Vietnam Foreign Policy Beliefs', *The Political Opinion Quarterly*, **44**, 1, Spring 1980, pp. 1–22.

38. President Bush, 'America's Stand Against Aggression', address to the 91st national convention of the Veterans of Foreign Wars, Baltimore, Maryland, 20 August 1990, *US Department of State Dispatch*, **1**, 1, 3 September 1990, pp. 55–7.

The 'never again' historical syndrome is analyzed by Earl C. Ravenal, *Never Again: Learning from America's Foreign Policy Failures* (Philadephia: Temple University Press, 1978).

39. President Bush, 'The Arabian Peninsula: US Principles', address to the nation from the Oval House of the White House, 8 August 1990, *US Department of State Dispatch*, **1**, 1, 3 September 1990, pp. 52–3.

40. Secretary Baker, 'America's Stake in the Persian Gulf', prepared statement before the House Foreign Affairs Committee, 4 September 1990, *US Department of State Dispatch*, **1**, 2, 10 September 1990, pp. 69–71. The proper historical referent of Baker's 'small, faraway country . . .' phrase is Czechoslovakia. British Prime Minister Neville Chamberlain on 27 September 1938, described its confrontation with Germany as 'a quarrel in a far-away country between people of whom we know nothing' (John Wheeler-Bennett, *Munich: Prologue to Tragedy*, New York: The Viking Press, 1963, p. 157). In the travel conditions of the 1980s Abyssinia/Ethiopia can be more plausibly said to be 'faraway'. Reference to that country perhaps was intended to conjure up the brave image of the victimized Emperor Haile Selassie, appealing to the League of Nations.

41. Thomas L. Friedman, 'Iraqis Are Hinting at a Compromise; US Reject Terms', *New York Times*, 17 October 1990.

42. '5 Points: The Iraqi Proposal', *Boston Globe*, 20 August 1990; Salah Nasrawi, 'Iraq Offers Conditions for Summit', *Boston Globe*, 12 November 1990. For Yasir Arafat's and Yevgeny Primakov's early conceptions of how various Middle Eastern issues might be interrelated, see Youssef M. Ibrahim, 'Arafat Stresses Linkage in Settling Gulf Crisis', *New York Times*, 26 November 1990, and Paul Lewis, 'Soviet Aide Urges Delay on U.N. Move on Force in Gulf', *New York Times*, 16 November 1990.

43. The four 'principles', frequently reiterated, were stated originally by President Bush in his address to the nation from the Oval Office of the White House, 8 August 1990.

44. Gerald F. Seib, 'Bush Hints US to Seek War-Crimes Trial of Iraq's Leaders for Actions in Kuwait', *Wall Street Journal*, 16 October 1990.

45. Thomas L. Friedman, 'No Compromise on Kuwait, Bush says', *New York Times*, 24 October 1990. A telephone call by the author to the White House determined, after further internal inquiry there, that the book the President referred to is Martin Gilbert, *The Second World War: A Complete History* (New York: H. Holt, 1989).

46. There was in fact some interest in a 'negotiated peace' in Great Britain in late 1939 and 1940, but the dominant temper of the time there was against it.

47. Maureen Dowd, 'President Seeks to Clarify Stand', *New York Times*, 13 November 1990. Bush had served as head of the US liaison office (later an embassy) in Beijing (1974–5) and also had been the US Permanent Representative to the United Nations (1971–3).

48. 'Excerpts From Speech By Bush at Marine Post', *New York Times*, 23 November 1990.

49. The Civil War was prominent in the American consciousness in 1990 because of the Public Broadcasting System's moving television series, 'The Civil War', and its companion volume by Geoffrey C. Ward, *The Civil War: An Illustrated History* (New York: Knopf, 1990). A reminder of the seizure of Americans for ransom by the Barbary coast states was given in Richard D. Lyons, 'Since Ancient Times, Hostages Have Been Used, and Misused, in Wars', *New York Times*, 22 August 1990.

50. 'Excerpts From Speech by Bush at Marine Post'.
51. H. D. S. Greenway, 'The Mixed Signals the US Sent to the Mideast', *Boston Globe*, 28 September 1990; 'Kuwait: How the West Blundered; The Signals That Were Sent — And the One That Wasn't', *The Economist*, **316**, 7674, 29 September 1990, pp. 19–22; Robert S. Greenberger, 'How the Baker Plan for Early Sanctions Against Iraq Failed', *Wall Street Journal*, 1 October 1990. A brief 'Who lost Kuwait?' discussion arose that carried historical overtones of the 'Who lost China?' debate in the late 1940s and 1950s. See 'The Search for Scapegoats', *Newsweek*, **116**, 14, 1 October 1990, pp. 24–5.
52. Greenway, 'Mixed Signals'.
53. At a minimum, the outbreak of the Gulf crisis in August 1990 constituted a failure of 'deterrence', as noted by Strobe Talbott, 'The Deterrence Vacuum', *Time*, **136**, 7, 13 August 1990, p. 24.
54. Baker, 'America's Stake in the Persian Gulf', p. 70.
55. President Bush, 'Toward a New World Order', address before a joint session of Congress, 11 September 1990, *US Department of State Dispatch*, **1**, 3, 17 September 1990, pp. 91–3. A joint statement issued by Bush and Gorbachev at Helsinki is on p. 92.
56. Baker, 'America's Stake in the Persian Gulf', p. 69.
57. ibid., p. 71.
58. Alan K. Henrikson, 'The Global Foundations for a Diplomacy of Consensus', in Alan K. Henrikson, ed., *Negotiating World Order: The Artisanship and Architecture of Global Diplomacy* (Wilmington, Del.: Scholarly Resources, 1986), p. 243.
59. Beisner, 'History and Henry Kissinger', p. 514.
60. See William Z. Slany, 'The Foreign Relations Series: Challenge and Response', The Society for Historians of American Foreign Relations *Newsletter*, **21**, 3, September 1990, pp. 46–9. The Office of the Historian has been able to start, on a 'pilot project' basis, a program of exit-interviews with selected ambassadors coming from, for comparative purposes, large and small embassies. As a visiting professor at the Center for the Study of Foreign Affairs in the State Department's Foreign Service Institute in 1986–87, I drafted, for the Department's potential use, an outline for a policy-relevant program of oral history.
61. Correspondence with the author. This was contrasted, interestingly, with the attitude toward history of the average US military officer, characterized as being too deferential toward formal historiography and the professional historian.
62. Alan K. Henrikson, 'The Geographical "Mental Maps" of American Foreign Policy Makers', *International Political Science Review*, **1**, 4, October 1980, pp. 495–530, contains a discussion of geographical perspective and policy-making.
63. An example of the recommendations of the 'Track Two' approach, based in part on previous high-level official experience, is Saunders, 'Reconstituting the Arab–Israeli Peace Process'. On the 'Track Two' concept see John W. McDonald and Diane B. Bendahmane, eds., *Conflict Resolution: Track Two Diplomacy*, (Washington, D.C.: Center for the Study of Foreign Affairs, Foreign Service Institute, Department of State, 1987).

Index